Living in Different Worlds Simultaneously

"This book is a great source of inspiration for what the world needs so desperately: honoring each other's contextuality while at the same time searching for inter-contextuality as a basis for our common humanity. There is no better way to honor a biblical scholar who has devoted his scholarly life to showing that such an approach is possible."

—**Heinrich Bedford-Strohm**, Moderator, World Council of Churches

"A wonderful volume, bringing together Western and African scholarship in biblical exegesis, reception history, and hermeneutics. The contributions honor Louis Jonker, a globally renowned South African Bible scholar who has devoted his academic life to integrating these areas into the cultural contexts from which they emerged."

—**Konrad Schmid**, Professor of Old Testament, University of Zürich

"This book honors Professor Louis Jonker for his significant contributions to Old Testament scholarship. It highlights his rigorous and nuanced approach to hermeneutics, engaging with the complexities and contextual issues of biblical texts. The book showcases various hermeneutical approaches that reflect the multidimensionality of exegesis. This book is ideal for readers interested in exploring different methods for interpreting Old Testament texts."

—**Hulisani Ramantswana**, Chair of Department, Biblical and Ancient Studies, University of South Africa

"This important volume closes a gap between Western/Northern and African hermeneutical approaches and exegesis. It is dedicated to Louis C. Jonker whose research and teaching was characterized by bridging different scientific traditions, Africa and Europe, historical-critical exegesis, hermeneutics, and reception history. His large horizon is perfectly mirrored in the contributions of this book which unites scholars of diverse disciplines covering a broad range of sources, methods, and applications."

—**Angelika Berlejung**, Professor of Old Testament, University of Leipzig

"This insightful and inspiring collection of essays is an excellent tribute to Louis Jonker and to his remarkable scholarship. . . . The individual contributions to the volume deal with a great variety of topics—from Chronicles to contemporary African biblical hermeneutics—but what makes the volume more important than its separate chapters is that it underscores Jonker's point of 'living in different worlds simultaneously' and the insights that emerge from living that way."

—**Ehud Ben Zvi**, Professor Emeritus of History, Classics, and Religion, University of Alberta

Living in Different Worlds Simultaneously

Essays on Biblical Hermeneutics in Celebration of Louis C. Jonker

EDITED BY
Ntozakhe S. Cezula,
Benjamin D. Giffone,
Knut Holter, AND
Lerato L. D. Mokoena

WIPF & STOCK · Eugene, Oregon

LIVING IN DIFFERENT WORLDS SIMULTANEOUSLY
Essays on Biblical Hermeneutics in Celebration of Louis C. Jonker

Wipf & Stock
An Imprint of Wipf and Stock Publishers
199 W. 8th Ave., Suite 3
Eugene, OR 97401

www.wipfandstock.com

PAPERBACK ISBN: 979-8-3852-5190-2
HARDCOVER ISBN: 979-8-3852-5191-9
EBOOK ISBN: 979-8-3852-5192-6

VERSION NUMBER 11/25/25

For Louis Jonker: careful teacher,
brilliant colleague, faithful friend

Contents

List of Figures

Preface

THE PAST DECADE OR SO has witnessed a significant resurgence and flourishing of identity politics in knowledge production across various disciplines. At the heart of this is how we write ourselves and our experiences into existence through myriad hermeneutical tools at our disposal, including Old Testament studies. Old Testament studies are no longer solely focused on narratives concerned with historical criticism; they are increasingly being fully integrated into the social sciences and engaged in documenting and investigating diverse experiences.

This book is dedicated to Louis C. Jonker, Distinguished Professor of Old Testament at Stellenbosch University—our colleague, teacher, supervisor, mentor, and friend. The book title, *Living in Different Worlds Simultaneously*, borrowed from Louis's own work, captures some crucial aspects of what Louis has shared with the guild of critical biblical studies. The core idea of the book is to explore the tension between two hermeneutical approaches standing at the crossroads, where one has a dominant hegemonic function and the other is described as pioneering and ambitious. As one reads the essays, almost every single contribution feels the need to directly or indirectly define what hermeneutics is and establish some sort of validity for every perspective across different periods; hence, the most important element of the book is how it brings together different generations of scholars.

The book is a convergence of ideas from diverse contributors who care about biblical interpretation that is context-informed and specific in the face of absolute truths and globalized ideas, text reception, and transmission. The richness and diversity of the approaches add significantly to our broader comprehension of Old Testament theology, while also increasing awareness of the complexities that cloud the understanding of the Old Testament and its hermeneutic practices, revealing insights about social and ideological frameworks of thought. The product of this volume expresses the complex nature of Old Testament theology: the Jonker way, living in different worlds simultaneously, with the mission to strengthen African biblical hermeneutical lenses and confront established practices of knowledge. Jonker himself would argue that these modes are not contradictory or competing.

The book is divided into three parts. In the first part, the essays set the scene by beginning where Jonker concludes: contemporary hermeneutics. From different perspectives, Solomon Amao, Ntozakhe Simon Cezula, Beth E. Elness-Hanson, Knut Holter, and Gerald O. West investigate the applications of contemporary hermeneutics beyond the Eurocentric matrix and concepts associated with sovereignty. The collective expressions begin by acknowledging that pluralism has its pitfalls, especially regarding the self-determination of contexts, as Amao argues. Cezula examines and underscores the importance of confronting the operational function of exegetical methods while engaging in a new emancipatory vocabulary of progressive politics: which tools do we adopt, and which do we discard? It is crucial to recognize that we all carry intellectual baggage that frequently obscures hidden biases; Elness-Hanson offers a possible foundation for radical intercultural politics. Holter and West partake in unique yet similar stances, focusing on specific methods of interpretation within contextual African biblical hermeneutics—one examining African proverbs as interpretive tools and the other exploring a contextual Bible study methodology.

In the second part, contributors Marta Høyland Lavik, Christo Lombaard, and Slindile Thabede analyze several texts and their formats, engaging with debates that surround reception of those texts. They focus on the epistemological debates of our times concerning the ongoing relationship between the text and the receiver, illustrating how texts themselves exist in different worlds simultaneously, depending on who is reading and from where. These approaches contextualize readings: Lavik using Ps 23 in relation to cancer patients, Lombaard examining the reception of Gen 22 through various traditions, and Thabede analyzing multidimensional and traditional interpretations of Hagar in Judaism, Christianity, and Islam.

The third part of this volume features contributions from Johann Cook, Jaco Gericke, Hendrik Bosman, Marius J. Nel, Jeremy Punt, Gerrie F. Snyman, and Benjamin D. Giffone, concluding with what Jonker begins with: the text. Cook, Gericke, Bosman, and Nel represent a grassroots movement of historical criticism, demonstrating their alignment with the concept and continuing the traditional knowledge associated with it. Punt, Snyman, and Giffone adopt a more intertextual and intertestamental approach to illuminate the streamlined representations of hermeneutics.

The ups and downs of all these essays create a network reflecting the objectives of Jonker's fundamental way of thinking. This coordination, structured from context, and reception to text, satisfies all the conditions needed to align with the way Jonker approaches his biblical interpretation. In closing, we must recognize all the contributions that made this special volume possible. Our utmost gratitude goes to Louis Jonker, whose contributions to Old Testament studies have provided us with an archive for engagement, along with sharing his intellectual property so generously with the world. Let me also extend my thanks to the authors: Solomon Amao, Ntozakhe Simon Cezula, Beth E. Elness-Hanson, Knut Holter, Gerald O. West, Marta Høyland Lavik, Christo Lombaard, Slindile Thabede, Johann Cook, Jaco Gericke, Hendrik Bosman, Marius Nel, Jeremy Punt, Gerrie Snyman, and Benjamin Giffone. This volume would not have materialized without your dedication to this project.

Lerato L. D. Mokoena
Pretoria, May 2025

PART I
Contemporary Hermeneutics

1

Retelling Bible Stories for Christian Ethics and Social Actions

Revisiting Narratology in West African Biblical Scholarship

Solomon Amao

West African people groups and contexts appear to resonate more with and readily learn from narratives than other literary genres in the Bible. The attraction is to the descriptive or informative language employed to challenge a rethink of life's choices and redefine life's values by encouraging the formation of virtues and discouraging vices. The preferences of West Africans toward biblical narratives seem to mirror those of biblical writers who made historical narratives oversee other genres, particularly in the Old Testament. More than half of the Old Testament, of the Protestant Bible, is narrative literature, and other genres commonly combine with it to present the Bible as a divine election/redemption narrative. Barton writes, "About half of the Old Testament, after all, consists not of overt moral teachings but of narrative histories, legends, stories, whatever we want to call it. And the narrative is always particular, concerned with connected chains of actions and events which always befall particular people."[1]

1. Barton, *Ethics and the Old Testament*, 20. Each biblical literary genre retains

West African cultures are primarily oral and built on shared cultural heritage.[2] The sources of knowledge that drive morality are commonly passed down through generations by elders and other custodians of the "ideals" in each community. The origins and the makeup of indigenous knowledge uniquely and readily provide for moral development and character formation in each context. Louise Grenier observes that indigenous knowledge is compelling and operative because it "is shared and communicated orally, by specific examples and through culture" and "stored in people's memories and activities."[3] George Dei, Budd Hall, and Dorothy Rosenberg contribute that such indigenous sources of knowledge "speak to questions about location, politics, identity, and culture, and about the history of peoples and lands."[4] The answers to these questions grant any resultant indigenous knowledge an unforced acceptance by the particular people group.

In West African contexts, stories, proverbs, and folklores[5] serve many purposes. One of which is to be conduits to preserve and transmit

---

different contexts, audiences, and purposes, employs different conventions and forms, and has different literary histories, backgrounds, authors, interpreters, tolerance of ambiguity, and social and cultural functions. For discussions on how to interface with the different features of the biblical genres, see Levinson, *Right Chorale*, 41–42; Olojede, "Storytelling as an Indigenous Resource," 4–6; DeRouchie, *How to Understand and Apply*, 22; and the section on "Sources and Sources Behind Sources of the Ethics in Israel" in Barton, *Ethics in Ancient Israel*, 25–40.

2. These include indigenous languages, songs, poems, stories, proverbs, illustrations and analogies, histories, folklores, dances, myths and legends, cultural values, beliefs, rituals, community laws, taxonomies, local events, customs, norms and practices, and persons and models.

3. Grenier, *Working with Indigenous Knowledge*, 1.

4. Dei et al., *Indigenous Knowledges in Global Contexts*, 74.

5. Many contexts have stories of mythological animals—lions, tortoises, rabbits, elephants, spiders—as heroes and villains in popular fables and riddles. For example, the Akan people of Ghana have Ananse (Mr. Spider), who is often a model of good behavior but can sometimes be a crafty character. The Yoruba people of Nigeria have Ijapa (Mr. Tortoise), the slow but crafty character who always outwits the fast but arrogant Mr. Hare and the strong but dim-witted Mr. Elephant. Furthermore, the Yorubas in Nigeria promote the use of proverbs, as a half-speech, for ethical teachings over a long speech. Two maxims convey the kinship between Yoruba proverbs and their formulation of ethics. The first, "Abo oro laa so fun omo nuabi, ti oba denu re aadi odindi," translates, "You only need to tell a half-speech to a well-trained person; when it gets into his/her stomach, it becomes a complete message." It declares that a proverb is a half-speech that becomes a full message for a prudent person. The second maxim is "Owe lesin oro; oro lesin owe. Bi oro ba so nu owe la fi nwa." This translates, "A proverb is the horse for a discussion; a discussion is a horse for a proverb. When a discussion is lost you recover it with a proverb." This is equivalent to saying, "A proverb is worth a thousand words."

histories, form values, and define identities. This approach also has bearings on biblical scholarship in West Africa. A narrative unit can be a veritable academic industry that addresses relationships between knowledge and narrative to shape human behaviors. The current dominating and permeating writing frameworks and cultures of knowledge (the scientific and philosophical methods) are still fundamentally modern. Bruce Birch provides an explanation that may suffice for West African preferences for the genre of narratives:

> [People] find identity by learning and developing their own story, becoming conscious of its dimensions and adding to it as life goes on through adulthood. . . . Our lives participate in the plot of many stories. The power of biblical stories is their ability to help us see the many stories of our lives as part of larger stories which integrate our life story into stories of ultimate meaning.[6]

Therefore, this essay revisits issues in narratives as they continue to be regularly and effectively used by West Africans to both generate, preserve, and transmit attainable grassroots moral values and address deeper issues of virtue and ethics, and social concepts and actions. It also analyses a variety of approaches in narratology for West African biblical scholarship in its search for a responsible hermeneutical approach in the process of formulating Christian ethics and directing social actions.

Current Drifts in West African Biblical Scholarship and Ethics

Political, social, economic, moral, and religious developments in recent histories further shape West African people groups, contexts, biblical scholarship, and formulation of ethics.[7] The colonial regimes had forced an artificial and capitalist coalition of people groups with diverse and clashing worldviews into nations. Then colonial regimes introduced new and often clashing worldviews to the prevalent different identities, cultures, and the typical social ontology of the people groups. Nigeria

6. Birch, *Let Justice Roll Down*, 55.

7. Giffone recognises biblical scholarship's dual task of "generating insight and sharing insights." He explains, "Generating new insights consists of uncovering new data and reinterpreting and reapplying existing data or truths according to new methods and/or in new contexts. Sharing insights includes teaching students (insights shared and explained) and writing (insights encapsulated and presented across time and space)." Giffone, "(Ir)Relevance of Biblical Scholarship," 3.

has journeyed as a primitive society, to becoming a slave society, then a colonialised society, to the era of decolonisation, and now a neocolonialisation.[8] These altered the different mechanisms the people employ for coping with prevalent socio-political challenges. Bosman has argued that Africa is a continent that lost its sense of self-worth over the last five hundred years.[9] The factors of her oppression—the slave trade, colonialism, postcolonial misrule, and a global economic system—have become major historical forces that shape Africa in the twenty-first century.

The major drift in biblical scholarship and formulation of morality resulted from a deliberate effort to dislodge and replace West African worldviews with a scientific and systematised reading of Scripture. It was further accelerated by compartmentalisation of life and issues. Kunhiyop expatiates, "The introduction of Christianity by the West introduced a new way of reality. Life was compartmentalised into theory and practice, classroom and practical life, knowledge and wisdom, abstract and practical, etc. This compartmentalisation was fundamentally alien to Africa. Life to the African is basically interpreted holistically."[10]

Approaches in Narratology for West African Biblical Scholarship

Hermeneutical varieties exist logically in narratology because communicating biblical faith from historical narratives requires a specific and responsible hermeneutical approach.[11] John Barton has noted that the "Old Testament narrative is well known to be sometimes reticent in drawing moral conclusions from the stories it presents."[12] The task of drawing conclusions from Old Testament narratives has been a problem for biblical critics and Christian ethicists alike. The task commonly requires a grasp of the rules of language, literary composition,

8. Alliyu et al., "Nigeria's Cobweb of Corruption," 102–27; Abdulrahman, "Colonialism," 294; Olarewaju, "Understanding Nigerian Development Crisis," 1; Alumona, *Understanding the Crisis of Development*, 1; Ochefu and Ogbogbo, "Role of Historical Societies," 77–78; Todd, "Attitudes of the Evangelical Church," 7; Okolo and Raymond, "Corruption in Nigeria," 31.

9. Bosman, "Bookends of Old Testament Ethics."

10. Kunhiyop, "Challenge of African Christian Morality," 68.

11. Moore, "Biblical Narrative Analysis," has critiqued a new narratology from its foundations as narrative criticism in the 1980s.

12. Barton, *Ethics in Ancient Israel*, 171. See also Meyer and Pietersen, "Old Testament Stories," 1.

structural and rhetorical developments, literary elements, clear and unquestionable statements, fixed starting points of reference to develop arguments, and the meaning of each text. These would then accomplish the primary task of comprehending the text's grammar, semantics, composition, style, and imageries, before moving to the secondary task of historical understanding of the text.[13]

Furthermore, hermeneutical varieties are due to the different interpretive approaches employed in the past. Wright chronicles the impact that the approaches of the early church, Marcion, the Alexandrian school, the Antiochene fathers, the Reformation era—marked by the teachings of Luther and Calvin—the Anabaptists, the dispensationalists, and Theonomism had on biblical interpretation and the development of Christian ethics.[14] Others have also emphasised the impact of the patristic interpreters, apostolic fathers of the Reformation era, the post-Reformation interpreters, and the contemporary interpreters on biblical interpretations and biblical ethics.[15] Determining a methodology and a framework for ethical principles in the Old Testament narratives has been divisive and arduous.[16] Some interpreters circumvent the process and merely draw out ecclesiological and pastoral principles from the texts. This brings misgivings about the academic integrity of such principles on Christian faith and mission. Wright suggests that some interpreters easily plunge into Old Testament ethical considerations with a proof-texting method and impose counter texts that lack hermeneutics and methodology.[17] The goal of such interpreters seems to be to seek what is relevant to their agenda.

13. Jonker and Lawrie, "Focusing on the Texts," 67–69.

14. Wright, *Old Testament Ethics*, 387–412. Carson, *Exegetical Fallacies*, takes the discussion further by listing and analysing the following exegetical fallacies and pitfalls: word study fallacies, grammatical fallacies, logical fallacies, and presupposition and historical fallacies.

15. Duvall and Hays, *Grasping God's Word*; Kaiser, *Preaching and Teaching*; Blomberg, *Interpreting Parables*; Bock and Fanning, *Interpreting the New Testament*; Goldsworthy, *According to Plan*; McCartney and Clayton, *Let the Reader Understand*; and Reid, *Study to Show Yourself Approved*. Goldsworthy, McCartney and Clayton, and Reid also discuss other pitfalls of biblical interpretation that emerged during these periods: errors in eisegesis, allegorical interpretation, fragmentation, and proof-texting and traditional interpretive methods that isolate texts from contexts.

16. Davies, *Immoral Bible*, has discussed some of the methods used earlier in the history of the development of Christian ethics.

17. Wright observes that an adequate interpretation wrestles with "getting there from here: methodological problem, getting back here from there: ideological problem, and the question of authority in the Bible stories." *Old Testament Ethics*, 44

Many of the interpreters have been simplistic and inadequate in their methodology and hermeneutical approaches.[18]

Moreover, the issues of imposing the reader's response (context) exist because some drifts in biblical scholarship have altered interpretive approaches of the present. Bosman warns,

> The current emphasis on contextual understanding is both healthy and exciting. But there are disturbing signs that point to a certain "orthopraxis," which is considered to be the only acceptable position from which to understand the biblical text. Without denying the important influence of the reader's context on the process of understanding, exegetes will have to be on the alert to the real danger that the historicity of the reader is over-emphasized at the cost of the historicity of the author. A qualified utilizing of authorial intent is not more of a hypothetical exercise than the reconstruction of the context of the reader and might even help to liberate interpreters from their view of "orthopraxis," as it once set them free from crippling orthodoxy.[19]

Giffone compared the (ir)relevance of biblical scholarship to the relevance of areas of humanities (history, philosophy, literature) in modern societies. Though the work exposed undue influences on biblical scholarship in Eastern Europe, South Africa, and the North Atlantic World, the undue influence of funding and sponsorship also accurately touched on current problems in African biblical scholarship. Giffone analysed not only the impact of incentive structures on the preservation and sharing of biblical and related texts but also on the methods or topics that reflect the scholarly agendas of the sponsors.[20]

Another challenge is the emergence of plurality (and fragmentation of knowledge) in the twentieth and twenty-first centuries. Plurality allows diverse interpretations and future possibilities. Plurality has introduced "innumerable changes, even revolutions, in biblical scholarship."[21] Yet, it is an inevitable and necessary aspect of biblical interpretation. Conradie and Jonker explain that "there can be no single fully adequate interpretation of any biblical text. Interpretation is necessarily an ongoing task if

18. Wright, *Old Testament Ethics*, 44. For example, see Jonker, "Further Interrogation" for evaluation of applications of the comparative paradigm by three modern African biblical interpreters: Erneste Nyirimana of Rwanda (1 Kgs 5:1–18); Yaw Adu-Gyamfi of Ghana (Josh 22); and Alexander Abasili (1 Sam 1).

19. Bosman, "Fallacy or Fountainhead," 30–31.

20. Giffone, "(Ir)Relevance of Biblical Scholarship," 10.

21. Giffone, "(Ir)Relevance of Biblical Scholarship," 7.

this implies the need to embody the significance of the text in forever changing circumstances."[22]

Two other challenges concern terminologies in narratology. Fludernik's section on "Some Dos and Don'ts: How to Avoid Narratologically Infelicitous Phrases" addresses first, errors of mixing up narratological models, and second, in remarks made about a narrator figure.[23] Fludernik also provides a glossary of narratological terms.[24]

Biblical Narratives for Christian Ethics and Social Actions: In Search of a Responsible Hermeneutical Approach

A responsible hermeneutical approach ensures that each biblical interpretation has historical consciousness, legitimacy, fruitfulness, sophistication, relevance/validity, openness, inclusiveness, and rhetorical efficacy.[25] Given this goal, I am advancing Jonker's review of the comparative paradigm identified by Knut Holter.[26] Jonker used Holter's comparative paradigm as the entry point to progressing an analogical hermeneutical approach to applying Old Testament texts, including narrative texts, to contemporary ethical discussions.[27] He then emphasised the dynamics of appropriation of Old Testament texts based on continuities and discontinuities in ways that retain the life interests that drive modern-day interpretations.

The analogical paradigm is a useful multidimensional approach. Jonker has described an analogical paradigm,[28] which is an interrogation of the modes of, and further qualification of the comparative paradigm of, West and Gadamer.[29] The analogical paradigm calls for a

22. Conradie and Jonker, "Determining Relative Adequacy," 448.

23. Fludernik, *Narratology*, 144–49.

24. Fludernik, *Narratology*, 150–60.

25. Conradie and Jonker, "Determining Relative Adequacy," 452–54.

26. Jonker, "Further Interrogation."

27. A discussion of the elements in a narrative is beyond the scope of this essay. See DeRouchie, *How to Understand and Apply*, 32–33; Mui, "Contemporary Scholars," 2–4; Mills, *Biblical Morality*, 9, 21, 24, 119–25; and Jonker and Lawrie, "Focusing on the Texts," 95–102. See also Moore, "Biblical Narrative Analysis," 29; Fludernik, *Narratology*; and Bal, *Narratology*.

28. Jonker, "Further Interrogation." Jonker recognises that a biblical scholar's biographies (social and academic locations) always influence his/her interpretations.

29. Jonker explains the comparative paradigm of West via Gadamer as an attempt to establish "a direct relationship between biblical texts and African contexts," "comparing

"historical consciousness" that demonstrates the analogies between the ancient and modern processes of reception.[30] The model strives for both contextual integrity and a community approach that reflects the rise of African cultures. Since history matters in African interpretations, biblical texts are not to be treated as contextless. The analogical method "will do justice to African interpretive interests without neglecting the life interests that drive African interpretations" and "would facilitate interculturality between ancient writer(s) and contemporary reader(s) as it brings the dynamics of appropriation of texts in ancient versus contemporary contexts" in relation to one another.[31]

To fully implement the analogical paradigm, an exegete is required to uncover the ancient writers' specific socio-historical, socio-economic, and socio-cultural realities. These would then be compared with the socio-historical, socio-economic, and socio-cultural realities of the contemporary reader. It is important to discover the realities in the text so that the contemporary reader dialogues with the Bible exegetically rather than the Bible being subordinated to the reader's context. In this way, the exegete avoids "the temptation to construct a socio-historical world without a trace, or with little trace, to the socio-rhetoric world within which the text originates and communicates."[32]

Jonker subsequently proposes the use of an analogical paradigm as a basis for the comparative paradigm often used in African biblical scholarship. Such an analogical paradigm prevents exegetes from either ascribing meaning exclusively to the authorial intentions of the biblical writers, or to the reception of modern-day readers. Thus, he endorses a contemporary application of a social-historical interpretation of a text derived from its socio-historical, socio-economic, and religio-cultural implications in ancient times. He regards the socio-historical, socio-economical, and religio-cultural implications of an ancient text as predilections that would resonate with the life interests of Africans.

---

worlds constructed in the biblical texts and different African contexts." Jonker, "Further Interrogation," 77.

30. Jonker, "Why History Matters," 1–7. Jonker concludes that an interpretation without a historical dimension cannot be contextual, and an interpretation without a sensitivity to the context cannot be historical. Levinson also emphatically declares, "The future is not hermeneutically closed: it is hermeneutically open. The canon is radically open. It invites innovation, it demands interpretation, it challenges piety, it questions priorities, it sanctifies submission and it enables critique." *Legal Revision*, 94.

31. Jonker, "Further Interrogation," 89.

32. Jonker, "Further Interrogation," 82.

Narrative texts can then address life struggles and unhealthy political, social, and cultural issues of ancient times that are similar to our shared West African experiences.

It is possible to reinforce the analogical model by bridging gaps between the worlds of Old Testament authors and the worlds of modern-day readers with the model proposed by Barton.[33] Andersen scrutinised the principles of Old Testament ethics as advanced by Janzen, Wright, and Barton and was able to articulate and lend credence to the use of the three models proposed by Barton:

1. An "Obedience of God's word" model that emphasises divine guidance yet recognises the value of human interests that underline the laws in the community. It acknowledges Israel as the medium of God's words even if Israel was not a perfect model because of her excesses of nationalism.
2. A "Natural law" model that should not be mistaken for Western natural laws. Rather these are ethical principles that are inherent in the nature of things. They are in the form of biblical moral laws but are distinct from biblical law codes that are more positive.
3. An "Imitation of God" model that manifests as ethics of obligations. First, it benchmarks and obligates emulating God's character and deeds. Second, it obligates valuing human dignity and encountering the "other."[34]

Andersen further analyses five themes proposed by Janzen: (1) the familial theme, (2) the priestly theme, (3) the wisdom theme, (4) the royal theme, and (5) the prophetic theme. These themes echo in every narrative text to varying degrees and will help strengthen the models discussed above.[35]

Each Bible text is to pass the test of contextual integrity as explained by Jonker and Lawrie in their communal analogical paradigm (communality approach), which is a progression of the multidimensional approach to biblical interpretation. The test concerns a realisation of the need for an alternative attitude in biblical interpretation—an attitude that does not isolate exegesis and actualisation as binary oppositions.[36]

33. Barton, *Understanding Old Testament Ethics.*
34. Andersen, "Biblical Laws."
35. Andersen, "Biblical Laws."
36. Jonker and Lawrie, "Focusing on the Texts."

I myself have elsewhere written in support of a communal approach to formulating biblical frameworks for ethics:

> Interpretation of the Bible is a communal effort (in constant interaction with the fathers and mothers of the past who brought about the biblical texts and applied them to their contexts, and with the brothers and sisters who strive to apply biblical values to their contemporary modern contexts); interpretation of the Bible should be done analogically, to avoid the danger of jumping directly from the texts to the modern-day contexts; the implications of using an analogical paradigm for the interpretation, are that one should attend to those themes that emerged in the socio-historical, socio-economic, and religio-cultural discussions of the worlds within which the texts originated, for the benefit of applying them to modern-day contexts. . . . In this way, it is possible to reach contextual integrity where the interpreter is responsible in terms of the contexts of the Bible, but also accountable in terms of modern-day contexts of faith.[37]

Conclusion

This essay proposes that West African biblical scholars and preachers do adequate and responsible biblical and hermeneutical scholarship in the area of narratology. I have argued that West Africans have a proclivity for narratives because the dominant cultures are oral in nature. Besides, West Africans also have local settings like "tales by moonlight" and other practices where indigenous origins, histories, civic and religious duties, moral values, crafts, and skills are passed down through generations using oral traditions. As such it can be viable in transmitting Christian values. I also contend that the major shifts in pedagogy, from the teacher-centred to the student-centred, demand that Christian teaching and learning progress from the deductive (analytical, philosophical, and essay-like) to, at the least, the inductive (scientific, probability theory that is concerned with rules of soundness of inferences) and at best, the analogical (paradigmatic, story-like). The aim is not to present the genre of biblical narratives as more "inspired" or of greater value than other genres, but to draw greater attention to the magnetism and optimal didactic potentials of biblical narratives for ethical formations of Christians in West Africa. Furthermore, it is to contribute to the ongoing discourses

37. Amao, "Reading Deuteronomy 16–18," 157.

in narratology and make them available for both biblical scholars (academic and informed reading) and the homilist (lay reading) who does spiritual formation for individuals, families, churches, and societies. For indeed, "to be human is to tell and interpret stories, to conceive of ourselves as living out and living by stories, and to see our individual stories as components of, as contributions to larger family, social, institutional, or national stories." Additionally, narratives "function as powerful and basic tools for thinking" and also work at "constructing and representing the rich and messy domain of human interaction."[38]

Bibliography

Abdulrahman, D. "Colonialism, Development Paths, Globalization, and Social Inequality: The Sources of Social Conflict in Nigeria." In *Nigeria and Globalization: Discourses on Identity Politics and Social Conflict*, edited by S. D. Oni et al., 29–326. Lagos: CBAAC, 2004.

Alliyu, N., et al. "Nigeria's Cobweb of Corruption and the Path to Underdevelopment." *International Journal of Arts and Humanities* 3 (2014) 102–27.

Alumona, I. *Understanding the Crisis of Development in Africa: Reflection on Bedford Umez's Analysis*. Awka: Anambra State University Press, 2009.

Amao, Solomon. "Reading Deuteronomy 16–18 Within the Context of Nepotism and Corruption in ECWA, Nigeria: A Theological-Ethical Study." PhD diss., Stellenbosch University, 2021.

Andersen, Cheryl B. "Biblical Laws: Challenging the Principles of Old Testament Ethics." In *Character Ethics and the Old Testament: Moral Dimensions of Scripture*, edited by Daniel M. Carroll R. et al., 37–50. London: Westminster John Knox, 2007.

Bal, Mieke. *Narratology: Introduction to the Theory of Narrative*. 3rd ed. Toronto: University of Toronto Press, 2009.

Barton, John. *Ethics and the Old Testament*. Harrisburg, PA: Trinity, 1998.

———. *Ethics in Ancient Israel*. Oxford: Oxford University Press, 2014.

———. *Understanding Old Testament Ethics: Approaches and Explorations*. 1st ed. Louisville: Westminster John Knox, 2003.

Birch, Bruce C. *Let Justice Roll Down: The Old Testament, Ethics, and Christian Life*. Louisville: Westminster John Knox, 1991.

Blomberg, Craig. *Interpreting Parables*. 2nd ed. Downers Grove, IL: IVP, 2012.

Bock, Darrell L., and Buist M. Fanning, eds. *Interpreting the New Testament: Introduction to the Art and Science of Exegesis*. Wheaton, IL: Crossway, 2006.

Bosman, Hendrik L. "Bookends of Old Testament Ethics: The First and Tenth Commandments and Human Dignity." *Scriptura* 106 (2011) 93–100.

———. "Fallacy or Fountainhead? Authorial Intention and Historical Critical Interpretation." In *Old Testament Science and Reality*, edited by W. Wessels et al., 20–32. Pretoria: Verba Vitae, 1992.

38. Bruner, "Narrative Construction of Reality," 4; Herman, "Stories as a Tool," 163.

Bruner, Jerome. "The Narrative Construction of Reality." *Critical Inquiry* 18 (1991) 1–21.

Carson, D. A. *Exegetical Fallacies*. 2nd ed. Grand Rapids: Baker, 2006.

Conradie, Ernst M., and Louis C. Jonker. "Determining Relative Adequacy in Biblical Interpretation." *Scriptura* 78 (2001) 448–55. https://doi.org/10.7833/78-0-695.

Davies, Eryl W. *The Immoral Bible: Approaches to Biblical Ethics*. London: T&T Clark, 2010.

Dei, George J. Sefa, et al. *Indigenous Knowledges in Global Contexts: Multiple Readings of our World*. Toronto: University of Toronto Press, 2000.

DeRouchie, Jason S. *How to Understand and Apply the Old Testament*. Phillipsburg, NJ: P&R, 2017.

Duvall, Scott J., and Daniel J. Hays. *Grasping God's Word: A Hands-On Approach to Reading, Interpreting, and Applying the Bible*. Grand Rapids: Zondervan, 2005.

Fludernik, Monika. *Narratology: An Introduction to Narratology*. London: Routledge, 2009.

Giffone, Benjamin D. "The (Ir)Relevance of Biblical Scholarship? A Challenge, and an Opportunity." *Scriptura* 120 (2021) 1–15.

Goldsworthy, Graeme. *According to Plan: The Unfolding Revelation of God in the Bible*. Downers Grove, IL: InterVarsity, 2002.

Grenier, Louise. *Working with Indigenous Knowledge: A Guide for Researchers*. Ottawa: International Development Research Centre, 1998. https://idrc-crdi.ca/en/books/working-indigenous-knowledge-guide-researchers.

Herman, David. "Stories as a Tool for Thinking." In *Narrative Theory and the Cognitive Sciences*, edited by David Herman, 163–92. Stanford, CA: CSLI, 2003.

Jonker, Louis C. "Further Interrogation of the Comparative Paradigm in African Biblical Scholarship: Towards an Analogical Hermeneutics for Interpreting the Old Testament in Africa." In *Reading Writing Right: Essays Presented in Honour of Prof Elna Mouton*, edited by Jeremy Punt and Marius J. Nel, 73–97. Stellenbosch: Sun, 2018.

———. "Why History Matters: The Place of Historical Consciousness in a Multidimensional Approach Towards Biblical Interpretation." *Verbum et Ecclesia* 34.2 (2013) 1–7. http://dx.doi.org/10.4102/ve.v34i2.775.

Jonker, Louis C., and Douglas Lawrie. "Approaches Focusing on the Texts Themselves." In *Fishing for Jonah (Anew)*, edited by Louis C. Jonker and Douglas G. Lawrie, 67–108. Stellenbosch: Sun, 2005.

Kaiser, Walter C., Jr. *Preaching and Teaching from the Old Testament: A Guide for the Church*. Grand Rapids: Baker, 2003.

Kunhiyop, Samuel Waje. "The Challenge of African Christian Morality." *Conspectus: Journal of the South African Theological Seminary* 7.3 (2009) 60–80.

Levinson, Bernard M. *Legal Revision and Religious Renewal in Ancient Israel*. Cambridge: Cambridge University Press, 2008.

———. *"The Right Chorale": Studies in Biblical Law and Interpretation*. Winona Lake, IN: Eisenbrauns, 2008.

McCartney, Dan, and Charles Clayton. *Let the Reader Understand: A Guide to Interpreting and Applying the Bible*. Phillipsburg, NJ: P&R, 2002.

Meyer, Esias, and Leonore Pietersen. "Old Testament Stories and Christian Ethics: Some Perspectives from the Narrative of Judah and Tamar." *Stellenbosch Theological Journal* 2 (2016) 241–59. http://dx.doi.org/10.17570/stj.2016.v2n1.a12.

Mills, Mary E. *Biblical Morality: Moral Perspectives in Old Testament Narratives*. Aldershot: Ashgate, 2001.

Moore, Stephen D. "Biblical Narrative Analysis from the New Criticism to the New Narratology." In *The Oxford Handbook of Biblical Narratives*, edited by Doanna Nolan Fewell, 27–50. New York: Oxford University Press, 2016.

Mui, Daisy Ying Mei. "How Do the Contemporary Scholars John Barton, Gordon Wenham, and Mary Mills Use Old Testament Narratives in Forming Christian Ethics?" Master's thesis, Wycliffe College and Toronto School of Theology, 2018.

Ochefu, Yakubu A., and Chris B. N. Ogbogbo. "The Role of Historical Societies in Nigeria's Development." *Afrika Zamani: Revue Annuelle d'Histoire Africaine* 13–14 (2005) 73–85.

Okolo, Philips O., and Akpokighe Okiemute Raymond. "Corruption in Nigeria: Possible Way Out." *Global Journal of Human-Social Justice* 14.7 (2014) 30–38.

Olarewaju, John Shola. "Understanding Nigerian Development Crisis." *Afro-Asian Journal of Social Sciences* 6 (2015) 1–8.

Olojede, Funlola. "Storytelling as an Indigenous Resource in the Interpretation of Old Testament Ethics and Religion." *Scriptura* 113 (2014) 1–9.

Reid, David R. *Study to Show Yourself Approved*. Dubuque, IA: Emmaus Correspondence School, 2007.

Todd, William P. "The Attitudes of the Evangelical Church of West Africa Towards Islam in Light of Ethnic and Religious Violence." Master's thesis, Queens University, 2010.

Wright, Christopher J. H. *Old Testament Ethics for the People of God*. Downers Grove, IL: InterVarsity, 2004.

2

Who Says We Do Not Need Historical Analysis?

Let Them Raise Their Hands

Ntozakhe Simon Cezula

Louis Jonker recalls the development of contextual approaches to biblical interpretation "since the 1960s, particularly in the wake of independence movements in the global south throwing-off the shackles of colonial oppression under European imperialism."[1] The implication thereof is accentuated in Knut Holter's remark: "Historical-critical methodology as we know it from Old Testament studies cannot escape the impression of being a typically western approach, an exponent of a western epistemology and hermeneutics of the eighteenth to twentieth centuries."[2] Holter distinguishes a category of African Old Testament scholars who long to reject "historical-critical methodology as a dogmatically intolerable way of responding to the revealed Word of God." Adhering, more or less, to fundamentalist theological contexts and claims of the inerrancy of Scripture, "they attempt to develop textual approaches that are free from the presuppositions of traditional historical-critical interpretation."[3] If I

1. Jonker, "Context[,] All Over[,] Again," 28.
2. Holter, "Historical-Critical Methodology," 382.
3. Holter, "Historical-Critical Methodology," 378.

may add, some suggest doing away with teaching the background to the Old Testament and do not regard dissertations using historical exegetical methods as African Biblical Hermeneutic (ABH). Conscious of these developments, Jonker is reminded of "the biblical interpretation trends in apartheid South Africa, where white and male (contemporary) *reception* dominated biblical interpretation to the detriment of its historical and literary dimensions." He is also reminded of "the devastating socio-political and socio-economic effects of apartheid biblical interpretation [by] not taking all three dimensions into account."[4]

In response, he suggests a "communal" approach to biblical interpretation, the core element of which is historical consciousness. However, he realises that his suggestion has been misinterpreted in some quarters of biblical interpretation. This chapter, therefore, aims to demonstrate the benefit of historical consciousness the "communal" approach suggests. It aims to read Gen 9:18–29 applying the elements of the communal approach. Special attention will be paid to the diachronic structure of the receiver. This will entail looking at the reading of Gen 9:18–29 during early Judaism in the late postexilic period and the rabbinic period in the Christian era. Since the rabbinic literature introduces a new element of skin colour, I will also examine the early encounter of amaXhosa on the one hand and the Khoi and the San people on the other, to make sense of the rabbinic sentiments towards Black skin. The discussion will start by describing the communal approach. It will then attend to the synchronic and diachronic structures of the text and the sender. After that, it will examine the receiver's synchronic and diachronic structures. Concluding remarks will bring the discussion to the end.

Jonker's "Communal" Approach

Jonker may not be impressed to see a subtitle that says "Jonker's 'Communal' Approach." The reason is that he does not see it as a new method distinct from what exists. He just uses the word *communal* to exhibit the spirit behind attending to all the different dimensions of the text. Nevertheless, from October 13 to 16, 1999, an international symposium on "Africa and the Old Testament" was held in Karen, outside Nairobi, Kenya. Jonker presented a paper titled "Towards a 'Communal' Approach

4. Jonker, "Context[,] All Over[,] Again," 31; emphasis original.

for Reading the Bible in Africa."[5] "The theme of the third session was 'Using Africa to Interpret the OT.' . . . Louis Jonker advocated the need for a 'communal' approach for reading the Bible in Africa."[6] He describes the communal approach as not something new but an emphasis on the multidimensionality of biblical interpretation. Importantly, he views historical consciousness as of "cardinal importance in the interpretation process."[7] Somehow bemoaningly, he says,

> Some participants in the discussion thought that I was arguing for some sort of a reconstruction of *the original context*, or that I was stepping into the trap of trying to identify the *intention of the author*. Some thought that I was confusing the *real author* and the *implied author* of texts, and indicated that the real author can never be recovered.[8]

The historical consciousness entailed by the communal approach, therefore, is not "a longing for a past which is forever lost, or with an optimism that the intentions of the original authors can be reconstructed." Rather, "historical consciousness is . . . the reader- or context-oriented appreciation of the contexts of textual production and of textual reception (from ancient times, throughout the ages, up to modern-day receptions in various and differing circumstances)."[9] He identifies the three elements of communication—namely, sender (author), medium (text), and receiver (reader). He argues that all three bear both diachronic and synchronic features. The author's context is synchronic, while the long process that involves the initial author, the subsequent editor(s), and the final compiler(s) forms a diachronic process. Similarly, how the text is understood by a given generation of readers is synchronic, whereas the different understandings of the text by different generations in their different contexts over the years form a diachronic structure. In the same vein, the context of readers is synchronic, while the different contexts of the successive generations of readers throughout their history also form a diachronic structure. Imagined together, these elements form what he calls "a hermeneutical map of the dynamic process of biblical

5. Jonker, "Towards a 'Communal' Approach."
6. Holter, "Symposium in Nairobi," 8.
7. Jonker, "Why History Matters," 1.
8. Jonker, "Why History Matters," 1.
9. Jonker, "Why History Matters," 6.

interpretation."[10] The engagement with all the six elements of this hermeneutical map is what historical consciousness entails. In different publications, he has advocated this approach in different ways.[11] By reading Gen 9:18–29 from a "communal" approach, I hope to demonstrate that historical consciousness can also help counter interpretations that distort the text motivated by discriminatory tendencies.

Synchronic and Diachronic Analysis of the Medium

The text as we have it today starts with Noah and his three sons who came out of the ark as the only survivors of the flood (verse 18) and ends with Noah dying at 950 years old (verse 29). Like in other instances, the order of the sons is Shem, Ham, and then Japhet.[12] The consistency of this order gives the impression that it descends from the oldest to the youngest. Expressing the same sentiment, Robert R. Wilson says the word *tôlēdôt*, which is frequently used to introduce genealogies in Biblical Hebrew, is derived from the root *yld* and "seems to mean literally 'the order in which people are born.'"[13] The impression of the descending order by age expressed here might be the same impression that leads Ephraim Isaac to describe Ham as "the name of the second son of Noah, and the brother of Shem and Japheth."[14] David Whitford blatantly expresses this confusion: "His 'youngest son' here means Ham, even though the text makes clear earlier that Ham is actually his middle child."[15] Nevertheless, the text continues to present these three sons of Noah as the ones from whom people of the whole earth descended (verse 19). There are no genealogical details before or after these names, but their outlook is genealogical. Maybe the author, in constructing the structure of his composition, did excerpt from a genealogical text. Of course, as Wilson asserts, genealogies played an important role in the life of the Israelites and the priestly writer also used them "to give the book a

10. Jonker, "Towards a 'Communal' Approach," 79.

11. Jonker, *Exclusivity and Variety*; Jonker, "Reading Jonah Multi-Dimensionally"; Jonker, "Towards a 'Communal' Approach"; Jonker, "Why History Matters," 1–7; Jonker, "Context[,] All Over[,] Again"; Jonker, "Contextual Interpretation, Then and Now."

12. Gen 5:32, 6:10, 7:13, 9:18, 10:1; 1 Chr 1:4.

13. Wilson, "Genealogy," 2:929.

14. Isaac, "Ham," 3:31.

15. Whitford, *Curse of Ham*, 3.

literary structure."[16] *Eye-catching* is how the list is presented. As if it is an afterthought, Canaan's name is thrust next to Ham's name, to designate Ham the father of Canaan. The other two brothers are not presented as fathers. It leaves one wondering why Ham alone is presented as a father and not his brothers too. Why are the other brothers' children not included, but Canaan alone? Why does the author choose the youngest son of Ham if he has to introduce him by a son? Normally, the first son is the one by whom a father is called. Sensing the anomaly, David H. Aaron propounds that the inclusion of Canaan is a gloss. He even suggests that the gloss serves the socio-political agenda of the redactor. He intimates that the redactor channels the story towards his own purpose.

Anyway, the story shifts focus from the sons of Noah to Noah himself. In verses 20–23, Noah is presented as the first person to plant a vineyard. He drank wine, got drunk, slept, and in the process exposed his nakedness. Ham saw him naked and told his brothers, Shem and Japhet, who covered their father without looking at his nakedness. For the second time, all three sons are involved, but only Ham is called by his son, the youngest son at that. The repetition of this odd designation of Ham as the father of Canaan starts to arouse curiosity. Aaron's suspicion above starts to gain traction. Among other things, repetition is a literary device to emphasise or to draw the attention of the listener. This repetition, coupled with the oddity of Canaan's presence as the son among the parents, makes Canaan's inclusion awkward and thus suspicious. Recognising this oddity, Gunther Wittenberg, echoing Aaron, perceives Canaan in verses 18 and 22 as an insertion.[17] Nevertheless, Noah woke up and "knew what his youngest son had done to him" (verse 24).[18] Even more astonishing, the "innocent" Canaan is cursed instead of the transgressor, Ham. The curse is announced three times in three verses, 25–27. On this, Christoph Uehlinger comments, "Canaan, the son of Ham, is also mentioned because of the particular outcome of the following story. . . . Canaan thus represents from the beginning an almost tragical character in a play that calls him on stage only to be submitted to the permanent fate of slavery."[19] Uehlinger's observation confirms Aaron's suspicion. Aaron suggested that "the original passage must simply have read that all human beings

16. Wilson, "Genealogy," 2:929.

17. Wittenberg, "Is Ham Also Cursed," 47.

18. Unless otherwise noted, all Scripture quotations in this chapter are from the ESV.

19. Uehlinger, "'Pre-Israelite' Peoples," 567–68.

were descendants from these three men."[20] Instead, the redactor inserted this "anachronistic gloss" as a foreshadowing of Canaan's curse. Canaan, it has now become clear, is thrust in just to be cursed. Having said all that has been said, in its final form, the text presents Canaan as the one who is cursed, and that is what is recorded. Emphasis is needed here. It is nobody else but Canaan that is cursed by Noah. This is what the analysis of the synchronic structure of the text yields.

From a diachronic point of view, Claus Westermann postulates that Gen 9:18–29 is a composite text that brings together (1) a genealogical tradition, (2) a history of civilisation, (3) a crime and punishment tradition, and (4) the tradition of curses and blessings.[21] Genealogies have their own function of tracing the origin of people and their relations. The names of the sons of Noah belong to this tradition. A history of civilisation is a tradition that traces developments within a given culture and its civilisation. The notice of Noah as the first man to grow a vine falls into this tradition of a history of civilisation. This notice is then attached to the genealogy as a note in a genealogy. Notes do get inserted in a genealogy to share some brief information about a certain person within the family tree. From this note in a genealogy develops a story. The story itself belongs to another tradition, a tradition of crime and punishment. This story develops from verses 21 to 24. In this story, a son dishonours his father whose faculties have been impaired by wine. In so doing, he incurred the father's curse. Stories of this nature, in fact, are common in primaeval events. Now we have a story formed by bringing together different traditions to focus on a particular family. From another tradition of blessings and curses, the redactor brings in a curse. Verse 25, which says, "Cursed be Canaan; a servant of servants shall he be to his brothers," is from a tradition of blessings and curses. The disagreement between the name *Ham* in verse 22 and the name *Canaan* in verse 25 indicates the different layers of this story. In the previous analysis, it was indicated that this insertion is absurd. Roughly, there might be three layers already in the story: the independent traditions in their original contexts, their coming together to form this story, and the introduction of the curse of Canaan.

It could be a story of the first family of the first man to grow the vine who got drunk from the wine and got dishonoured by his son and he

20. Aaron, "Early Rabbinic Exegesis," 730.

21. Westermann, *Genesis*, 68.

cursed him. Westermann endorses this probability when he says, "One can conjecture that there was an older form of the narrative which told only of the son of Noah the winegrower, and which ended with the curse over his son."[22] He views the story as belonging "to the group of crime and punishment stories characteristic of the primeval event and is close to the family stories of the patriarchal history."[23] Verse 25 is connected to the story by thrusting in verses 18 and 22: "Ham was the father of Canaan," and "the father of Canaan," respectively. The disagreement of the names of Ham in verse 22 and Canaan in verse 25 has kept biblical readers talking up to this day. The different elements of this story from independent traditions could have been composed by whomever. Their combination until verse 24 could also be a redaction of whomever. But the inclusion of Canaan, specifically, is very highly probable to be the Yahwist's work. The fact that it does not agree with the name of Ham in verse 22 is telling. To crown it all, the Yahwist brought in the blessings of Shem and Japhet. This addition transformed a family-oriented story into a politically oriented one. The story took on political overtones. Canaan stands for the Canaanites and Shem for the Israelites. As Robert B. Coote connected the dots, the conquest of Canaan is the climax of the curse of Canaan in Gen 9:25–26, reinforced with the promise to Abraham in Gen 12:1–3 and 6–7.[24] This analysis confirms the previous analysis that it is Canaan that was cursed and not Ham.

Synchronic and Diachronic Analysis of the Sender

Now that it has been established from the text that it is Canaan that the author is mainly interested in and not Ham, a synchronic analysis of the sender may strengthen or weaken this argument. In its final form, the compiler of Gen 9:18–29 is identified as the Yahwist. Barbara Green describes the Yahwist as "typically recognized as the most brilliant of the pentateuchal storytellers . . . from the origins of human existence to the eve of entrance into the Promised Land."[25] The Documentary Hypothesis came up with this designation of the Yahwist. Providing more about the Yahwist, Green says, "The Yahwist may be presumed to have been active

22. Westermann, *Genesis 1–11*, 485.

23. Westermann, *Genesis 1–11*, 485.

24. Coote, "Conquest," 275.

25. Green, "Yahwist," 1402.

in the Davidic court, hence writing ca. the 10th century BCE. . . . The Jerusalem location and early date suggest to some that the Yahwist is an apologist for the Davidic monarchy and enterprise, the epic recounting the tribal roots of the emergent state."[26] Nadav Na'aman says, "The ethnic/gentilic name 'Jebusite' appears in almost all lists of the pre-Israelite nations. In many cases it closes the list, probably due to the fact that according to biblical historiography David subdued the Jebusites, and hence they were the last group among the six/seven nations that the Israelites subjugated."[27] Alternatively, Niels Peter Lemche says the Yahwist source "was formerly attributed to the work of a scribe, or a circle of scribes, who lived in the days of King Solomon at the end of the 10th century BCE."[28] Solomon is also implicated in the subjugation of the Canaanites. Lemche evokes 1 Kgs 9:20–21 when Solomon conscripted "the surviving 'Amorites, Hittites, Perizzites, Hivites and Jebusites' to corvée workers."[29] For von Rad, the Yahwist is connected to both David and Solomon.[30] Nevertheless, whether it is David or Solomon, it seems the tenth century, generally, is somehow connected with the subjugation of the Canaanites. This is compatible with the curse of Canaan to be the slave of Shem. The circumstances of the author depicted here concerning the Canaanites conform to the intention of the author to direct the curse to Canaan. As Day said earlier concerning the curse of either Ham or Canaan, the editor of Gen 9:25 "presumably had some view on the matter."[31] I conclude that this view is the subjugation of the Canaanites and not the Curse of Ham. While some scholars reject the date of the tenth century, the claim of the land of Canaan for the Israelites remains. In a paper titled "The Elusive Yahwist," Römer says, "Today one may find proposals for virtually each century between the tenth and the sixth centuries BCE"[32] for the date of the Yahwist. However, whether the Yahwist is preexilic (von Rad), exilic (Levin), or postexilic (Persian era; Lemche), the land of Canaan is central. After doing an overview of the discussion on the Yahwist, Jean-Louis Ska says, "To conclude: along with the Elohist, the Yahwist has also lost credit. This is why certain scholars prefer to speak about 'nonpriestly

26. Green, "Yahwist," 1402–3.
27. Na'aman, "Jebusites and Jabeshites," 481.
28. Lemche, *Canaanites*, 65.
29. Lemche, *Canaanites*, 120.
30. Von Rad, *Genesis*, 30, 98.
31. Day, *From Creation to Babel*, 141.
32. Römer, "Elusive Yahwist," 22.

texts.'"[33] However, even if the Yahwist is removed from the stage and replaced with non-priestly sources, as Ska indicates, Canaan remains in the centre because of the need to recover the lost land during the exile and in the postexilic periods. The "Curse of Ham," therefore, cannot have been derived from the Bible but from somewhere else.

Synchronic and Diachronic Analysis of the Receiver

No matter how anachronistic the gloss the Yahwist attached to Ham's name, saying, "Ham being the father of Canaan," it served the purpose of the Yahwist to establish his socio-political agenda. His intended audience must have grappled with the same questions that the Yahwist grappled with. Therefore, just as the Yahwist "didn't need a 'Curse of Ham', but . . . a 'Curse of Canaan,'"[34] so did his audience. Whether it was the tenth-century audience, the exilic, or the postexilic (Persian era) audience, the land of Canaan was their area of interest. As Edith R. Sanders puts it, "Ideas have a way of being accepted when they become useful as a rationalization of an economic fact of life."[35] Considering this statement, it may not be far-fetched to argue that the discrepancy between Ham and Canaan in Gen 9:22 and verse 25, respectively, might not have been a contention for the Yahwist's audience. As Philip E. Satterthwaite avers, Israel's inheritance of Canaan was integral to the themes of election and promise.[36] Canaan's importance to the people of Judah underscores its central role in their narrative and identity. Understanding the situation from this sense, some remarks from Lemche may be proper to conclude this part of the discussion:

> The Canaanites may be considered a kind of ideological prototype of an ethnic phenomenon which was very much a reality in the period when the historical narratives were reduced to writing, and, furthermore, it is obvious that the Canaanites represented a phenomenon which was considered to be extraneous and hostile to the Israelites. . . . Such anti-Canaanite sentiments were nourished among the historians who wrote the Pentateuch

33. Ska, *Introduction to Reading the Pentateuch*, 145.
34. Aaron, "Early Rabbinic Exegesis," 730.
35. Sanders, "Hamitic Hypothesis," 522.
36. Satterthwaite, "Genealogies in the Old Testament," 222.

> . . . and concerned the religious, ethnic and political conditions of their own time.[37]

If the expressed sentiments are anything to go by, the "Curse of Ham" cannot have been derived from the Bible but from an external source. The Bible actually projects the curse of Canaan.

A diachronic examination of the structures of the receiver may provide information that may help place the "Curse of Ham" into perspective. The author of the book of Jubilees is one interesting reader in his interpretation of Gen 9:18–29. The author of Jubilees is not known. VanderKam says about the author of Jubilees, "He does not disclose to the reader his name, where he lived, his family connections, his education, or his position in society."[38] Nevertheless, the book of "Jubilees was likely written at some point between c. the 170s (or even 164) and c. 125 BCE (the upper date limit for the earliest copy). It is difficult to be more precise than that."[39] James L. Kugel describes the author of Jubilees as having lived when his community was despairing for Israel's future. This community brooded over the downfall of the Northern Kingdom of Israel and the successive subjugations of Judah; first the Babylonian exile, then "ruled over . . . by Persia, then Ptolemaic Egypt, then by Seleucid Syria." The community concluded that "the apparently unending years of foreign domination were a clear indication that Israel had fallen into God's disfavour."[40] As a "conscientious" interpreter, the author of Jubilees rewrote Genesis "principally to combat any such reading of history." The author of Jubilees found retelling the book of Genesis "the ideal instrument for communicating" that their historic bond with God had not ended.[41] They will always be God's people. The stories of "Israel's remote ancestors, Abraham and Sarah, Isaac and Rebekah, and Jacob and his wives and children,"[42] are evidence of God's commitment to his relationship with Israel. To prove his claim, he points to the land of Canaan, which he describes as God's tangible grant to the ancestors and their descendants.

37. Lemche, *Canaanites*, 165.

38. VanderKam, *Book of Jubilees*, 38.

39. VanderKam, *Book of Jubilees*, 37–38.

40. Kugel, *Walk Through Jubilees*, 6.

41. Kugel, *Walk Through Jubilees*, 6.

42. Kugel, *Walk Through Jubilees*, 6.

According to Michael Segal, one of the elements of the ideology of the author of Jubilees is that the land called Canaan originally belonged to the Israelites.[43] To purport this idea, the author of Jubilees introduces the second curse of Canaan for occupying the land allotted to Shem and his descendants in Jubilees 10:28–36. The narrative structure of Jubilees presents both the departure from Egypt and the arrival in Canaan as having happened on the fiftieth Jubilee, depicting the release of slaves to claim their lost land. From this perspective, there is no way that another person other than Canaan could have been cursed. The "Curse of Ham" cannot, therefore, have been derived from this text. Another "conscientious" interpreter of early Judaism is the author of the Genesis Apocryphon. In fact, he is not that much different from the author of Jubilees. According to Machiela, "the Genesis Apocryphon shares Jubilees' concern for defending Israel's claim to the land called Canaan in the Pentateuch."[44] "According to both texts, the eventual conquest of this land by the Israelites merely restored to Shem's descendants what was rightfully theirs from the beginning."[45] The author of the Genesis Apocryphon made it his duty "to alleviate difficulties in Genesis" by bringing in Noah's dream and the earth's division.[46] He made sure there was no ambiguity about the curse of Canaan and removed Ham from what became the curse conundrum of Genesis. Now it has become clear that if there is anywhere to find building blocks for the "Curse of Ham," it is not in early Judaism.

Other interesting readers of Gen 9:18–29 for this discussion are the rabbinic circles of around the sixth century CE. Responding to Gen 9:19, the rabbinic literature introduced the Curse of Ham. Until this point, we have been dealing with the *curse of Canaan*. For the first time now, Ham is introduced as also cursed. Sanhedrin 108b of the Babylonian Talmud records that all the occupants of the ark during the flood were forbidden to engage in sexual intercourse. David M. Goldenberg provides both the version of the Babylonian Talmud and the Jerusalem Talmud:

> The Palestinian version tells it this way: "Ham, the dog, and the raven had sexual relations [in the ark]. Ham went forth darkened/blackened [*mefuham*], the dog went forth with the characteristic of publicly copulating [or, of copulating in a well-known manner]; and the raven went forth different from other

43. Segal, *Book of Jubilees*, 7.

44. Machiela, *Dead Sea Genesis Apocryphon*, 99.

45. Machiela, *Dead Sea Genesis Apocryphon*, 131.

46. Machiela, *Dead Sea Genesis Apocryphon*, 131.

> creatures." The Babylonian version: "Three had sexual relations in the ark and they were all punished; the dog, the raven, and Ham. The dog is connected, the raven spits, and Ham was punished in his skin [*laqah be-Goro*]."[47]

Goldenberg then writes a commentary on these two versions of the Talmudîm as follows:

> It would appear that the Palestinian and Babylonian versions do not disagree in the various elements of the story except, possibly, regarding the dog's punishment. And although the Palestinian account is clear enough, if not always specific ("different from other creatures"), the Babylonian is specific but unclear. What do "connected," "spit," and "punished in skin" mean? By the ninth to eleventh century a set of explanations for these three expressions seems to have become well accepted and is commonly found in Jewish literature from that period onward. Accordingly, "connected" refers to the dog's physiological inability to disengage from the bitch immediately after ejaculation; "spit" refers to what was believed to be the raven's unique manner of inseminating the female by spitting the semen into her mouth; and "punished in skin" means that Ham's skin turned dark, as stated in the Palestinian version.[48]

So, for copulating in the ark, the dog was punished to remain tied after mating, the raven to inseminate through the mouth, and Ham to be Black-skinned.

To grasp the gravity of this narrative, we must identify its genre first. This story is what is called an aetiology. The word *aetiology* is the combination of the Greek words *aitia* (reason, cause) and *logos* (reasoning). One can literally say *reasoning about a cause*. In the case of this story, we have an aetiological story. An aetiological story is meant to answer questions people might ask concerning the things they see in their environment and wonder why they are the way they are. Describing aetiology, Goldenberg says,

> Stories of origins are common. They serve to explain the state of the world, especially natural phenomena that appear unusual or strange (e.g., "How did the tiger get its stripes?"). The Bible itself provides several well-known examples. The story of Adam and Eve in the Garden of Eden accounts for the unusual, legless

47. Goldenberg, *Race and Slavery*, 103.

48. Goldenberg, *Race and Slavery*, 103.

> feature of the snake. The Tower of Babel narrative explains the multiplicity of languages in the world. Noah's curse of slavery is also an etiology, explaining the (actual or imagined) subservient position of the Canaanites in later Israelite society ("It came about when Israel became strong, that they put the Canaanites to forced labor."—Judges 1:28).[49]

So, the story of the dog, raven, and Ham in the ark is an aetiology explaining why the dog and the raven do as they do. Concerning Ham, the story makes sense if one considers that from Ham, who is presumably white, descended Kush and Egypt, who are dark-skinned. Commenting on this story's genre, Goldenberg says, "This story . . . is an aetiology accounting for the darker skin of some of the descendants of Ham."[50]

Before grappling with this aetiology, a perspective is needed. It is, indeed, puzzling that we have people of different skin colours on earth while we are all descended from the same couple—namely, Noah and his wife. It is therefore not abnormal that the rabbis of the Talmudîm concerned themselves with this conundrum. An aetiology is a logical consequence of one's interaction with their environmental context and circumstances of their origin generally. It is of paramount importance, therefore, that it is examined within the parameters of its context of origin. Goldenberg provides a helpful perspective in this regard, "that these folktales are concerned with skin color, not race."[51] Isaac argues that "racialism, the doctrine that some people are biologically and inherently superior to others, is alien to their thinking."[52] An example of what is being expressed here is Bereshit Rabbah 37:2:

> "And the sons of Ḥam: Kush, and Mitzrayim, and Put, and Canaan"—Rabbi Shimon ben Lakish said: We might have been under the impression that the family of Put was assimilated [into other nations]. But Ezekiel came and stated explicitly [otherwise]: "Kush, Put and Lud and all the intermingled people, Cub (*sic*) and the children of the land of the covenant, will fall with them by the sword" (Ezekiel 30:5).[53]

49. Goldenberg, *Black and Slave*, 28.
50. Goldenberg, *Black and Slave*, 19.
51. Goldenberg, "Case of Rabbinic Racism," 24.
52. Isaac, "Genesis," 6.
53. Bereshit Rabbah 37:2 (Sefaria ed.); brackets original.

In the mind of Rabbi Shimon ben Lakish, Put was absorbed in other branches of the family, but Ezekiel reminded him that Put belonged to the family of Ham. Another example is Vayikra Rabbah 17:6. It states as follows:

> Who came and told the Canaanites that Israel was entering the land? Rabbi Yishmael bar Naḥman said: Joshua sent three missives to them. One who wishes to evacuate, let him evacuate. One who wishes to make peace, let him make peace. One who wishes to wage war, let him do so. The Girgashite stood and evacuated; therefore they were given a land as fine as their [previous] land. That is what is written: "Until I arrive and take you to a land like your land" (Isaiah 36:17); this is Africa.[54]

As much as the Girgashites are presented in a negative light—particularly in Deuteronomy—this passage, as well as the previous one, is not hostile. Isaac comments,

> Inasmuch as the Israelites who sin against God can be accursed, the Canaanites who obey God can be blessed; in other words, there is no dogmatic view on the curse of Canaan. Thus the *Canaanite* Eliezar, the servant of Abraham, succeeded in escaping the curse because of his service to Abraham. One Canaanite tribe, called the Girgashites, left Canaan of their own accord and went to North Africa; so God blessed them by giving them a land "as beautiful as theirs."[55]

An interpretation of this aetiology that is based on racism as it is known today is misplaced. Whether the thinking of the rabbis is sensible for our respective contexts is a different issue, that has to do with our own challenges, than the text. This is the perspective for this aetiology.

All cultures have aetiologies. AmaXhosa also have their own aetiologies. Some of the amaXhosa myths of origin are recorded by Janet Hodgson in her PhD dissertation titled "Ntsikana: History and Symbol Studies in a Process of Religious Change Among Xhosa-Speaking People." Hodgson records this myth of origin as follows:

> The first man and woman, together with their animals, appeared on earth from a previous existence. The so-called "Creator," perhaps better, originator, is conceived as enabling them to emerge. Common to the different versions of the Xhosa cosmogonic

54. Vayikra Rabbah 17:6 (Sefaria ed.).

55. Isaac, "Genesis," 7; emphasis original.

myth is the idea that men and animals formerly existed in caverns in the bowels of the earth. At length they are said to have come forth out of this underworld through an immense hole, the opening of which was either in a cavern or else in a marsh overgrown with reeds. . . . Xhosa oral traditions refer to their place of origin as *Eluhlangeni* or *Umhlanga*.[56]

Ntongela Masilela explains *Eluhlangeni* or *Umhlanga* as "the place of reeds" where *abantu bomlambo* (the mythical river people) reside. According to Masilela, "although this myth of origins about *umhlanga* has affinities with other African myths of origins, in Xhosa oral traditions it took on a particular distinctiveness: this distinctiveness is that of incorporation, amenability, expansion and constant metamorphoses."[57] What Masilela means is that this myth accommodates the Bantu-speaking people only. When amaXhosa encountered the Khoi people and the San people, these new encounters had to be accounted for. Hodgson has a longer version of this adjusted myth, but I prefer to use a shorter version told by Robert Balfour Noyi, published in the *Glasgow Missionary Record, 1848*, and included as an appendix in a book edited by John Knox Bokwe:

"A certain man," say they, "had three sons, whose names were Ibranana, Xosa, and Twa. Ibranana was a keeper of cattle, sheep, and goats, as was also Xosa, while poor Twa was satisfied with his honey bird and his game in the desert. Ibranana (the ancestor of the Hottentots[58]) was not a tall man, and his complexion was sallow. Twa (the ancestor of the Bushman[59]) was shorter still and more slender, and also of a sallow

56. Hodgson, *God of the Xhosa*, 6–7.

57. Masilela, "Modern World of Xhosa Folklore," 4.

58. The term *Hottentots* was used by Europeans to refer to Khoi people. It is now regarded as offensive. According to Hodgson, "available linguistic and archaeological evidence indicates that they had occupied . . . [West of the Kei] for many centuries. There was some active resistance among the Khoi to the Xhosa advance; but on the whole friendly relations were established between them and they lived side by side for many years." Hodgson, *God of the Xhosa*, 3.

59. The term *Bushmen* was used by Europeans to refer to San people. It is now regarded as offensive. According to Hodgson, "the land east of the Kei was originally occupied by roving bands of 'hunter-gatherers' generally known as San or Bushmen. As the Xhosa penetrated further the San were driven from their hunting grounds to seek refuge in the mountain strongholds of the Drakensberg. But some established a symbiotic relationship with the Xhosa and continued to occupy the same territory. Intermarriage took place on a limited scale." Hodgson, *God of the Xhosa*, 3.

> complexion, but a shade lighter. And Xosa was a tall, muscular man, and dark coloured."[60]

Three points deserve highlighting in this aetiology—namely, Twa is referred to as "poor Twa." This exhibits some condescension, an attitude of patronising superiority. The complexion of Twa and Ibranana is said to be sallow, implying they are unhealthy somehow. It is thus viewed as not normal. The dark complexion seems to be viewed positively. It is the complexion that is normal. These attitudes exhibit ethnocentrism.

It does not need to be stated that these isiXhosa myths of origin have nothing to do with ancient Israel and the Jewish life of the Christian era. The differences are obvious. However, there are similarities as well. First, both these myths point to one couple from which all humanity descended. Genesis 9:18–25 presents Noah and his wife as the couple from which humanity descended. The isiXhosa myth refers to the first man and the first woman, who came with their animals from a cavern, from whom humanity descended. This is a phenomenon that permeates all humankind. Second, the myths of the origin of humanity raised expectations that all people of the world would resemble the first couple in all respects. The existence of dark-skinned Cushites and Egyptians on the one hand, and light-skinned Khoi and San, on the other, were social realities that needed an explanation. For this reason, the second myths are responses to such questions. Goldenberg asserts that such "etiological myths are common to all cultures." He relates a Cameroonian folktale about two children who were sent to the sea to wash because they were dirty. The one jumped into the water and came out white again. The other one only made the soles of the feet and palms of the hands wet. The father said to him, "May you therefore become black and may your children and your children's children all become black. Only the soles of your feet and the palms of your hands will remain white." The point being emphasised is that the Ham story is in line with worldwide trends. There is no reason to understand it other than an aetiology to explain how Cush became Black. Third, both aetiologies consider the skin colour of the communities from which they originate as normal and the preferred one; the other colour is abnormal. For the Jewish story, dark skin is a punishment, while for the isiXhosa, dark skin is expressed with appreciation. This situation is not peculiar to a particular community but permeates all communities. Goldenberg eloquently says, "Such human conceit is universal. People everywhere find most desirable

60. Noyi, "Ama-Xosa History," 37.

that which most closely resembles themselves."[61] This point leads to the fourth: both aetiologies exhibit some degree of negative sentiments toward the other skin colour. The Jewish aetiology presents dark skin as a curse, and isiXhosa aetiology presents the light skin as sallow, denoting unhealth somehow. In this sense, they both exhibit ethnocentrism. Goldenberg explains this as "an ethnocentric manifestation of conformism to dominant aesthetic tastes."[62] He then makes an interesting point: "Ethnocentrism is not tantamount to racism. The former recognises physical reality, the latter orders that reality into a hierarchy of domination."[63] His point is that disparagement of the other's somatic features "is not in and of itself racist. Only when a society's internal structures are discriminatory and its ideology justifies such discrimination can that society be considered racist."[64] Lastly and importantly, none of these aetiologies are racist.

To demonstrate that these aetiologies are not racist, I start with the isiXhosa story. The isiXhosa myth, as already indicated, considers the dark skin normal and the light skin not normal. This leads to negative sentiments about light skin. For example, light skin is said to be sallow, connoting unhealth. This is an expression of ethnocentrism. Historical details corroborate this ethnocentric attitude. According to historian Jeffrey B. Peires, "a Khoi who entered the Xhosa society did so on terms of distinct inferiority."[65] However, Peires qualifies this statement: "But since this inferiority was expressed in economic terms and not in social or racial ones, it passed within the course of a generation."[66] Hodgson corroborates:

> Extensive intermarriage, led by the respective royal lineages, opened the way for cultural diffusion. . . . Mixed Khoi and Xhosa communities are recorded by European travellers in Ciskei and Transkei from the eighteenth century on. . . . The "clicks" or implosive consonants in the Xhosa language indicate the extent of Khoisan influence on Xhosa culture.[67]

61. Goldenberg, "Curse of Ham," 25.
62. Goldenberg, *Race and Slavery*, 110.
63. Goldenberg, *Race and Slavery*, 198.
64. Goldenberg, *Race and Slavery*, 198.
65. Peires, *House of Phalo*, 23.
66. Peires, *House of Phalo*, 23.
67. Hodgson, *God of the Xhosa*, 3.

These details confirm Goldenberg's assertion that "ethnocentrism is not tantamount to racism."[68] Ethnocentrism is based on norms that are influenced by the specific historical, social, and cultural contexts in which they arise. As these contexts change, so too can the norms. However, racism is rooted in the belief in the inherent superiority or inferiority of certain races, which is not open to change or adaptation. These beliefs are often maintained despite evidence to the contrary.

Let us now examine the Jewish story. Dark skin was presented as a punishment and a curse. This is an expression of ethnocentric sentiments. However, they are not necessarily racist. An exploration of other rabbinic writings might be helpful in this regard. Narrating the same story narrated by the Babylonian Talmud about the Curse of Ham, the Midrash Tanḥuna-Yelammedenu states as follows:

> Thereupon Noah cursed his seed, saying: Cursed be Canaan (Gen. 9:25). . . . This happened to him because the Holy One, blessed be He, exacts retribution measure for measure. Nevertheless, the Holy One, blessed be He, relented and had mercy upon him, for His tender mercies are over all His works (Ps. 145:9).[69]

After Noah cursed Canaan, God "relented and had mercy upon him." This is because "His tender mercies are all over His works." Canaan is regarded as part of "all His works." There is no attitude to view Canaan as inferior to other works of God, as racism operates. Another example is in Vayikra Rabbah 17:5. The rabbis say Eliezer who was the servant of Abraham was a Canaanite. "But because he served that righteous one, he emerged from the category of cursed and came into the category of blessed." Racism does not care what you achieve, you remain condemned because you are inherently inferior. In Vayikra Rabbah 17:6 when the Canaanite Girgashites heeded God's warning, they were blessed with a land like their previous land. As Isaac indicated, "Inasmuch as the Israelites who sin against God can be accursed, the Canaanites who obey God can be blessed; in other words, there is no dogmatic view on the curse of Canaan." The dogmatic view is a racist one. These details should suffice to exonerate these texts from racism. The interpretation of skin colour in these rabbinic texts in racist terms by the "Curse of Ham" does not derive from this literature but from the

68. Goldenberg, *Race and Slavery*, 198.

69. Berman, *Midrash Tanhuma-Yelammedenu*, 67.

ideologies of the adherents of this myth. Moreover, the issue of Black skin is not connected to slavery in the rabbinic literature.

Conclusion

To conclude our discussion, the Curse of Ham, with its thesis that Black people were divinely destined to be slaves to other races, is not based on the Old Testament, early Judaism, or rabbinic literature. This contention has been demonstrated from different dimensions of Gen 9:18–29—thanks, particularly, to the historical data that surfaced during the multidimensional analysis. The various traditions that came together to shape the final form of Gen 9:18–29, especially the repeated anachronistic insertion of Canaan in verses 18 and 22, bespeak the strong determination to have Canaan cursed. As Uehlinger describes it, Canaan is mentioned merely to shape the outcome of the story so that he is called on stage only to "be submitted to the permanent fate of slavery." Further, the socio-political and historical circumstances of the author/editor at the centre of which was the land of Canaan, whether the editor is located in the preexilic, exilic, or postexilic (Persian) era, conformed to the strong desire to curse Canaan in the text. The later readers of Gen 9:18–29 during early Judaism—namely, the authors of Jubilees and the Genesis Apocryphon—went out of their way to eliminate any distraction away from Canaan to ensure, unambiguously, that it was none other than Canaan that was cursed. The even later readers—namely, the rabbinic fraternity—explaining how dark-skinned people descended from the supposed white people, composed aetiologies to reconcile Gen 9:19 with their social reality which included dark-skinned people. By comparing this rabbinic creativity with worldwide trends, it was shown that it is inappropriate to understand these aetiologies apart from being aetiologies because it is a phenomenon that permeated all communities. Also, it was acknowledged that these aetiologies did exhibit ethnocentric sentiments. However, these ethnocentric sentiments are not racist but products of their cultural context, and may change when the context changes. To dispel any notion of racism, the discussion appealed to religious precepts discernible in other rabbinic explanations. It also appealed to amaXhosa's encounter with the Khoi and the San people to demonstrate that the discernible ethnocentric sentiments are not equal to racism. Historical data proved to be resourceful in this regard. The outcome of the analysis demonstrated that Ham was not cursed to slavery, and the Curse of Ham to be dark-skinned served an aetiological purpose and had nothing to do with slavery. The thesis that Black people, especially Africans, were divinely destined to be slaves is *eisegesis*.

According to Benjamin Braude, the theme of "the Hamitic origin of servitude" was extensively explored in medieval Christian exegesis.[70] Ham was then viewed as the ancestor of serfs and slaves. "Slaves and serfs, as one knew from daily experience, were Europeans, not Africans."[71] However, as the fifteenth, sixteenth, and seventeenth centuries progressed, "in response to the rising European trade in sub-Saharan African slaves," this theme was directed to Africans.[72] This haphazard use of biblical themes, reading ideological meanings into the biblical text, is the consequence of the lack of historical consciousness in biblical interpretation. Considering such mishaps, it is concerning to hear Justin Ukpong's observation: "In the African context, it has also been argued that since biblical studies in Africa are interested in the message of the text, historical criticism, which is interested more in the history of the text than in its message, should be abandoned."[73] However, Ukpong contends, agreeably so, that African academic reading of the Bible must be critical. "For this reason the historical critical method is more appropriate for African academic reading of the Bible."[74] Those who raised their hands can drop them now.

Bibliography

Aaron, David H. "Early Rabbinic Exegesis on Noah's Son Ham and the So-Called 'Aaron.'" *Journal of the American Academy of Religion* 63 (1995) 721–59.

Berman, Samuel A., ed. *Midrash Tanhuma-Yelammedenu: An English Translation of Genesis and Exodus from the Printed Version of Tanhuma-Yelammedenu with an Introduction, Notes, and Indexes*. Hoboken, NJ: KTAV, 1996.

Braude, Benjamin. "The Sons of Noah and the Construction of Ethnic and Geographical Identities in the Medieval and Early Modern Periods." *William and Mary Quarterly* 54 (1997) 103–42.

Coote, Robert. "Conquest: Biblical Narrative." In *Eerdmans Dictionary of the Bible*, edited by David N. Freedman et al., 274–76. Grand Rapids: Eerdmans, 2000.

Day, John. *From Creation to Babel: Studies in Genesis 1–11*. London: Bloomsbury, 2014.

70. Braude, "Sons of Noah," 134.

71. Braude, "Sons of Noah," 134.

72. Braude, "Sons of Noah," 134.

73. Ukpong, "Historical Critical Approach," 4.

74. Ukpong, "Historical Critical Approach," 4.

Goldenberg, David M. *Black and Slave: The Origins and History of the Curse of Ham*. Studies of the Bible and its Reception 10. Berlin: de Gruyter, 2017.

———. "The Curse of Ham: A Case of Rabbinic Racism?" In *Struggles in the Promised Land: Toward a History of Black-Jewish Relations in the United States*, edited by Cornel West and Jack Salzman, 21–51. New York: Oxford University Press, 1997.

———. *The Curse of Ham: Race and Slavery in Early Judaism, Christianity, and Islam*. Princeton: Princeton University Press, 2009.

———. "What Did Ham Do?" In *The Words of a Wise Man's Mouth Are Gracious*, edited by Mauro Perani, 21–70. Berlin: de Gruyter, 2023.

Green, Barbara. "Yahwist." In *Eerdmans Dictionary of the Bible*, edited by David N. Freedman et al., 1402–3. Grand Rapids: Eerdmans, 2000.

Hodgson, Janet. *The God of the Xhosa*. Cape Town: Oxford University Press, 1982.

Holter, Knut. "Report: Symposium in Nairobi, October 1999." *Newsletter on African Old Testament Scholarship* 7 (1999) 8–9.

———. "The Role of Historical-Critical Methodology in African Old Testament Studies." *Old Testament Essays* 24 (2011) 377–89.

Isaac, Ephraim. "Genesis, Judaism, and the 'Sons of Ham'?" *Slavery and Abolition* 1 (1980) 3–17.

———. "Ham." In *The Anchor Bible Dictionary*, 6 vols., edited by David N. Freedman, 3:31–32. New York: Doubleday, 1992.

Jonker, Louis C. "Context[,] All Over[,] Again! A Hermeneutical Reflection on Some Feminist Receptions in South African Biblical Studies." In *Authorising Authentic African Readings of the Bible: Socially Engaged and Contextually Rooted*, edited by Ntozakhe Cezula and Peter Nagel, 21–70. Wellington: Biblecor, 2023.

———. "Contextual Interpretation, Then and Now: Overhearing Inner-Biblical Discourses to Enrich Contemporary Contextual Interpretations." In *Context Matters: Old Testament Essays from Africa and Beyond Honoring Knut Holter*, edited by Madipoane Masenya (Ngwan'a Mphahlele) et al., 239–51. Atlanta: SBL, 2023.

———. *Exclusivity and Variety: Perspectives on Multidimensional Exegesis*. Contributions to Biblical Exegesis and Theology 19. Kampen: Kok Pharos, 1996.

———. "Reading Jonah Multi-Dimensionally: A Multidimensional Reading Strategy for Biblical Interpretation." *Scriptura* 64 (1998) 1–16.

———. "Towards a 'Communal' Approach for Reading the Bible in Africa." In *Interpreting the Old Testament in Africa*, edited by Mary Getui et al., 77–88. New York: Lang, 2001.

———. "Why History Matters: The Place of Historical Consciousness in a Multidimensional Approach Towards Biblical Interpretation." *Verbum et Ecclesia* 34.2 (2013) 1–7. http://dx.doi.org/10.4102/ve.v34i2.775.

Kugel, James L. A *Walk Through Jubilees: Studies in the Book of Jubilees and the World of Its Creation*. Leiden: Brill, 2012.

Lemche, Niels P. *The Canaanites and Their Land: The Tradition of the Canaanites*. Sheffield: Sheffield Academic, 1991.

Levin, Christoph. *The Old Testament: A Brief Introduction*. Translated by Margaret Kohl. Princeton: Princeton University Press, 2005.

Machiela, Daniel A. *The Dead Sea Genesis Apocryphon: A New Text and Translation with Introduction and Special Treatment of Columns 13–17*. Studies on the Texts of the Desert in Judah 79. Leiden: Brill, 2009.

Masilela, Ntongela. "The Modern World of Xhosa Folklore." 2009. https://pzacad.pitzer.edu/NAM/general/essays/xhosa.pdf.

Na'aman, Nadav. "Jebusites and Jabeshites in the Saul and David Story-Cycles." *Biblica* 95 (2014) 481–97.

Noyi, Robert Balfour. "Ama-Xosa History." In *Ntsikana: The Story of an African Convert*, 2nd ed., edited by John Knox Bokwe, 36–39. Alice: Lovedale, 1914.

Peires, Jeffrey B. *The House of Phalo: A History of the Xhosa People in the Days of Their Independence*. Berkeley: University of California Press, 1982.

Römer, Thomas. "The Elusive Yahwist: A Short History of Research." In *A Farewell to the Yahwist? The Composition of the Pentateuch in Recent European Interpretation*, edited by Thomas B. Dozeman and Konrad Schmid, 9–27. Atlanta: SBL, 2006.

Sanders, Edith R. "The Hamitic Hypothesis: Its Origin and Functions in Time Perspective." *Journal of African History* 10 (1969) 521–32.

Satterthwaite, Philip E. "Genealogies in the Old Testament." In *A Guide to Old Testament Theology and Exegesis*, edited by Willem A. VanGemeren, 222–34. Grand Rapids: Zondervan, 1999.

Sefaria Midrash Rabbah. Translated by Joshua Schreier. Sefaria, 2022. https://www.sefaria.org/texts/Midrash/Aggadah/Midrash%20Rabbah.

Segal, Michael. *The Book of Jubilees: Rewritten Bible, Redaction, Ideology and Theology*. Leiden: Brill, 2007.

Ska, Jean-Louis. *Introduction to Reading the Pentateuch*. University Park: Eisenbrauns, 2006.

Uehlinger, Christoph. "The 'Canaanites' and Other 'Pre-Israelite' Peoples in Story and History (Part I)." *Freiburger Zeitschrift für Philosophie und Theologie* 46 (1999) 567–68.

Ukpong, Justin. "Can African Old Testament Scholarship Escape the Historical-critical Approach?", *Newsletter on African Old Testament Scholarship* 7 (1999): 2–5.

VanderKam, James C. *A Commentary on the Book of Jubilees Chapters 1–21*. Hermeneia. Minneapolis: Fortress, 2018.

Von Rad, Gerhard. *Genesis: A Commentary*. Rev. ed. Old Testament Library. Philadelphia: Westminster, 1972.

Westermann, Claus. *Genesis*. Translated by David E. Green. London: T&T Clark, 2004.

———. *Genesis 1–11: A Commentary*. Translated by John J. Scullion. Minneapolis: Augsburg, 1984.

Whitford, David M. *The Curse of Ham in the Early Modern Era: The Bible and the Justifications for Slavery*. Farnham: Ashgate, 2009.

Wilson, Robert R. "Genealogy, Genealogies." In *The Anchor Bible Dictionary*, 6 vols., edited by David N. Freedman, 2:929–32. New York: Doubleday, 1992.

Wittenberg, Gunther. "'Let Canaan Be His Slave' (Genesis 9:26). Is Ham Also Cursed?" *Journal of Theology for Southern Africa* 74 (1991) 46–56.

3

Looking for Blind Spots

Dimming Implicit Bias Through Spotlighting Contextual Models

Beth E. Elness-Hanson

> "A father and his son are in a car accident. The father dies at the scene and the son, badly injured, is rushed to the hospital. In the operating room, the surgeon looks at the boy and says, 'I can't operate on this boy. He is my son.'"
>
> If your immediate reaction is puzzlement, that's because automatic mental associations caused you to think "male" on reading "surgeon." The association surgeon [equals] male is part of a stereotype. In this riddle, that stereotype works as the first piece of a mindbug. The second piece is an error in judgment—in this case a failure or delay in figuring out that the surgeon must be the boy's mother.[1]

This story and puzzlement explanation appear in the book *Blindspot: Hidden Biases of Good People*, written by psychologists Anthony Greenwald and Mahzarin Banaji. When listening to the audiobook form of their research—knowing the book was about implicit bias and that this

1. Banaji and Greenwald, *Blindspot*, 71.

story appears at the beginning of chapter five—I, a feminist and one who has a sister that is a physician, still was caught in a stereotype that unconsciously assumed the surgeon was a male. I started wondering if the surgeon was a stepdad or a boy with two gay dads.

Everyone has implicit biases, and we do not like them to be pointed out to us.[2]

The research of psychologists Greenwald and Banaji has demonstrated that these so-called "blind spots" influence our perception and behaviour toward others in various social groups, while we can remain unaware of these hidden biases. Yet, these predilections are often not benign. Rather, they frequently incubate negative generalisations that cultivate misunderstandings. As Victor Hugo represents in the words of Bishop Monseigneur Bienvenu, "Prejudices are the real robbers. . . . The great dangers lie within ourselves."[3] This is a reality for me and others engaging in intercultural biblical hermeneutics, especially when we do not realise our negative prejudices.[4]

Louis Jonker understands this, and in his honour, this essay continues in his work of intercultural biblical hermeneutics. While discussing how identity and context influences biblical interpretation, Jonker writes, "Without being aware of how our unique approaches have developed, we will not only be unable to identify our own strengths, but *also our own weaknesses*."[5] He advocates avoiding the "dangers of reductionism and essentialism" and encourages that we be sensitised "to the unique contribution that all the participants in global hermeneutics bring to the interpretation process."[6] Indeed, understanding our weaknesses or biases can sensitise us to the Other and open us up to their enriching contributions.

2. Gadamer, *Truth and Method*, 275, 301, 327. This concept is nuanced from Gadamer's "horizon," where each interpreter has limited experiences and thus has a limited "horizon" of understanding. The limitation is not inherently negative. See also footnote 14 below, which aligns with Gadamer's "fore-conception of completeness" and a disconnect in understanding that can result. The disconnect is not automatically an unhelpful prejudice. It is necessary to distinguish helpful prejudices from unhelpful prejudices.

3. Hugo, *Les Misérables*, 28–29.

4. Fortunately, the academic disciplines do encourage critical analysis. Seminars and, especially, the double-blind review process can make explicit one's implicit bias.

5. Jonker, "Global Context," 49; emphasis added.

6. Jonker, "Global Context," 53.

Thus, this examination explores a method for making implicit bias explicit in order to mitigate miscommunication in intercultural Bible reading and scholarship. Below, I engage the intersection of an inquiry of implicit bias as described by Greenwald and Banaji and Stephen Bevans's analysis in his book *Models of Contextual Theology* (2002).[7] This juncture develops a framework for intercultural biblical hermeneutics, which is engaged for foregrounding cultural or contextual aspects that can reduce unexamined biases. While Bevans's models of contextual theology have been fruitful for the discipline of contextual theology, this synthesis appropriates his insights for intercultural biblical exegesis. This analysis asserts that self-reflection upon Bevans's models can help one discover negative cultural and theological leanings that can hinder intercultural engagement and comprehension. These biases can then be compensated by higher-level cognitive reasoning, intercultural engagement, and the transformation of the Holy Spirit. These pathways can then reduce misunderstandings and build bridges of understanding across cultures in support of intercultural biblical hermeneutics.

This exploration begins with a brief description of the source of the blind spot metaphor from physiological eyesight, with a comment about ableism, and then discusses blind spots in normal brain function that affect human interactions. Next, I overview Greenwald and Banaji's research and describe two of Bevans's six "Models of Contextual Theology." Finally, I synthesise this examination into an analysis for intercultural biblical hermeneutics, integrating insights from Jonker's work with intercultural Bible reading, as well as drawing upon the transformational work of the Holy Spirit.

Blind Spots in Eyesight

The term *blind spot* comes from our eyesight, and it is similar in all vertebrate animals. Physiologically named a *scotoma*, the natural blind spot in the retina of each eye is a result of the lack of rod or cone receptors where the optic nerve leaves the eye, as Richard Gregory and Patrick Cavanagh describe.[8] However, our brains are amazing, and they fill in the gap with information from the other eye.

We can discover our physical blind spot through a simple test:

7. Bevans, *Models of Contextual Theology*.

8. Gregory and Cavanagh, "Blind Spot."

1. Using the diagram below, look straight ahead and place your face approximately three times the distance between the *R* and *L*.
2. Close your LEFT eye.
3. Focus upon the *R* with your RIGHT eye.
4. Move your face towards or away from the image (about 15 cm or 6 in) until you notice the *L* disappear.
5. Also, try closing the RIGHT eye and look at the *L* with your LEFT eye.

Diagram to Find Your Blind Spot[9]

R	L

Figure 1: Diagram to Find Your Blind Spot

The brain is wired to fill in the information missing because of the blind spot. Farther or closer than the disappearing *L* distance, we see the *L* through the brain's interpolation. This is the natural way that our brain makes associations, which is a normal part of brain function.

This physical scotoma is the source of the blind spot metaphor found in psychological discourse and beyond. While everyone has implicit bias, in an effort to eschew language of ableism or insensitivity to people with visual impairments, the language of *blind spot* is replaced hereafter with *implicit bias* and related synonyms.

Implicit Bias Due to Standard Brain Function

Neuropsychological studies confirm that the brain makes assumptions with what is already known to fill cognition gaps when in new experiences. Dan Ariely, a behavioural economist, writes, "The brain cannot start from scratch at every new situation. It must build on what it has seen before. For this reason, stereotypes are not intrinsically malevolent. They provide shortcuts in our never-ending attempt to make sense of complicated surroundings."[10] Psychologists James Hilton and William von Hippel define stereotypes as "beliefs about the characteristics, attributes, and

9. Author's rendering of a common blind spot diagram.
10. Ariely, *Predictably Irrational*, 199–200.

behaviours of members of certain groups."[11] They continue, "Stereotypes operate much like object schemas, allowing easier and more efficient processing of information about others."[12] Similarly, psychologist Brené Brown states, "That's human nature. That's wiring. In the absence of data, we will always make up stories."[13] This *cognitive bias* is a practical strategy to seek to understand the world and not be overwhelmed by an inordinate amount of information. Until there is a cognitive dissonance that conflicts with an experience, the assumption goes unchecked.[14]

While this is not inherently meant to be a negative prejudice, it is not uncommon to find tendencies for stereotyping and the reality of implicit bias.[15] Psychologists Greenwald and Banaji identify that we are more likely to see negative aspects in groups than we are to attribute to individuals, stating, "Group stereotypes typically consist of traits that are noticeably more negative than those we would attribute to our friends."[16]

The scientific analysis of stereotyping is identified by psychologist Gordon Allport in his 1954 book *The Nature of Prejudice*. Allport wrote, "The human mind must think with the aid of categories. . . . Once formed, categories are the basis for normal prejudgment. We cannot possibly avoid this process. Orderly living depends on it."[17]

Further analysis on bias by Nobel laureates in economics, Daniel Kahneman and Amos Tversky, appeared in their landmark 1974 article "Judgment Under Uncertainty: Heuristics and Biases." Psychologists Kahneman and Tversky are considered among the vanguards at the intersection of psychology and economics, now known as behavioural economics. Kahneman and Tversky demonstrated "that people rely on a limited number of heuristic principles which reduce the complex tasks of assessing probabilities and predicting values to simpler judgmental operations."[18] The issue of concern for this examination is addressed by

11. Hilton and Hippel, "Stereotypes," 240.

12. Hilton and Hippel, "Stereotypes," 240–41.

13. Brown, "Leaves the Audience Speechless."

14. Gadamer, *Truth and Method*, 294. Gadamer also addresses this in his "fore-conception of completeness" related to texts. When one reads a text, one assumes their understanding as complete. Only when there is a disconnect in understanding does one become aware of the other viewpoint.

15. Amodio, "Neuroscience of Prejudice," 670.

16. Banaji and Greenwald, *Blindspot*, 78; Hilton and Hippel, "Stereotypes," 239.

17. Allport, *Nature of Prejudice*, 20.

18. Tversky and Kahneman, "Judgment Under Uncertainty," 1124. This research in behavioural economics is more complex, but it is appropriated here to identify the

their heuristic of *representativeness*. Tversky and Kahneman argue that people assess others, i.e., the description of others, by the degree to which they "are similar to, or representative of, the stereotype" that the assessor holds. However, this simplification of heuristic principles applied in decision-making can lead to errors.[19] Indeed, behavioural economist Pedro Bordalo (et al.) confirmed that Kahneman and Tversky's identification of simplifying representations is intimately related to stereotyping and sometimes causes errors in judgment.[20]

To help make explicit what is implicit or unconscious in our thinking, Greenwald and Banaji developed research based on the Implicit Association Test, hereafter the IAT. This assessment detects unconscious associations between mental representations of objects (concepts) without requiring a deliberative act of introspection.[21] There are several assessments using this model that identify different kinds of bias, such as racial groups, gender, sexuality, age, religion, and political views. More recently, the IAT has been used in implicit bias trainings, which work to decrease the unconscious bias and any resulting discriminatory behaviour. While not without critique,[22] the IAT testing concept has been made available in thirty-nine countries and twenty-four languages by the time of the 2013 publication. The IAT is available for free at implicit.harvard.edu.

Be aware that there may be an unexpected outcome from taking the IAT. For example, the biracial author and public intellectual Malcolm Gladwell discussed the results of taking the Race IAT in an interview with Oprah Winfrey. Gladwell stated,

> I took it the first time, and it told me that I had a moderate preference for White people. . . . I was biased—slightly biased—against Black people, toward White people, which horrified me because my mom's Jamaican. . . . The person in my life who I love more than almost anyone else is Black, and here I was taking a test, which said, frankly, I wasn't too crazy about Black people, you know? So, I did what anyone else would do: I took the test

human tendency of simplification that results in representationalism or stereotyping. For example, if research subjects knew of prior probabilities without descriptions, then probabilities were made more accurately. "Judgment Under Uncertainty," 1125.

19. Tversky and Kahneman, "Judgment Under Uncertainty," 1124.

20. Bordalo et al., "Stereotypes," 1755; Hilton and Hippel, "Stereotypes," 239.

21. Nosek et al., "Implicit Association Test," 166.

22. Houwer, "Structural and Process Analysis"; Hahn et al., "Awareness of Implicit Attitudes."

> again! Maybe it was an error, right? Same result. Again, same result, and it was this creepy, dispiriting, devastating moment.[23]

Thus, taking the IAT should be engaged with appropriate caution. Yet, Greenwald and Banaji write,

> When it comes to seeking change, the reflective, conscious side of the brain—the side that is unique to humankind—is more than capable of doing the necessary work. Its power derives from its ability to observe itself and to use those observations to guide conscious action. . . . Knowledge is indeed power, and self-knowledge achieved by taking the IAT can exert its power by unsettling existing views of one's mind. If that happens, the melancholy produced by the IAT will indeed be useful.[24]

Greenwald and Banaji identify that hidden biases are widespread, and thus, they are inherent in "good people"[25] like themselves—and like myself—who intend to do well and strive to align behaviour with good intentions. Thus, I now engage Bevans's "Models of Contextual Theology" as a self-reflective tool[26] for an exercise in identifying negative presuppositions that can impede constructive dialogues in intercultural biblical hermeneutics.

Models of Contextual Theology

The revised text by Stephen Bevans, *Models of Contextual Theology*, is a seminal classic. Originally published in 1992, the revised and expanded

23. Oprah, "Overcoming Prejudice"; Banaji and Greenwald, *Blindspot*, 57.

24. Banaji and Greenwald, *Blindspot*, 70.

25. While "good people" may be language that assumes a problematic opposite counterpart, Greenwald and Banaji clarify their meaning: "It is with some trepidation that we refer to 'good people' in this book's subtitle. We have no special competence (let alone the moral authority) to judge who is good and who is not. By 'good people' we refer to those, ourselves included, who intend well and who strive to align their behavior with their intentions. Our highest aim for this book is to explain the science sufficiently so that these good people will be better able to achieve that alignment." Banaji and Greenwald, *Blindspot*, xv.

26. I am aware there are different methodologies for identifying implicit biases than that used by Greenwald and Banaji. The Greenwald and Banaji research exemplifies that we all have negative presuppositions, even "good people," (see footnote above) and that our new awareness can aid self-reflection. They write, "The reflective aspects of our mind allow us to imagine a future that improves on the present state of affairs, and to achieve settled-upon and consciously chosen goals and values." Banaji and Greenwald, *Blindspot*, 70.

edition, published in 2002, exists in multiple reprints and is still a standard in contextual theology and other intercultural courses.[27] The cogency of his writing is seen in a collection of essays on contextual theology published in 2021, where Bevans's *Models of Contextual Theology* is quoted by at least three of the authors.[28]

Bevans's understanding of models is that they are *constructions*.[29] He continues,

> Models are not mirrors of a reality "out there"; they are "ideal types," either logically constructed theoretical positions ("You could do this, and then things would look so") or abstractions formed from concrete positions ("So and so does this this way; someone else proceeds this way").[30]

In *Models of Contextual Theology*, Bevans describes the use of the various models as the theoretical type that are either inclusive or descriptive, yet as operative in the way they develop theological methods.[31] The revised and expanded edition has six models[32] that he elucidates with a description, a critique, the title's conceptualisations, core presuppositions, a diagram of each model, and a discussion of the advantages and disadvantages of each model. Finally, Bevans reviews the writings of two theologians who represent the model.

Bevans's six models are placed on a continuum with the emphasis of the two poles being the following:

- Experiences of the Present (Context), exemplified in
  - human experience
  - culture

27. It is a textbook in a VID Specialized Universities course in contextual theology as of this writing in 2023. I use the book or Bevans's summary chapter (Bevans, "Contextual Methods in Theology") for my intercultural biblical hermeneutics courses. Once, an African-descent Swedish student queried why we read a theology book for a biblical hermeneutics course. My answer and convictions are that if we do not have a framework to understand culture, then the unexamined stereotypes from the dominant culture will control our presuppositions and result in unhelpful reductionism.

28. See Bergmann and Vähäkangas, *Contextual Theology*.

29. Bevans, *Models of Contextual Theology*, 29.

30. Bevans, *Models of Contextual Theology*, 29.

31. Bevans, *Models of Contextual Theology*, 31.

32. See also Rapisarda, *Oaths of Peace*, for the framework for a seventh model. Thus, Bevans's six models do not represent an exhaustive list, but they provide a language to have an important conversation.

  - social location
  - social change
- Experiences of the Past, exemplified in
  - Scripture
  - tradition[33]

Bevans locates the six models on the continuum as thus:[34]

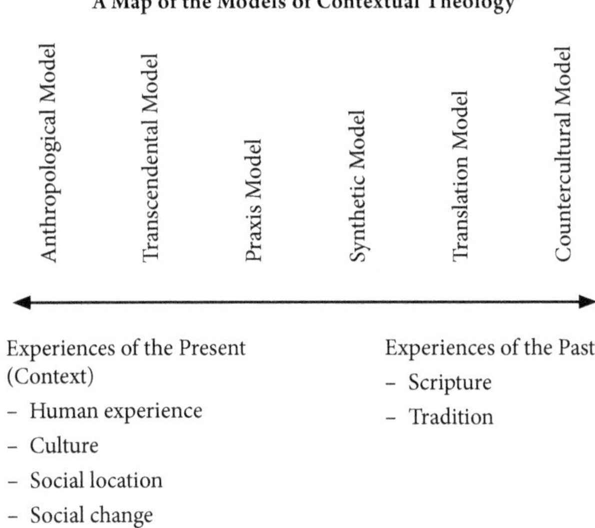

Figure 2: A Map of the Models of Contextual Theology

Bevans identifies that each model is distinct, but they can be used in combination with other models.[35] In fact, Bevans continues and argues that no one model can be used exclusively, as overemphasis on one model will warp "the theological enterprise," because there is not just one "completely adequate" way of practicing theology.[36] So, the context

33. Bevans, *Models of Contextual Theology*, 32.

34. Bevans, "Contextual Methods in Theology," 8. Author's rendering of content from Bevans.

35. Bevans, *Models of Contextual Theology*, 32.

36. Bevans, *Models of Contextual Theology*, 32, 33.

will determine which model or blended models are appropriate. Thus, Bevans encourages a "healthy pluralism."[37]

The scope of this chapter will not allow a full analysis of all six models. Thus, I start the conversation by looking at two models on different ends of the continuum, the Translation Model and the Anthropological Model, which can stimulate a self-reflection to potentially reveal our hidden biases of how theology and culture intersect.

The Translation Model

A desperately oversimplified summary of the Translation Model is that it is one of the most common ways of doing theology in a context, and it follows the example found in Paul's speeches at Lystra and Athens (Acts 14:15–17 and 17:22–31). Taking the context of theologising seriously, there is an "insistence on the message of the gospel as an unchanging message," and it seeks to be faithful to "an essential content."[38] The contexts, with their thought forms and changing social structures, are not "good in themselves, but [they are] convenient vehicles for this essential, unchanging deposit of truth."[39] "Experience, culture, social location, and social change" are indeed important, though just not as important as the gospel message.[40] In translation with a focus on meaning, this model presupposes that the gospel message is supracultural or supracontextual,[41] and therefore, "the gospel is the judge of all contexts," and the contextual situation "is the vehicle of the message."[42]

The strength of this model is that no other model takes the gospel message so seriously, believing that the gospel does have something to offer a broken and hurting world.[43] Another asset is that this contextual theologising can hold the ambivalence within contextual realities, accepting "the good in all cultures or contexts while still being committed to the transforming and challenging power of the gospel."[44]

37. Bevans, *Models of Contextual Theology*, 139.

38. Bevans, *Models of Contextual Theology*, 37.

39. Bevans, *Models of Contextual Theology*, 37.

40. Bevans, *Models of Contextual Theology*, 41.

41. Bevans, *Models of Contextual Theology*, 38, 40.

42. Bevans, *Models of Contextual Theology*, 41.

43. Bevans, *Models of Contextual Theology*, 42.

44. Bevans, *Models of Contextual Theology*, 43. A third strength is that it can be engaged by "any person committed to a particular culture or situation, nonparticipant

However, there are several critiques of the Translation Model. First, is there ever such thing as a supracultural, "naked gospel"?[45] Second, can we have access to the gospel without some form of cultural mediation? The message of Christianity is always enculturated, and—imagining culture in the onion metaphor with various layers, as used by Krikor Haleblian—is it possible to discover an essential core?[46] A third critique deals with what is perceived as a propositional nature of the Translation Model, which will not be addressed here due to the limited scope of this analysis.

A table describes various aspects of the Translation Model:[47]

Aspect	Translation Model
Other Titles	Accommodation; adaptation
Basis in Scripture and Tradition	Acts 14:15–16, 17:2–31 Cyril and Methodius; Ricci; de Nobili; John 23 at Vatican II
Revelation	Tends to be interpreted as propositional, content-oriented
Scripture/Tradition	Supracontextual (Scripture above context); complete
Context	Basically good and trustworthy
Method	Kernel/husk; know the context so as to effectively insert the gospel
Analogy	Bring seeds, plant in native ground
Legend	"Putting the gospel into" (Bruce Fleming)
Critique Pro	Takes Christian message seriously; recognises contextual ambiguity; can be used by participants and nonparticipants in culture
Critique Con	Naïve notions of culture and gospel; propositional notion of revelation

Figure 3: Aspects of the Translation Model

or participant. With a relatively brief introduction to a particular culture or society, one can begin 'making the good news relevant' in homilies, religion classes, counseling sessions, and so forth.'" Bevans, *Models of Contextual Theology*, 43.

45. Bevans, *Models of Contextual Theology*, 43.

46. Bevans, *Models of Contextual Theology*, 43; Haleblian, "Problem of Contextualization," 102. Bevans cites Haleblian.

47. Bevans, *Models of Contextual Theology*, 141. Recreated by author.

The Anthropological Model

Another streamlined summary is that of the Anthropological Model. Almost located on the polar opposite end of Bevans's continuum (the fifth of six models) is the Anthropological Model with its focus on the "experience of the present" (context: human experience, culture, social location, social change) in contrast to the Translation Model's focus on the "experience of the past" (Scripture and tradition).

A way of crystallising this "establishment or preservation of cultural identity by a person of Christian faith"[48] is the illustration Bevans gives:

> The answer to the question as to whether one is aiming to become a Christian Filipino or a Filipino Christian is very definitely the former option. What is important in this model is the understanding that Christianity is about the human person and her or his fulfilment. This does not mean that the gospel cannot challenge a particular context, but such a challenge is always viewed with the suspicion that the challenge is not coming from God as such, but from a tendency of one (Western, Mediterranean) contextual perspective to impose its values on another.[49]

This model presumes the "goodness of *anthropos*, the human person," in whom and in every context God manifests God's divine presence.[50] Making use of social sciences, especially anthropology, the language of *indigenisation* or *enculturation* demonstrates "the importance of culture in the construction of a true contextual theology" that engages the human stuff of life—wholeness, healing, and relationships—through which one can examine whether or not a theological expression is sound.[51]

Core assumptions of this model start with a quote by M. A. C. Warren: "Our first task in approaching another people, another culture, another religion, is to take off our shoes, for the place we are approaching is holy. Else we may find ourselves treading on [another's] dreams. More serious still, we may forget that God was here before our arrival."[52] As a creation-centred theology (distinct from redemption-centred), there is

48. Bevans, *Models of Contextual Theology*, 54.

49. Bevans, *Models of Contextual Theology*, 54.

50. Bevans, *Models of Contextual Theology*, 55.

51. Bevans, *Models of Contextual Theology*, 55.

52. Bevans, *Models of Contextual Theology*, 56. Bevans cites Warren, with this quote appearing in the preface of the seven-book Christian Presence series published by SCM Press between 1959 to 1966. However, there is no record in WorldCat.org.

a conviction of the goodness of creation, and the starting point is the present human experience with a focus on culture, whether secular or religious,[53] such that culture is equal to Scripture and tradition for understanding the gospel.[54] Thus, "it is culture that shapes the way Christianity is articulated,"[55] such that language is significant for understanding the culture along with learning from the wisdom of interreligious dialogue.[56] Ultimately, "context affects content."[57]

The strength of this model is grounded in the seriousness by which it regards human reality. It recognises that Christianity is not a propositional message, but rather that revelation comes through an encounter with God's love and power that brings healing in the midst of daily life. Because the Christian message is not first the introduction of a "foreign" message, this model presents Christ in a fresh perspective that integrates with people in a specific cultural and historical context. It gives personal views on how to live one's life faithfully in their own settings, starting right where they are.[58]

Yet, the primary danger of the Anthropological Model is a romanticism about culture, tilting toward the propensity to make God in own's own image. In addition, it is more easily said than done, as Scripture and tradition need to be integrated into the lives of Christian Filipinos or into whatever context.[59]

A summary of the Anthropological Model is as follows:[60]

Aspect	Anthropological Model
Other Titles	Indigenisation; ethnographic model
Basis in Scripture and Tradition	Matt 15:21–28; Mark 7:24–30; John 3:16; movement of Acts; Justin Martyr "seeds of the word"

53. Bevans, *Models of Contextual Theology*, 57.

54. Bevans, *Models of Contextual Theology*, 61.

55. Bevans, *Models of Contextual Theology*, 57.

56. Bevans, *Models of Contextual Theology*, 58–59.

57. Bevans, *Models of Contextual Theology*, 58. Consider a corollary by Schüssler Fiorenza, "What we see depends on where we stand. One's social location or rhetorical context is decisive of how one sees the world, constructs reality, or interprets biblical texts." Schüssler Fiorenza, "Ethics of Biblical Interpretation," 5.

58. Bevans, *Models of Contextual Theology*, 59–60.

59. Bevans, *Models of Contextual Theology*, 60–61.

60. Bevans, *Models of Contextual Theology*, 141.

Aspect	Anthropological Model
Revelation	Tends to be understood as "personal presence"
Scripture/Tradition	Culturally conditioned; like all human expressions; incomplete
Context	Basically good and trustworthy; equal to Scripture and tradition
Method	Know the culture to "pull the gospel out of it"
Analogy	Seeds are already in the ground; just need to be watered to sprout
Legend	"take off your shoes" (Max Warren)
Critique Pro	Takes context seriously; provides fresh perspective of Christianity; starts with where people are
Critique Con	Prey to cultural romanticism; more easily said than done

With this foundation, I turn to an analysis for intercultural biblical hermeneutics.

Overview and Further Analysis

Above, I have discussed that all of us have implicit biases, as exemplified by the research of Greenwald and Banaji, who developed the Implicit Association Test, the IAT. These implicit biases are normal, as they are the way the brain functions, so that even "good people"[61] who want to align their noble values to behaviours are subconsciously influenced by these biases.

However, often the IAT test identifies biases of which one is already aware. This is the critique of social psychologists Adam Hahn et al., whose research indicates that many are actually attuned to their own biases.[62] Understandably, there is additional social science research that identifies that even if one has biases, they may not be acted upon, especially in

61. See footnote 25 on how Banaji and Greenwald use "good people."

62. Hahn et al., "Awareness of Implicit Attitudes."

the presence of a person from that group, which Greenwald and Banaji confirm.[63]

For these known and unknown biases, I discuss four pathways for mitigation.

Higher-Level Reasoning

The first of four pathways for mitigating bias—especially for which one is aware—is that higher-level cognitive reasoning can overlay values and ethical frameworks upon intercultural situations which can override the bias in lived experience. This is demonstrated in Greenwald and Banaji's research, affirming that one's new awareness can aid choosing constructive responses to counteract unhelpful biases. They write, "The reflective aspects of our mind allow us to imagine a future that improves on the present state of affairs, and *to achieve settled-upon and consciously chosen goals and values*."[64] This capacity of higher-level reasoning is supported by the research of Kahneman, who identified that the implicit "fast" impressions can be mitigated by deliberative, more demanding, and conscious "slow" judgments.[65] As Kahneman writes, "Salience can be overcome by deliberate attention."[66]

Bevans's Models for Self-Reflection

The second pathway I propose for mitigating unconscious bias is using Bevans's six "Models of Contextual Theology" for self-reflection. When reading Bevans's models, one can recognise where one is unsettled or disagrees with these six different approaches of how theology and culture intersect in intercultural contexts. My suggestion is that reflection upon the pros and cons (the positive and negative critique) of each model is a strategy for discovering negative presuppositions.[67]

63. Banaji and Greenwald, *Blindspot*, 108–9.

64. Banaji and Greenwald, *Blindspot*, 70; emphasis added.

65. Kahneman, "Perspective on Judgment and Choice," 698–99, 716.

66. Kahneman, "Perspective on Judgment and Choice," 701. Kahneman writes, "When people become aware of using a heuristic, they correct their judgment accordingly and may even overcorrect." "Perspective on Judgment and Choice," 711.

67. On the flip side, negative assumptions may have a mirror image of positive assumptions that privilege some people groups based upon gender, ethnicity, height, etc. that are unfounded.

While reflecting upon the Translation Model and the Anthropological Model, perhaps you resonated with aspects of one of the models that reflected your biblical-theological hermeneutical framework and personal values. Perhaps you discovered aspects of both models that you affirmed as important, and therefore, you see the value of holding these differing perspectives in a creative tension. Even more so, you can identify that a dialogue partner with a differing model is not invalid, but rather, you can strengthen an awareness that this is part of a "healthy pluralism."[68] These are starting points for a deeper reflection and can serve to make explicit one's implicit biases related to intercultural dialogues. This foundation can be in the background of other scholarly critical thinking and reflections, such that other aspects can be identified.

While not using Bevans's model, Jonker similarly exemplifies that self-reflection and reasoning in identifying one's context and hermeneutical frameworks is important for stronger intercultural outcomes. He writes,

> When we include the earlier stages in our own traditions of interpretation in our *reflection* on our hermeneutical task, we not only discover our continuities with the past, but also our discontinuities and differentiations. We then get a *better perspective on our own strengths, but also on our deficiencies and weaknesses.*[69]

Thus, both higher-level reasoning and self-reflection upon cultural issues are important to counteract one's biases when engaging other scholars from different contexts.

Intercultural Engagement

The third pathway to mitigate bias is intercultural engagement or crossing boundaries that holds transformative potential. In an overview of the *Through the Eyes of Another: Intercultural Reading of the Bible* project, which Jonker coedited, he summarises that "intercultural approaches lead to transformation."[70] Through sharing and receiving Bible study insights across cultures, transformational aspects included

68. Bevans, *Models of Contextual Theology*, 139.

69. Jonker, "Global Context," 50; emphasis added.

70. Jonker, "Crossing Boundaries," 7; Wit, "Through the Eyes of Another."

developing "a basic attitude of openness, trust, vulnerability, and *willingness to criticize oneself*."[71]

Jonker demonstrates this transformation through an empirical study of an intercultural Bible reading project with eight distinct cultural groups in the complicated landscape of the Western Cape of South Africa. In this project, Jonker identified that interculturality is a strategy to overcome "othering," where I note that biases are both implicit and explicit. Prior to the encounter, there were participants who wrote, "The apartheid past still causes division," and "Cultural differences cause division [in society]."[72] Jonker notes that the majority of the statements were negative.

However, after the encounter, Jonker identifies that the responses were overwhelmingly positive to two core questions related to "attitude" and "changes of knowledge and insight." While differences were still acknowledged, there was "appreciation and respect for 'the other.'"[73] With regard to "attitude" questions, responses included, "Our appreciation for them increased," and "We got to realize the similarities between us."[74] Related to "changes of knowledge and insight," participants affirmed, "*Our biases disappeared*," and "We discovered our shared (spiritual) needs."[75] Jonker overviews,

> These positive responses contrast dramatically with the negative understanding of the South African nation in terms of "family" and "hospitality" observed before the intercultural exposure. Although the project included only a single intercultural Bible reading meeting, one may state with confidence from the data presented above that significant transformation took place in all groups, as well as in the individual group members, in their *openness toward and understanding of "the other*."[76]

In summary, Jonker writes, "The project confirmed clearly that the tool of intercultural Bible reading has transformative power."[77] In more recent analysis of intercultural Bible reading, Jonker identifies that a core criterion for this transformation is that "interculturality thus

71. Jonker, "Crossing Boundaries," 8; emphasis added.
72. Jonker, "On Becoming a Family," 400.
73. Jonker, "On Becoming a Family," 404.
74. Jonker, "On Becoming a Family," 405.
75. Jonker, "On Becoming a Family," 405; emphasis added.
76. Jonker, "On Becoming a Family," 407; emphasis added.
77. Jonker, "On Becoming a Family," 411.

results on *self-insight*."[78] The self-insight that is provoked by intercultural encounters is crucial, and it can be enhanced with thoughtful self-reflection upon Bevans's models.

Transformation by the Holy Spirit

The fourth pathway—or perhaps support for the journey on the three previous pathways—is the transforming work of the Holy Spirit for those who are followers of Jesus Christ. While the IAT is generally considered a scientific method for identifying implicit bias, and self-reflection can expand our self-understanding of areas for growth, my concern is that awareness does not automatically result in behavioural change and—even less often—transformation. The inwardly bent and selfish human nature needs a redeemer.[79] Indeed, the knowledge of the negative biases does not enable one to live a non-biased life. We know what we should do but are not empowered to do the things we want to do.[80] The transformation comes through walking by the Holy Spirit (Gal 5:16); that produces the fruit of the Spirit (Gal 5:22–23), which includes patience, kindness, and gentleness among others—all core values in intercultural Bible reading and interpretation.

Conclusion

While Greenwald and Banaji have demonstrated that our natural implicit biases influence our perception and our unconscious behaviour toward others, Bevans's "Models of Contextual Theology" are fruitful for intentional self-reflection in order to identify negative presuppositions related to our intercultural dialogue partners. Indeed, our higher-level reasoning can help us overcome negative biases with intentional application of our values and ethical frameworks, reducing the adverse effects of our

78. Jonker, "Crossing Boundaries," 8; emphasis added.

79. Jeremiah 17:9 describes the human condition as, "Most devious is the heart; It is perverse—who can fathom it?" (JPS).

80. See Rom 7:7–26, where Paul writes, "For I do not do the good I want, but the evil I do not want is what I do" (verse 19, NRSV). The text ends with the good news that the deliverance from this state is through Jesus Christ (verses 24–25). This is paralleled in Gal 3, where Paul writes, "Are you so foolish? Having begun with the Spirit, are you now trying to attain perfection by human effort?" (verse 3, Longenecker's translation; Longenecker, *Galatians*, 98–99).

unacknowledged prejudices. Furthermore, intercultural encounters can help us become aware of implicit bias and—if holding an openness and self-insight—it can lead to transforming one's biases toward the Other. Yet, this journey can be a difficult one, leaving a sense of melancholy or worse, unless we recognise that the work of the Holy Spirit is supporting the work of transformation. This transformation will help us to build bridges of understanding across cultures within the guild of intercultural biblical hermeneutics—and beyond.

Bibliography

Allport, Gordon W. *The Nature of Prejudice*. 25th anniv. ed. Reading, MA: Basic, 1979.

Amodio, David. "The Neuroscience of Prejudice and Stereotyping." *Nature Reviews Neuroscience* 15 (2014) 670–82. https://doi.org/10.1038/nrn3800.

Ariely, Dan. *Predictably Irrational: The Hidden Forces That Shape Our Decisions*. Rev. and expan. ed. New York: Harper Perennial, 2010.

Banaji, Mahzarin R., and Anthony G. Greenwald. *Blindspot: Hidden Biases of Good People*. New York: Delacorte, 2013.

Bergmann, Sigurd, and Mika Vähäkangas, eds. *Contextual Theology: Skills and Practices of Liberating Faith*. London: Routledge, 2021.

Bevans, Stephen B. "Contextual Methods in Theology." In *Essays in Contextual Theology*, edited by Stephen B. Bevans, 1–29. Boston: Brill, 2018.

———. *Models of Contextual Theology*. Rev. and expan. ed. Maryknoll, NY: Orbis, 2002.

Bordalo, Pedro, et al. "Stereotypes." *Quarterly Journal of Economics* 131 (2016) 1753–94.

Brown, Brené. "Brené Brown Leaves the Audience Speechless: One of the Best Motivational Speeches Ever." Motivational Instinct, Jan. 5, 2023. https://www.youtube.com/watch?v=5vphihopa1A.

Gadamer, Hans-Georg. *Truth and Method*. Repr. ed. London: Bloomsbury Academic, 2013.

Gregory, Richard, and Patrick Cavanagh. "The Blind Spot." *Scholarpedia* 6 (2011) 9618. https://doi.org/10.4249/scholarpedia.9618.

Hahn, Adam, et al. "Awareness of Implicit Attitudes." *Journal of Experimental Psychology: General* 143 (2014) 1369–92. https://doi.org/10.1037/a0035028.

Haleblian, Krikor. "The Problem of Contextualization." *Missiology* 11 (1983) 95–111. https://doi.org/10.1177/009182968301100108.

Hilton, James L., and William von Hippel. "Stereotypes." *Annual Review of Psychology* 47 (1996) 237–71. https://doi.org/10.1146/annurev.psych.47.1.237.

Houwer, Jan De. "A Structural and Process Analysis of the Implicit Association Test." *Journal of Experimental Social Psychology* 37 (2001) 443–51. https://doi.org/10.1006/jesp.2000.1464.

Hugo, Victor. *Les Misérables*. Translated by Christine Donougher. New York: Penguin Classics, 2016.

Jonker, Louis C. "Crossing Boundaries: The Transformative Potential of Intercultural Bible Reading in Secular/Post-Secular Contexts." *Scriptura* 120 (2021) 1–13. https://doi.org/10.7833/120-1-1982.

———. "The Global Context and Its Consequences for Old Testament Interpretation." In *Global Hermeneutics? Reflections and Consequences*, edited by Knut Holter and Louis C. Jonker, 47–56. Atlanta: SBL, 2010.

———. "On Becoming a Family in South Africa: Intercultural Bible Reading as Transformative Power in Society (Luke 11:1–13)." In *Bible and Transformation: The Promise of Intercultural Bible Reading*, edited by Hans de Wit and Janet Dyk, 387–413. Atlanta: SBL, 2015.

Kahneman, Daniel. "A Perspective on Judgment and Choice: Mapping Bounded Rationality." *American Psychologist* 58 (2003) 697–720. https://doi.org/10.1037/0003-066X.58.9.697.

Longenecker, Richard N. *Galatians*. Word Biblical Commentary 41. Waco, TX: Nelson, 1990.

Nosek, Brian A., et al. "Understanding and Using the Implicit Association Test: II. Method Variables and Construct Validity." *Personality and Social Psychology Bulletin* 31 (2005) 166–80. https://doi.org/10.1177/0146167204271418.

Oprah. "Overcoming Prejudice." Jan. 1, 2006. https://www.oprah.com/oprahshow/overcoming-prejudice/all.

Rapisarda, Daniela Lucia. *Oaths of Peace: Theology of Peacebuilding in Southern Sudan*. New York: Lang, 2020.

Schüssler Fiorenza, Elisabeth. "The Ethics of Biblical Interpretation: Decentering Biblical Scholarship." *Journal of Biblical Literature* 107 (1988) 3–17.

Tversky, Amos, and Daniel Kahneman. "Judgment Under Uncertainty: Heuristics and Biases." *Science* 185 (1974) 1124–31.

Wit, Hans de. "Through the Eyes of Another: Objectives and Backgrounds." In *Through the Eyes of Another: Intercultural Reading of the Bible*, edited by Hans de Wit et al., 3–53. Elkhart, IN: Institute of Mennonite Studies, 2005.

4

The Stones of the Cooking Fire Are Three

African Proverbs as an Interpretive Resource in African Biblical Proverbs Studies[1]

Knut Holter

In his monograph *Bible and Theology in African Christianity* (1986)—now part of the canon of critical biblical studies in Africa—John S. Mbiti notices that, when reading the Bible, "Africans hear and see a confirmation of their own cultural, social and religious life in the life and history of the Jewish people as portrayed and recorded in the pages of the Bible."[2] One of his textual examples of this interpretive experience and strategy relates to "traditional wisdom as collected in the Book of Proverbs," and the key role of Proverbs is then empirically demonstrated

1. This article is dedicated to an esteemed colleague, Professor Louis C. Jonker, in gratitude for allowing me to walk some steps together with him in his journey throughout landscapes of critical biblical scholarship. I use the opportunity to go into dialogue with two scholarly ancestors, Mbiti and Ukpong, and while I reread the two, I look at pictures that Louis took of me together with the two at a conference in Stellenbosch thirty years ago, and I am reminded of the importance of meeting physically, not only digitally as we do more and more nowadays.

2. Mbiti, *Bible and Theology*, 26.

with a reference to its frequency in Harold W. Turner's material of eight thousand sermons from the Aladura tradition in West Africa.[3]

The following reflections will take a closer look at the interface between certain experiences and concerns as they are reflected in African proverbial material and corresponding themes in the biblical book of Proverbs.[4] The focus, however, will not be on sermons in the Aladura tradition or what Mbiti elsewhere in the same book refers to as an "oral theology," produced in open air by the masses, but rather on what he calls a "written theology," produced by the few and privileged ones allowed into academic institutions.[5] This will be the case because a contextualising reading of the Bible, enabling African readers—in the words of Mbiti—to "hear and see a confirmation of their own cultural, social and religious life," is no longer a practice and strategy of the masses only. During the last half century, and in particular since the 1980s, biblical scholarship in Africa has gradually developed into an *African* scholarship, both institutionally and hermeneutically, and its key characteristic is a comparative approach, reflecting on the relationship between African experiences and concerns and the ancient texts of the Bible.[6]

This process of Africanising biblical scholarship is not least visible concerning the book of Proverbs. In the following, I will therefore analyse the work of a few African biblical scholars who have read Proverbs from consciously African perspectives, and I will ask what roles African proverbial material plays in their studies. I will do the analysis in four steps. First, a brief discussion of the actors involved. Second, a close reading of the main publications of five African biblical scholars. Third, a survey of the reception of African proverbs and African biblical proverbs studies in Western biblical scholarship. And fourth, some concluding remarks.

The Three Stones of the Cooking Fire

Those who are familiar with placing a pot on the stones of a cooking fire will intuitively understand the Oromo proverb saying that "the stones

3. Mbiti, *Bible and Theology*, 35.

4. The article develops some perspectives that I sketched nearly two decades ago in Holter, "Left Hand Washes the Right," 45–55.

5. Mbiti, *Bible and Theology*, 46–47.

6. Holter, *Old Testament Research*; Holter, *Contextualized Old Testament Scholarship*, 83–115; Ukpong, "Developments in Biblical Interpretation."

of the cooking fire are three."[7] If we use only two stones, the result will probably be that the pot turns over, and if we use four stones, the pot will easily be unstable. Accordingly, three is the perfect number.

Three is also the number of actors when African biblical scholars make comparative use of African proverbs for interpreting biblical proverbs. The first actor is the biblical text, the key object of analysis in biblical studies. Proverbs and other examples of wisdom literature are attested in various parts of the Bible. An illustrative example from the prophetic literature—also reflecting familiarity with Africa, though hardly expressing the negative view on Africans it used to be accused of—is found in Jer 13:23: "Can a Cushite change his skin or a leopard its spots?"[8] Nevertheless, the major bulk of biblical proverbs are found in the Old Testament book which is simply titled Proverbs. The book is a collection of various groups of proverbs, different concerning form as well as content, still conceptualised as being part of the same genre. Some of those groups that Proverbs is made up of are linked to King Solomon, whose affinities with wisdom are praised also in other parts of the Bible. The explicit link between Proverbs and Solomon is hardly historically correct, but it fits into the more overall, biblical portrayal of Solomon as having strong international connections, in the sense that wisdom traditions and even wisdom texts floated across the cultural and political borders of the ancient Near East. I will return to an example of this below: the reception of the Egyptian "Instructions of Amenemope" in Proverbs.

The second actor is the African proverb. Proverbs have "always" been a part of African traditional culture and wisdom,[9] but for quite some time the genre has received attention also from critical, research perspectives. An illustrative example of this is that nearly one-quarter of a century has passed since Wolfgang Mieder was able to publish his annotated bibliography on African proverb scholarship.[10] The research referred to by Mieder builds on local and regional proverbs collections that were published from the nineteenth and throughout the twentieth century, and more recently from the more extensive and systematically carried out "Africa Proverbs Project."[11]

7. Cotter, *Ethiopian Wisdom*, 186.

8. Unless otherwise indicated, Scripture quotations in this chapter are from the CSB.

9. See for example Wanjohi, *Wisdom and Philosophy*, 75–93.

10. Mieder, *African Proverb Scholarship*.

11. Saayman, *Embracing the Baobab Tree*; Mbiti, "African Proverbs Project," 256–63.

The third actor is then the biblical scholar, in this case the African biblical scholar who for various reasons makes comparative use of African proverbial material in her or his interpretation of Proverbs. The academic discipline of biblical studies has for the last couple of centuries had a strong historical flavour, focusing on the religio-cultural background of the texts. In the last decades, though, the discipline has opened for a wider set of interpretive approaches, with interpretive models from literary studies and the social sciences. The opening up for a wider set of approaches happened to coincide with the establishment of biblical scholarship in Africa. As noticed above, the consciously African biblical scholarship that emerged from the 1960s, and especially from its institutionalisation in the 1980s, is characterised by a comparative approach that has developed strategies for reading the ancient texts of the Bible—such as Proverbs—against traditional and contemporary African experiences and concerns.[12]

Five African Recipes for Interpreting Biblical Proverbs in Dialogue with African Proverbs

Now, as the pot is steadily placed on the three stones of the cooking fire, it is time to take a closer look at how the cook allows the ingredients that are put into the pot to boil together and share "flavours." In other words, the question is how the cook—*in casu* the African biblical scholar—arranges the two major ingredients in the pot: the biblical and African proverbs. In this section, I will discuss five such cooks, that is five African biblical scholars who have read biblical proverbs comparatively with African proverbs. All five cases are monographs that are based on the author's doctoral studies. The material is too small to talk about representativity. Nevertheless, it should be noted that the five include scholars from West Africa (Naré and Akoto-Abutiate), East Africa (Kimilike), Central Africa (Nzambi), and Southern Africa (Masenya), and it includes two females (Masenya and Akoto-Abutiate) and three males (Naré, Kimilike, and Nzambi).

For pragmatic reasons, I will discuss the five chronologically. The first example is Laurent Naré (Burkina Faso), who in 1986 published his monograph *Proverbes salomoniens et proverbes mossi: Étude comparative*

12. Holter, *Contextualized Old Testament Scholarship*, 83–115.

à partir d'une nouvelle analyse de Pr 25–29.[13] Naré compares the so-called "Solomonic" collections in Prov 25–29 with proverbs of the Mossi of Burkina Faso. The two traditions are examined separately, and then they are exposed to each other. Naré notices similarities with regard to form and style—for example, various cases of rhythm, sound, and parallelism. Moreover, when it comes to content, he emphasises that the parallels between the two traditions not only cover practical wisdom (for example, laziness and mendacity) but also more theological wisdom (for example, concerning God as the Creator and God as the source of justice). However, apart from noticing such kinds of parallels, the investigation has a rather static profile, and its ambitions are somewhat meagre:

> Dans une telle problématique, l'idée d'une comparaison assez poussée sur le plan exégétique entre la sagesse biblique et une sagesse non-biblique d'une aire culturelle aussi éloignée, dans l'espace et dans le temps, par rapport à Israël, que celle, précisément, du pays mossi, revêt déjà peut-être un certain caractère de nouveauté.[14]

For Naré, the point that two proverbial traditions have a lot in common is in itself an important result, and he sees no need for going further, such as interpreting one of the two proverbial traditions in the light of the other.

The second example is Philippe Dinzolele Nzambi (Democratic Republic of the Congo), who in 1992 published his voluminous study *Proverbes bibliques et proverbes kongo: Étude comparative de Proverbia 25–29 et de quelques proverbes kongo.*[15] The book first analyses Congolese proverbs, arranging them according to topics. Emphasis is placed on certain stylistic aspects such as grammar and syntax. A selection of Proverbs—chapters 25–29, here too, like in Naré's investigation—is then analysed, again with a particular and meticulous focus on stylistic aspects. A final comparison follows up this focus on stylistic phenomena, arguing that the expressions we can observe in Prov 25–29 to a high degree resemble corresponding expressions in the Congolese proverbial material:

> Les nombreuses ressemblances formelles qui existent entre Proverbia 25–29 et les proverbs kongo peuvent étonner plus d'un. Cet étonnement ne doit cependant pas conduire à une

13. Naré, *Proverbes salomoniens.*

14. Naré, *Proverbes salomoniens*, 1–2.

15. Nzambi, *Proverbes bibliques.*

> sorte de révolte. En effet, nous nous trouvons ici dans le domaine de la sagesse; domaine dans lequel l'élément humain joue un rôle de premier plan. La sagesse, c'est ce qui le plus unit toute l'humanité.[16]

However, Nzambi, like Naré, stops here, as if he is satisfied with simply pointing out (a large number of) stylistic parallels between the two proverbial traditions—though with one exception, as he briefly touches on the question of the origin of the biblical proverbs, arguing that they, like their Congolese counterparts, probably reflect a popular rather than royal context.

The third example is Madipoane Masenya (Ngwan'a Mphahlele; South Africa), who in 2004 published her *How Worthy Is the Woman of Worth? Reading Proverbs 31:10–31 in African South-Africa.*[17] Masenya reads the text about the supposedly ideal woman in Prov 31:10–31 from what she calls a *bosadi*—that is womanhood—perspective of a Northern Sotho woman. The perspective is developed by an analysis of how women are portrayed in Northern Sotho proverbs, with attention to liberating as well as oppressive aspects. These *bosadi* insights are then used in the interpretation of the Proverbs text, and it is noticed that

> the text of Proverbs 31:10–31 is liberative since it elevates the significance of the family (for African men and women), an important institution in traditional Africa.... The text is also problematic due to its separation between what appears to be the womanly sphere of the home and the more significant (public) sphere of men, the gates of the city. Such a traditional division between these spheres, on the basis of gender, should be rejected as it does women and men themselves injustice.[18]

In other words, the African context—as it is constructed based on Northern Sotho proverbs—is here made the explicit interpretive subject of the biblical text.

The fourth example is Lechion Peter Kimilike (Tanzania), who in 2008 published his *Poverty in the Book of Proverbs: An African Transformational Hermeneutic of Proverbs on Poverty.*[19] Kimilike is concerned with what he finds to be a rather static tendency of Western biblical

16. Nzambi, *Proverbes bibliques*, 733.

17. Masenya, *How Worthy.*

18. Masenya, *How Worthy*, 161–62.

19. Kimilike, *Poverty.*

scholarship about proverbs on poverty in the book of Proverbs. It neglects the ethical challenge of poverty, he argues:

> The impetus for undertaking this study was the conviction that the predominant interpretation of poverty proverbs in the Book of Proverbs displayed a conservative outlook. Such a *status quo*–oriented socio-economic outlook was not helpful for the transformation of the life and livelihood of the poor in my African Christian context.[20]

Against this, Kimilike suggests a more dynamic interpretation of the biblical proverbs on poverty. A comparative approach, reading the biblical texts in the light of African proverbial material on poverty allows him to create an interpretive strategy of transformation into contemporary contexts of poverty.

Finally, the fifth example is Dorothy BEA Akoto-Abutiate (Ghana), who in 2014 published her *Proverbs and the African Tree of Life: Grafting Biblical Proverbs on to Ghanaian Eve Folk Proverbs*.[21] The book aims to develop a metaphor of "grafting" about African biblical hermeneutics, with Ewe proverbs (Ghana) as her material base. Trying to avoid typically academic jargon like inculturation, acculturation, indigenisation, etc., she makes use of a concrete and well-known image from agriculture, and the major point of her African "hermeneutic of grafting" is that biblical texts and motifs can and should be explicitly related to already existing counterparts in Africa. Basing her thinking on the hermeneutics of Gadamer, she argues,

> [The] translation of meaning from one world to another is accomplished by taking some "shoots" from the world of Proverbs 25–29 and "grafting" them on to the world of the African Ghanaian Eve folk proverbs. In other words, "shoots" from the tree of life, the biblical Book of Proverbs, are grafted on to the Eve folk proverbial tree of life.[22]

On her way through the material, Akoto-Abutiate touches important discourses in African proverbs scholarship (e.g., form and function) as well as biblical proverbs scholarship (e.g., the question of social location), but the concept of "grafting" is repeatedly used as an overall

20. Kimilike, *Poverty*, 308; emphasis original.

21. Akoto-Abutiate, *African Tree of Life*. Akoto-Abutiate uses the spelling "Eve" in place of "Ewe."

22. Akoto-Abutiate, *African Tree of Life*, 13.

interpretive perspective. The aim is no longer to demonstrate parallels between the two proverbial traditions, but rather,

> as a result of this blending, a new and hybridized fruit is created with a completely different flavor than either of the traditions or trees of life when viewed individually.[23]

A completely new flavour, resulting from a conscious grafting, Akoto-Abutiate suggests. Or, in the image I have used above, a new flavour resulting from two different ingredients boiling together in a pot on the three stones of the cooking fire. The gardener and the cook—and indeed the African biblical scholar—have facilitated a mutual sharing of "flavours," and the question is now how the five recipes discussed above relate to each other.

Reading the five studies chronologically, one soon observes that they represent quite individual endeavours. With one exception, they are not genetically related. The five come from different geographical, cultural, and institutional contexts, and they did the research that resulted in the five monographs in university and research environments that—again with one exception—probably have little to do with each other. Moreover, neither do the five explicitly build upon each other's work. On the contrary, they more or less ignore each other. Naré (1986) was the first of the five, but Nzambi (1992) does not refer to Naré; Masenya (2004) does not refer to Naré or Nzambi; and Akoto-Abutiate (2014) only makes a brief reference—without doing anything out of it—to Naré. The only exception in the list of lacking interaction is Kimilike (2008), who was supervised by Masenya (and myself) and to some extent built on her work.[24] In other words, one can hardly talk about an institutionalised "school" of African biblical scholars making use of African proverbial material in their analysis of biblical proverbs.

Nevertheless, there are obvious parallels between the interpretive strategies of the five. All of them take for granted that African proverbial material may serve as an entry to a closer understanding of biblical Proverbs. When there is no "school" that can explain their parallel approach to Proverbs, there must be another reason. I believe that they developed their interpretive strategies quite intuitively; the time was simply ripe for these kinds of approaches. As noticed above, African biblical scholarship can probably be said to have been born in the 1960s

23. Akoto-Abutiate, *African Tree of Life*, 13.

24. Kimilike, *Poverty*, 73–75.

and then to have experienced an institutionalised breakthrough in the 1980s.[25] The key characteristic of the guild of African biblical scholarship that emerged in the latter decades of the twentieth century was what is often referred to as a comparative paradigm, emphasising the interpretive potential of the African context.[26] This paradigm developed in response to the quest for contextualisation that came from the churches throughout the 1960s and onwards, but it also developed in response to the focus on the African heritage that was emphasized at the same time by African post-independence academia. As far as biblical studies were concerned, we can see a strong focus on comparative research projects from the 1980s on,[27] and when the five studies being analysed here chose to read Proverbs from the perspective of African proverbial material, it was probably simply an example of a broader trend.

However, not only are there obvious parallels between the interpretive strategies of the five, but there are also some clear differences. The most striking difference can be found between the two former ones—Naré and Nzambi—on the one hand, and the three latter ones—Masenya, Kimilike, and Akoto-Abutiate—on the other. As I have indicated above, the two former ones have a rather static approach to the two proverbial traditions. Throughout hundreds of pages and in minutiae, they discuss all possibly imaginable examples of stylistic parallels between the two. But then, when they have demonstrated all the parallels, they simply stop and conclude. Proving the existence of such parallels seems to be their main interpretive strategy and goal.

On the other hand, the three latter do not at all show interest in style; their focus is a supposed set of parallels concerning content. These parallels are then conceptualised as interpretive clues, enabling one set of proverbs to shed light on the other. If the term *static* could be used about the approaches of Naré and Nzambi, the term *dynamic* should probably be used about the approaches of Masenya, Kimilike, and Akoto-Abutiate. They aim to let the two proverbial traditions interact, often from two perspectives that are different but not mutually exclusive: one is to let the African proverb serve as a kind of exegetical tool for understanding the biblical proverb, and the other is to let the biblical proverb serve as a kind

25. Holter, *Contextualized Old Testament Scholarship*, 83–115.

26. Anum, "Comparative Readings."

27. Holter, *Old Testament Research*, 88–100.

of hermeneutical tool for understanding the contemporary context and function of the African proverb.[28]

The Use of African Proverbs and African Biblical Proverbs Studies in Western Recipes

After the above discussion of five monographs that interpret Proverbs from the perspective of African proverbial material, I will now in the last part of the article briefly turn to the reception of the African material in the Western guild of biblical scholarship. If we are to remain in the image of ingredients in a pot that is placed on the stones of the cooking fire, the question is then how the African material—that is, both the African proverbs *per se* and African biblical Proverbs studies—is being used in Western recipes of Proverbs studies.

The Western reception of African material to Proverbs studies can roughly be grouped into three. First, Western biblical scholars have for nearly a century acknowledged close parallels between Proverbs 22:17—23:11 and the so-called "Instruction of Amenemope," a text dating back to the late second millennium BCE Egypt. It can certainly be discussed whether ancient Egypt is part of Africa and Amenemope thus is an "African text." What is nevertheless interesting is that we here have two proverbial texts where there probably is a genetic relationship—that is, a historical, cultural influence between Egypt and Israel. When biblical scholars make use of Amenemope to interpret Proverbs, it is, therefore, part of a broader interpretive strategy, that of reading biblical texts in the light of other available examples of literature from the ancient Near East, including Northeast Africa.

Second, some exponents of Western biblical scholarship have realised the interpretive potential of traditional and contemporary proverbial material from Africa for the study of Proverbs. An early example was the German biblical scholar Claus Westermann. He was in a sense predisposed to this; being a son of the German Africanist Diedrich H. Westermann, he grew up in a context that was familiar with African languages and oral traditions. Westermann does not claim a genetic relationship between African proverbial material and its biblical counterpart, such as in the case of Amenemope. Rather, he acknowledges the phenomenological correspondence between the two proverbial

28. Holter, *Old Testament Research*, 88–100.

traditions and suggests that African material can be used to illustrate biblical proverbs.[29] Westermann's seminal ideas were followed up by his student Friedemann W. Golka, who develops the idea that traditional and contemporary African proverbial material can be used comparatively to understand questions of meaning and genre in Proverbs.[30]

Third, when it comes to African biblical proverbs scholarship, Westermann refers positively to Naré's work, whereas Golka surprisingly ignores both Naré and Nzambi. A few years later, though, Golka invited African colleagues to join the research field with their particular background,[31] an invitation that was soon taken up by Kimilike.[32] In more recent Western commentaries to Proverbs, however, there seems to be a tendency to acknowledge the value of the approach made by African colleagues of the guild. One example is Roland E. Murphy, who briefly refers to the work of "native African scholars" like Naré and Nzambi.[33] Another example is Ernest W. Lucas, who in his Proverbs commentary discusses Naré and Nzambi and devotes several pages to Kimilike:[34]

> Kimilike's work shows the considerable influence of social context on the understanding of proverbs. It suggests that a dialogue between Western and African scholars could be fruitful in the study of biblical proverbs.[35]

Conclusion

In the pages above, I have asked what roles African proverbial material play in the Proverbs studies of Laurent Naré (Burkina Faso), Philippe Donzolele Nzambi (Democratic Republic of the Congo), Madipoane Masenya (South Africa), Lechion Peter Kimilike (Tanzania), and Dorothy BEA Akoto-Abutiate (Ghana). To conclude I will make a brief detour via the Nigerian biblical scholar Justin S. Ukpong. Nearly two decades ago he argued that African biblical scholarship is characterized by three relatively clear interpretive phases. One is a "reactive phase" (the 1930s–1970s), which through comparative studies aimed at legitimising African religion and culture vis-à-vis the Western tradition. The other is a

29. Westermann, *Wurzeln der Weisheit*, 152–59.

30. Golka, *Die Flecken des Leoparden*.

31. Golka, "Wisdom by (the) People," 78–79.

32. Kimilike, "Friedemann W. Golka," 255–61.

33. Murphy, *Proverbs*, 290.

34. Lucas, *Proverbs*, 39–40, 311–14.

35. Lucas, *Proverbs*, 313.

"reactive-proactive" phase (the 1970s–1990s), which more clearly made use of the African context as a resource for biblical interpretation. And the third is a "proactive" phase (the 1990s), which made the African context the explicit subject of biblical interpretation.[36]

Ukpong's model can be criticised for exaggerating a clear-cut chronology of phases vis-à-vis a material that is far more diverse. Nevertheless, the five studies analysed above clearly point to some important characteristics. On the one hand, when Naré and Nzambi insist that it is possible to find stylistic parallels between their respective Mossi and Congolese proverbs and those of the Bible, it is not difficult to see an early postcolonial reaction to traditional Western oppression and marginalisation of African culture, such as in Ukpong's "reactive" phase.

I suspect that behind Naré and Nzambi's insistence of stylistic parallels between African and biblical proverbs, there is a strategy of demonstrating that Africa is able to come up with cultural expressions that are on the "same level" as the book that—wrongly, of course—was conceptualised as *the* Western book.

On the other hand, when Masenya, Kimilike, and Akoto-Abutiate more or less ignore Naré and Nzambi's stylistic emphasis, instead highlighting how the two proverbial traditions may enlighten each other, the interpretive strategy reflects what Ukpong refers to as "reactive-proactive" and "proactive" phases. In the Proverbs studies of the three latter scholars, African experiences and concerns have indeed become resources for biblical interpretation and even an explicit subject of biblical interpretation. Both interpretive characteristics—the focus on stylistic parallels in the works by Naré and Nzambi, and the focus on Africa as an interpretive subject in the works by Masenya, Kimilike, and Akoto-Abutiate—reflect African experiences and concerns, and both deserve more attention from Western scholarship working with Proverbs.

Bibliography

Akoto-Abutiate, Dorothy BEA. *Proverbs and the African Tree of Life: Grafting Biblical Proverbs on to Ghanaian Eve Folk Proverbs*. Studies in Systematic Theology 16. Leiden: Brill, 2014.

Anum, Eric. "Comparative Readings of the Bible in Africa: Some Concerns." In *The Bible in Africa: Transactions, Trajectories and Trends*, edited Gerald O. West and Musa W. Dube, 457–73. Leiden: Brill, 2000.

Cotter, Georg. *Ethiopian Wisdom: Proverbs and Sayings of the Oromo People*. African Proverbs Series 1. Pretoria: Unisa, 1997.

36. Ukpong, "Developments in Biblical Interpretation."

Golka, Friedemann W. *Die Flecken des Leoparden: Biblische und afrikanische Weisheit im Sprichwort*. Arbeiten zur Theologie 78. Stuttgart: Calwer, 1994.

———. "Wisdom by (the) People for (the) People: Eine Antwort an J. A. Loader." *Zeitschrift für die alttestamentliche Wissenschaft* 112 (2000) 78–79.

Holter, Knut. *Contextualized Old Testament Scholarship in Africa*. Nairobi: Acton, 2008.

———. "The Left Hand Washes the Right and the Right Hand Washes the Left: Some Remarks to the Use of African Proverbs in Old Testament Scholarship." *African Journal of Biblical Studies* 26 (2008) 45–55.

———. *Old Testament Research for Africa: A Critical and Annotated Bibliography of African Old Testament Dissertations, 1967–2000*. Bible and Theology in Africa 3. New York: Lang, 2002.

Holter, Knut, and Louis C. Jonker, eds. *Global Hermeneutics? Reflections and Consequences*. International Voices in Biblical Studies 1. Atlanta: SBL, 2010.

Jonker, Louis C. *From Adequate Biblical Interpretation to Transformative Intercultural Hermeneutics: Chronicling a Personal Journey*. Intercultural Biblical Hermeneutics Series 3. Elkhart, IN: Institute of Mennonite Studies, 2015.

Kimilike, Lechion Peter. "Friedemann W. Golka and African Proverbs on the Poor." *Zeitschrift für die alttestamentliche Wissenschaft* 114 (2002) 255–61.

———. *Poverty in the Book of Proverbs: An African Transformational Hermeneutic of Proverbs on Poverty*. Bible and Theology in Africa 7. New York: Lang, 2008.

Lucas, Ernest C. *Proverbs*. Two Horizons Old Testament Commentary. Grand Rapids: Eerdmans, 2015.

Masenya, Madipoane (Ngwan'a Mphahlele). *How Worthy Is the Woman of Worth? Reading Proverbs 31:10–31 in African South-Africa*. Bible and Theology in Africa 4. New York: Lang, 2004.

Mbiti, John S. "The African Proverbs Project and After." *Lexikos* 12 (2002) 256–63.

———. *Bible and Theology in African Christianity*. Nairobi: Oxford University Press, 1986.

Mieder, Wolfgang. *African Proverb Scholarship: An Annotated Bibliography*. Colorado Springs, CO: African Proverbs Project, 1994.

Murphy, Roland E. *Proverbs*. Word Biblical Commentary 22. Nashville: Nelson, 1998.

Naré, Laurent. *Proverbes salomoniens et proverbes mossi: Étude comparative à partir d'une nouvelle analyse de Pr 25–29*. Publications Universitaires Européennes 23/283. Frankfurt: Lang, 1986.

Nzambi, Philippe Dinzolele. *Proverbes bibliques et proverbes kongo: Étude comparative de Proverbia 25–29 et de quelques proverbes kongo*. Religionswissenschaft 5. Frankfurt: Lang, 1992.

Saayman, Willem, ed. *Embracing the Baobab Tree: The African Proverb in the 21st Century*. African Proverbs Series 5. Pretoria: Unisa, 1997.

Ukpong, Justin S. "Developments in Biblical Interpretation in Africa: Historical and Hermeneutical Directions." *Journal of Theology for Southern Africa* 108 (2000) 3–18.

Wanjohi, Gerald J. *The Wisdom and Philosophy of the Gikuyu Proverbs*. Nairobi: Paulines Publications Africa, 1997.

Westermann, Claus. *Wurzeln der Weisheit: Die ältesten Sprüche Israels und anderer Völker*. Göttingen: Vandenhoeck & Ruprecht, 1990.

5

Enabling Biblical Text in African Communities

From Socio-Historical Production to Literary-Narrative Reception

Gerald O. West

Much of my own work and much of the work of Louis Jonker, whose contribution we celebrate in this volume, has been shaped by the complex relationship between biblical reception hermeneutics and/as biblical production hermeneutics. We are both creatures of method. Indeed, we are both interested in theoretical discussion about method, recognising that theory shapes method and that method summons theorising. The focus of our PhDs was on theory about method,[1] and we both recognised the importance of teaching method in our biblical studies pedagogy.[2] Most importantly, perhaps, we have both been concerned about the inclusion of ordinary, non-specialist Bible readers in reception and/as production hermeneutics.[3]

1. Published respectively as West, *Biblical Hermeneutics of Liberation*; Jonker, *Exclusivity and Variety*.

2. Conradie et al., *Fishing for Jonah*; Jonker and Lawrie, *Fishing for Jonah (Anew)*.

3. Conradie et al., "Biblical Interpretation"; Draper and West, "Anglicans and Scripture." We have both contributed essays to various projects of intercultural Bible reading: Jonker, "Jesus Among the Ancestors"; West, "Artful Facilitation"; Jonker, "On Becoming

Given the praxeological community-based orientation of my own work, where "accountability"[4] to local African communities is a contextual reception priority, the aspect of Jonker's work that has challenged me most has been his call for "contextual integrity,"[5] where his emphasis is on contextual production. In another of our joint projects, Jonker presented this analysis as part of a process in which African and European interpreters constructed a dialogue about biblical interpretation. Our collaborative dialogue, both in person and in the published form, was methodological in orientation, as we wrestled for "a shared meaning."[6] Jonker took up and developed a notion I had borrowed from the work of Stephen Fowl, in which we (each of us in dialogue with each other) distinguish between "life interests" and "interpretive interests."[7] Jonker helpfully integrates the concepts of interpretive and life interests with his concept of "seven contextualities."[8] "Who we are ['interpretive contextuality'], for whom we are interpreting ['didactic contextuality'] and with which methods we are doing our interpretations ['meta-theoretical contextuality'], are inevitable motivations in our scholarship." "These life interests," continues Jonker, "cannot be ignored or sidestepped."[9]

Having fully embraced the place of life interests (and life contexts) in our biblical interpretation, Jonker reminds us of the other four contextualities he has identified, insisting that these textual contexts—"productive, rhetorical, literary and canonical contextuality," these interpretive interests—must be integrated with each other and with the contexts that shape our life interests.[10]

In my understanding, Jonker is making a general plea for "inter-contextual" "contextual integrity" within a "multi-dimensional" approach to biblical interpretation,[11] and a particular plea for an interpretive integrity between textual production and textual reception.

---

a Family"; West, "Heterotopic Intercultural Site."

4. West, *Biblical Hermeneutics of Liberation*, 2nd rev. ed., 88, 91, 101.

5. Jonker, "Living in Different Worlds Simultaneously."

6. Wit and West, *African and European Readers*.

7. Fowl, "Ethics of Interpretation," 385; West, *Biblical Hermeneutics of Liberation*, 2nd rev. ed., 132–34; Jonker, "Plea for Contextual Integrity," 112–13.

8. Jonker, "Plea for Contextual Integrity," 110.

9. Jonker, "Plea for Contextual Integrity," 113, wherein I have integrated concepts from 110–12.

10. Jonker, "Plea for Contextual Integrity," 113.

11. Jonker, "Plea for Contextual Integrity," 113–14.

Both pleas provide a useful framework for reflecting on the Contextual Bible Study (CBS) praxis of the Ujamaa Centre. However, before I engage with CBS praxis in detail, I want to describe the biblical studies context and the intersecting community-based Bible reading context that framed the emergence of the Ujamaa Centre's "Contextual Bible Study" interpretive process in the late 1980s.

Reception Hermeneutics and/as Production Hermeneutics

In what has proved to be a prescient article, shaping both Jonker's work and my own, Bernard Lategan offered South African biblical scholars an astute historical analysis of biblical interpretive methodology across the eras of biblical studies as a discipline.[12] Among its many points of insightful analysis, Lategan notes the following point with respect to the paradigm switch within biblical studies to the "receptor": "Oddly enough, the concentration on the reader [as the third vector of biblical interpretation, including 'source-message-receptor'] also caused the return of the historical problem, be it on a different level and in a different form. . . . It appears in the form of a renewed 'sociological' interest in the setting of text and reader."[13] Real flesh and blood readers are located within a thick sociological history, not merely a linear chronological history, and if real flesh and blood readers are so situated, then so too are real flesh and blood authors (as "source").[14] Questions of textual reception generate questions of textual production.

This is the biblical studies world of the mid-1980s that framed the work of what is now the Ujamaa Centre for Community Development and Research at what is now the University of KwaZulu-Natal.[15] Sociological-historical analysis was the primary methodological emphasis of Gunther Wittenberg, the founder of what has become the Ujamaa Centre. As a socially engaged biblical scholar, Wittenberg's interpretive interests were socio-historical, as is evident in this scholarship over many decades. For Wittenberg biblical reception in South Africa required understanding biblical production in the ancient world. His particular socio-historical

12. Lategan, "Current Issues."
13. Lategan, "Current Issues," 4.
14. Lategan, "Current Issues," 3.
15. For an account of this early history, see West, "Contextual Bible Study."

interest was in the emergence of what he called "resistance theology" in the early monarchic period among "the people of the land," the עם הארץ.[16]

When Wittenberg went to Brazil in 1988, his own socio-historical methodological emphasis found resonance in the work of Centro de Estudios Biblicos (CEBI). He was especially moved by how biblical scholars who shared his socio-historical methodological commitments were "greatly involved in the grassroots Bible Movement of ordinary people." This "fascinated" Wittenberberg.[17] "I saw how liberation theology was a living, dynamic concern and how it reached the people," he reports, through the many courses and projects offered by socially engaged seminaries and CEBI. "Things that I saw in Brazil resonated with me, and everything started to come together in my mind. I was convinced that we needed something similar in South Africa."[18] On his return to South Africa Wittenberg began the process what would lead to the establishment of what is now the Ujamaa Centre.[19] For Wittenberg, resistance to South African apartheid as biblical reception required ancient resistance theology as biblical production.

The Ujamaa Centre was established within such an understanding of a relationship between biblical reception hermeneutics and biblical production hermeneutics. What Lategan astutely recognised in his 1984 analysis was how socio-historical textual interests were shaped by reception-oriented hermeneutics. "The most extreme example of reception-oriented hermeneutics," he argues, "is no doubt 'materialistic' exegesis." "The term itself," he continues, "implies a critique of the so-called 'idealistic' exegesis, which is supposed to be more interested in concepts, meaning, and an intellectual approach to interpretation. In contrast, materialistic exegesis is primarily interested in the empiric situation, in the 'material conditions' which give rise to the production of a specific text."[20] Lategan understands the role of Marxist theory within this form of reception-history when he states, "The text is the result of certain production factors. It is a 'superstructure' built on a basis which is determined in the last analysis by socio-economic factors."[21] "The text is

16. The title and content of a significant collection of his essays demonstrates this: Wittenberg, *Resistance Theology*.

17. Wittenberg, *Visit to Brazil*, 14–15.

18. Institute for the Study of the Bible, *Tenth Anniversary Celebration*, 16.

19. West, "Contextual Bible Study," 5–6.

20. Lategan, "Current Issues," 6.

21. Lategan, "Current Issues," 7.

understood as an ideological product, shaped by specific socio-economic forces and serving certain interests. The task of interpretation is to lay bare these (often concealed) interests."[22]

Lategan is clear that this kind of biblical textual analysis belongs to reception hermeneutics. "It is important to notice," he insists, "that although the focus is on the situation of production, this is done from a reader's perspective. What is at stake is the 'application' of these texts in a contemporary situation." "Claims made on the basis of traditional [historical-critical idealist] interpretation are overturned by revealing the bias which they harbour." In sum, says Lategan, "the reaction of materialistic exegesis against ruling conventions of exegesis is in fact a reaction against what is perceived as the ruling class."[23] South African Black theology biblical studies would articulate a similar sentiment a few years later. It is not incidental that White, socially engaged biblical scholars and Black, socially engaged biblical scholars were asking similar questions; it is part of the "interpretive contextuality,"[24] to use Jonker's term, of South Africa in the 1980s.

In the prologue to his landmark 1989 book, *Biblical Hermeneutics and Black Theology in South Africa*, the published version of his 1987 PhD thesis,[25] Itumeleng Mosala declares that he has chosen to use "the historical-materialist method of analysis usually associated with the name of Karl Marx rather than the idealist framework."[26] Though Mosala does not cite Lategan, he does cite a White, socially engaged, compatriotic scholar who was doing similar hermeneutical work within South African Old Testament / Hebrew Bible at the time, Ferdinand Deist. Mosala uses Deist to demonstrate the ideological orientations of biblical text production. Deist is overt about how older texts are ideologically reused in order "to authorize the new."[27] Deist, like Mosala, insists on South African biblical scholarship being attentive to the ideological dimensions of the Bible, at a time when much of White South African biblical scholarship was avoiding the ideological dimensions of biblical

22. Lategan, "Current Issues," 7.

23. Lategan, "Current Issues," 7.

24. Jonker, "Plea for Contextual Integrity," 110.

25. Mosala, "Biblical Hermeneutics and Black Theology."

26. Mosala, *Biblical Hermeneutics and Black Theology*, 4.

27. Deist, "Idealistic Theologiegeschichte," 65; Mosala, *Biblical Hermeneutics and Black Theology*, 101.

interpretation.[28] Both Mosala and Deist are particularly interested in three of Jonker's contextualities and their relationships: "productive contextuality," "literary contextuality," and "canonical contextuality,"[29] in this order of priority. What connects these three contextualities is that they each designate a feature of biblical textual production; what Mosala and Deist would hasten to add is that these three contextualities each designate a feature of biblical textual *ideological* production!

For both, though my focus is on Mosala, a biblical ideological reception hermeneutics requires a biblical ideological production hermeneutics. Indeed, this is perhaps Mosala's single most significant argument. In introducing his work in the prologue, Mosala states, "Two main issues form a structure for the development of my thought in this work." He continues, "First, there is the question of the historical-cultural foundations and links of black theology and how these affect black theology's biblical-hermeneutical assumptions, which I regard as very important in developing a biblical hermeneutics of liberation."[30] In Jonker's terms, Mosala is arguing that "interpretive contextuality" is critical in establishing a "meta-theoretical contextuality."[31] Mosala argues for a particular interpretive contextuality, contending that "in order to become a weapon of struggle for oppressed black people, black theology needs to relocate itself within the historical and cultural struggles of these people."[32]

"Second," says Mosala, turning to his second main issue, "black theology must openly declare where it stands ideologically and theoretically," "specifically with respect to the biblical-hermeneutical aspect I deal with here,"[33] which are the three related contextualities of production I indicated above. Again, Mosala is clear that there is what I have referred to as "an analogy of method"[34] that connects a hermeneutics of reception and

28. Smit, "Ethics of Interpretation"; Draper, "For the Kingdom Is Inside."

29. Jonker, "Plea for Contextual Integrity," 110, 111, 112.

30. Mosala, *Biblical Hermeneutics and Black Theology*, 3.

31. Jonker, "Plea for Contextual Integrity," 110, 112.

32. Mosala, *Biblical Hermeneutics and Black Theology*, 4. Mosala critiques Latin American liberation theology of this period because "it presupposes European history and culture and not the indigenous Latin American history and culture," and Western social and political theologies because "they have been premised on the dominant and patriarchal class histories and cultures at the expense of the oppressed and women's histories and cultures." *Biblical Hermeneutics and Black Theology*, 3–4.

33. Mosala, *Biblical Hermeneutics and Black Theology*, 4.

34. West, *Biblical Hermeneutics of Liberation*, 2nd rev. ed., 75–76.

a hermeneutics of production within Black theology's meta-theoretical contextuality. In Mosala's terms,

> I give priority to this [historical-materialist] method of exposing fundamental social relationships because, in the case of both the Bible and black theology, there are communities and networks of relationships that must be brought to the fore. Only such an exposure of the underlying material relationships can throw light on the problems of which the biblical texts are a solution and can enable black theology to become the kind of critical discourse that is capable of contributing meaningfully to black liberation struggle.[35]

I have done extensive reflection on Mosala's analogy of method, and how Mosala's hermeneutic of textual reception requires a particular hermeneutic of textual production.[36] I will not reiterate that work here. My purpose here is to add Mosala to the voices of Wittenberg and Lategan. These were among the formative biblical hermeneutical voices that guided the early CBS work of the Ujamaa Centre as it was being summoned to hear the voices of Black South Africans struggling with the Bible in the midst of their struggle against apartheid. Significantly, the methodological emphasis was on the socio-historical dimensions of biblical texts.

An Insufficient Final Form: Socio-Historical Method

I return in this section to Jonker's plea for contextual integrity by turning to his dialogue with the comparative approach of much of African biblical interpretation. The comparative approach, he reflects, "often establishes a direct relationship between biblical texts and African contexts, or to be more precise, between the worlds constructed in the biblical texts and different African contexts."[37] Using language similar to Mosala's, Jonker goes on to point out that "often African biblical scholars do not take into account the fact that the biblical texts are constructed realities that wanted to engage in dialogue with those socio-historical circumstances within which they were written."[38] "In short," he continues, "the compara-

35. Mosala, *Biblical Hermeneutics and Black Theology*, 4–5.
36. See for example West, "Serving the Sighs"; West, "Reception and Production."
37. Jonker, "Further Interrogation," 77.
38. Jonker, "Towards an Analogical Hermeneutics," 77.

tive paradigm in African biblical scholarship often falls prey—at least in my opinion—to a lack of historical consciousness."[39]

Significantly, in his recent book on African biblical studies, Andrew Mbuvi confirms Jonker's assessment. In discussing the relationship between "western Biblical Studies" and "African Biblical Studies," Mbuvi makes the point that while Western biblical studies grappled with the emergence of literary-narrative methods of interpretation, "African biblical scholars from the newly independent African countries were already engaging in post-colonial/postcolonial discourses of the Bible that already were focused less on the historical-grammatical and more on the final form of the text."[40] "Then and now," Mbuvi continues, "African scholars have found that the final form of the text provides a sufficient starting point for the interpretive process without necessarily denigrating historical analysis. The focus is less on 'what the biblical text meant for its ancient settings,' and more on 'what the text means for the current reader.'"[41] Mbuvi then goes on to elaborate, explaining how he understands this preference for the final form.

> So laden was the Bible with encumbrances of the colonial project that it could never simply be relegated to its ancient status. For the African biblical scholar, because the Bible is not simply an ancient text, but one that essentially finds its full expression in the reader's present, the need to understand how it applies to the contemporary realities precludes (but does not ignore) its historical provenance. For the African, the Bible has always been about the present, as the expectation is that it ably addresses the reader's current concerns. Because African readers received and experienced the Bible as a component of the colonizer's tool bag, the Bible was always about current affairs (dynamics of authority, power, subjugation, and oppression), and not ancient history.[42]

Mbuvi provides a compelling argument here for engaging the final form, and I will return to elements of his analysis later. However, given Mbuvi's historical interrogation of the embedded racism and colonialism within the formation of Western biblical studies, it is curious that he does not advocate for, with Mosala and other African biblical scholars like

39. Jonker, "Towards an Analogical Hermeneutics," 77.

40. Mbuvi, *African Biblical Studies*, 109.

41. Mbuvi, *African Biblical Studies*, 109.

42. Mbuvi, *African Biblical Studies*, 109.

Justin Ukpong,[43] a historical interrogation of the formation of the biblical text. Though Mbuvi does offer an overview of some of Mosala's method within a subsection dedicated to Mosala's work,[44] he does not engage with Mosala's primary concern—namely, that the final form cannot be trusted to serve African ideological interests, representing as it does dominant ideologies. Just as Africans must interrogate their colonial histories, so too Africans must interrogate the ruling-class colonising ideologies of the final form of the Bible. African biblical scholarship, Mosala and Wittenberg insist, must interrogate the final form.

Just as Jonker worries about African biblical scholars who disregard the historical "constructedness" of biblical texts, so Mosala too worries about Black theologians who receive the biblical text in its ideologically co-opted final form. A biblical hermeneutics of liberation, insists Mosala, "using the same tool of struggle as was used to interrogate the readers' history, culture, and ideology, must now address the question of the material conditions that constitute the sites of the struggles that produced the biblical texts."[45] Most Black theological biblical interpretation lacks, argues Mosala, echoing Jonker's analysis, a historical(-materialist) consciousness.[46]

Both Jonker and Mosala locate their African analogical biblical hermeneutics in the historical (or more accurately, in the socio-historical, in Lategan's sense). Jonker is explicit about a socio-historical analogical interpretive hermeneutic, which he reiterates in a recent essay, stating, "Historical consciousness assists us to relate the worlds-behind-the-texts with our contemporary realities—not directly, but rather analogically."[47] Mosala too rejects any direct interpretive engagement between contemporary context and biblical text. "I argue," he says, "that the category of [socio-historical] struggle provides the [analogical] lens for reading the text in a liberating fashion as well as the codes for unlocking the possibilities and limitations of the biblical texts."[48]

43. Ukpong, "Rereading the Bible," 6–7; Ukpong, "Parable of the Shrewd Manager."

44. Mbuvi, *African Biblical Studies*, 127–29.

45. Mosala, *Biblical Hermeneutics and Black Theology*, 9.

46. Mosala, *Biblical Hermeneutics and Black Theology*, 24.

47. Jonker, "Contextual Interpretation, Then and Now," 242.

48. Mosala, *Biblical Hermeneutics and Black Theology*, 8.

Socio-Historical Community-Based Rereading

Such socio-historical sentiments were uppermost in the early Contextual Bible Study (CBS) work of what is now the Ujamaa Centre. Wittenberg's biblical scholarship was thoroughly shaped by the socio-historical trajectories of Old Testament scholarship at the time, and his experience of CEBI in Brazil confirmed the usefulness of socio-historical scholarship for community-based forms of Bible "rereading." I use the term "rereading" precisely because what CEBI and the South African equivalent Wittenberg established, the Institute for the Study of the Bible (ISB),[49] did was to reread the Bible by reading behind-the-text. The German biblical scholarship, much of which lay behind both CEBI and ISB (now the Ujamaa Centre), was resolutely socio-historical in its orientation,[50] as was the formative (in both Latin America and South Africa) work of Norman Gottwald,[51] as was the emerging feminist work of that time.[52]

The earliest forms of CBS constructed an analogy of struggle between contemporary South African contexts of struggle and ancient struggles behind the biblical text. A good example of the Ujamaa Centre's earliest CBS work is Wittenberg's *Prophecy and Protest: A Contextual Introduction to Israelite Prophecy*.[53] In each chapter Wittenberg uses the work of a local South African artist to locate the CBS within an African analysis of the South African struggle. Wittenberg follows the meta-methodological framework of the See–Judge–Act process.[54] He carefully chooses local African art which engages with a particular feature of South Africa's socio-political struggle (See). He then brings this aspect of contemporary struggle reality into dialogue with the potentially resonant struggles behind particular biblical texts in order to discern (Judge) if the sacred text has resources to engage contemporary reality. If it does, a local community of struggle appropriates these biblical-theological resources for their community-based action for change (Act).

49. For a history of the early years of the ISB see West, "Contextual Bible Study."

50. Wittenberg was deeply influenced by the work of Frank Crüsemann; see Wittenberg, *Resistance Theology*, 174–75.

51. Gottwald, *Tribes of Yahweh*; Gottwald, *Hebrew Bible*.

52. Schüssler Fiorenza, "Towards a Feminist Biblical Hermeneutics"; Schüssler Fiorenza, *Bread Not Stone*.

53. Wittenberg, *Prophecy and Protest*.

54. Sands, "Cardijn's See–Judge–Act."

For example, the introductory CBS in the series uses an image by David Hlongwane in which a woman is protesting or lamenting a bulldozer which is busy demolishing her shack-home.[55] Participants are invited via rhetorical questions to imagine her reality, her anger, and her protest. Wittenberg continues the "See" moment by probing the lived reality of communities of faith at the time, asking, "Is it right for Christians to protest? Should they resist evil or should they accept it as God's will? . . . What is the role of the Church in situations of injustice? Should ministers remain quiet and attend only to spiritual matters, or should they get involved in protest action, like protest marches and other activities of resistance?"[56]

Having located the CBS within the realities of a community of faith struggling with such questions in the early 1980s,[57] Wittenberg then turns to the Bible (Judge), identifying an analogy: "The Bible records the experiences of God's people through a long period of history. God's people often suffered oppression and injustice and needed direction. In these difficult times they were guided by men and women specially chosen and appointed by God to help them and show them the way."[58] In this way Wittenberg invites participants to go behind the "difficulties" ordinary readers and hearers of the Bible may have had with "the prophetic books,"[59] offering them socio-historical resources to understand and make use of biblical prophetic literature.

Wittenberg provides a thorough CEBI-like socio-historical introduction to Old Testament prophetic literature[60] before offering participants a particular example, "The Message of Nathan" in 2 Sam 12:1–13, in order to illustrate the behind-the-text socio-historical detail he has reconstructed.[61] Throughout the first introductory CBS, Wittenberg identifies key aspects of biblical prophetic literature, illustrating each aspect with reference to particular texts. The input of socio-historical detail is considerable.

The CBS concludes as it began by inviting participation. Following the considerable socio-historical detail behind biblical prophetic literature,

55. Wittenberg, *Prophecy and Protest*, 13.

56. Wittenberg, *Prophecy and Protest*, 13.

57. Wittenberg, *Prophecy and Protest*, 5.

58. Wittenberg, *Prophecy and Protest*, 13–14.

59. Wittenberg, *Prophecy and Protest*, 15.

60. Wittenberg, *Prophecy and Protest*, 14–17; Lopes, *Livros proféticos*.

61. Wittenberg, *Prophecy and Protest*, 17–18.

Wittenberg invites participants to "Judge" whether such resources are useful in their own struggles (and then to "Act" if they are useful). He uses a particular biblical text, Amos 7:14–17, as a summative resource for the general socio-historical detail that has been provided:

> 1. Read Amos 7:14–17. Can you identify the following three sections: the protest and accusation of the prophet Amos; the messenger formula showing that Amos is God's messenger; the message itself?
>
> 2. If you are a member of a Bible study group discuss this question with others: Should the Church remain neutral in a situation of oppression and evil?[62]

A second example, "Protest Against the Politics of Security, Isaiah," follows the same format, whereby Wittenberg constructs an analogy between the reality of struggle behind Suzanne Louw's image of a military Ratel armoured troop carrier in the South African township of Langa, and the struggles in the eighth and seventh centuries BCE of Israel and Judah in the context of Assyrian military domination.[63] Wittenberg uses this ancient reality as the socio-historical context within which (First) Isaiah is produced. He focuses in detail on three successive socio-historical phases of struggle, characterised by different yet related forms of political-military contestation: Isa 7:1—8:15 (Ahaz, 735–733); Isa 31:1–3, 30:15–17, 28:14–18, 28:9–13 (in that order; Hezekiah, 715–701); and Isa 1:4–9 (The Disaster, 701). Each of these texts is cited, sometimes without the later editorial additions.[64] This is not the left-to-right final form version of the Bible most ordinary readers and hearers of the Bible are familiar with. The ordering reflects socio-historical realities behind-the-text. Central to Wittenberg's CBS is an analogical dialogue between the reality of South Africa's "low intensity conflict" version of "democracy"[65] in the 1980s and the ancient Near Eastern reality behind the text of Isaiah of the Assyrian empire's political-military governance.[66]

62. Wittenberg, *Prophecy and Protest*, 21.

63. Wittenberg, *Prophecy and Protest*, 47.

64. Wittenberg, *Prophecy and Protest*, 54 note (footnote number not provided; note marked by asterisk).

65. Metz, "Pretoria's 'Total Strategy'"; Gills and Rocamora, "Low Intensity Democracy."

66. Wittenberg, *Prophecy and Protest*, 47.

As in the other CBS in this series, Wittenberg concludes with questions inviting appropriation, such as, "How would you answer a person who claimed that Christians should not be involved in politics? Is the approach of Isaiah to politics still valid for Christians today?"[67] Participants have both the substantial socio-historical input, making up the bulk of the CBS, alongside the citation of fairly extensive material from the text of Isaiah (see above), with which to draw resources for this final exercise of appropriation.

We find a similar socio-historical orientation, but within a more explicitly participatory format, in a series of CBSs for the United Congregational Church in Southern Africa (UCCSA). UCCSA invited the Ujamaa Centre to provide them with a series of Bible studies on Exodus for the launch of their Pastoral Plan in 1990, and then to accompany UCCSA local churches with further follow-up CBS work on Exodus and facilitation training.[68] Unlike the previous CBS resource on Old Testament prophetic literature, this resource had a more extensive set of questions for Bible study group work. However, each CBS in the series had substantial socio-historical input. Wittenberg had produced a number of scholarship-based resources for the Pietermaritzburg CBS group which formed the core of early CBS practice, reflection, and construction, including a booklet, "Exodus and Settlement," as well as a set of notes which formed part of the CBS series.[69] The group used these resources to develop each CBS, which was then used in a local faith-based group, reflected on further, reworked, and finally published as a series.[70]

The second CBS in the Exodus series focuses on Exod 2:1–10. As with the series on prophet literature, this CBS is shaped by a considerable amount of socio-historical input, including an adapted version of the "Legend of Sargon." This is then followed by a series of three questions, inviting participants to compare and contrast the story of the birth of Moses and the story of the birth of Sargon. These questions are then followed by further socio-historical input, locating the Exodus story within the ancient context of Assyrian oppression. This input situates the story of Moses socio-historically:

67. Wittenberg, *Prophecy and Protest*, 61.

68. This work is described in West, "Contextual Bible Study," 8–9.

69. These were the published as Wittenberg, *I Have Heard the Cry*.

70. Nürnberger, *I Will Send You*.

> When the story of Moses was written down, the Egyptian oppression of the Hebrews had been ended long ago. Now it was the Assyrians who were oppressing the Israelites. . . . That was the situation when the story of Moses was written down. We can be sure that the story of the Hebrews under *Egypt* reminded the Hebrew readers of their own present situation under the *Assyrians*. Surely they were praying for another Moses, through whom God would liberate them from the Assyrians. What will *we* think of when we read this story in our own situation today?[71]

The CBS then goes on to conclude with a "task" of appropriation: "Together think out or write a short story of Moses' life as it if had happened in our country today."[72]

We find a similar See–Judge–Act process in these CBSs to the earlier prophetic literature series. What is distinctive about the Exodus series is that they are more overtly participatory, with discussion questions and concluding tasks. As we facilitated these CBSs in UCCSA churches, we recognised the need for a more participatory process and format. So while we had no doubts about the usefulness of socio-historical resources, in both the "See" and the "Judge" movements of CBS, we experimented with where to locate the socio-historical input within a CBS. The predominantly "Catholic" reading communities in Brazil seemed to have little problem with Bible study that began with socio-historical input. However, South Africa's predominantly "Protestant" reading communities were more familiar with final form of the biblical text, as Mbuvi notes. Though they appreciated socio-historical resources, they seemed unsettled by beginning a participatory Bible study with socio-historical input. Indeed, beginning in such a way reminded them of how their church leaders led Bible study, telling them what the Bible "said" rather than facilitating their own participatory reading of the Bible.

Over a period from 1990 to 1992, Wittenberg and I established a series of research projects, funded by the Centre for Science Development (CSD) in South Africa in which we analysed various methods within CBS praxis. Key findings of this research, relevant to this essay, were shared in the first (1991) "Consultation on Contextual Hermeneutics," organised by the Centre for Contextual Hermeneutics, hosted by Lategan. The proceedings of this conference were published, wherein I

71. Institute for the Study of the Bible, *Book of Exodus*, 12–13; emphasis original. I cite here from the prepublication version we used in the UCCSA churches.

72. Institute for the Study of the Bible, *Book of Exodus*, 13.

report on our research with three different methodological emphases: behind-the-text, on-the-text, in-front-of-the-text.[73] The first CBS was the one on Exod 2:1–10, cited above. The second CBS, on Mark 10:17–22, was one that Jonathan Draper and I had constructed as part of empirical research on how ordinary Anglicans, across the racially divided Anglican churches in Pietermaritzburg, engaged with a "prophetic"—in the sense of the Kairos Document[74]—Bible study.[75] The third CBS, on Matt 6:19–34, was based on a thematic approach to Bible study used by CEBI in the north of Brazil. Our CSD research took each of these CBSs, each of which had a history of community-based use,[76] and reused them in order to do empirical research on how ordinary African readers evaluated each of these methodological orientations.[77]

Two findings about socio-historical modes of reading used in the Exod 2:1–10 CBS are particularly relevant to this essay. First, there was overwhelming support among ordinary African readers for the kind of socio-historical input offered by behind-the-text–type CBS: such resources situated the text in its ancient real-life context; through such resources ancient social, political, economic, religious, and cultural realities became apparent; such resources minimised the abuse of biblical texts by those who used them out of their context of production; and the use of such resources enabled a transfer of socio-historical skills from ancient context to contemporary context. Second, there was caution concerning how (and where in a CBS) these resources were used: such resources were not available to the community itself, and so their use might develop dependency and even manipulation by outside experts; there was little opportunity for the community to participate in the production of such resources; there was a worry that such resources, inappropriately used, might cause confusion in their understanding of how the final form of the text was related to the socio-historically reconstructed version of the text; and such resources might trap the text in the past and so limit appropriation of the text for the present.[78]

Responses to the on-the-text CBS on Mark 10:17–22 offered us a way forward, for ordinary readers found these modes of reading useful,

73. West, "Different Modes of Reading."

74. Kairos Theologians, "Challenge to the Church."

75. Draper and West, "Anglicans and Scripture," 37.

76. For an overview of this use see West, "Contextual Bible Study," 8–11.

77. West, "Different Modes of Reading," 95–99.

78. West, "Different Modes of Reading," 96–97.

first, because they started with the biblical text as ordinary people knew it, and second, because they engaged in detail with the literary-narrative-linguistic context of the text, minimising the selective use of these texts.[79] Together, these findings led us to discern ways of introducing socio-historical input, but not as a starting point.

Literary-Led Socio-Historical Community-Based Rereading

Our regular experience of the Mark 10:17–22 CBS, in its various forms, made it clear that a close and careful rereading of the text, using narratological critical methods, provided both an egalitarian entry point to a biblical text for both trained and ordinary reader as they worked together in CBS, and as they reread the text carefully and closely, a call from participants for socio-historical resources. Even when socio-historical resources were not explicitly offered, as in this CBS, the relentless interrogation of the literary-narrative detail of the text within poor and marginalised communities enabled them to "feel the impulse of the struggle behind and in the text," to quote Mosala.[80] As facilitators we were summoned to share particular socio-historical detail about the text's context of production.

A series of CBSs on Mark's Gospel demonstrated the same impulse. We chose Mark in much of our early work because of scholarship which identified Mark's site of production as shaped by political and economic contestation,[81] and because of Mark's narrative tendency to use juxtaposition to "hide," in James Scott's sense,[82] a transcript of resistance. The Mark 10:17–22 CBS enabled communities of struggle to engage with Mark's analysis of economic systems of wealth in-the-text and behind-the-text and in their own contexts; a CBS on Mark 11:27—13:2 enabled communities of struggle to recognise institutional economic exploitation in-the-text and behind-the-text, and in their own contexts;[83] and a CBS on Mark 5:21—6:1 enabled women's groups to recognise systems which

79. West, "Different Modes of Reading," 97.

80. Mosala, *Biblical Hermeneutics and Black Theology*, 10.

81. Myers, *Binding the Strong Man*; Waetjen, *Reordering of Power*.

82. Scott, *Domination and the Arts of Resistance*.

83. West, "Contextuality."

exploited women in-the-text and behind-the-text, and in their own contexts.[84] In each of these cases Mark uses significant geographical shifts to signal a distinct narrative unit, and in each of these delimited literary units Mark uses juxtaposition to summon a socio-politically engaged reader. Though the final form of the text was the entry point, relentless rereadings of the narrative detail of the text deconstructed the final form, rendering it unstable. Our transgressing of chapter divisions in favour of a literary unit made small incursions into the stability of the final form, and our interrogation of Mark's juxtapositions generated a recognition of "something going on" behind-the-text, in the ancient reality that produced Mark's narrative. For example, the fifth question of our CBS on Mark 11:27—13:2 was as follows: What was the role of the temple in the time of Jesus? This question invited socio-historical reflection based on a narrative-juxtaposition-based rereading of the text, but quickly led to socio-historical discussion (led by the Ujamaa Centre facilitators) of the world that produced such a text. "Something socio-economic and socio-political is going on in the temple," participants said.

Even our apparently narrative-based work, such as our CBS on 2 Sam 13:1–22, separates this literary unit from its larger monarchic-oriented narrative about succession and the leadership of David,[85] acknowledging later ideological appropriations of what we discern to be a women-based source. As with all sources "from below," this source has been "reused"[86] for patriarchal purposes. In our most recent work on this literary unit, we ask form-critical questions about Tamar's voice, probing whether her elite voice has not co-opted "hidden" (again in Scott's terms) subaltern women's voices. We recognise that Tamar's story inhabits a larger "rhetorical contextuality" and "literary contextuality," in Jonker's terms.[87] However, we also recognise, with the many thousands of ordinary women who have engaged with the CBS version of this text, that the text has retained sufficient "internal contradictions," in Mosala's terms,[88] to discern ancient socio-historical women's struggles against gender-based violence behind-the-text.

Much of the Ujamaa Centre's socio-historical orientation with respect to the Tamar gender-based violence CBS, and the related

84. West, "Dumb Do Speak."

85. Higgins, "From Skilled Speech to Silence"; Kozlova, "2 Samuel," 24.

86. Mosala, *Biblical Hermeneutics and Black Theology*, 101.

87. Jonker, "Plea for Contextual Integrity," 111.

88. Mosala, *Biblical Hermeneutics and Black Theology*, 10.

alternative masculinities CBS using the same textual unit,[89] is not overtly apparent to CBS participants. Our facilitation processes, however, embody our recognition that biblical text is a site of socio-historical ideological struggle, intrinsically. For example, women participants almost always raise concerns about 2 Sam 13:13b, where Tamar says, "Now therefore, please speak to the king, for he will not withhold me from you."[90] Is this a ruse to deflect Amnon from his violence, enabling her escape from his chambers, or does she really want and imagine that David will legally permit Amnon to marry her? There is usually robust small-group and plenary discussion concerning this sentence, which our facilitation encourages, prompting discussion about the internal contestation within a textual unit. In our most recent version of the Tamar CBS,[91] where we recognise other subaltern voices behind Tamar's elite royal voice, this kind of site-of-production contestation will become even more apparent to participants.

While the Ujamaa Centre appreciates Mbuvi's arguments for the presence of the final form in the lives of African hearers and readers of the Bible, we are persuaded by Mosala's hermeneutic of absence,[92] whereby he argues that the redactional processes of text production are also processes of ideological co-optation, through which socio-historically marginalised voices are elided, though never fully eradicated. The final form, carefully and closely reread, bears the evidence of these sites-of-production struggles. But while Mosala would agree with Mbuvi that contemporary African eyes of struggle might recognise glimpses of kin struggles within a biblical text,[93] Mosala contends that African biblical hermeneutic work is not done until we have understood the context-of-production sites-of-struggle behind-the-text and laboured diligently to hear what has been rendered absent (or at best only partially present). A hermeneutic of reception must be accompanied by a hermeneutic of production. Mbuvi is correct insofar as he says, "The final form of the text provides a sufficient *starting* point for the interpretive process,"[94] but we

89. West, "Deploying the Literary Detail."

90. Unless otherwise noted, Scripture quotations in this chapter are from the NASB.

91. West, "Poetics of Redacted Absence."

92. Mosala, *Biblical Hermeneutics and Black Theology*, 188.

93. Mosala, *Biblical Hermeneutics and Black Theology*, 188.

94. Mbuvi, *African Biblical Studies*, 109; emphasis added.

must move on from this co-opted form, delving behind-the-text for the sites of struggle that have produced the text.[95]

In a recent CBS on 1 Kgs 12:1–16 (or 18), we work with a text which has a remarkable narrative composition, though disrupted by later interpolated redactional devices. What is significant about the recent version of this CBS is that we use the Masoretic version (1 Kgs 12:1–16) only as an introduction to a variant version of the narrative in 3 Reigns 12:24p–t. The final form is then disregarded. The CBS focuses on this even more coherent Septuagintal narrative, with no interpolation and a clear and unambiguous message of economic exploitation. While the place of this variant among the other variant versions is a matter of some complexity,[96] what is likely is that 3 Reigns 12:24p–t represents a different and earlier Hebrew source text version of this important historical and theological story.[97] Our CBS recovers this absent text (except in scholarly apparatuses) and returns it to the realm of faith-based communities. Within the CBS we are quite overt about our unstable canonical final-form Bibles Africans use.[98] We are also overt about the kinds of socio-historical economic contestations that produced this text and its sister variants.

Conclusion: Connecting Reception and Production

Texts like 3 Reigns 12:24p–t have an accessible narrative entry point for CBS participants, and a narrative that when carefully reread using literary-narrative methods, summons socio-historical behind-the-text analysis. This is our preferred CBS process, working with literary-narrative CBS questions as an egalitarian entry point into a biblical text, and then constructing short inputs and questions that generate participator-based socio-historical resources for rereading behind-the-text.

The overarching See–Judge–Act process that gives shape to the CBS processes is a useful resource for constructing both an analogy of method and an analogy of struggle—for constructing what Jonker refers to as "meta-theoretical contextuality."[99] Socio-historical forms of analysis are

95. A salutary example of the dangers of the final form, if left un-interrogated, is West, "Taming Texts of Terror."

96. Schenker, "Jeroboam"; Trebolle Barrera, "Textual Criticism."

97. West, "Economic Remnant of Resistance."

98. West, "Textual Criticism."

99. Jonker, "Plea for Contextual Integrity," 112. (Louis: May the conversation continue!)

used to "read" local contemporary contexts and to reread biblical texts. Socio-historical forms of analysis are not usually our way into a biblical text, as we practice our commitment to "read with" local communities, endeavouring to be accountable to their modes of interpretation. But we do not remain with their modes of reading. CBS is a collaborative process, working both with community-based interpretive resources and with (ideologically selective) biblical studies–based interpretive resources. We recognise a responsibility to the critical resources of biblical scholarship, even as we forge African forms of biblical scholarship.

Bibliography

Conradie, Ernst M., et al. "Biblical Interpretation in Established Bible Study Groups: A Chronicle of a Regional Research Project." *Scriptura* 78 (2001) 340–46.

Conradie, Ernst M., et al. *Fishing for Jonah: Various Approaches to Biblical Interpretation*. Bellville: University of the Western Cape, 1995.

Deist, Ferdinand. "Idealistic Theologiegeschichte, Ideology Critique and the Dating of Oracles of Salvation." Paper presented at the SA Society for the Study of the Old Testament Congress (22nd and 23rd), Pretoria (1979) and Johannesburg (1980), 1982.

Draper, Jonathan A. "'For the Kingdom Is Inside of You and It Is Outside of You': Contextual Exegesis in South Africa (Lk. 13:6–9)." In *Text and Interpretation: New Approaches in the Criticism of the New Testament*, edited by Patrick J. Hartin and Jacobus H. Petzer, 235–57. Leiden: Brill, 1991.

Draper, Jonathan A., and Gerald O. West. "Anglicans and Scripture in South Africa." In *Bounty in Bondage: The Anglican Church in Southern Africa; Essays in Honour of Edward King, Dean of Cape Town*, edited by Frank England and Torquil J. M. Paterson, 30–52. Johannesburg: Ravan, 1989.

Fowl, Stephen E. "The Ethics of Interpretation, or What's Left Over After the Elimination of Meaning." In *The Bible in Three Dimensions: Essays in Celebration of the Fortieth Anniversary of the Department of Biblical Studies, University of Sheffield*, edited by David J. A. Clines et al., 379–98. Sheffield: JSOT, 1990.

Gills, Barry, and Joel Rocamora. "Low Intensity Democracy." *Third World Quarterly* 13 (1992) 501–23.

Gottwald, Norman K. *The Hebrew Bible: A Socio-Literary Introduction*. Philadelphia: Fortress, 1985.

———. *The Tribes of Yahweh: A Sociology of the Religion of Liberated Israel, 1250–1050 B.C.E.* Maryknoll, NY: Orbis, 1979.

Higgins, Ryan S. "'He Would Not Hear Her Voice': From Skilled Speech to Silence in 2 Samuel 13:1–22." *Journal of Feminist Studies in Religion* 36.2 (2020) 25–42.

Institute for the Study of the Bible. *Bible Studies on the Book of Exodus*. Pietermaritzburg: Institute for the Study of the Bible, 1990.

———. *The Tenth Anniversary Celebration and Evaluation: April 2000*. Pietermaritzburg: Institute for the Study of the Bible, 2000. https://ujamaa.ukzn.ac.za/wp-content/uploads/2022/12/The-tenth-anniversary-celebration-and-evaluation-1.pdf.

Jonker, Louis C. "Contextual Interpretation, Then and Now: Overhearing Inner-Biblical Discourses to Enrich Contemporary Contextual Interpretations." In *Context Matters: Old Testament Essays from Africa and Beyond Honoring Knut Holter*, edited by Madipoane Masenya (Ngwan'a Mphahlele) et al., 239–51. Atlanta: SBL, 2023.

———. *Exclusivity and Variety: Perspectives on Multidimensional Exegesis*. Kampen: Pharos, 1996.

———. "Further Interrogation of the Comparative Paradigm in African Biblical Scholarship: Towards an Analogical Hermeneutics for Interpreting the Old Testament in Africa." In *Reading Writing Right: Essays Presented in Honour of Prof Elna Mouton*, edited by Jeremy Punt and Marius J. Nel, 73–97. Stellenbosch: Sun, 2018.

———. "Jesus Among the Ancestors: Continuity and Discontinuity." In *Through the Eyes of Another: Intercultural Reading of the Bible*, edited by Hans de Wit et al., 315–33. Amsterdam: Institute of Mennonite Studies and Vrije Universiteit, 2004.

———. "Living in Different Worlds Simultaneously, or: A Plea for Contextual Integrity." In Wit and West, *African and European Readers*, 105–19.

———. "On Becoming a Family in South Africa: Intercultural Bible Reading as Transformative Power in Society (Luke 11:1–13)." In *Bible and Transformation: The Promise of Intercultural Bible Reading*, edited by Hans de Wit and Janet Dyk, 387–413. Atlanta: SBL, 2015.

Jonker, Louis C., and Douglas G. Lawrie. *Fishing for Jonah (Anew): Various Approaches to Biblical Interpretation*. Stellenbosch: Sun, 2005.

Kairos Theologians. "Challenge to the Church: A Theological Comment on the Political Crisis in South Africa; The Kairos Document, 1985." South Africa History Online, last updated Sept. 1, 2019. https://sahistory.org.za/archive/challenge-church-theological-comment-political-crisis-south-africa-kairos-document-1985.

Kozlova, Ekaterina E. "2 Samuel and the Architecture of Poetic Justice." *Journal of Hebrew Scriptures* 22 (2022) 1–24.

Lategan, Bernard C. "Current Issues in the Hermeneutical Debate." *Neotestamentica* 18 (1984) 1–17.

Lopes, Eliseu. *Livros proféticos—Profetas posteriores*. Roteiros para Reflexão 4. São Leopoldo: CEBI/Paulus, 1996.

Mbuvi, Andrew M. *African Biblical Studies: Unmasking Embedded Racism and Colonialism in Biblical Studies*. London: Bloomsbury, 2022.

Metz, Steven. "Pretoria's 'Total Strategy' and Low-Intensity Warfare in Southern Africa." *Comparative Strategy* 6 (1987) 437–69.

Mosala, Itumeleng J. *Biblical Hermeneutics and Black Theology in South Africa*. Grand Rapids: Eerdmans, 1989.

———. "Biblical Hermeneutics and Black Theology in South Africa." PhD diss., University of Cape Town, 1987.

Myers, Ched. *Binding the Strong Man: A Political Reading of Mark's Story of Jesus*. Maryknoll, NY: Orbis, 1988.

Nürnberger, Margarete P. L., ed. *I Will Send You to Pharaoh: Bible Studies on Exodus 1–15*. Pietermaritzburg: Institute for the Study of the Bible, 1992.

Sands, Justin. "Introducing Cardinal Cardijn's See–Judge–Act as an Interdisciplinary Method to Move Theory into Practice." *Religions* 9.4 (2018) 1–10. https://doi.org/10.3390/rel9040129.

Schenker, Adrian. "Jeroboam and the Division of the Kingdom in the Ancient Septuagint: LXX 3 Kingdoms 12.24 a–z, MT 1 Kings 11–12; 14 and the Deuteronomistic History." In *Israel Constructs Its History: Deuteronomistic Historiography in Recent Research*, edited by Albert de Pury et al., 214–57. Sheffield: Sheffield Academic, 2000.

Schüssler Fiorenza, Elisabeth. *Bread Not Stone: The Challenge of Feminist Biblical Interpretation*. Boston: Beacon, 1984.

———. "Towards a Feminist Biblical Hermeneutics: Biblical Interpretation and Liberation Theology." In *The Challenge of Liberation Theology: A First World Response*, edited by B. Mahan and L. D. Richesin, 91–112. Maryknoll, NY: Orbis, 1981.

Scott, James C. *Domination and the Arts of Resistance: Hidden Transcripts*. New Haven: Yale University Press, 1990.

Smit, Dirk J. "The Ethics of Interpretation: And South Africa." *Scriptura* 33 (1990) 29–43.

Trebolle Barrera, Julio C. "Textual Criticism and the Literary Structure and Composition of 1–2 Kings / 3–4 Reigns: The Different Sequence of Literary Units in MT and LXX." In *Die Septuaginta: Entstehung, Sprache, Geschichte*, edited by S. Kreuzer, 55–78. Wuppertal: Mohr Siebeck, 2012.

Ukpong, Justin S. "The Parable of the Shrewd Manager (Lk 16:1–13): An Essay in the Inculturation of Biblical Hermeneutics." *Semeia* 73 (1996) 189–210.

———. "Rereading the Bible with African Eyes." *Journal of Theology for Southern Africa* 91 (1995) 3–14.

Waetjen, Herman C. *A Reordering of Power: A Socio-Political Reading of Mark's Gospel*. Minneapolis: Fortress, 1989.

West, Gerald O. "Artful Facilitation and Creating a Safe Interpretive Site: An Analysis of Aspects of a Bible Study." In *Through the Eyes of Another: Intercultural Reading of the Bible*, edited by Hans de Wit et al., 211–37. Amsterdam: Institute of Mennonite Studies and Vrije Universiteit, 2004.

———. *Biblical Hermeneutics of Liberation: Modes of Reading the Bible in the South African Context*. Pietermaritzburg: Cluster, 1991.

———. *Biblical Hermeneutics of Liberation: Modes of Reading the Bible in the South African Context*. 2nd rev. ed. Maryknoll, NY: Orbis, 1995.

———. "The Biblical Text as a Heterotopic Intercultural Site: In Search of Redemptive Masculinities." In *Bible and Transformation: The Promise of Intercultural Bible Reading*, edited by Hans de Wit and Janet Dyk, 241–57. Atlanta: SBL, 2015.

———. "Contextual Bible Study as a Form of Contextual Theology: An Early Conceptual History." *Studia Historiae Ecclesiasticae* 48.2 (2022) 1–17.

———. "Contextuality." In *The Blackwell Companion to the Bible and Culture*, edited by John F. A. Sawyer, 399–413. Oxford: Blackwell, 2006.

———. "Deploying the Literary Detail of a Biblical Text (2 Samuel 13:1–22) in Search of Redemptive Masculinities." In *Interested Readers: Essays on the Hebrew Bible in Honor of David J. A. Clines*, edited by James K. Aitken et al., 297–312. Atlanta: SBL, 2013.

———. "The Dumb Do Speak: Articulating Incipient Readings of the Bible in Marginalized Communities." In *The Bible and Ethics*, edited by John W. Rogerson et al., 174–92. Sheffield: Sheffield Academic, 1995.

———. "In Search of an Economic Remnant of Resistance: 3 Reigns 12:24p–t." *HTS Theological Studies* 78 (2022) 1–9.

———. "The Poetics of Redacted Absence as Presence: Kin Eyes Hearing Tamar (2 Samuel 13)." In *Narrating Rape*, edited by Rhiannon Graybill et al., 209–25. London: SCM, 2024.

———. "The Relationship Between Different Modes of Reading (the Bible) and the Ordinary Reader." *Scriptura* S9 (1991) 87–110.

———. "Serving the Sighs of the Working Class in South Africa with Marxist Analysis of the Bible as a Site of Struggle." *Rethinking Marxism* 32 (2020) 41–65.

———. "Taming Texts of Terror: Reading (Against) the Gender Grain of 1 Timothy." *Scriptura* 86 (2004) 160–73.

———. "Textual Criticism, Literary Criticism, and State Capture: Returning 3 Reigns 12:24p–t to the Canon of Local African Communities." *Journal for Semitics* 32.2 (2023). https://doi.org/10.25159/2663-6573/13518.

———. "Towards an Inclusive and Collaborative African Biblical Hermeneutics of Reception and Production: A Distinctively South African Contribution." *Scriptura* 119.3 (2020) 1–18.

Wit, Hans de, and Gerald O. West, eds. *African and European Readers of the Bible in Dialogue: In Quest of a Shared Meaning*. Leiden: Brill, 2008.

Wittenberg, Gunther H. *I Have Heard the Cry of My People: A Study Guide to Exodus 1–15*. Pietermaritzburg: Cluster, 1992.

———. *Prophecy and Protest: A Contextual Introduction to Israelite Prophecy*. Pietermaritzburg: Cluster, 1993.

———. *Report of a Visit to Brazil from 28 August to 12 September 1988*. Pietermaritzburg: University of Natal, 1988.

———. *Resistance Theology in the Old Testament: Collected Essays*. Pietermaritzburg: Cluster, 2007.

PART II
Reception

6

"There Is a Psalm I Don't Like!"

The Impact of Psalm 23 When Approaching Death

MARTA HØYLAND LAVIK

Contrasting Emotions About Ps 23

THE SITUATION AND CONTEXT of the reader in relation to the Bible is one of the research areas in which Louis C. Jonker has shown interest.[1] The reception and appropriation of biblical texts can be studied in many ways.[2] The present essay takes its point of departure in a qualitative data

1. It is a privilege to be part of a book that honours the distinguishing contributions of a dear colleague and friend. My family and I cherish all the shared memories with the honouree and his family. Thanks to one of the editors of this volume, Prof. Knut Holter, who first introduced us at the sixteenth congress of the International Organization for the Study of the Old Testament, held in Oslo, Norway, in 1998. It is commonly acknowledged that "literature emerges from real-life contexts." Jonker, "Crossing Boundaries," 5. It is also commonly acknowledged that interpretations of literature, such as the Bible, emerge from real-life contexts. African biblical scholarship has investigated the situation and context of Bible readers for decades, whereas the shift of interest in European biblical studies to the reception side of the Bible is still in its infancy. The present contribution is an example of this latter development.

2. Jonker pursues his research on the reception of biblical texts in dialogue with historically oriented approaches—to enhance mutual fertilisation between the approaches and to avoid ahistorical interpretations, see Jonker, "Crossing Boundaries," 6. From the same qualitative data material as this essay builds on, I have integrated ancient and contemporary understandings, see Lavik, "Do Not Fear." In the present

material where fourteen Norwegian adults diagnosed with incurable cancer were asked individually about the potential significance of the Bible in their pressing situation.[3] The general insight from these interviews is that the Bible became pivotal for all fourteen in trying to coming to grips with the traumatic experience of facing death. As part of their religious coping strategies, all participants chose to expose themselves to biblical texts carrying messages of comfort and consolation, and they avoided texts of suffering, sorrow, and lament. Several of the participants cherished and found consolation in Ps 23.[4] However, one participant, Kristin, was clear about the opposite: "There is a Psalm I don't like!" Her aversion towards Ps 23 stands in contrast especially to Simon, who experiences this psalm as "unbelievably consoling." The present essay seeks to understand what is at stake when Ps 23 is perceived in diametrically different ways by these two participants.

Since the 1960s, insights from trauma theory within the field of psychology and sociology have influenced biblical studies of individual and collective dimensions of traumatic experiences.[5] In 2013, a new programme unit of the Annual Meeting of the Society of Biblical Literature (SBL) was inaugurated: "Biblical Literature and the Hermeneutics

---

essay, however, historical approaches are not explicitly attended to. The situation and context of the readers are here sought to be understood from the perspectives of psychology and sociology.

3. All participants defined themselves within the Christian religion. However, two had previously never opened a Bible but had become attentive to biblical texts after they were diagnosed. The participants distributed themselves among the Lutheran Church of Norway, Lutheran lay-church organisations, traditional Pentecostal, and Pentecostal-charismatic congregations. The research was carried out in accordance with the professional standards of the National Committee for Research Ethics in the Social Sciences and the Humanities (NESH). The ethical principles of the World Medical Association Declaration of Helsinki were also followed. Before the research started, ethical approval was granted by the Regional Research Ethical Committee (with reference number 2010/458). The participants were promised anonymity and confidentiality in all aspects of the research and were informed that they could withdraw from the project at any time without any risks. Each participant gave their written consent to participate, and I obtained permission from each participant to publish analyses of the interview material. The data material has been interpreted from various angles before; see a selection of works listed by Lavik in the bibliography to this essay.

4. Other texts mentioned by the participants in the study were: Exod 15:26; Num 6:24–26; Deut 31:8; 33:25; Josh 1:9; Job 35:14; Pss 31:15; 91; 118:17; 139; Isa 41:10; 49:16; Jer 29:11; 30:16; Mark 11:23; John 7:38; Eph 6:13–17; Phil 1:6; 4:7; 1 Pet 2:24; 1 John 5:12; and Rev 21–22.

5. See Dickie, "Intersection of Biblical Lament," 885; and Boase and Frechette, "Defining 'Trauma,'" 12.

of Trauma." Ten years later, the SBL programme book shows a threefold call for papers to this unit: (i) historical events referred to in the biblical literature as traumatic and deeply disturbing, (ii) the use of trauma theory to interpret biblical literature, and (iii) interpretation of biblical texts through the lens of trauma theory. The present essay takes a slightly different direction as it is occupied with contemporary traumatic experiences and with understanding underlying psychological mechanisms when the ancient text of Ps 23 stirs up opposite emotions in contemporary readers.[6] What has come to be labeled *biblical trauma hermeneutics* is an interdisciplinary engagement of analysing ancient and contemporary contexts of suffering through the lens of trauma theory: "Trauma hermeneutics is used to interpret texts in their historical contexts, and as a means of exploring the appropriation of texts, in contexts both past and present."[7]

When the two participants in the study referred to here were interviewed about the potential significance of the Bible, their world had broken apart due to their lethal cancer diagnoses, and biblical texts had become central in their coping. As already mentioned, both Kristin and Simon talked about Ps 23, but in opposite terms.

> KRISTIN: There is a psalm I don't like very much. I don't know why. It is Psalm 23.
>
> RESEARCHER: You don't like that psalm very much?
>
> KRISTIN: No, because: Even though I walk through the valley of the shadow of death [verse 4].
>
> RESEARCHER: What do you think then?
>
> KRISTIN: Then I think that God is with me also in a process of death. And that [the process of death] I don't like to think of.

The day Simon had learned from the hospital that the cancer could not be cured, he and his wife stopped at a restaurant on their way home. When they opened the menu book, they found to their surprise a print of Ps 23 on the first page. He shared what impact this made on him:

6. Over the last decades there has been a growing interest among biblical scholars to engage in contemporary suffering and on how biblical texts have the potential to evoke meaning on various levels in readers, see for instance Rollins, "Bible and Psychology"; Boase and Frechette, *Bible Through the Lens of Trauma*; and Dickie, "Intersection of Biblical Lament," 887. Such empirical experiences about the Bible as are presented here have the potential to inform and illuminate scholarly knowledge on the Bible.

7. Boase and Frechette, "Defining 'Trauma,'" 2.

> I had to lie down over the table and my tears flooded. I experienced to *walk through the valley of the shadow of death*, and *I fear no evil* [verse 4]. . . . Unbelievably consoling! It was so sensational! . . . There we sit, in the restaurant, completely dejected—read, open up the menu book, and in the menu book we are met with Psalm 23—fantastic!

The Enduring Traumatic Condition of Approaching Death

Understanding the situation and context of the reader is essential when trying to grasp how people relate to the Bible. Kristin and Simon share the situation of living with incurable cancer and the context of belonging to Pentecostal congregations. Simon is in his sixties, and Kristin is in her forties. Simon's children are established with their own families. Simon has a lot of interesting projects at work he would love to accomplish. Kristin has a teenager who lives under her roof. After a long time of living in a difficult marital relationship, Kristin broke out and has recently met a man with whom she feels safe. Only shortly after she met him, she learned she had incurable cancer. The totally unexpected reality of being diagnosed with incurable cancer is a great disappointment to both Kristin and Simon, as it shines through in the interviews that they are eager to live. After she became diagnosed, Kristin chose to attach herself to a Pentecostal-charismatic congregation which is strongly influenced by the Word of Faith movement, whereas Simon attends the traditional Pentecostal congregation in which he was raised. They both receive prayers for healing in their respective congregations and anticipate being miraculously healed from their disease.

Trauma theory is used to understand some of what Kristin and Simon go through when approaching death. British psychoanalyst Caroline Garland articulates the psychoanalytical understanding of trauma, that "annihilation is man's most fundamental anxiety"; and further, "to conceive of a personal death is virtually impossible until we meet it face to face."[8] Before saying more about the psychologically informed understanding of trauma applied here, the personal story of the American scholar of Hebrew literature James L. Kugel will serve as a background example of how the situation of approaching death can be experienced, and how this situation can shape one's relation to the Bible.[9]

8. Garland, "Thinking About Trauma," 17.

9. I have earlier written an article where I touch upon Kugel's reading of biblical

Relating to the Bible in the Face of Death

At the age of fifty-four, Kugel was diagnosed with cancer, and the doctors gave him the prospects of two to four more years to live. Eleven years after he received this limited prediction, Kugel published the book *In the Valley of the Shadow: On the Foundations of Religious Belief (and Their Connection to a Certain, Fleeting State of Mind)*. In this book he goes back to the situation of facing death with the aim to "recapture a certain state of mind that one enters under such circumstances."[10] He explains,

> After the initial shock, I was, of course, disturbed and worried. But the main change in my state of mind was that—I can't think of a better way to put it—the background music suddenly stopped. It had always been there, the music of daily life that's constantly going, the music of infinite time and possibilities; and now suddenly it was gone, replaced by *nothing*, just silence. . . . This was definitely a different perspective. But how could I have ever thought that life would just go on forever? I did, of course; that's what the music does, and everyone is caught up in it.[11]

In this state of mind, Kugel explains how he encountered biblical and other texts. The value of the Bible as a resource for people going through hard times in life is commonly known.[12] According to the American Old Testament scholar David M. Carr, although all religions in some ways relate to trauma, what is unique to the religions of Judaism, Christianity, and Islam is that they "were founded on trauma and survival of it."[13] In his view, these traumatic origins enable these religions to help people who suffer.[14] For Kugel, when the unexpected and life-threatening reality of cancer emerged, his pressing reality added an existential layer to his accumulated academic knowledge. It becomes clear that he reads the biblical texts into his own experience of being

---

texts when he was ill with cancer, see Lavik, "Do Not Fear."

10. Kugel, *Valley of the Shadow*, 1–2.

11. Kugel, *Valley of the Shadow*, 2; emphasis original.

12. For examples of individual cases of cancer, see for instance Lavik, "Materiality of the Bible"; and Lavik, "Reading the Bible." On the Bible as a resource in intercultural-hermeneutic exercises in societal contexts, see Jonker, "Crossing Boundaries," 10.

13. Carr, *Holy Resilience*, 245.

14. "Jewish and Christian Bibles both emerged as responses to suffering, particularly group suffering. Both Judaism and Christianity offer visions of religious life that emphasize religious community, whether the people of Israel or the church." Carr, *Holy Resilience*, 2.

a cancer patient and his own experiences as a cancer patient into the texts, as seen in how he reflects on what Ps 102:24 says about dying before one's time. The psalmist's words seem to be interpreted in line with Kugel's deep desire of an intervention from God:

> But the person who wrote this psalm was not, I think, offering it as a philosophical justification for his premature death. He was trying to get God to intervene:
>
> "O Lord, hear my prayer, and let my cry come before You:
>
> Do not hide Your face from me in my time of trouble;
>
> hear me when I cry out, and answer me soon.
>
> For my life is drifting away like smoke, as my bones burn in a bonfire.
>
> My insides are fried up like grass, withered from lack of food.
>
> I've been groaning so much my ribs show through my skin" [Psalm 102]:1–5.[15]

Kugel continues with reading his own experiences into the psalm, and he uses the biblical text to deliver a subtle protest against the disease:

> Reading these lines now, I don't have any trouble imagining the person who wrote them. He was very sick, perhaps in the last stages of some form of cancer. There was a good chance he would be dead in a few weeks or months. . . . But he still had some hope. So he had dragged himself to the very place where God resides, the temple. If he could cry out there, he thought, perhaps God would hear him and intervene, since what was happening really wasn't normal, really didn't fit the pattern: "O my God, do not take me halfway through life."[16]

The title of Kugel's book is taken from Ps 23:4, and he thinks that the phrase *in the valley of the shadow* captures how most people relate to death: "Death is something shadowy that we push to the back of our minds. It's always there, but only as an idea, abstract and distant. But then suddenly, one day, it's not."[17] What Kugel shares about death in relation to Ps 23:4 correlates well with how I interpret Kristin's thoughts about Ps 23. She is aware of the shadow the incurable cancer symbolises

15. Kugel, *Valley of the Shadow*, 4–5; his translation.
16. Kugel, *Valley of the Shadow*, 5.
17. Kugel, *Valley of the Shadow*, 74.

in her life, but from the quotation above, it becomes clear that she neither wants to think of the cancer nor of death.

Both Kristin's and Simon's state of mind as cancer patients are probably not far from what Kugel describes this way: "As for you, you are small. Your life is winding down now, and you can clearly see its end point; your life has become a compact, *little* thing. Good-bye."[18] When the reality of death is encountered—as it is for Kristin and Simon—this can, according to a psychoanalytically informed understanding, be experienced as traumatising.[19] At the time when Kristin learns that she cannot be cured of the cancer, she recalls—speaking in the present tense—what her state of mind was like:

> Then I am desperate. I become very scared. I experience death anxiety. And then I start looking—where is my Bible? . . . I had a Bible earlier but where it was now, I didn't know. . . . I phoned my friend [who belongs to a Pentecostal-Charismatic congregation], and she asks: "What are you afraid of?" And I tell her how afraid I am of dying. . . . She says: "We will stand with you in prayer. God is good. God has healed. We believe in healing! We go for healing!" And I think that this sounds completely idiotic. In my world as a health professional, I knew all this [about cancer]. It sounded totally insane.

Despite her initial scepticism, Kristin chooses to attend a Pentecostal-charismatic congregation in her desperate struggle for life. Whenever her death anxiety becomes strong, she is helped by medication and the words from Eph 6:10–17:

> Then I put on the whole armour of God as a protection and am ready to fight! I felt that when I now become anxious—because I was full of anxiety—I am ready to meet that anxiety. It can come, but I have a protection in me which means that the anxiety can arrive, but it shall not crush me.

Kristin shares how important the support from the Christian fellowship she has chosen is:

> [The congregation shows me an] enormous care, a lot of care. I love going there, and what makes it so good is that they help [me] carry the hope for healing.

18. Kugel, *Valley of the Shadow*, 3; emphasis original.

19. Garland, "Thinking About Trauma," 25.

Simon does not mention the word *healing* once in the interview, but it is evident that he has a very strong hope of becoming well, and preferably through God's miraculous intervention:

> It would have been more elegant if God had intervened miraculously because this had been great to tell people. But it may very well be that God uses medicine. There are many examples of it happening medically—that things happen in remarkable ways via medicine.

Simon has, as already mentioned, not searched for a new fellowship but continues to attend the same congregation he has belonged to his entire life. He shares how the Bible study group which he leads is important also now:

> It has been amazing. We are a group of eight people, and we have been together for many years. They are close friends, or close acquaintances. I experience extraordinary care from that group.

A Psychologically and Sociologically Informed Understanding of Trauma

The word trauma comes from a Greek word for "wound." In physical medicine, trauma means damage to tissue, and in psychology it denotes "how the mind too can be pierced and wounded by events."[20] Being overwhelmed is an essential part of traumatic experiences:

> Trauma is the unique individual experience of an event or enduring condition in which the individual experiences a threat to life or to her or his psychic or bodily integrity, and experiences intense fear, helplessness, or horror. A key aspect of what makes something traumatic is that the individual's coping capacity and/or ability to integrate their emotional experience is overwhelmed. Trauma often impacts individuals in multiple domains, including physical, social, emotional, and/or spiritual.[21]

Kristin and Simon experience both the physical and spiritual effects of trauma: the cancer disease has injured their flesh, and they are shaken in their inner parts. The focus in this essay is on understanding

20. See Garland, "Thinking About Trauma," 9, who refers to Freud's expression from 1920.

21. National Resource Center on Domestic Violence, "Definitions."

Simon and Kristin's individual emotional responses to Ps 23 when being wounded by incurable cancer.

It goes beyond the scope of this essay to trace its development, but the origins of the contemporary Western concept of trauma goes back to the nineteenth century and the psychoanalyst Sigmund Freud.[22] Since then the concept has evolved into a multifaceted and interdisciplinary network of knowledge. From the 1980s, trauma is a vital part of the medical diagnosis PTSD, post-traumatic stress disorder, about individual suffering.[23] Although originated in the West, the concept of trauma plays a part in the broader societal and political discourse used to describe a universal human response to individual or collective disasters.[24]

A basic insight from a psychoanalytically informed understanding of trauma is, as already stated, that some events can overwhelm the normal capacity of human beings to take care of their own well-being and self. Not all traumatic events disturb ordinary functioning, but there is a potential risk of being thrown into disorder and confusion when one is subject to something traumatic.[25] For emotionally difficult experiences to find expression, they ought to be processed. In the process of digesting something which overwhelms a human being, the concept of containment is central. The British psychoanalyst Wilfred R. Bion takes the example of what happens between the infant and its mother to illustrate this process he calls containment.[26] When the baby expresses raw, unarticulated feelings, the mother serves the function of digesting the unspoken feelings, such as frustration or anxiety, that the baby cannot hold on its own. To be digested, the baby's experiences need to be contained by the adult, and then given back in a processed form. According to Bion, human beings need to build this capacity of containment to make sense of themselves and their experiences. When

22. For a survey of trauma studies in psychology, see Boase and Frechette, "Defining 'Trauma,'" 3n3.

23. The diagnosis PTSD was developed on the background of a wide range of earlier research on suffering which overwhelmed the individual and put the capacity to cope in jeopardy; see Boase and Frechette, "Defining 'Trauma,'" 3.

24. The idea of the PTSD diagnosis as universal has been criticised for acting as a new form of Western colonialism. The critics point to its culture-specific origin and shape and show how the diagnosis has been unable to acknowledge and understand local ways of suffering in societies outside the Western; see Carr, *Holy Resilience*, 260–62, with references.

25. Garland, "Thinking About Trauma," 9.

26. Bion, *Learning from Experience*. The present description of Bion's concept of containment is taken from Ramvi et al., "Who Thinks About Death," 334.

people are able to digest difficult experiences, they can eventually be able to think about them. This process of containment and digestion of experiences does not end in childhood but is a life-long process in which human beings make sense of themselves and their experiences.[27] To build capacity in this process of developing reflective self-containment, people need others, and human beings' socio-cultural context thus plays an important role in this endeavour.[28]

Due to the development of diagnostic categories, there is a relative consensus to description of individual experience and recovery of trauma in the field of psychology.[29] Sociological understandings of trauma correspond to and build on psychological insights on individual suffering but expand and transfer the knowledge to communal settings. Although there is no single sociological definition of collective or social trauma, there seems to be agreement that communal traumas in one or the other way deal with "ruptures in social fabric that certain events can cause."[30] Despite a lack of consensus, there is a shared interest among sociologists interested in trauma to describe how social processes after traumas work to fragment and/or (re)construct communal identity.[31] Collectives tend to create a narrative "to name and account for the suffering."[32] Such narratives have the potential to form and influence the identity of the collective. On the contrary, if the collective does not adopt a narrative to represent the suffering, there is less identity formation, and there is a risk that the ruptures of the social fabric remain open.

Using the Bible in a Defensive Strategy or as a Means of Containment?

The interview with Kristin was done one year after she had learned about her incurable cancer diagnosis, and one and a half years after Simon received his diagnosis. From what they share, they seem to be functioning quite well in their visible, outer world. The first shock of the event has perhaps lessened a little; however, their identity as human beings

27. Bion, *Learning from Experience.*
28. See Ramvi et al., "Who Thinks About Death," 334.
29. See American Psychiatric Association, "Diagnostic and Statistical Manual."
30. Boase and Frechette, "Defining 'Trauma,'" 8–9.
31. Boase and Frechette, "Defining 'Trauma,'" 8–9.
32. Boase and Frechette, "Defining 'Trauma,'" 9.

is shaken.[33] According to Simon and Kristin, the Bible in general is a resource which assists them in a fundamental way when the distressing news is sought to be digested. Their use of the Bible is an example of how texts *can* cultivate safety and well-being in people experiencing distressing times: "Texts may represent and interpret trauma, thus functioning as a means of facilitating recovery and resilience for both individuals and communities."[34] However, biblical texts can also evoke anxiety, as we have seen from Kristin's encounter with Ps 23. Although both Kristin and Simon believe they will be miraculously healed, it shines through in the interview that Simon—at the same time as anticipating healing—somehow has accepted the situation of approaching death. To borrow the language from Bion, it is as if Simon's raw emotions are contained by the Bible and his Christian fellowship and then given back to him in a more processed form. When Simon finds words for his experiences in the biblical texts, this helps him in making sense of his own situation and in turn enables him to think about death. Psalm 23 functions as a text which assists Simon in his process of digesting what his enduring traumatic condition entails.[35]

Psalm 23 does not have the same effect on Kristin. Psalm 23 reminds her of what she is not able to think about, and she thus shies away from the text. She seems not to have come to an acceptance of the situation, and for her, the psalm is a painful reminder of what she has not yet processed. Biblical texts create both order and disorder in Kristin at the same time. It seems difficult for her to hold texts of healing (Ps 118:17) together with texts mentioning death (Ps 23). Kristin says she does not know why she dislikes Ps 23. In my interpretation, this has to do with the unconscious. Kristin is protecting herself by engaging in defensive strategies. It is well-known from psychoanalysis that death anxiety is part of the human condition and something with which people often do not have conscious contact.[36] And it is well-known from psychotherapy that denial can help individuals to absorb distressing news gradually. The sense of being

33. Garland, "Thinking About Trauma," 10.

34. Boase and Frechette, "Defining 'Trauma,'" 11.

35. For examples of other biblical texts that can serve the same function, see Dickie, "Intersection of Biblical Lament."

36. See Garland, "Thinking About Trauma," 11; and Ramvi et al., "Who Thinks About Death," 333.

overwhelmed can in this sense be reduced when individuals follow their own pace in a bit-by-bit digestion of the shocking news.[37]

Religious Contexts as Places to Experience Containment?

The context in which people belong impacts their understanding of the biblical texts, and this is not something new. The Bible itself is, according to Louis C. Jonker, "a dynamic illustration of the re-interpretation and re-appropriation of cultural and religious values in changed and changing socio-political and socio-religious circumstances."[38] For both Kristin and Simon, the traumatic experience of being diagnosed with lethal cancer represents a breakdown of their established beliefs about the predictability of the world.[39] The damage the diagnosis has done to them is not temporary but permanent, and they seek help in the Bible and in their Christian fellowships to be validated, as well as to get help to familiarise the extraordinary and integrate the devastating message into their autobiography. "Thus, the safe and supportive presence of others as witnesses and dialogue partners is crucial for advancing the process of reinterpreting the traumatic experience."[40] Their strategies vis-à-vis the Bible are fueled by the theology they meet in their respective congregations. As Kristin's understanding of Ps 23 is unlike the other participants', I will in the following look at her religious environment and suggest some influences of her interpretation of Ps 23.

Kristin's drive towards a Christian fellowship which can understand her situation and take away her despair by praying for healing underlines the fact that "psychology is powerful for explaining immediate reactions to trauma across cultures, while culture and social support provide important explanatory paradigms for how recovery occurs after trauma."[41] In seeking help in the Pentecostal-charismatic congregation, Kristin's consciousness most likely works towards a transformation of the enduring traumatic condition into a shape that is recognisable. But does the congregation provide her with containment and assistance in recreating some order? In her congregation, Kristin experiences great spiritual

37. Garland, "Thinking About Trauma," 10.

38. Jonker, "Crossing Boundaries," 10.

39. Garland, "Thinking About Trauma," 11.

40. See Dickie, "Intersection of Biblical Lament," 891, with references.

41. Marten W. deVries quoted in Boase and Frechette, "Defining 'Trauma,'" 7.

and social support but seems not to be met theologically in her deepest anxiety—the loss of her very life. The hesitance from both Kristin and her congregation to go into her anxiety can be seen as a way of reducing her pain of being reminded of the threat of death. This strategy from her spiritual context makes sense when knowing that the congregation has strong theological relations to the Word of Faith movement as developed in the United States from the 1970s on. In short, the narrative about life and death which prevails in Kristin's congregation holds that death before a human being reaches the age of seventy to eighty is not acceptable.[42] According to this theology, Christians have the same authority that Jesus, according to the New Testament, had. Sicknesses are curses, and people can thus take authority over diseases and cast them out of their bodies.[43] This theological thinking can be understood in a variety of ways, and here I suggest an understanding of the resistance towards accepting death as a part of the human condition through the lens of trauma theory.[44]

From trauma theory it is well-known that "certain thoughts or feelings can from a functional point of view become 'forgotten' or sealed-off, existing as foreign bodies within the rest of the mind's functioning until released intact, perhaps by treatment, perhaps by particular events, or by time itself, years later."[45] In my interpretation, Kristin's mind is sealed off when it comes to the traumatic message of death she has received from the hospital. When she chooses a congregation which preaches miraculous healing also for palliative cancer patients, this works as a reinforcement of the alienation. Kristin finds herself frightened, helpless, and enraged by the fact that her life will be shortened by the disease. Instead of helping her to integrate the shocking news and to release or at least negotiate with her thoughts and feelings, the congregation boosts and intensifies her repression and sealing-off of emotions by theologically keeping her imprisoned in the hope for healing. On the

42. See the theology of one of the founders of the Word of Faith movement, Hagin, *Turning Hopeless Situations Around*, 29–30. An article in Norwegian (Lavik, "Forsvinn i Jesu namn") discusses the Word of Faith movement in relation to another participant in the interview material.

43. Hagin, *Redeemed from Poverty*, 23–65; Hagin, *Believer's Authority*.

44. Lack of communication about death is, however, not exclusive to Pentecostal-charismatic congregations influenced by the Word of Faith movement. Also studies among staff working in nursing homes—where patients die on a regular basis—reveal a hesitance to speak openly about death; see Ramvi et al., "Who Thinks About Death," with references.

45. Garland, "Thinking About Trauma," 13.

basis of what she is taught in the congregation, it is not surprising that Kristin—instead of being comforted by Ps 23—experiences this very text as a trigger. In verse 4, the phrase *the valley of the shadow* can be perceived as a metonym for death. These words thus remind Kristin of her mortality and open up the possibility of capitulation. This verse thus questions her capacity for resistance towards her enemy, death, and she needs to keep it out of reach if she is to build resistance: "Indeed, through its use of metonymic images, a poem can bring to consciousness the whole trauma experience through a single word."[46] Psalm 23 produces death anxiety in Kristin, and she avoids it, as death is not part of the theological discourse to which she exposes herself.

As explained earlier, to be able to process emotionally difficult experiences, human beings need others who can contain unarticulated feelings and return them in a more digested form.[47] Such a digestion has the potential to put the anxiety into verbal form as "language can encode and respond to traumatic experiences."[48] Instead of containment, Kristin is presented with a counternarrative, that of a miraculous healing. This narrative keeps her spirits high but also disturbs her coping, as she needs to keep away all that can make her think of the unthinkable, i.e., her aversion of Ps 23. Kristin is in need of help to integrate the distressing news into her autobiography, but the congregation's theological basis distorts her in developing a language for her suffering: "Trauma leads to the disintegration of language yet relies on language in its more integrative capacity."[49]

Sociologically speaking, the congregation needs a language for what the occurrence of death does to the fellowship. When the alerted death of Kristin one day becomes a reality, this will result in a rupturing of social bonds between Kristin and her fellowship and the other way around.[50] Subsequently, the fellowship needs a narrative that can rebuild the theological identity of the congregation concerning death. I do not know how the congregation worked in this sense, as the research was done on cancer patients only, but from a sociological point of view, when communal narratives are created, "such narratives serve to construct identity and solidarity in ways that can restore healthy assumptions about the self in

46. Dickie, "Intersection of Biblical Lament," 892–93, with references.

47. Bion, *Learning from Experience.*

48. Boase and Frechette, "Defining 'Trauma,'" 13.

49. Boase and Frechette, "Defining 'Trauma,'" 11.

50. Boase and Frechette, "Defining 'Trauma,'" 9.

relation to the world."[51] In my interpretation, Kristin's congregation's narrative about life and death based on the Word of Faith movement's ideas most likely makes the ruptures that death creates in the fabric difficult to mend. From what Kristin shares of her individual experiences, the theological thinking does not seem capable of providing a language that can contain and name the suffering when death occurs.[52]

A strategy of building resistance and sealing off thoughts and feelings to avoid thinking of the unthinkable is not exclusive to Kristin's congregation but well-known from historical situations where collectives live through traumas. That unmanageable realities can be met with excessive or radical defence is well-known from psychotherapy.[53] The self-defence she develops when experiencing the threat to her existence can be understood in terms of a trauma-induced amnesia. Trauma-induced amnesia of approximately two decades is, for instance, typical for groups experiencing traumatic events.[54] The memory about the trauma is kept silent to reduce the pain of being reminded of shameful or painful events such as threats, intimidation, and persecution. There were, for instance, approximately twenty years where the discussion in Europe about the Holocaust after World War II was scarce, also in the emerging Israeli national identity. Instead of inducing public discourse about the recent traumatic events, the Israeli collective focused on "events seen to exhibit resolute resistance, such as the story of Jewish rebels at Masada choosing suicide over surrender to the Romans in 70 CE."[55] This collective strategy of dealing with traumatic events is not very far from the strategy Kristin is taught in her fellowship.

In place of going through painful victimisation as a dying cancer patient, Kristin, together with her congregation, concentrates on developing resistance—with the Bible as a companion. The shocking information that she is going to die is indigestible both to her and her congregation—the thought of death can neither be absorbed and comprehended by the conscious mind nor by the theological system.[56] Kristin is re-traumatised by Ps 23 as it brings her back to the devastating news about her imminent

51. Boase and Frechette, "Defining 'Trauma,'" 9, 15.
52. Boase and Frechette, "Defining 'Trauma,'" 9.
53. Garland, "Thinking About Trauma," 10.
54. On trauma-induced amnesia, see Hart and Brom, "When the Victim Forgets."
55. Carr, *Holy Resilience*, 266.
56. Garland, "Thinking About Trauma," 10.

death.[57] Instead, she uses biblical texts which in her view can develop her resistance and—metaphorically speaking—dress her in armour to avoid surrender to the enemy: Ps 118:17 and Eph 6:10–17. This strategy nurtures her hope for healing but pushes away her need for processing the fact that her life will be shortened by the disease. Using trauma as a hermeneutical lens underlines the fact that traumatic experiences are overwhelming, and that there is a potential risk for both individuals and collectives of being thrown into disorder and confusion.

Conclusion

This essay deals with the emotions concerning one biblical text in a contemporary context and attributes to the understanding of the broader hermeneutical reception and appropriation of biblical texts. From the qualitative data material referred to here, it is evident that biblical texts have the potential to resonate in various ways in people's suffering, and the situation and context of the reader is determinative for what biblical texts are read and how they are interpreted. Psalm 23 is used as an example, as this psalm is perceived in diametrically different ways by two participants who share the situation of having their life shortened due to an incurable cancer diagnosis. In such a situation, Ps 23 is consoling for Simon, as it functions to interpret and help him integrate the enduring traumatic experience of approaching death. For Kristin, the same psalm is discomforting and traumatising, as it represents her deepest anxiety, death. The present data material is thus a reminder of the constant need for a deeper ethical and theological awareness of the complexities in human beings' experiences and contexts.

From the psychologically and sociologically informed understandings of trauma, the ideas of containment and processing are central to comprehend what is at stake when the same biblical text is perceived so differently. The socio-religious contexts in which people belong impact their understanding of biblical texts, and Christian communities serve as interpretative horizons. Seen through the lens of trauma theory, the different emotions towards Ps 23 in the participants deal with to what degree the enduring traumatic situation of facing death is contained and processed in the individual and in their socio-religious context. Both Simon and

57. For an opposite result, see for instance how Ps 78 can be used in terms of recovery; see Poe Hays, "Trauma, Remembrance, and Healing."

Kristin wrestle with the thought of death, but unlike Simon's congregation, Kristin's setting provides her with a strategy of opposition, denial, and resistance instead of offering her containment. The Christian fellowship thus boosts her repression of the thought of death, instead of helping her with the transformation of the unassimilable into something she can process mentally and eventually integrate into her autobiography.

Bibliography

American Psychiatric Association. "Diagnostic and Statistical Manual of Mental Disorders (DSM-5-TR)." https://www.psychiatry.org/psychiatrists/practice/dsm.

Bion, Wilfred R. *Learning from Experience*. London: Karnac, 1991.

Boase, Elizabeth, and Christopher G. Frechette, eds. *Bible Through the Lens of Trauma*. Semeia Studies 86. Atlanta: SBL, 2016.

———. "Defining 'Trauma' as a Useful Lens for Biblical Interpretation." In Boas and Frechette, *Bible Through the Lens of Trauma*, 1–23.

Carr, David M. *Holy Resilience: The Bible's Traumatic Origins*. New Haven: Yale University Press, 2014.

Dickie, June Frances. "The Intersection of Biblical Lament and Psychotherapy in the Healing of Trauma Memories." *Old Testament Essays* 32 (2019) 885–907.

Garland, Caroline. "Thinking About Trauma." In *Understanding Trauma: A Psychoanalytical Approach*, edited by Caroline Garland, 9–31. London: Karnac, 1998.

Hagin, Kenneth E. *The Believer's Authority*. Tulsa, OK: Faith Library, 1986.

———. *Redeemed from Poverty, Sickness and Spiritual Death*. Tulsa, OK: Faith Library, 1983.

———. *Turning Hopeless Situations Around*. Tulsa, OK: Faith Library, 1981.

Hart, Onno van der, and Danny Brom. "When the Victim Forgets: Trauma-Induced Amnesia and Its Assessment in Holocaust Survivors." *Attachment: New Directions in Psychotherapy and Relational Psychoanalysis* 7 (2013) 40–47.

Jonker, Louis C. "Crossing Boundaries: The Transformative Potential of Intercultural Bible Reading in Secular/Post-Secular Contexts." *Scriptura* 120 (2021) 1–13. https://doi.org/10.7833/120-1-1982.

Kugel, James L. *In the Valley of the Shadow: On the Foundations of Religious Belief (and Their Connection to a Certain, Fleeting State of Mind)*. New York: Free, 2011.

Lavik, Marta Høyland. "'Do Not Fear for I Am with You': The Use of Isaiah 41:10 in Times of Incurable Illness." In *New Studies in the Book of Isaiah: Essays in Honor of Hallvard Hagelia*, edited by Markus Zehnder, Perspectives on Hebrew Scriptures and Its Contexts 21, 157–81. Piscataway, NJ: Gorgias, 2014.

———. "'Forsvinn i Jesu namn!' Om sjukdom, bibelbruk og impulsar frå global trusteologi." In *Levende religion: Globalt perspektiv—lokal praksis*, edited by Anne Kalvig and Anna Rebecca Solevåg, 192–210. Stavanger: Stavanger University Press, 2015.

———. "'I Bring It with Me Everywhere': The Materiality of the Bible in Critical Illness." In *A Critical Study of Classical Religious Texts in Global Contexts: Challenges of a

Changing World, edited by Beth Elness-Hanson and Jon Skarpeid, 69–83. New York: Lang, 2019.

———. "Reading the Bible in Present-Day Norwegian Contexts: The Case of Cancer Patients." In *Context Matters: Old Testament Essays from Africa and Beyond Honoring Knut Holter*, edited by Madipoane Masenya (Ngwan'a Mphahlele) et al., International Voices in Biblical Studies 16, 223–36. Atlanta: SBL, 2023.

National Resource Center on Domestic Violence. "Definitions." VAWnet. https://vawnet.org/sc/definitions.

Poe Hays, Rebecca W. "Trauma, Remembrance, and Healing: The Meeting of Wisdom and History in Psalm 78." *Journal for the Study of the Old Testament* 41 (2016) 183–204.

Ramvi, Ellen, et al. "Who Thinks About Death? A Psychoanalytically Informed Interpretive Study of Communication About Death Among Nursing Home Staff." *Journal of Social Work Practice* 36 (2022) 331–44.

Rollins, Wayne G. "The Bible and Psychology: New Directions in Biblical Scholarship." *Pastoral Psychology* 45.3 (1997) 163–79.

7

Sin and Atonement in the *Akedah*

When Genesis 22 Is Reread in Short Stories in the Modern Period

Christo Lombaard

The Text of Gen 22 and the *Agnus ex Machina*[1]

In the text on which the argument below will be based,[2] the italics in verses 1a and 15–18 should be noted; they denote the editorial insertions that brought the text to its current, and theologically speaking difficult, form:

1. This contribution is an expanded version of a paper presented at the "Literatūra un reliģija: Grēks un pestīšana" conference, Faculty of Humanities, University of Latvia, February 23, 2023 (Latvijas Universitāte, "Konference"). I am honoured herewith to dedicate this contribution to colleague Louis Jonker, who has devoted much of his academic life to the interaction between exegesis and interpretation. From this, as much as from his personal energies and his strong administrative skills, many of us have benefitted—in my case, also through publication of a monograph in a series he coedits and through an admirable example that he has set for me on collegial relations. Colleague Jonker is a true gift to us.

2. From Lombaard, "Issues in or with Genesis 22," 3.

Biblia Hebraica Stuttgartensia	New Revised Standard Version (italics added to verses 1 and 15–18)
וַיְהִ֗י אַחַר֙ הַדְּבָרִ֣ים הָאֵ֔לֶּה וְהָ֣אֱלֹהִ֔ים נִסָּ֖ה אֶת־אַבְרָהָ֑ם וַיֹּ֣אמֶר אֵלָ֔יו אַבְרָהָ֖ם וַיֹּ֥אמֶר הִנֵּֽנִי׃	1 After these things *God tested Abraham*. He said to him, "Abraham!" And he said, "Here I am."
וַיֹּ֡אמֶר קַח־נָ֠א אֶת־בִּנְךָ֨ אֶת־יְחִֽידְךָ֤ אֲשֶׁר־אָהַ֙בְתָּ֙ אֶת־יִצְחָ֔ק וְלֶךְ־לְךָ֔ אֶל־אֶ֖רֶץ הַמֹּרִיָּ֑ה וְהַעֲלֵ֤הוּ שָׁם֙ לְעֹלָ֔ה עַ֚ל אַחַ֣ד הֶֽהָרִ֔ים אֲשֶׁ֖ר אֹמַ֥ר אֵלֶֽיךָ׃	2 He said, "Take your son, your only son Isaac, whom you love, and go to the land of Moriah, and offer him there as a burnt offering on one of the mountains that I shall show you."
וַיַּשְׁכֵּ֨ם אַבְרָהָ֜ם בַּבֹּ֗קֶר וַֽיַּחֲבֹשׁ֙ אֶת־חֲמֹר֔וֹ וַיִּקַּ֞ח אֶת־שְׁנֵ֤י נְעָרָיו֙ אִתּ֔וֹ וְאֵ֖ת יִצְחָ֣ק בְּנ֑וֹ וַיְבַקַּע֙ עֲצֵ֣י עֹלָ֔ה וַיָּ֣קָם וַיֵּ֔לֶךְ אֶל־הַמָּק֖וֹם אֲשֶׁר־אָֽמַר־ל֥וֹ הָאֱלֹהִֽים׃	3 So Abraham rose early in the morning, saddled his donkey, and took two of his young men with him, and his son Isaac; he cut the wood for the burnt offering, and set out and went to the place in the distance that God had shown him.
בַּיּ֣וֹם הַשְּׁלִישִׁ֗י וַיִּשָּׂ֨א אַבְרָהָ֧ם אֶת־עֵינָ֛יו וַיַּ֥רְא אֶת־הַמָּק֖וֹם מֵרָחֹֽק׃	4 On the third day Abraham looked up and saw the place far away.
וַיֹּ֨אמֶר אַבְרָהָ֜ם אֶל־נְעָרָ֗יו שְׁבוּ־לָכֶ֥ם פֹּה֙ עִֽם־הַחֲמ֔וֹר וַאֲנִ֣י וְהַנַּ֔עַר נֵלְכָ֖ה עַד־כֹּ֑ה וְנִֽשְׁתַּחֲוֶ֖ה וְנָשׁ֥וּבָה אֲלֵיכֶֽם׃	5 Then Abraham said to his young men, "Stay here with the donkey; the boy and I will go over there; we will worship, and then we will come back to you."
וַיִּקַּ֨ח אַבְרָהָ֜ם אֶת־עֲצֵ֣י הָעֹלָ֗ה וַיָּ֙שֶׂם֙ עַל־יִצְחָ֣ק בְּנ֔וֹ וַיִּקַּ֣ח בְּיָד֔וֹ אֶת־הָאֵ֖שׁ וְאֶת־הַֽמַּאֲכֶ֑לֶת וַיֵּלְכ֥וּ שְׁנֵיהֶ֖ם יַחְדָּֽו׃	6 Abraham took the wood of the burnt offering and laid it on his son Isaac, and he himself carried the fire and the knife. So the two of them walked on together.
וַיֹּ֨אמֶר יִצְחָ֜ק אֶל־אַבְרָהָ֤ם אָבִיו֙ וַיֹּ֣אמֶר אָבִ֔י וַיֹּ֖אמֶר הִנֶּ֣נִּֽי בְנִ֑י וַיֹּ֗אמֶר הִנֵּ֤ה הָאֵשׁ֙ וְהָ֣עֵצִ֔ים וְאַיֵּ֥ה הַשֶּׂ֖ה לְעֹלָֽה׃	7 Isaac said to his father Abraham, "Father!" And he said, "Here I am, my son." He said, "The fire and the wood are here, but where is the lamb for a burnt offering?"
וַיֹּ֙אמֶר֙ אַבְרָהָ֔ם אֱלֹהִ֞ים יִרְאֶה־לּ֥וֹ הַשֶּׂ֛ה לְעֹלָ֖ה בְּנִ֑י וַיֵּלְכ֥וּ שְׁנֵיהֶ֖ם יַחְדָּֽו׃	8 Abraham said, "God himself will provide the lamb for a burnt offering, my son." So the two of them walked on together.
וַיָּבֹ֗אוּ אֶֽל־הַמָּקוֹם֮ אֲשֶׁ֣ר אָֽמַר־ל֣וֹ הָאֱלֹהִים֒ וַיִּ֨בֶן שָׁ֤ם אַבְרָהָם֙ אֶת־הַמִּזְבֵּ֔חַ וַֽיַּעֲרֹ֖ךְ אֶת־הָעֵצִ֑ים וַֽיַּעֲקֹד֙ אֶת־יִצְחָ֣ק בְּנ֔וֹ וַיָּ֤שֶׂם אֹתוֹ֙ עַל־הַמִּזְבֵּ֔חַ מִמַּ֖עַל לָעֵצִֽים׃	9 When they came to the place that God had shown him, Abraham built an altar there and laid the wood in order. He bound his son Isaac, and laid him on the altar, on top of the wood.
וַיִּשְׁלַ֤ח אַבְרָהָם֙ אֶת־יָד֔וֹ וַיִּקַּ֖ח אֶת־הַֽמַּאֲכֶ֑לֶת לִשְׁחֹ֖ט אֶת־בְּנֽוֹ׃	10 Then Abraham reached out his hand and took the knife to kill his son.

Biblia Hebraica Stuttgartensia	New Revised Standard Version (italics added to verses 1 and 15–18)
וַיִּקְרָ֨א אֵלָ֜יו מַלְאַ֤ךְ יְהוָה֙ מִן־הַשָּׁמַ֔יִם וַיֹּ֖אמֶר אַבְרָהָ֣ם ׀ אַבְרָהָ֑ם וַיֹּ֖אמֶר הִנֵּֽנִי׃	11 But the angel of the LORD called to him from heaven, and said, "Abraham, Abraham!" And he said, "Here I am."
וַיֹּ֗אמֶר אַל־תִּשְׁלַ֤ח יָֽדְךָ֙ אֶל־הַנַּ֔עַר וְאַל־תַּ֥עַשׂ ל֖וֹ מְא֑וּמָה כִּ֣י ׀ עַתָּ֣ה יָדַ֗עְתִּי כִּֽי־יְרֵ֤א אֱלֹהִים֙ אַ֔תָּה וְלֹ֥א חָשַׂ֛כְתָּ אֶת־בִּנְךָ֥ אֶת־יְחִידְךָ֖ מִמֶּֽנִּי׃	12 He said, "Do not lay your hand on the boy or do anything to him; for now I know that you fear God, since you have not withheld your son, your only son, from me."
וַיִּשָּׂ֨א אַבְרָהָ֜ם אֶת־עֵינָ֗יו וַיַּרְא֙ וְהִנֵּה־אַ֔יִל אַחַ֕ר נֶאֱחַ֥ז בַּסְּבַ֖ךְ בְּקַרְנָ֑יו וַיֵּ֤לֶךְ אַבְרָהָם֙ וַיִּקַּ֣ח אֶת־ הָאַ֔יִל וַיַּעֲלֵ֥הוּ לְעֹלָ֖ה תַּ֥חַת בְּנֽוֹ׃	13 And Abraham looked up and saw a ram, caught in a thicket by its horns. Abraham went and took the ram and offered it up as a burnt offering instead of his son.
וַיִּקְרָ֧א אַבְרָהָ֛ם שֵֽׁם־הַמָּק֥וֹם הַה֖וּא יְהוָ֣ה ׀ יִרְאֶ֑ה אֲשֶׁר֙ יֵאָמֵ֣ר הַיּ֔וֹם בְּהַ֥ר יְהוָ֖ה יֵרָאֶֽה׃	14 So Abraham called that place "The LORD will provide"; as it is said to this day, "On the mount of the LORD it shall be provided."
וַיִּקְרָ֛א מַלְאַ֥ךְ יְהוָ֖ה אֶל־אַבְרָהָ֑ם שֵׁנִ֖ית מִן־הַשָּׁמָֽיִם׃	15 *The angel of the LORD called to Abraham a second time from heaven,*
וַיֹּ֕אמֶר בִּ֥י נִשְׁבַּ֖עְתִּי נְאֻם־יְהוָ֑ה כִּ֗י יַ֚עַן אֲשֶׁ֤ר עָשִׂ֙יתָ֙ אֶת־הַדָּבָ֣ר הַזֶּ֔ה וְלֹ֥א חָשַׂ֖כְתָּ אֶת־בִּנְךָ֥ אֶת־יְחִידֶֽךָ׃	16 *and said, "By myself I have sworn, says the LORD: Because you have done this, and have not withheld your son, your only son,*
כִּֽי־בָרֵ֣ךְ אֲבָרֶכְךָ֗ וְהַרְבָּ֨ה אַרְבֶּ֤ה אֶֽת־זַרְעֲךָ֙ כְּכוֹכְבֵ֣י הַשָּׁמַ֔יִם וְכַח֕וֹל אֲשֶׁ֖ר עַל־שְׂפַ֣ת הַיָּ֑ם וְיִרַ֣שׁ זַרְעֲךָ֔ אֵ֖ת שַׁ֥עַר אֹיְבָֽיו׃	17 *I will indeed bless you, and I will make your offspring as numerous as the stars of heaven and as the sand that is on the seashore. And your offspring shall possess the gate of their enemies,*
וְהִתְבָּרְכ֣וּ בְזַרְעֲךָ֔ כֹּ֖ל גּוֹיֵ֣י הָאָ֑רֶץ עֵ֕קֶב אֲשֶׁ֥ר שָׁמַ֖עְתָּ בְּקֹלִֽי׃	18 *and by your offspring shall all the nations of the earth gain blessing for themselves, because you have obeyed my voice."*
וַיָּ֤שָׁב אַבְרָהָם֙ אֶל־נְעָרָ֔יו וַיָּקֻ֛מוּ וַיֵּלְכ֥וּ יַחְדָּ֖ו אֶל־ בְּאֵ֣ר שָׁ֑בַע וַיֵּ֥שֶׁב אַבְרָהָ֖ם בִּבְאֵ֥ר שָֽׁבַע׃ פ	19 So Abraham returned to his young men, and they arose and went together to Beer-sheba; and Abraham lived at Beer-sheba.

Figure 4: The Text of Gen 22

The classic Hebrew title for the Gen 22 account (technically, only verses 1–19 of that chapter), the *Akedah* (עֲקֵדָה), meaning "the binding (of Isaac [by Abraham])," is usually said to relate to the Isaac figure in this narrative who is bound—that means, who is tied up by the Abraham figure in preparation for the human sacrifice commanded by God. On a literal level, that Hebrew title of course depicts the narrative accurately, viz., as a summary-in-title of what occurs in this account. However, to expand the meaning of "the binding" to other aspects, *in* the text, *of* the text, and *to* the text, is equally possible (if a literary-interpretative moment may be allowed), even if that was evidently not the initial intent with the title, the *Akedah*:

a. Related to "*in* the text": some interpreters, from different religious traditions, apply the metaphor of the binding to other characters in the unfolding plot of this narrative—for instance to God (who is bound to Abraham and his progeny) or to the ram (which is bound instead of Isaac).
b. Related to "*of* the text": the hold the text has on the mind of its readers throughout the ages, given the psychologically and theologically disturbing nature of its subject matter.
c. Related to "*to* the text": the beholdenness of a range of literary texts, which find as part of their artistic impulses this basis text or ground text.

It is the latter that will be expanded in what follows.

What is fully clear about the Gen 22 text in the Bible is that already *there*, within the text itself, it was retold. Famously called the "earliest commentary on the Akedah" by Moberly,[3] he with that formulation summarised what had by then been part of the stock of knowledge of historical-critical exegetes of the Old Testament. These later additions, verses 1a and 15–18, are found already in the canonised text, indicated in the English translation above by means of the italics. The third point immediately above, "Related to '*to* the text,'" hence commences already in the Hebrew text itself. When these italicised sections are read on their own, an apologetic intent is clear on the part of the editorial hand: there was—akin to the Latvian subtitle of the conference at which this contribution was first presented, "Grēks un pestīšana" (sin and salvation)—some manner of iniquity that had to be atoned for and compensated for, to the mind of that

3. Moberly, "Earliest Commentary on the Akedah."

redactor. This, because the sin (wickedness, immorality, depravity are the kind of concepts applied here by critics of the religiosity encountered in Gen 22) related in the text seemed just too great: it was theologically-morally unpalatable.[4] Whereas the *that* of this redaction history is quite clear, the *why* of such emendations is however less so, with the editorial purposes usually related to how the historical background of this Bible chapter is reconstructed. This kind of reconstruction is notoriously delicate but remains, hermeneutically speaking, indispensable.[5]

The dramatic motifs of the Gen 22 chapter are often remarked upon. It has all the makings of an ancient Greek celestial "soap opera": the thematic parallels between Gen 22 and, for instance, the Greek myth in which Cronus eats his children have to be noted, with Zeus surviving because Cronus eats a rock instead of devouring Zeus, who would in time become the head of the Greek pantheon.[6] As a story with no morality, when stripped of the attempts at apologetics in verses 1a and 15–18, disturbing themes present themselves more clearly. In Gen 22, God commands child sacrifice. The later so-called father of all believers, Abraham, is a deliberate misleader, also colluding in the planned murder. Only by means of the forced ancient stage technique of—in this case—*agnus ex machina* is human blood not spilt. No wonder that apologetics (italicized, in the text above) were required already within Gen 22!

The unambiguously harsh theology in the earlier textual layer here is approached in foulness by the endless ethical wranglings on this text, each of which tries to impose a morality on an account that initially had no such intentions. To be sure, the attempted 1a and 15–18 interpretative framing itself fails to render a morally wholesome text: What kind of God would require such a test of faith from a believer? (That kind of Deuteronomistic-derivative theology seems to have indeed been a part of the religious history in ancient Judea for a while, perhaps slightly before and during the early Hellenistic era.[7]) All of these reinterpretative wranglings show surprising naïveté of engagement with the biblical text, expecting it to voice ethics, primarily—in a way, parallel to

4. For an overview of these theological-moral difficulties, see Čapek, "Philosophical Discourse on Genesis 22," and Stoker, "God se Opdrag aan Abraham."

5. See, e.g., Jonker, *Historiography and Identity (Re)Formulation*; Jonker, *Texts, Contexts and Readings*; Jonker, *From Adequate Biblical Interpretation*; Jonker, *Exclusivity and Variety*.

6. Abramovitch, "Akeda."

7. Lombaard, "Testing Tales."

the much later and equally sanitised eventual versions of the Brothers Grimm's famous folktale collections.[8] This, as if moralisms had been the intent with such a text. This expectation or assumption in relation to the Akedah most often devolves into appreciation for the obedience of Abraham,[9] whose piousness is somehow, illogically, taken to stand in the stead of the objectionable subject matter. This is at times also lessened, in a way, by indicating the thematic parallels of Gen 22 with the crucifixion of Jesus.[10] Notwithstanding any and all such attempts at "sanitising" the text, unmistakably Gen 22 in its pre-emendation version (*sans* verses 1a and 15–18) had a different purpose.

Genesis 22 is a myth, in the sense that it is an identity-giving account, meant to draw by association the original hearers or readers into the frame of reference which it sets out to create. Not meant to be an edifying tale, this account sets out to *create* history, in the sense that those who accept what it relates would understand themselves anew, then as a part of that history. In order to set up this different kind of "creation history," the confessed founding father of the faith of the Judeans (the historical origins of what would in time become the Jewish faith are of course much more complex[11]), Abraham, is placed in the role of human protagonist, along with the more prominent, activating divine protagonist. God is in this account variously referred to as אלהים (verses 1, 3, 8, 9, and 12), as מלאך יהוה (verses 11 and 15), and as יהוה (verses 14 and 16). This variation counts among the indicators of a more complex editorial history than the simplified version related above. The alteration in divine epithets equally indicates that these three holy names had in time come to be regarded as synonymous appellations for God.[12]

On what had indeed historically been the intent with this identity-giving account, there are substantially divergent scholarly views, four of which had been very briefly summarised in an earlier publication of mine.[13] Genesis 22, then,

8. See, e.g., Zipes, *Original Folk and Fairy Tales.*

9. See, e.g., Neef, "Abraham! Abraham!"; and Kruger, "God Tests Abraham."

10. See, e.g., Bekker and Nortjé, "Die Gebruik."

11. See, e.g., Römer, *Invention of God*; and Albertz, *Religionsgeschicte Israels,* vol. 1.

12. On the history of the divine names in the Hebrew Bible, see, e.g., Fleming, *Yahweh Before Israel.*

13. Lombaard, "Graphic Text, Graphic Depiction," 263.

- polemicizes against the possibility of child sacrifice in ancient Israel,[14] rather than legitimising such a religious act, as is often popularly assumed;
- memorialises ancient initiation rites within Israel;[15]
- philosophically prepares the way, through a relatively unrefined treatment of the theodicy issue—namely, as antecedent text—for the more mature dealing with the problem of suffering by the book of Job;[16]
- reflects tensions on social and geographical matters between the postexilic carriers of the respective patriarchal traditions, in which the Abrahamite groupings here put paid to the diminutive Isaacite groups' claims to a distinct theological and geographical identity.[17]

These are the extant historically oriented exegetical attempts at understanding the Akedah account, which are important for weighing other kinds of interpretation. However, a greater focus below falls on non-exegetical renderings, in the form of high-quality literary receptions of the Akedah. These receptions take the text of Genesis as point of departure, but then in both senses of that expression: they begin in some ways thematically related to the Gen 22 account, but then they take their leave of it—depart from it—almost immediately. These literary texts do not try to reimagine and re-present what may historically have happened in the events recounted in the Gen 22 text, as a Hollywood motion picture or a missionary movie might do. Nor do they seek to explain the text to modern readers, as exegetical writings attempt, or to explain away some worrisome contents of the story, as typically engaged in by philosophical-ethical wranglings. These modern stories tell their own story, drawing on the Akedah, though, as an inspirational moment, amongst many other such steering influences.

A kind of chorus in support of such narrativised orientations to meaning *from* Gen 22 can be provided by three aspects, here indicated from the broadest to the smallest of such yardsticks. First, the Bible as literature may, on the ground of literary-aesthetic qualities, be regarded

14. Boehm, "Child Sacrifice," 145, on, classically, Westermann, *Genesis 12–36*, 363, and especially Gunkel, *Genesis*, 240–43.

15. White, "Initiation Legend of Isaac"; White, "Where Is the Lamb."

16. Veijola, "Abraham und Hiob."

17. Lombaard, "Isaac Multiplex."

as second only to the oeuvre of Shakespeare in the history of human writing, as viewed by the influential literary critic Harold Bloom.[18] Second, the Old Testament narratives convey spirituality in a particularly appealing manner.[19] Third, the literary genre of the Akedah itself may be characterised as a "short short story."[20] As good literature frequently leads to ancillary literature, with creativity inducing creativity, it should come as no surprise to us that biblical narratives in general and Gen 22 in particular have produced literary offspring.[21]

That should not lead us, as latter-day readers, to assume that for these reasons, amongst others, our expectations of what constitutes a literary work should one-directionally be pressed upon a biblical text. Our refinement of expectations on the nature of literature, after more than three millennia of reading, are certainly valid as interpretative tools for texts that came into being within broadly the same intellectual milieu as us. Such refinements may moreover aid us in understanding texts that came into being in different milieux. If such current understandings, however, become the most authoritative criteria for evaluating an ancient text (for instance),[22] the reciprocity inherent to the communicative act of reading, where a text also shapes our comprehension, would be lost. Such a loss would be ours.

These orienting remarks lead to the following section: a briefest review of some such literary appropriations of the Gen 22 narrative.

Narrative Re-Narrated

Five short retellings of the Gen 22 account will now be listed,[23] in chronological order, with brief descriptions of the contents of each so that their relation to the Akedah is indicated. The at times extensive debates on the

18. Bloom, *Western Canon*.

19. McCarthy and Riley, *Old Testament Short Story*; see Alter, *Art of Biblical Narrative*.

20. Lombaard, "Isaac in the Old Testament," 100; see, however, Lombaard, "Problems of Narratological Analyses."

21. See Noort and Tigchelaar, *Sacrifice of Isaac*.

22. See Jonker, "Crossing Boundaries."

23. It would certainly be worthwhile in another forum to explore all of these, and others, in greater detail, as well as musical receptions of Gen 22, such as Igor Stravinsky's "Abraham and Isaac" (1962–1963) and Leonard Cohen's "Story of Isaac" (1969), the Edmund McMillen computer game *The Binding of Isaac* (2011), and other receptions in various genres of expression.

interpretation of each of these texts are not traced here. The point being made here is more modest, that Gen 22 inspired (in the nontheological sense) these literary works, at times clearly directly and at times in a more culturally derived and literarily meandering manner.

Søren Kierkegaard, *Frygt og Bæven* (1843)

Itself a text thoroughly conversant with the major philosophers and ideas of the era, *Fear and Trembling*[24] soon itself became a formative text for subsequent philosophy. Hardly has an influential philosopher since Kierkegaard not acknowledged the effect *Fear and Trembling*, in its various translations, has had on the development of their thoughts.[25]

This substantial work opens with a number of retellings of the Gen 22 narrative, each offering a new literary take on this basis text. What is offered is, first, a wishful admiration of the Abraham figure, from a Danish perspective. Thereupon follows a version of the Akedah in which Abraham does not conceal from Isaac his intended fate, and in which the source of the idea of the sacrifice is transferred from God to Abraham. The implied apologetics is clear: in order not to taint God with such an act, the "sin" is put on the account of the human actor, who himself is in doing so absolved from deception, though not from murderous intent. Third, a shorter version of the retelling is offered, in which Abraham, after sacrificing the ram, retreats to a life of depression. (Could this be Kierkegaard's reflection of his own life?) A fourth and more meditative vignette follows, of Abraham reflecting on his two lost sons: Ishmael, whom he had abandoned, and Isaac, whom he would slaughter. Perhaps to counter the expectation of further apologetics, in a fifth retelling Isaac, after the almost-sacrifice, loses his faith, with the suggestion that this was because Abraham did not carry through the sacrificial act. Upon these retellings follows a longer praise text on Abraham and then a series of involved, at times relatively pious, arguments on aspects of faith, drawing on the example of Abraham and in discussion with major philosophers and authors of Kierkegaard's time.

The relation here to the Gen 22 account is clear. Through multiple retellings and reflections, the disturbing aspects of the subject matter

24. Kierkegaard, *Frygt og Bæven*; originally published under the pseudonym Johannes de silentio.

25. See, e.g., Conway, *Kierkegaard's Fear and Trembling*; Dreyer, "Transcending Fear and Anxiety"; Lippitt, *Routledge Philosophy Guidebook*.

of the basis text are recast, though not in any predictable direction. The recounted Akedah is at times somewhat surprising in its positive twists, at times soothing, and at times as disturbing as the original, though in different ways.

The conclusion is, however, clear in this instance. Without the impulse of the Gen 22 text in the Bible, the entire *Fear and Trembling* volume would not have come into being.

This is not meant to imply, here, that much of modern Western(ised) philosophy is either directly or indirectly beholden to the Gen 22 account. However, the recent theological turn in philosophy[26] does enable us to see the trajectory of influence, as one fundamental thought leads to another—not in any predictable or logically unfolding sense,[27] yet certainly as a recognisable, reconstructable literary train of thought, which has as its originating moment the Akedah.

Franz Kafka, "Das Urteil" (1913)

In this short story,[28] a mere fourteen pages, the author most associated with the idea of the absurd in modern Western literature (though perhaps not in philosophy, which characterisation could accrue to the mid-twentieth-century existentialist, usually French, philosophers), Kafka, touches in some aspects on the narrative contents of Gen 22. In "The Judgement,"[29] the father-son relationship of Gen 22 is, however, reversed, in that here the father suspects that the son seeks his (the father's) death.

Both main characters are in correspondence with, what in current parlance may be termed, an *other*. This has the possible metaphysical counterfoil of an Other, with either possibility, with or without the capital

26. Vanhoutte, "Word Once More Turned."

27. As written memorably on philosophical reinterpretation by culturally the most visible philosopher of our time: "All great 'dialogues' in the history of philosophy were so many cases of misunderstanding: Aristotle misunderstood Plato, Thomas Aquinas misunderstood Aristotle, Hegel misunderstood Kant and Schelling, Marx misunderstood Hegel, Nietzsche misunderstood Christ, Heidegger misunderstood Hegel. . . . Precisely when one philosopher exerted a key influence upon another, this influence was without exception grounded in a productive misreading—did not the entirety of analytic philosophy emerge from misreading the early Wittgenstein?" Žižek, *Organs Without Bodies*, ix.

28. Original publication: Kafka, "Das Urteil."

29. See Corngold, *Lambent Traces*, 13–36; Hartwich, "Böser Trieb."

letter, relating to a non-present yet compelling figure. The theological inference, though created by themes only, is nevertheless strong.

Towards the end of the account, the son does die—against the dual initial possibility of the story and contrary to the expectation from Gen 22 (but perhaps as a possible reverberation of the fifth version of Kierkegaard's, related above?). The son's death is, however, by suicide, committed after a prompt in this regard by the father. This too is related with the connection that both of these figures have with the far-off but significantly influential friend (Friend).

The parallels, initial role reversals and later re-reversals, make this narrative a thematically parallel rendering, in some respects, of Gen 22, but with quite a few surprises. These correspondences are neither copied nor forced, but with the subtleties of reinterpretation indicated, once noticed, such derivations cannot be overlooked.

Jean-Paul Sartre, "L'Enfance d'un chef" (1939)

A novella, rather than a short story,[30] in typical Sartrean style—extensive and complex; self-searching for meaning, though futilely so, with substantive parallels to his own experiences as a youth;[31] by no means shy to touch on matters of sexuality—the theme of self-development unto leadership qualities is treated here in a way no modern management textbook would dare. In "The Childhood of a Leader," the self-sacrifice in different manners of exploration parallels thematically the Gen 22 account.[32] It entails the main character coming to hone his anti-Semitic attitudes and practices, which is of course ironic given that the Gen 22 narrative is found in the Hebrew Bible. Other role reversals occur too. The son, here, grows to become the perpetrator; the victim becomes anyone who is Jewish. The possibilities of suicide by the main character echo similar themes in the Kierkegaard and Kafka narratives referred to above, with the futility of relationships of any kind to give meaning to life.[33]

The relationship to Gen 22 is more tenuous here than in the previous instances; the inspirational echoes are more contextual (just before World War II) and autobiographical. Yet the idea of sacrifice and the

30. Sartre, "L'Enfance d'un chef," 314–88.

31. Daigle and Golomb, *Beauvoir and Sartre*.

32. More broadly, Kirkpatrick, *Sartre on Sin*.

33. See Sartre, *L'Être et le néant*.

echoes of older Gen 22, re-narrativised texts place this novella too in the wake of the Akedah.

Flannery O'Connor, "The River" (1953)

Centred on the topic of US religious revivalism and faith healing, a youth as the main character in this short story[34] is first baptised and then baptises himself, which ends in his death. The latter, paradoxically, saves him from a less than fulfilling life.

Though no mention is made in this short story of the Akedah or any of its characters, the parallels of a youth dying for the sake of faith, as the killing of Isaac would demonstrate with respect to Abraham in the Akedah, renders this narrative a further exploration of some of the themes from Gen 22. Not a male but a female caretaker is, in "The River," the initiator of and chaperone during the perilous (the reader knows, during each subsequent reading after the initial) journey. This gender variation, however, does not substantively alter the dynamics of the flow of story, culminating as it does in this instance more dramatically than in Gen 22, in the drowning of the youth.

The themes of salvation underscore the biblical link, with overtly Christian links, not all of the revivalist kind,[35] in the language of some of the paragraphs in the story. Bible books are referred to often, enhancing the intertextual nature of this text, as are repeated mentions of key Christian concepts such as the kingdom of Christ and, central to the story, baptism, with the latter that occurs in the River of Life / Faith / Jesus' Blood.[36]

Albert Camus, *Le Renégat ou un esprit confus* (1957)

An allegory in the form of (mostly) a monologue on religion, conversion, and the dubious value of non-reasonable faith, in this short story[37] a few

34. O'Connor, "River."

35. "They joked a lot where he lived. If he had thought about it before, he would have thought Jesus Christ was a word like 'oh' or 'damn' or 'God,' or maybe somebody who had cheated them out of something sometime." O'Connor, "River," 462. This sounds, in the current different intellectual ambience, much like a post-secular, positively religious comment; on which, see Jonker, "Crossing Boundaries."

36. See McHugh, "Nomads of Desire," 62–63.

37. Camus, *Le Renégat*.

absurdities—typical of the author's general approach[38]—are combined: violence, faith convictions, politics, colonialism, speech, and more. The speaker in *The Renegade or a Confused Spirit* is a Christian missionary who converts to the local faith in Mali. He experiences torture, cruelly murders another missionary for the sake of redemption, and is himself then killed for that act. The first two actions parallel vicariously key aspects of the Akedah narrative, with the latter, similar to the instances discussed above, inverting the culmination. Yet, with the latter, salvific tones remain, though not in any traditionally Christian sense.

In this retelling, the self-sacrifice by the main character for the sake of God and others turns out disastrously, thus pushing the topic of sacrifice to its extreme (again in the style typical to Camus).[39] Such extremity is not alien to the Akedah, with Gen 22 understood as being amongst the most disturbing of the canonical texts (along with, e.g., Gen 34, Deut 13, and the book of Revelation). Parallels with the crucifixion of Christ are also drawn in, though creatively rather than with intentions of piety. Genesis 22 remains a reverberating text here, with aspects of its shock value affirmed and others upended, though no less surprisingly.

Outstanding

The term *outstanding* in English is ambiguous: it can mean either a positive attainment—a superlative position achieved, which is raised in stature beyond others so that it *stands out* in the proverbial crowd—or something incomplete, something that has not been finished, which has *not* been handed *in* or submitted. Both these meanings relate to Gen 22.

First, the Akedah clearly is raised to a position of what Thiselton called a "writerly text":[40] it is one that inspires authors to compose; it is a text that generates more texts; a writerly text becomes influential; it is not eliminated by silence, as poor writing would be, but creates life. This is the kind of influence that in relation to scholarship might be called being "of heuristic value." The literary qualities of the Gen 22 account are plainly such that, as we have seen, it inspired much of worth which followed in its wake.

38. McGregor, "Camus's 'Le Renégat.'"

39. With Camus, *Le mythe de Sisyphe* as the classic text in this regard.

40. Thiselton, *New Horizons in Hermeneutics*, 98.

However, the other sense of *outstanding* also relates to the Akedah, and to an equal extent as the first sense: it is a story that has not been told to completion. The Gen 22 narrative is not a story that has reached its end in retelling.[41] There remains more to be said.

What has been said in the pages above is, equally, far from exhaustive. Genesis 22 is too much of a *Text* to have been captured adequately here—and that is a human condition for which we could never properly atone.

The value of literary reinterpretations by one text of another, namely, lies herein: the later inventiveness does not pretend to recoup the basis text, in the sense of giving it its "true," or perhaps original (historical), meaning. Rather, in short stories, for instance, that take as inspiration a basis text or ground text such as Gen 22, it is clear that the newer interpretation is wholly that of the later author. The engagements with the basis text (Gen 22, in this case) are those of the modern authors.

The nod of recognition in the direction of the basis text acknowledges the creative stimulus. The new rendition as a very loose reinterpretation stretches the possibilities of meaning in whichever direction the later author chooses (or is led, by the proverbial "muse" of inspiration).[42] The new meaning and the interplay between older and new meanings are all to the credit of the modern author, who does not attempt to unveil hidden historical meaning in the basis text, as if that ground text were a kind of mystic script that had been awaiting unlocking by a gifted diviner of sorts. Such engagements occur often enough in popular circles and, alas, in circles that ought to be better informed.

Whereas exegetes may try to find viable historical (ancient) meanings in a text, such literary interpreters, however, create new *current* (rather than ancient) possibilities of meaning—doing overtly so.

Bibliography

Abramovitch, Henry. "Akeda and the Psychology of the Spiritual Revolutionary: A Jungian Reading Based on a Hebrew Text of Genesis 22." In *Gesetz und Begehren: Theologische, philosophische und psychoanalytische Perspektiven*, edited by Angelica Löwe et al., 41–59. Freiburg: Karl Alber, 2018.

Albertz, Rainer. *Religionsgeschicte Israels in alttestamentlicher Zeit*. 2 vols. Göttingen: Vandenhoeck & Ruprecht, 1992.

41. Hence, e.g., Noort and Tigchelaar, *Sacrifice of Isaac*; Sagi, "Meaning of the 'Akedah.'"

42. See Von Solms, "Ingenuity's Engine."

Alter, Robert. *The Art of Biblical Narrative*. Updated ed. New York: Basic, 2011.

Bekker, C. J., and Susara Nortjé. "Die Gebruik van die Offer van Isak as 'n Motief vir die Verkondiging van Jesus as die lydende Christus." *HTS Theological Studies* 51 (1995) 454–64.

Bloom, Harold. *The Western Canon: The Books and School of the Ages*. London: Papermac, 1994.

Boehm, Omri. "Child Sacrifice, Ethical Responsibility and the Existence of the People of Israel." *Vetus Testamentum* 542 (2004) 145–56.

Camus, Albert. *Le mythe de Sisyphe: Essai sur l'absurde*. Paris: Éditions Gallimard, 1942.

———. "*Le Renégat ou un esprit confus*." In *L'exil et le royaume*, edited by Albert Camus, 43–72. Paris: Éditions Gallimard, 1957.

Čapek, Filip. "Philosophical Discourse on Genesis 22—Akedah Reflected by Kant, Fichte and Schelling." *Communio Viatorum* 52 (2010) 217–27.

Conway, Daniel, ed. *Kierkegaard's Fear and Trembling: A Critical Guide*. Cambridge: Cambridge University Press, 2015.

Corngold, Stanley. *Lambent Traces: Franz Kafka*. Princeton: Princeton University Press, 2004.

Daigle, Christine, and Jacob Golomb, eds. *Beauvoir and Sartre: The Riddle of Influence*. Bloomington: Indiana University Press, 2009.

Dreyer, Yolanda. "Transcending Fear and Anxiety: The Great Cleanup." *Pastoral Psychology* 67 (2018) 475–91.

Fleming, Daniel. *Yahweh Before Israel: Glimpses of History in a Divine Name*. Cambridge: Cambridge University Press, 2020.

Gunkel, Hermann. *Genesis*. Göttingen: Vandenhoeck & Ruprecht, 1910.

Hartwich, Wolf-Daniel. "Böser Trieb, Märtyrer und Sündenbock Religiöse Metaphorik in Franz Kafkas Urteil." *Deutsche Vierteljahrsschrift für Literaturwissenschaft und Geistesgeschichte* 67 (1993) 521–40.

Jonker, Louis C. "Crossing Boundaries: The Transformative Potential of Intercultural Bible Reading in Secular/Post-Secular Contexts." *Scriptura* 120 (2021) 1–13. https://doi.org/10.7833/120-1-1982.

———. *Exclusivity and Variety. Perspectives on Multidimensional Exegesis*. Contributions to Biblical Exegesis and Theology 19. Kampen: Kok Pharos, 1996.

———. *From Adequate Biblical Interpretation to Transformative Intercultural Hermeneutics: Chronicling a Personal Journey*. Intercultural Biblical Hermeneutics Series 3. Elkhart, IN: Institute for Mennonite Studies, 2015.

———, ed. *Historiography and Identity (Re)Formulation in Second Temple Historiographical Literature*. New York: T&T Clark, 2010.

———. *Texts, Contexts and Readings in Postexilic Literature: Explorations into Historiography and Identity Negotiation in Hebrew Bible and Related Texts*. Tübingen: Mohr Siebeck, 2011.

Kafka, Franz. "Das Urteil." In *Arkadia: Ein Jahrbuch für Dichtkunst*, edited by Max Brod, 53–65. Leipzig: Kurt Wolff, 1913.

Kierkegaard, Søren. *Frygt og Bæven: Dialektisk Lyrik*. Copenhagen: C. A. Reitzel, 1843.

Kirkpatrick, Kate. *Sartre on Sin: Between Being and Nothingness*. Oxford: Oxford University Press, 2018.

Kruger, H. A. J. "God Tests Abraham: The Command to Sacrifice Isaac." *Ned. Geref. Teologiese Tydskrif* 32 (1991) 187–200.

Latvijas Universitāte. "Konference 'Literatūra un reliģija: grēks un pestīšana.'" Feb. 16, 2023. https://www.hzf.lu.lv/par-mums/lu-mediji/zinas/zina/t/76441/.

Lippitt, John, ed. *The Routledge Philosophy Guidebook to Kierkegaard and Fear and Trembling*. New York: Routledge, 2003.

Lombaard, Christo. "Graphic Text, Graphic Depiction: Genesis 22 and Its Interpretation on a Louvre Miniature Plaque." *Missionalia* 4 (2019) 255–68.

———. "Isaac in the Old Testament. A New Interpretation from Genesis 22, Based on Hermeneutical-Methodological and Exegetical Investigations." DDiv thesis, University of Pretoria, 2009.

———. "Isaac Multiplex: Genesis 22 in a New Historical Representation." *HTS Theological Studies* 64 (2008) 907–19.

———. "Issues in or with Genesis 22: An Overview of Exegetical Issues Related to One of the Most Problematic Biblical Chapters." *Verbum et Ecclesia* 34.2 (2013) 1–5.

———. "Problems of Narratological Analyses of Genesis 22:1–19." In *Thinking Towards New Horizons. Collected Communications to the XIXth Congress of the International Organization for the Study of the Old Testament, Ljubljana 2007*, edited by Matthias Augustin and Hermann Niemann, 49–62. Bern: Lang, 2008.

———. "Testing Tales: Genesis 22 and Daniel 3 and 6." In *Prayers and the Construction of Israelite Identity*, edited by Susanne Gillmayr-Bucher and Maria Häusl, 113–23. Atlanta: SBL, 2019.

McCarthy, Carmel, and William Riley. *The Old Testament Short Story: Explorations into Narrative Spirituality*. Wilmington, DE: Glazier, 1986.

McGregor, Rob. "Camus's 'Le Renégat': An Allegory of the Existentialist Pilgrimage." *French Review* 66 (1993) 742–51.

McHugh, Kevin. "Nomads of Desire." In *Multiple Dwelling and Tourism: Negotiating Place, Home and Identity*, edited by Norman McIntyre et al., 51–66. Cambridge: CAB International, 2006.

Moberly, Walter. "The Earliest Commentary on the Akedah." *Vetus Testamentum* 38 (1988) 302–23.

Neef, Heinz-Dieter. "'Abraham! Abraham!' Gen 22,1–19 als theologische Erzählung." *Journal of Northwest Semitic Languages* 24.2 (1998) 45–62.

Noort, Ed, and Eibert Tigchelaar, eds. *The Sacrifice of Isaac: The Aqedah (Genesis 22) and Its Interpretations*. Leiden: Brill, 2002.

O'Connor, Flannery. "The River." *Sewanee Review* 61 (1953) 455–75.

Römer, Thomas. *The Invention of God*. Translated by Raymond Geuss. Cambridge: Harvard University Press, 2015.

Sagi, Avi. "The Meaning of the 'Akedah' in Israeli Culture and Jewish Tradition." *Israel Studies* 3 (1998) 45–60.

Sartre, Jean-Paul. "L'Enfance d'un chef." In *Le Mur*, edited by Jean-Paul Sartre, 314–88. Paris: Éditions Gallimard, 1939.

———. *L'Être et le néant*. Paris: Éditions Gallimard, 1943.

Stoker, Henk. "God se Opdrag aan Abraham om sy Kind te Offer eties bekyk." *Journal for Christian Scholarship* 51 (2015) 77–92.

Thiselton, Anthony. *New Horizons in Hermeneutics*. Grand Rapids: Zondervan, 1992.

Vanhoutte, Kristof. "And the Word Once More Turned into Flesh; or, On the Various 'Theological Turns' in Contemporary Continental Philosophy." *Ceļš* 65 (2015) 156–76.

Veijola, Timo. "Abraham und Hiob: Das literarische und theologische Verhältnis von Gen 22 und der Hiob-Novelle." In *Vergegenwärtigung des Alten Testaments: Beiträge zur biblische Hermeneutik*, edited by Christoph Levin et al., 127–44. Göttingen: Vandenhoeck & Ruprecht, 2002.

Von Solms, Charlayne. "Ingenuity's Engine: An Overview of the History and Development of the Concept of the Muse." MPhil thesis, University of Stellenbosch, 2003.

Westermann, Claus. *Genesis 12–36*. Grand Rapids: Eerdmans, 1987.

White, Hugh. "The Initiation Legend of Isaac." *Zeitschrift für die alttestamentliche Wissenschaft* 91 (1979) 1–30.

———. "Where Is the Lamb for the Burnt Offering? Genesis 22." In *Narration and Discourse in the Book of Genesis*, edited by Hugh White, 187–203. Cambridge: Cambridge University Press, 1991.

Zipes, Jack, ed. *The Original Folk and Fairy Tales of the Brothers Grimm*. Princeton: Princeton University Press, 2014.

Žižek, Slavoj. *Organs Without Bodies*. New York: Routledge, 2004.

8

Constructing Politics of Identity from Judaism, Christianity, and Islam

An Afrocentric Exploration into the Intertextuality of the Hagar Narratives

Slindile Thabede

Hagar, the ambiguous figure in the narratives of Judaism, Christianity, and Islam, stands at the crossroads of these monotheistic religions, weaving a complex and intricate tapestry of meaning and interpretation.[1] Her story has long been utilized by adherents of these faiths as a cornerstone for identity construction and ideological reinforcement. However, within this intricate mosaic of religious heritage, Hagar's narrative reveals a troubling underbelly, a dark reflection of society's penchant for crystallizing or upholding systems of oppression through kyriarchy.[2]

Hagar/Hajar's narrative is a profound tale of a woman navigating the harsh realities of the ancient world, a journey that holds profound

1. This contribution is adapted from chapter 6 of the PhD dissertation, Thabede, "Navigating the Threshold," supervised by Professor L. C. Jonker with Professor N. Davids.

2. Schüssler Fiorenza introduced the term *kyriarchy* to characterize a system of "interlocking structures of domination" that extend beyond patriarchy and aid in understanding more intricate power structures. Schüssler Fiorenza, *But She Said*, 8.

resonance for our modern society. Within these narratives, we encounter the insidious influence of patriarchy, the stain of racism, the shadow of gender inequality, the specter of ethnocentrism, the menace of classism, and the ignominy of slavery.[3] It is a story fraught with layers of discrimination, from cultural and economic racism to religious bigotry and myriad other forms of prejudicial tendencies. Hagar's tale is unique in that it exposes how hegemonic powers, deeply entrenched in these religions, used an African female figure to perpetuate and justify the injustices that would condition the very socialization processes of our societies. The use of the African woman's body to drive insidious agendas is a norm originating from the Western empires. According to Preston, the Roman Empire exhibited hostility toward women, a perspective shaped by earlier Greek philosophers like Plato and Aristotle, who asserted that women were inherently inferior to men. Male Roman citizens even held legal authority to kill their wives, and daughters were similarly regarded as expendable.[4] Since Greece and Rome were misogynistic societies which sought to normalize this agenda by creating societal systems that accommodated the same agenda, it comes as no surprise that they could use Hagar to inscribe their political agendas using race.

The system of ideas and beliefs that shape a society is imposed and maintained not just through physical control over bodies but also by influencing people's thoughts, consciousness, and perceptions.[5] Subsequently, power operates through both physical discipline and ideological control to shape societies. It suggests that what we accept as "normal" or "natural" is constructed through systems of power and knowledge and that these constructs are always changing as society evolves. The power rhetoric associated with the female body involves the use of symbolic or actual violence against women as a means of exerting control, sending messages, or achieving political objectives. Consequently, the intertwining of gender, power, and politics reflects a complex relationship where the African female body becomes a contested terrain in the broader political landscape.

In examining Hagar's ambiguous nature, we are compelled to explore the various systems that enable her discrimination in Judaism and Christianity, while the Islamic tradition emphasizes her strength and resilience. It becomes clear that the systems involved in her subjugation

3. Thabede, "Navigating the Threshold," 180.

4. Preston, "Kandake," 16–17.

5. Foucault, *Discipline and Punish*, 195–228.

within the first two traditions are not isolated but interconnected, mutually reinforcing each other to uphold structures of power and domination. It is then in the interplay of these systems that we begin to understand the depths of injustice that simultaneously affect the negative representation of African women.

The Challenge with Religious Texts

Hassan states that "the deepest truth and insights that lie at the heart of each major religious tradition are represented myths and symbols that can inform, form and transform the inner and outer lives of millions of human beings through the ages."[6] This assertion maintains that our scriptural stories carry deep cultural, spiritual, and moral meanings which serve as vehicles for conveying complex religious concepts and values in a way that is accessible and memorable. They not only inform individuals about their faith but also have the power to shape and mold their beliefs, values, and behavior. Furthermore, Scriptures can also bring about transformative experiences, altering one's perspective and inner life. This indicates that these religious myths and symbols have a long-lasting and far-reaching influence. They impact the thoughts, emotions, and actions of countless individuals over many generations, both on a personal level and within the broader society.

Initially, religion has historically played a significant role in strengthening systems of oppression by endorsing imperialism, capitalism, slavery, segregation, and the subjugation of women. Jiménez asserts that "the planning of a patriarchal utopia as a delimited and organised space supports attempts to structure nature according to individual will in order to control it."[7] Jiménez's statement rings true here; religion belongs under one of the institutions of the state that generates hegemonic patriarchal power, and such institutions play a significant role in shaping and conditioning public opinion and disseminating cultural value, as well as influencing how people think about various aspects of life. What negative fabrications are the religious narratives we read conditioning our societies to understand about African women, or is this a mythical etiology of the colonizer's history?

6. Hassan, "Islamic Hagar," 149.
7. Jiménez, "On Utopus' Uterus," 49.

Hagar as an African princess originating from Egypt becomes the perfect body on which to inscribe the Jewish, Christian, and Islamic cultural norms, due to her race and gender; her character allows for setting an example of the denunciation to strangers who differ from the Israelite and Christian racial and ethnic identities. The choice to highlight a Kemet woman was a political act, especially in light of the West's defeat in wars against Kemet. Kandake Amantitere's triumph over Rome did more than disrupt Roman military ambitions, it directly challenged their reputation as an unbeatable empire. In an effort to preserve this image, Rome sought to erase Kush from historical records, obscuring the significant challenge presented by the powerful and autonomous Kandake queens.[8]

According to Dove, throughout history, African women have played pivotal roles as spiritual, military, and political leaders in resisting foreign occupation and defending land, resources, and autonomy. Their military and political skill, as demonstrated by leaders such as Amanirenas, successfully defended Kush from being conquered by both the Greeks and the Romans.[9] Therefore, based on these historical findings, it can be inferred that Hagar's use here could not be because she was a vulnerable woman from a subjugated colony, as portrayed. Given the evidence of women from Kemet defending their nations, the construction of Hagar's story appears to be a deliberate counternarrative rather than a reflection of historical truth. Preston has argued above that the omission of Kemet from historical records may reflect an attempt by Western powers to conceal the discomfort of having been outmatched by African queens in past conflict—hence, the creation and dissemination of narratives like Hagar as a purpose in maintaining Western dominance.

Looking at Hagar under the colonial intertextual script, the categorization of bodies follows a hierarchical structure wherein those belonging to dominant groups enjoy greater power and privilege. Initially, bodies that deviate further from the Western norm[10] or who indicate greater divergence are granted progressively fewer advantages and less privilege.[11] For example, the Hagar/Hajar traditions from Judaism and Islam both cohere in unearthing Hagar's origins towards a certain

8. Preston, "Kandake," 16–17.

9. Dove, "African Womanism," 532.

10. Individuals belonging to the dominant groups (i.e., white, male, able-bodied, cisgender).

11. Butts, "Global Body Politics."

tyranny.[12] Interestingly, the early fifth-century Genesis Rabbah 45:1 asserts that Hagar was the daughter of Pharaoh: after being reprimanded by God for taking Abraham's wife, Pharaoh took his daughter and gave her to Sarah. He said, "It is better for my daughter to be a maidservant in this house than a mistress in another."[13] Nonetheless, the Genesis Rabbah's rendition reveals that from the hierarchy of the social order, Hagar's class was initially above that of Sarah and Abraham's; however, observed from the framework of racial politics, Hagar is at the bottom of this hierarchy because her ethnicity and race does not comply with the same category of the dominant group or the owners of the colonizing script.[14]

This was a strategic move to reinforce the notion of racial superiority and legitimize control.[15] The portrayal of individuals or groups as threats or villains can provide a justification for repressive measures, whether in the form of discrimination or even violence; this can make it easier to justify the denial of rights and freedoms to these individuals. Therefore, based on the above evidence, how do we then navigate through narratives within our religious texts that perpetuate institutions of violence, division, subjugation, and dominance? How do we confront the enduring negative impact of these narratives in our societies as readers of these texts? What strategies can be employed to address the lasting effects of such stories in our worlds and religions? Can we mitigate the deep-seated pain and trauma associated with these violent biblical stories every time they are invoked?

Afrocentric Womanist Theoretical Framework

This chapter will first adopt a multidimensional exegetical approach which will be employed in dealing with these three narratives that have emerged from various contexts.[16] A multidimensional exegetical

12. Thabede, "Navigating the Threshold," 89–95, 166–71.

13. Bakhos, *Family of Abraham*, 109.

14. Africa and Africans, along with their political, social, religious, military, and economic roles, are frequently ignored, diminished, or narrowly portrayed through the lens of slavery. See Adamo, "Teaching the History," 474.

15. This research acknowledges that the intersection of colonialism and racism historically originated in Western nations long before spreading to African territories. This implies that Hagar's character may be found to represent women beyond African women's experiences; however, the focus here is African women.

16. Thabede, "Navigating the Threshold," 24.

approach encompassing the use of multiple hermeneutical theories[17] to interact with each narrative within its cultural and religious context was employed in performing an intertextuality for the three Hagar narratives.[18] The objective of this approach was to gain a comprehensive understanding of the narratives within the unique contexts of their respective religious traditions, thus capturing their intended messages in their cultural and religious settings.

Secondly, the Afrocentric approach will be employed, which proposes that Blacks (at home and abroad) must look at knowledge from an African perspective.[19] It suggests looking at matters at hand from an African viewpoint, that we misunderstand Africa when we use viewpoints and terms other than that of the African to study Africa. When Africans view themselves as centered and central in their own history, they see themselves as agents, actors, and participants rather than as marginal and on the periphery of political or economic experience. Asante defined Afrocentricity as a manner of thought and action in which the centrality of African interests, values, and perspectives predominate.[20] According to Amenyedzi, the Afrocentric-Womanist Paradigm emphasizes that culture is inseparable from gender discussions within the African socio-cultural framework, as culture permeates all aspects of life in Africa.[21] Therefore, given the prominence of debates surrounding gender and sexuality, it is essential to examine cultural viewpoints when conducting gender research.

17. Jonker and Lawrie, "Where Does This Leave Us?," 235.

18. Many scholars identify the Russian literary scholar Mikhail Bakhtin as the first to describe in the early twentieth century how texts never have meanings in themselves but are the product of relations with other kinds of texts. French post–World War II philosophers like Roland Barthes and Julia Kristeva picked up and developed this idea, with Kristeva in particular introducing the concept of intertextuality itself: "Any text is a mosaic of quotations; any text is the absorption and transformation of another." Kristeva, *Desire in Language*, 37.

19. The origin of the Afrocentric philosophy cannot be established with certainty. The most influential book advocating it was published in 1954. Marcus Garvey was one of the most influential propagators of the ideology. The abstract noun *Afrocentricity* dates to the 1970s and was popularized by Asante during the 1980s, when he developed epistemological and methodological foundations for an Afrocentric curriculum based on an African perspective but aiming at global understanding.

20. Asante, *Afrocentricity*. Among the Temple Circle of Afrocentrists are scholars such as C. Tsehloane Keto, Kariamu Welsh Asante, Abu Abarry, Ama Mazama, Theophile Obenga, and Terry Kershaw.

21. Amenyedzi, "Afrocentric Reflection," 124.

These hermeneutical frameworks above take into account what Jonker argues for. The first is the importance of contextual integrity in biblical interpretation.[22] He emphasizes that understanding the Bible requires acknowledging and navigating the different contexts in which it exists and is interpreted. These contexts include the context within and for which biblical interpretation takes place. The second is the context of the interpreter, including their own experiences, beliefs, and biases. The last is the broader theoretical frameworks and assumptions that shape interpretation. For Jonker, these different contexts are not separate or isolated but rather interact and influence each other. He emphasizes the need for interpreters to be aware of these different contexts and to engage with them in a thoughtful and critical manner. He also argues that a failure to acknowledge and address these different contexts can lead to misinterpretations and misunderstandings of the Bible. By advocating for contextual integrity, Jonker seeks to promote a more nuanced and insightful approach to biblical interpretation that considers the complexities of the text and the interpreter.

Identity Construction by the Abrahamic Religions[23]

I have argued elsewhere that the three Abrahamic religious identities were constructed under the influence of the Persian and Roman empires, and it becomes interesting that the imperial traces live within the gaps of their Hagar stories.[24] These traces will be observed in the delineation of the Hagar narratives below.

According to Foucault, "each society has its regime of truth, its 'general politics' of truth: that is, the types of discourse which it accepts and makes function as true; the mechanisms and instances which enable one to distinguish true and false statements; the means by which each is sanctioned; the techniques and procedures accorded value in the acquisition of truth; the status of those who are charged with saying what counts as true."[25] For Foucault, truth is deeply intertwined with power; those in positions of authority define and maintain what counts as truth to reinforce their power. This concept challenges the idea of

22. Jonker, "Living in Different Worlds Simultaneously."

23. All translations are the author's own unless otherwise indicated.

24. Thabede, "Navigating the Threshold," 199.

25. Foucault, *Power/Knowledge*, 131.

objective, immutable truths, emphasizing instead that truth is fluid, context-dependent, and shaped by societal structures and practices. This interplay is observed in the three stories of Hagar found in Judaism, Christianity, and Islam; each religion carved its own truth based on their geopolitical contexts from the details of the original story and made that their adherents' and national state truth.

The Jewish Hagar: Kyriocentric

The story of Hagar found in Gen 16 and 21[26] is embedded within the Abrahamic narrative that has been used by Judaism, Christianity, and Islam for their religious identity formation. According to Crotty, the initial purpose of the Hagar narrative was to solidify the assertion of a migrant community's connection to a specific territory and their ancestral heritage.[27] Significantly, the three distinct religious traditions employed the narrative of Abraham and his descendants to shape their individual religious identities. Identity, as described by Hogg and Abrams, primarily pertains to individuals' concepts of self, including their understanding of who they are, the type of people they identify as, and how they relate to others.[28] In the context of the biblical narrative of Hagar, these concepts of identity become critical, particularly as they relate to diverse aspects like ethnicity, gender, race, culture, and religion.

From the Hebrew story found in Gen 16 (verses 1–15; also 21:8–21), Hagar is portrayed as Sarah's Egyptian slave. She is given to Abraham by Sarah due to her infertility issues. However, tensions and conflicts between Hagar and Sarah intensify, leading to Hagar's expulsion into the wilderness of Paran with her son Ishmael.

The Hagar narrative in Judaism thrives within the framework of multiple oppressive systems identified as patriarchy, racism, ethnocentrism, classism, and slavery, as well as cultural, economic, gender, religious, and political divides. Hagar provides a lens through which we can examine the construction of this Israelite identity politics at play between the methods of relations of the main characters—Abraham, Sarah, and Hagar. Reading Sarah's treatment of Hagar, we are brought

26. The linguistic inquiry of Gen 16, 21; Gal 4:21–31; and hadith can be found in chapters 3–5 of Thabede, "Navigating the Threshold."

27. Crotty, "Hagar/Hajar," 180.

28. Hogg and Abrams, *Social Identifications*, 2.

to the understanding that Hagar is only valuable for what she can do for Sarah, being a surrogate.

While Sarah does not have a son, through Hagar Sarah can rid herself of the stigma of infertility. The shame of barrenness was dominant in ancient Near Eastern marriages since they had various laws in place that were implemented in order to prevent divorce for women; one of them was using their slaves as surrogates. However, the derogatory terms that came with being childless, the depreciation, and having failed at being a woman were a constant reality in Sarah's life. It is common that in cultural settings "women are held accountable for the reproductive challenges of a couple. Infertility evolves into a crisis not only impacting the couple but also extending to the larger family and society."[29] Hence, Sarah takes the role of finding the surrogate in her handmaid because it is she who endures the stigma more than Abraham. Therefore, in accordance with the cultural expectations, Sarah's infertility was perceived as a setback for the entire Jewish clan.

Consequently, the racial and ethnic distinctions of Hagar became inconsequential, as the primary concern was ensuring the continuation of the Abrahamic lineage. It is only upon completing the entire narrative that one comes to the realization that, despite initial impressions, the identity markers of Hagar did in the end matter. The conclusion leaves us with the awareness that these markers played a significant role in the manner in which the story unfolded. Hagar and Sarah's story is not the only story revolving around infertility and surrogacy agenda in Genesis. Interestingly, Zilpah and Bilhah in Gen 29 (verses 24, 29) also assisted their mistresses in the same predicament; however, regardless of the jealousy wars they endured, there is no animosity that threatens the right of either the wife or mistress, and there are no expulsions caused by their children. Theirs is the battle of the classes rather than ethnicity and race.

Some scholars also argue that it was not Hagar that agitated Sarah as much as Ishmael. According to Exum, Ishmael being Abraham's flesh and blood posed a threat to the fragile boundaries of Israel since he was born to a woman considered "other to the Jewish identity."[30] However, the conversation of Abraham and God in Gen 15 (verses 4–5) about who will inherit his estate does not specify which son; secondly, the promise of numerous offspring was also not racially or ethnically bound to a certain

29. Mabasa, "Sociocultural Aspects of Infertility," 65–66.

30. Exum, "Hagar En Procès," 5.

son. One wonders how Sarah could have had an inkling of what God was referring to when he promised Abraham many generations.

Crotty explicates that this double rejection in Hagar's story found in Gen 16 and 21 signifies a covenant common in the Near Eastern religious societies, which excludes Abraham's progeny via Ishmael from the contract with the High God and instead privileges Abraham's progeny via Isaac, the son of Sarah.[31] Crotty's explanation is a good attempt to make sense of what transpired between the privileging of one son over another in a cultural setup. Does this mean Ketura's children born with Abraham are also dismissed from Abraham's will because she was not Jewish? If mothers are what sons are identified through, is this culture still patriarchal, or matrilineal? Notably, even the genealogy of Jesus is constructed the same way: the sons are recognized through their mothers rather than their fathers.

Nevertheless, God has proven not to be a part of this culture of excluding one son over another, because he promises Abraham and Hagar at different times that he will make Ishmael great too because he is Abraham's seed, as God had reiterated in Gen 15.[32] Therefore, this is not at all a loss for both Hagar and Ishmael. However, the question remains, had Isaac not miraculously been born to Sarah, since Hagar had already been coerced into surrogacy, what would have been the Jewish stance on this matter?

My argument is derived from what Weber and Parra-Medina expound, that matters around race, class, gender, and sexuality are historically contingent constructs that represent social hierarchies of dominance—essentially, power relationships. Weber and Parra-Medina highlight these as "power hierarchies" where one group wields control over another, securing its dominant position within the system.[33] Alternatively, they assert that the interconnected nature of race, gender, and sexuality hierarchies becomes particularly evident to those experiencing oppression along multiple dimensions of inequality.[34] In this context, the dominant Western culture plays a role in defining categories within race, gender, and sexuality as opposites, such as white/Black, men/women, heterosexual/homosexual, in order to establish social rankings of good or bad, worthy or unworthy, right or wrong.

31. Crotty, "Hagar/Hajar," 169.

32. Thabede, "Navigating the Threshold," 82–83.

33. Weber and Parra-Medina, "Intersectionality and Women's Health," 20.

34. Weber and Parra-Medina, "Intersectionality and Women's Health," 15.

Schüssler Fiorenza coined a term that encapsulates all these systems: *kyriarchy*.[35] According to Schüssler Fiorenza, this system is a phenomenon of "interlocking structures of domination" that extends beyond patriarchy, and aids in understanding more intricate power structures. Kyriarchy builds upon colonization and patriarchy by encompassing the multiple, intersecting, and co-constitutive structures of power and oppression that shape the experiences of individuals.[36] Kyriarchy acknowledges that power relations are not exclusively dictated by men over women but involve a complex interplay of various axes of difference. These axes encompass not only gender but also factors such as race, class, sexuality, and more. Kyriarchy underscores that individuals can occupy different positions within these various axes of difference, and power dynamics can manifest differently depending on the specific combination of these factors.

While there are common patterns and characteristics shared among oppressive structures, they are not uniform and do not operate in identical ways.[37] Rather, they are interconnected, interactive, and mutually constitutive, drawing from each other to reinforce their respective powers. As bell hooks aptly phrases it, different structures of oppression are not "synonymous"; instead, they are linked yet distinct.[38] Moreover, an individual's experience of a particular structure is inevitably complicated by the presence of other structures in their lives through the concept of intersectionality.

Subsequently, through this narrative Hagar's identity is shaped and transformed by the specific social, economic, and political circumstances in which she finds herself within the Israelite household. Hagar's story highlights, as Powell argues, "the ways in which the elements of ethnicity and class coupled with sexuality and gender can produce, reinforce, and undermine the structures through which the covenant is established."[39] Therefore, this suggests that the covenant is not neutral or universal but is influenced by social constructs like ethnicity, class, sexuality, and gender. These elements can either perpetuate or disrupt the systems of power and inequality embedded within the covenant's framework. According to Latvus this folktale is burdened with political ideologies because of

35. Schüssler Fiorenza, *But She Said*, 8.

36. Aquino, "Feminist Intercultural Theology," 25.

37. Matsuda, "Beside My Sister," 1188.

38. hooks, *Yearning*, 125.

39. Powell, "Sor Juana's Critique," 90.

its history of inception.[40] The narratives of Hagar found in Gen 16 and 21 were constructed during exile and postexilic moments of the Israelite nation, hence the political burdens they carry.

The Christian Hagar: Hegemonic

The New Testament, which has the Christian Bible's narrative on Hagar, found in Gal 4 (verses 21–31), revisits the same Genesis story but offers a somewhat altered narrative. In the Christian context, the focus is on Sarah and Hagar as two distinct covenants along with their two sons; not much attention is given to Abraham. Sarah is equated to the new Jerusalem, and Hagar to Mount Sinai, which symbolizes the old covenant.

The Christian interpretation of the Hagar narrative reinforces a hegemonic structure by establishing and sustaining dominance within social, political, and cultural contexts. Hegemony entails the assertion of power and influence by a dominant group or institution, shaping societal norms, values, and beliefs.[41] This dynamic is evident in how the Christian retelling of Hagar's story serves to create marginalized groups, such as Judaism and Islam, while simultaneously privileging Christianity. By building upon a narrative already rooted in various forms of oppression, the Christian version introduces additional layers of domination without addressing the harm perpetuated by the original Jewish narrative.

The Christian perspective on the Hagar narrative, as found in Gal 4 (verses 21–31), introduces a unique dimension of identity politics within the broader context of the Abrahamic narratives. This interpretation of Hagar's story, which is distinct from the Jewish and Islamic traditions, presents a condensed yet thought-provoking allegorical perspective that plays a pivotal role in the formation of Christian identity. In his letter to the Galatians, Paul uses Hagar and Sarah as symbolic figures representing two covenants: Hagar symbolizes the old covenant associated with the Mosaic law and the earthly Jerusalem, while Sarah embodies the new covenant, characterized by Christian grace and the heavenly Jerusalem.

Alternatively, Paul's argument overturns the Jewish story by denying the Jews the privilege of being Sarah's children and rather asserts that the blessings promised to Abraham are now available to non-Jews, the gentiles, through Jesus who was the offspring of Abraham; Jesus

40. Latvus, "Reading Hagar in Contexts," 14.

41. Thatcher, *God, Sex, and Gender*, 27.

was now the "New Isaac." Previously, in the Jewish tradition, Hagar had been recognized as the mother of all non-Jews, and they were considered the siblings of Ishmael.[42] However, in the Christian narrative, the Jews are the children of Hagar.

Notably, after Jesus' death, Sarah's role undergoes a transformation, and she becomes the mother of non-Jews who embrace faith in Jesus. These individuals then become the siblings of Isaac. Nevertheless, within the Christian context, Hagar remains the outsider—the mother of those who are not part of the Christian faith, whether they are gentiles or Jews who choose to adhere to Jewish customs and reject Jesus.[43] The relationship between Hagar and Sarah in this Christian interpretation becomes a symbolic representation of the transition from the old to the new, from the earthly to the heavenly. It reinforces the notion that the identity of the Christian community is not bound by the constraints of the Mosaic law but rather founded on grace and faith in Christ. While this interpretation underscores the boundaries of Christian identity, it also prompts contemplation on the complexities and nuances of identity politics in the context of religious traditions and their relationship with their historical and theological predecessors.

Tajfel and Turner emphasize that the effect of identification increases when groups pose a threat to one another.[44] In a similar vein, the Israelites initially employed the narrative to distinguish themselves from neighboring ethnicities. However, later during the rule of the Greco-Roman Empire years, the same narrative became a focal point of struggle for the Jewish community. The Romans, aiming to assert dominance, strategically used the Jewish identity narrative to craft their own master narrative. According to Tajfel and Turner, social identity begins with the premise that individuals define their own identities in relation to social groups, and that such identifications work to protect and bolster self-identity. Nevertheless, the maneuver executed by the Romans transformed this tactic into an act of marginalizing and oppressing Jews, thereby stripping them of their once-held power and privilege.

Consequently, it can be concluded that borders are crafted through political, social, and cultural processes within specific historical contexts.[45] These deliberately constructed borders create distinctions and

42. Crotty, "Hagar/Hajar," 175.

43. Crotty, "Hagar/Hajar," 175.

44. Tajfel and Turner, "Integrative Theory of Intergroup Conflict."

45. Magyar-Haas, "Ambivalent Concepts of the Border," 3.

delineate the boundaries of inclusion and exclusion. Passi contends that the significance of power dynamics is underscored by the fact that boundaries and borders encompass the politics of setting limits, the politics of portrayal, and of identity.[46] They serve to separate entities from one another, express their meanings in specific contexts, and permit the existence of particular forms of identity while frequently hindering others. There is an assumption of superiority and dominance by Christians, while regarding Jews as inferior and thereby allocating a low slave status and class to them.

Moreover, there is a notion of racialization at play hidden in the layers of the narrative. According to Grosfoguel, racialization is a process that manifests through the categorization of individuals, where some are assigned a superior racial identity, while others are categorized as having an inferior racial identity.[47] Those individuals identified as superior are said to inhabit the "zone of being," whereas those considered inferior are placed in the "zone of non-being" because they are viewed as nonhuman or subhuman. The latter group is seen as lacking established norms, rights, or civility. This implies that actions such as violence, rape, and appropriation are allowed, actions that would otherwise be deemed unacceptable for individuals belonging to the "zone of being." Within the realm of non-being, racial oppression compounds the numerous forms of oppression. Subsequently, both Jewish and Christian traditions convey the idea that identities typically emerge through the interaction of power, representation, and distinctions, which can manifest either as negative constructs involving exclusion or marginalization.

The Islamic Hajar: Subversive

In contrast to Judaism and Christianity above, the Islamic Hajar version found in the hadith adheres closely to the Gen 16 and 21 story; however, it carves its story from Hajar's banishment in Ibrahim's house. Hajar, as she is known, is recognized as the second wife of the prophet Ibrahim and the mother of the prophet Ishmael. Her departure from Ibrahim's household into the desert is interestingly not a banishment as described in Gen 21, rather it is Hajar's expulsion from the home of Ibrahim. She was commanded by God to go and start a new religion.

46. Passi, "Political Boundaries," 217.

47. Grosfoguel, "What Is Racism," 11.

This led to the construction of the hajj praxis in the city of Mecca as Muslims celebrate it to this day.

The Hajar narrative found in Islam reconstructs a praxis of subversion. Subversive stories are politically transformative because they reject the master narrative and its systems of oppression. The Hajar story, found in Islamic tradition and sacred texts, unfolds a narrative that is both rich in symbolism and intrinsically connected to Islamic identity and spirituality. Hajar, the central character in the Islamic retelling of the story, is an Egyptian woman who holds a significant place in Islamic history and spirituality. She assumes a significant position in Islamic awareness, as her narrative is intertwined with the "hajj rituals," as explained.[48]

According to Yusuf, the most iconic aspect of Hajar's identity in the Islamic narrative is her connection to the holy city of Mecca.[49] Islamic tradition maintains that Hajar and her son Ishmael were left in the desolate valley of Mecca by the prophet Ibrahim as an act of obedience to God's command. Hajar's journey through the harsh desert landscape, her desperate search for water, and the miraculous appearance of the sacred Zamzam well are central elements of Islamic identity. The Zamzam well, a symbol of divine mercy, remains a vital spiritual and physical resource for Muslim pilgrims visiting the Kaaba, the most sacred site in Islam, located in the center of Mecca.

This aspect of the Hajar narrative plays a pivotal role in the construction of the Islamic identity. The annual Hajj pilgrimage, where millions of Muslims retrace Hajar's footsteps in the desert, underscores the spiritual and physical connection that Muslims have with Hajar's story. It serves as a powerful reminder of the importance of faith, trust in God, and the endurance of hardships, all integral components of the Muslim identity.[50]

As mentioned above, in this narrative Hajar is neither expelled by Sarah nor due to Isaac's inheritance. The Islamic story does not put blame on any parties involved in the plot to construct a negative agenda. Instead, God is in control for calling Hajar. Hajar's character, therefore, embodies resilience, faith, and the pursuit of divine purpose, which have a profound impact on the shaping of Islamic identity. Her identity as a woman, the mother of Ishmael, and an Egyptian is intertwined

48. Chande, "Islam and Qur'anic Figures," 8.

49. Yusuf, "From Hebrew 'Slave,'" 3.

50. Arguetta, "Reimagination of Hagar," 12.

with the spiritual and historical identity of Muslims; nothing about her identity markers is shameful.[51]

The process of identity formation underscores that constructing an identity is inclusive, involving the internalization of the values of the identifier, but it is also an exclusive process that involves the elimination of other identities.[52] The former is evident in the construction of the Islamic Hajar narrative, while the latter is evident in the Jewish and the Christian Hagar narrative. In contrast to Judaism and Christianity, the Islamic tradition is constructing its identity without stigmatizing any gender, race, class, ethnicity, culture, ethnicity, or religion. Thatcher characterizes the Jewish and Christian approach as an exercise of "power-over," signifying absolute domination. However, by refusing to perpetuate negative connotations through the Hajar narrative, this maneuver can be seen as a reconstruction of "power-with," defined by Thatcher as power that operates through negotiation and consensus.[53] The Islamic master narrative does not entail oppression or marginalization. Rather, it can be regarded as a subversive narrative of resistance.

As previously discovered by the researcher, the Hagar/Hajar narrative found in Judaism, Christianity, and Islam bears the imprint of the Persian and Roman Empires. It is interesting to note that remnants of imperialism strive within the narratives of the first two traditions but not within Islam. Despite the historical ties of the Arab region to the formidable Persian and Roman Empires, the Hajar narrative in Islam surprisingly refutes the distinct influences of these imperial powers. Substantial evidence strongly supports the notion that Hagar and Ishmael are not truly the enemies, idolaters, violent people, or depraved beings they have been portrayed to be. Rather, these negative associations can be attributed to the socio-political dynamics of the initial Jewish narrative;[54] however, its negativity is further used and developed by the New Testament to mimic similar tendencies of division. One does ponder how much each tradition was using the historical reality of Kemet to shape their narrative. Is Islam's justice to the Hajar narrative connected to the Islamic invasion of Egypt? Or is the justice connected to the relations the Palestinians shared with ancient Egypt long before plundering them? How much of actual history is hidden in the three narratives of Hagar?

51. Dolbeare, *Reading in American Ideologies*, 195.

52. İnaç and Ünal, "Construction of National Identity," 224.

53. Thatcher, *God, Sex, and Gender*, 26.

54. Firestone, "Hagar and Ishmael," 416.

Constructing Global Politics on an African Female Body

As reiterated above, the Greco-Roman Empire exhibited hostility toward women, a perspective shaped by earlier Greek philosophers like Plato and Aristotle, who asserted that women were inherently inferior to men. Male Roman citizens even held legal authority to kill their wives and daughters; they were similarly regarded as expendable.[55] Rome was a misogynistic society which sought to normalize this agenda by creating societal systems that accommodated this ideology. This implies that this gruesome phenomenon was first experienced by the Western women in those ancient empires long before it was implemented on African female bodies.

The dynamics within body politics involve various forms of power: institutional power, seen in government and laws; disciplinary power, present in economic production; discretionary power, exercise; and personal power, negotiated in intimate relations.[56] Graham posits that hegemonic institutions employ a mix of moral, religious, and psychological discourses to regulate and shape the population.[57] These ideologies are not confined to theoretical concepts but also manifest in the tangible, physical aspects of people's lives, including health, sexual practices, and ethical choices.

Butts asserts,

> Because identities are read from bodies . . . [they] are used to divide and classify [people] into socially constructed racial groups. Within these groups, [people] are further divided and classified again based upon constructs such as class, gender, sexual identity and expression, age, religion, nationality, and ability. Consequently, we subscribe meaning to human bodies based upon our perceptions and interpretations of each of these groupings and subgroupings, where we are socialized and taught how to perform as members of the various communities to which we belong, through body rules.[58]

Therefore, it comes as no surprise why the interpretation of Hagar and Ishmael by the adherents of Judaism and Christianity continue to perpetuate the negative stereotypes; reading the Scriptures has also

55. Preston, "Kandake," 16–17.
56. Shaw, "Body Politics."
57. Graham, *Making the Difference.*
58. Butts, "Global Body Politics."

become a political agenda because they situate the reader according to their age, race, gender, and cultural position.

This shows that Hagar was not used here due to helplessness or vulnerability; the use of her in this manner was rather continuing an existing discourse regarding how women were viewed since the Eurocentric society already deemed them inferior to men.[59] Her body is constructed into a site of oppression for political purposes in this manner, which is a strategy designed to further political objectives or sow discord and conflicts within societies of multiple identities. Bellows-Blakely says African girlhood has been politicized and used as a site upon which Western hegemony has projected its ideologies, justified interventions, and shaped policies.[60] While Bellows-Blakely's argument is valid, it tends to speak for the experiences of African women, which can vice versa inadvertently mirror the very systems of oppression she criticizes. Black women have frequently been positioned as topics within Western feminist discourses to date. Nonetheless, Hagar's body is a text purposefully made ambiguous to produce the conflicting feelings and disgust around her and the groups she represents. Not only that, but Hagar is also the perfect tool to police and condition global societies regarding the markers and boundaries of identity that are meant to keep us at odds with one another. This is readily accepted because the separation grants power and advantage to those who benefit from the ideology promoted by the narrative. Subsequently, for those beings the maintenance of their privilege relies on the continued oppression of African women to this day.[61] However, while her narrative actively shapes the identities of those who engage with it, it simultaneously exposes the complicity and positionality of individuals who derive power or legitimacy from the very systems of oppression that the story critiques and sustains.

The Liberation Movement of the African Matriarchs

Dove asserts the recovering and retelling of the history of African women "herstory" is crucial.[62] Could the Hagar narrative be a counternarrative

59. The adaptable gender systems that once existed in Africa were overtaken by strict and hierarchical frameworks, establishing entrenched inequalities related to sex, class, and gender roles through Western invasion. See Amenyedzi, "Engaging Ifi," 50.

60. Bellows-Blakely, "Girlhood in Africa," 14.

61. Young, "Justice," 96.

62. Dove, "African Womanism," 532.

of the West? Preston argues that the Kandake's (African queen's) victory over the Roman army not only posed a military threat but also challenged Rome's image as an invincible superpower.[63] To maintain this image, Rome sought to erase Kush from historical records. This suppression aimed to conceal the threat posed by the Kandakes, powerful female rulers who challenged Roman patriarchy. It has been said that history is often written by the victors, and victors may intentionally or unintentionally present a biased version of events, downplaying their own mistakes and emphasizing their own heroism. And if this is the case, what would sifting history from Hagar's narrative reveal?

Hagar's story offers a lens through which we can critically interrogate African culture beyond the distortions imposed by European interpreters. Colonial interpretations have historically constructed a false discourse around Hagar, obscuring the realities of African history and experience. Yet the narrative of Hagar does more than reflect oppression, it rather illuminates the dual process: first, by revealing how systems of dominance maintain their power, and second, by exposing the inherent fragility and instability of white supremacist structures.

Hajar, read from the three traditions, dismisses the validity of the dominant power structures of Judaism and Christianity. To her they only are true if one believes in their ideologies; hence, she resists them by exiting both contexts. From an Afrocentric womanist perspective, historical evidence suggests that the Europeanization of Africa has often resulted in negative consequences rather than improvements in quality of life on a global scale. Historically, feminists in Judaism and Christianity had painted Hagar's departure negatively as a banishment, which has been a form of denying womanists their modes of autonomy. However, Dove does note the problem is that some individuals, both Black and white, either actively or inadvertently, serve as instruments of oppression by contributing to the process of White supremacy's deculturation of Africa.[64]

However, the stories of African women's bravery are numerous, yet many remain untold in literature due to the dominance of narratives shaped by kyriarchy and racism. Despite this, remarkable figures have emerged, such as Nanny, the legendary Maroon military leader and strategist from eighteenth-century Jamaica. From Africa, leaders like Queen Nzinga of Angola (1581–1663), Dona Beatrice of the Kongo (1682–1706),

63. Preston, "Kandake," 16.

64. Dove, "African Womanism," 534.

and Yaa Asantewaa of Ghana (1840/60–1920) demonstrated extraordinary courage.[65] They stand out as a symbol of resilience. According to Dove, these women's strength and determination have played a pivotal role in advancing Pan-Africanism and Black Nationalism, even though their contributions often go unacknowledged or underappreciated.

Foucault said that "power is everywhere" and "comes from everywhere," meaning it cannot be confined to a specific agency or structure.[66] This suggests that power is not exclusive to a particular group; rather, it is something both oppressors and the marginalized possess. Each group wields power in its unique ways, employing different methods to exercise it. Subsequently, the Hagar narrative from the Islam perspective proves Foucault's argument. It exposes the power of African queens that were able to emasculate the Western empires of the past. Subsequently, according to Kartzow, "marginalized subjects have an epistemic advantage";[67] individuals or communities who experience marginalization, discrimination, or exclusion from mainstream societal structures possess unique insights or knowledge regarding their own experiences and the broader social dynamics that impact them. In essence, those situated at the margins of society may offer perspectives and understandings that are valuable for analyzing power structures, inequalities, and social issues around them.

Subsequently, by engaging with texts of African women's past stories to examine the present, African women gain a platform through which they can navigate contemporary realities, asserting their existence and identities afresh. This process is both dynamic and transformative, enabling them and their community's agency to reclaim their heritage and confront oppressive narratives. It serves as a powerful act of resistance, fostering self-empowerment and revitalizing African cultural traditions.

Conclusion

As argued above, discourse can be both a tool of power and a means of challenging that power; it can be used to control and manipulate, but it can also be used to resist oppression and advocate for change. In this case, Hagar's narratives are not merely an academic exercise; they

65. Dove, "African Womanism," 534.

66. Foucault, *History of Sexuality*, 63.

67. Kartzow, "Asking the Other Question," 370.

are a profound exploration of the methods in which religions shape our understanding of identity, power, and justice. Secondly, they are a means of historical exposure. The same narratives challenge us to confront the uncomfortable truths that lie at the heart of these religious traditions, while also holding out the promise of transformation and renewal. In exploring Hagar's narratives, African women are embarking on a journey of self-discovery, both for the individual believer and for larger religious communities.

The exploration of her story within the three monotheistic religions prompts us to engage in a process of critical reflection on the narratives, beliefs, and practices that have perpetuated discrimination and injustice. Consequently, by shedding light on the darker aspects of these religious traditions, this article invites us to reexamine the foundations of our faith and consider how the oppressive narratives can be read in a transforming manner to promote justice and equality.

Bibliography

Adamo, David T. "Teaching the History of Ancient Israel from an African Perspective: The Invasion of Sennacherib of 701 B.C.E." *Old Testament Essays* 23 (2010) 473–501.

Amenyedzi, Seyram B. "An Afrocentric Reflection on the Rape of Tamar in 2 Samuel 13." In *African Womanhood and the Feminist Agenda*, edited by Constantine Maxwell et al., 123–36. London: IGI Global, 2024.

———. "Engaging Ifi Amadiume's Findings Through an Afrocentric-Womanist Lens." In *Sankofa: Liberation Theologies of West African Women (Circle Jubilee Volume 1)*, edited by Seyram B. Amenyedzi et al., 41–62. Bamberg: University of Bamberg Press, 2023. https://doi.org/10.20378/irb-91400.

Aquino, M. P. "Feminist Intercultural Theology: Toward a Shared Future of Justice." In *Feminist Intercultural Theology: Latina Explorations for a Just World*, edited by M. P. Aquino and M. J. Rosado-Nunes, 9–28. Maryknoll, NY: Orbis, 2007.

Arguetta, Amanda. "The Reimagination of Hagar in the Hebrew Bible and Islamic Scripture." *Say Something Theological: The Student Journal of Theological Studies* 2.2 (2020) 1–13.

Asante, Molefi Kete. *African Culture: The Rhythms of Unity*. Trenton, NJ: African World, 1990.

———. *Afrocentricity*. Buffalo, NY: Amulefi, 1980.

Bakhos, Carol. *The Family of Abraham: Jewish, Christian, and Muslim Interpretations*. Cambridge: Harvard University Press, 2014.

Bauer, Greta R., et al. "Intersectionality in Quantitative Research: A Systematic Review of Its Emergence and Applications of Theory and Methods." *SSM—Population Health* 14 (2021). https://doi.org/10.1016/j.ssmph.2021.100798.

Bellows-Blakely, Sarah. "Girlhood in Africa." *Oxford Research Encyclopedia of African History*, Mar. 31, 2020. https://doi.org/10.1093/acrefore/9780190277734.013.654.

Butts, Tracy. "Global Body Politics." In *Women Worldwide: Transnational Feminist Perspectives*, edited by Tracy Butts et al., 51–78. Corvallis, OR: Oregon State University, 2022. https://open.oregonstate.education/womenworldwide/chapter/global-politics/.

Cele, Sofía, and Danielle van der Burgt. "Children's Embodied Politics of Exclusion and Belonging in Public Space." In *Politics, Citizenship and Rights*, edited by Kirsi Kallio and Sarah Mills, 1–14. Singapore: Springer, 2016

Chande, Abdin. "Islam and Qur'anic figures in Africa: Prophets, Sages and Disciples." *Journal of Islamic and Middle Eastern Multidisciplinary Studies* 2 (2012) 1–16.

Cole, E. R. "Intersectionality and Research in Psychology." *American Psychologist* 64.3 (2009) 170–80.

Crotty, Robert. "Hagar/Hajar, Muslim Women and Islam: Reflections on the Historical and Theological Ramifications of the Story of Ishmael's Mother." In *Women in Islam: Reflections on Historical and Contemporary Research*, edited by Terence Lovat, 165–84. New York: Springer, 2012.

Dione, Saliou. "Scrutinizing the Construction of the Black Female Persona in African-American Narratives." *International Journal on Studies in English Language and Literature* 10.8 (2022) 23–29.

Dolbeare, Kenneth M. *Reading in American Ideologies*. Edited by Patricia Dolbeare and Jane A. Hadley. Chicago: Markham, 1973.

Dove, Nah. "African Womanism: An Afrocentric Theory." *Journal of Black Studies* 28 (1998) 515–39.

Ewick, Patrick, and Susan S. Silbey. "Subversive Stories and Hegemonic Tales: Toward a Sociology of Narrative." *Law and Society Review* 29 (1995) 117–226.

Exum, C. J. "Hagar En Procès: The Abject in Search of Subjectivity." In *From the Margins 1: Women of the Hebrew Bible and Their Afterlives*, edited by Peter S. Hawkins and Lesleigh C. Stahlberg, 1–16. Sheffield: Sheffield Phoenix, 2009.

Firestone, Reuven. "Hagar and Ishmael in Literature and Tradition as a Foreshadow of Their Islamic Personas." In *Abraham's Family: A Network of Meaning in Judaism, Christianity, and Islam*, edited by Lukas Bormann, 397–420. Tübingen: Mohr Siebeck, 2018.

Foucault, Michel. *Discipline and Punish: The Birth of the Prison*. Translated by Alan Sheridan. New York: Random, 1995.

———. *Power/Knowledge: Selected Interviews and Other Writings, 1972–1977*. Edited by Colin Gordon. New York: Pantheon, 1980.

Frye, Victoria, et al. "Whither Gender in Urban Health?" *Health and Place* 14 (2008) 616–22.

Graham, Elaine. *Making the Difference: Gender, Personhood and Theology*. London: Mowbray, 1995.

Grosfoguel, Ramon. "What Is Racism?" *Journal of World-System Research* 22 (2016) 10–15.

Hassan, Riffat. "Islamic Hagar and Her Family," In *Hagar, Sarah, and Their Children: Jewish, Christian and Muslim Perspectives*, edited by Phyllis Trible and Letty M. Russell, 149–67. Louisville: Westminster John Knox. 2006.

Hills Collins, Patricia. *Black Feminist Thought: Knowledge, Consciousness and the Politics of Empowerment*. New York: Routledge, 1991.

Hogg, Michael, and Dominic Abrams. *Social Identifications: A Social Psychology of Intergroup Relations and Group Processes*. London: Routledge, 1988.

hooks, bell. *Yearning: Race, Gender, and Cultural Politics*. Boston: South End, 1990.

İnaç, Hüsamettin, and Feyzullah Ünal. "The Construction of National Identity in Modern Times: Theoretical Perspective." *International Journal of Humanities and Social Science* 3.11 (2013) 223–32.

Jiménez, Almudena M. "On Utopus' Uterus: The Colonisation of the Body and the Birth of Patriarchal Utopia in Thomas More's Utopia." *Coolabah* 31 (2021) 48–66.

Jonker, Louis C. "Living in Different Worlds Simultaneously, or: A Plea for Contextual Integrity." In *African and European Readers of the Bible in Dialogue: In Quest of a Shared Meaning*, edited by Gerald O. West and Hans de Wit, 105–19. Leiden: Brill, 2008.

Jonker, Louis C., and Douglas G. Lawrie. "Where Does This Leave Us?" In *Fishing for Jonah (Anew): Various Approaches to Biblical Interpretation*, edited by Louis C. Jonker and Douglas G. Lawrie, 229–44. Stellenbosch: Sun, 2005.

Kartzow, Marianne B. "Asking the Other Question: An Intersectional Approach to Galatians 3:28 and the Colossian Household Codes." *Biblical Interpretation* 18 (2010) 364–84.

Kim, Grace Ji-Sun, and Susan M. Shaw. *Intersectional Theology: An Introductory Guide*. Minneapolis: Fortress, 2018.

Kristeva, Julia. *Desire in Language: A Semiotic Approach to Language and Art*. New York: Columbia University Press, 1980.

Latvus, K. "Reading Hagar in Contexts: From Exegesis to Inter-Contextual Analysis." In *Genesis: Texts and Contexts*, edited by Athalya Brenner et al., 247–74. Minneapolis: Fortress, 2010.

Mabasa, Langutani F. "Sociocultural Aspects of Infertility in a Black South African Community." *Journal of Psychology in Africa* 12 (2002) 65–79.

Magyar-Haas, Veronika. "Ambivalent Concepts of the Border: Political Borders—Bodily Boundaries." *Social Work and Society* 10.2 (2012) 1–13.

Matsuda, Mari J. "Beside My Sister, Facing the Enemy: Legal Theory out of Coalition." *Stanford Law Review* 43 (1991) 1183–92.

Passi, A. "Political Boundaries." In *International Encyclopedia of Human Geography*, edited by Rob Kitchen and Nigel Thrift, 217–27. Amsterdam: Elsevier, 2009. https://doi.org/10.1016/B978-008044910-4.00793-8.

Powell, Lisa D. "Sor Juana's Critique of Theological Arrogance." *Journal of Feminist Studies in Religion* 37.2 (2011) 11–30.

Preston, Hilarry. "The Kandake: A Missing History." *Priscilla Papers* 37.2 (2023)16–19.

Schüssler Fiorenza, Elisabeth. *But She Said: Feminist Practices of Biblical Interpretation*. Boston: Beacon, 1992.

Shaw, Carolyn Martin. "Body Politics." *Encyclopedia of Race and Racism*, 2021. Encyclopedia.com. https://www.encyclopedia.com/social-sciences/encyclopedias-almanacs-transcripts-and-maps/body-politics.

Stoddart, Mark C. J. "Ideology, Hegemony, Discourse: A Critical Review of Theories of Knowledge and Power." *Social Thought and Research* 28 (2007) 191–225.

Tajfel, Henri, and John C. Turner. "An Integrative Theory of Intergroup Conflict." In *The Social Psychology of Intergroup Relations*, edited by W. G. Austin and S. Worchel, 33–47. Monterey, CA: Brooks, 1979.

Thabede, Slindile. "Navigating the Threshold: An African Feminist Reading of the Hagar Narrative in Judaism, Christianity and Islam." PhD thesis, Stellenbosch University, 2022.

Thatcher, Adrian. *God, Sex, and Gender: An Introduction*. Hoboken, NJ: Wiley-Blackwell, 2011.

Weber, Lynn, and Deborah Parra-Medina. "Intersectionality and Women's Health: Charting a Path to Eliminating Health Disparities." In *Advances in Gender Research: Gender Perspectives on Health and Medicine*, edited by V. Demos and M. T. Segal, 183–226. Amsterdam: Elsevier Science, 2003.

Yoo, Peter. "Hagar the Egyptian: Wife, Handmaid, and Concubine." *Catholic Biblical Quarterly* 78 (2016) 215–35.

Young, Iris Marion. "Justice and the Politics of Difference." In *Gender and Planning: A Reader*, edited by S. F. Fainstein and L. J. Servon, 86–103. New Brunswick: Rutgers University Press, 2005.

Yusuf, Julius B. "From Hebrew 'Slave' to Arabian 'Sage': Linking the Jewish and Muslim Narratives in the Story of Hagar, the African in Pre-Islamic Arab History." *Claremont Journal of Religion* 4 (2017) 1–34.

PART III
Text

9

Plato and the Hebrew Bible

Johann Cook

There is a definite trend among scholars to identify Platonic influences in the Greek and Hebrew Bibles.[1] Few scholars have published as much as Russell Gmirkin on ancient Near Eastern and Greek creation topics. He has already written three books on this theme. The current study (*Plato and the Making of the Hebrew Bible*, 2017) is a sequel to *Berossus and Genesis, Manetho and Exodus: Hellenistic Histories and the Date of the Pentateuch* (2006) In these books, novel literary source-critical methods were brought to bear on the questions of dating, provenance, and authorship of the Pentateuch.[2] Gmirkin brings novel arguments to the discussion. He firstly suggests a new methodological frame of reference. Secondly, he has a novel perspective on the constitution of sources. Thirdly, he has a creative view on the site where texts and sources were created and extended—in this case the Alexandrian library. In what follows, these arguments are outlined and evaluated.

1. It is an honor to dedicate this contribution to Prof. Louis Jonker, one of the brilliant students I was privileged to work with. It was especially true for our collaboration in respect of the organizing of the IOSOT congress that took place in Stellenbosch. He is a colleague, collaborator, academic partner, and friend. I acknowledge the financial and other assistance that I received from the SANRF (South African National Science Foundation) and the University of Stellenbosch for this research. I am solely responsible for the findings of this research. I thank Prof. Edwin Hees for improving my English.

2. Gmirkin, *Berossus and Genesis*, 2.

Gmirkin deals with the following aspects:[3]

1. A novel methodological frame
2. The role of the Bibliotheca Alexandriana
3. Athenian and pentateuchal legal institutions
4. Biblical, ancient Near Eastern, and Greek laws
5. Greek and ancient Near Eastern law collections
6. Greek and biblical legal narrative
7. The creation of the Hebrew Bible

A New Methodological Framework

An unmistakably novel development in this research field is the understanding of the Hebrew Bible / Old Testament as a Hellenistic text, which was formulated in a 1993 article ("The Old Testament—A Hellenistic Book?") by Niels Peter Lemche.[4] According to Gmirkin, this development actually inaugurated the modern study of the Pentateuch as a Hellenistic-era composition, noting that external evidence for the biblical text in the form of preserved manuscript fragments or references in extrabiblical texts of known date appear only in the third century BCE and later.[5] Taking the groundbreaking, at the same time devastating, impact of Alexander the Macedonian on the ancient Near Eastern / Greek context into account, Lemche questioned whether the common assumptions about the antiquity of the biblical text were correct.[6] In the process he suggested that the Hebrew Bible might have been composed in the Hellenistic era, after the penetration of Greek culture into the east. Such a late date, according to Gmirkin,[7] implied a definitive rejection of the historical criticism which posited that the Pentateuch evolved over time with phases of the biblical text dated by means of an acceptance of biblical stories whose historical value and significance had never been independently established. Instead of imagining the creation of the biblical text as taking place during the biblical period itself, according to Gmirkin, this new model postulated

3. It is not possible to deal with all these aspects in the limited space available here.
4. Gmirkin, *Berossus and Genesis*, 16.
5. Gmirkin, *Berossus and Genesis*, 9.
6. Lemche, "Old Testament," 189.
7. Gmirkin, *Berossus and Genesis*, 9.

that most of the Hebrew Bible, although conceivably preserving some ancient sources and traditions, were written centuries after the fact (*ex eventu*), in the third century BCE or even later.[8]

Semitic and/or Greek Sources

Fundamental to this new development is Gmirkin's view on sources. According to him the scientific world of textual studies primarily made use of Semitic sources, which have the implication that interpretation of source material focuses on earlier data and more problematic hypotheses that operate with dating. Gmirkin has a different approach. He finds space for the Septuagint (LXX) as the first earlier significant source for the biblical studies under discussion.[9] Two implications flow from this contention: first, that the LXX should be used in source-critical research, and second, that biblical texts could also be used for the later dating of source material.

According to Gmirkin, the evidence of the sources has been misused by applying it culturally only to the ancient Near East.[10] This testifies to a bias towards older datings and interpretations. Since 1990, Greek perspectives from the Alexandrian library have appeared progressively.

The Alexandrian Library

The Great Library of Alexandria in Egypt was one of the best equipped and significant libraries in the ancient world.[11] It was part of a larger research institution, the Mouseion of Alexandria dedicated to the Muses, the nine goddesses of the fine arts. It was probably constructed by one of the Ptolemies, presumably Ptolemy II Philadelphos. According to legend, the Septuagint was written during his reign in Koine Greek and is a Jewish Hellenistic document proper.[12] One should be careful not to think of this library in modern terms. The library was a formidable structure and apparently housed between forty thousand and four hundred thousand

8. Gmirkin, "Historical Context of the Septuagint," 33–34.
9. Gmirkin, *Berossus and Genesis*, 34.
10. Gmirkin, *Berossus and Genesis*, 9.
11. MacLeod, "Alexandria in History and Myth"; Collins, *Library in Alexandria*.
12. Wright, *Letter of Aristeas*, 22.

scrolls at its peak.[13] It consisted of a cluster of buildings, including depots where books were housed. Unfortunately very little is known about the functioning of the library and of the works kept in the library.[14] According to legend, books from various countries were included in the library. These seemingly would have included Greek literature, such as the Septuagint. Fraser thinks it possible that Greek texts, inter alia the Greek translations of the various Hebrew Biblical texts, were added to the library as they were created, according to the Letter of Aristeas.[15]

The Aristeas Letter/Book

This source is significant as it is the only one related directly to the Septuagint, especially septuagintal origins.[16] Almost all scholars recognize that it was written sometime in the second century BCE and that the translation of the Pentateuch had most likely been done in the third century.[17]

As to be expected, there are various possible reasons why the Aristeas text was created. Some scholars search for historical data in it, and there has accordingly been a concerted effort to "mine" the text for historical facts.[18] However other scholars, such as van der Kooij, hold more nuanced views. He discusses various models and opts for a historical one.[19] According to van der Kooij, the Jewish community in Alexandria was hardly involved in the project to produce a Greek version of the Torah.[20] Rather, it was an initiative of the Ptolemaic court, on the one hand, and the Jewish authorities in Jerusalem, on the other.

Another issue, that is related to this one, is identifying who the translators were. Another question was determining to which milieu or circles they belonged. For van der Kooij, there is just one answer: they are to be found in learned, *scribal* circles.[21] This means that the transla-

13. MacLeod, "Alexandria in History and Myth," 9.

14. Fraser, *Ptolemaic Alexandria*, 330.

15. Fraser, *Ptolemaic Alexandria*, 330.

16. It is not necessary here to be exhaustive. See especially Wright, *Letter of Aristeas*, with commentary.

17. Wright, *Letter of Aristeas*, 5.

18. Wright, *Letter of Aristeas*, 5.

19. Kooij, "Septuagint of the Pentateuch"; Honigman, *Septuagint and Homeric Scholarship*.

20. Kooij, "Study of the Septuagint."

21. Kooij, "Study of the Septuagint," 229.

tion of biblical texts was done in the setting of the "school." Other settings are the religious one[22] and the interlinear[23] one, which according to Pietersma is also a school setting.[24]

Discussion

One of my main criticisms concerns Gmirkin's view on the Alexandrian library[25] and the seventy/seventy-two persons mentioned in the Aristeas Letter.[26] There is no historical evidence to substantiate some of his claims.[27] However, this should not prevent us from endeavoring to retrovert these artifacts/texts. Arie van der Kooij has indicated the way. His focus on the learned activity of scribes in translations, etc. is well-known.[28] He imagines that the work of translation could only have been done by scholars imported from Jerusalem for the express purpose of placing these translations in the library because "it was only natural to make the Greek version of the Pentateuch available in the library."[29] For this view there is also no proof, even though the probability is high.

According to Gmirkin, texts from this library had an impact on the Septuagint as well as on the Hebrew Bible.[30] He proposes that the Pentateuch was written ca. 270 BCE, drawing on a variety of sources written in Greek and housed in the Library of Alexandria.[31] This in turn led to the conclusion that the authors of the Pentateuch were the same group of seventy/seventy-two aristocratic, Greek-educated, Jewish scholars that ancient tradition credited with having translated the Pentateuch into Greek at Alexandria at almost exactly the same time (ca. 273–269 BCE). I have already demonstrated that I fail to understand how this could have happened.[32] The main problem remains the lack of available sources.

22. Cf. also Nodet, "Editing the Bible."

23. Cook, "Interpreting the Septuagint," 7.

24. Pietersma, "Interlinear Model," 357.

25. Gmirkin, "Historical Context of the Septuagint," 36.

26. Wright, *Letter of Aristeas*, 9.

27. Cook, "Judaism and Hellenism," 60.

28. Kooij, "Study of the Septuagint."

29. Kooij, "Study of the Septuagint," 229.

30. Gmirkin, *Berossus and Genesis*, 3.

31. The *Bibliotheca Alexandrina* is a modern commemoration of the ancient library in Alexandria that was lost in antiquity.

32. Cook, "Judaism and Hellenism," 67.

Unfortunately, we have no reliable extant sources. This is the result of the Romans (specifically under Julius Caesar)[33] apparently having accidentally burned the Mouseion down, or it may have been other groups; it is even possible that it simply deteriorated over the course of time. Even though it is possible that the library could have housed between forty thousand to four hundred thousand scrolls at one time, this cannot be used as decisive proof that the Greek and Hebrew Bibles came into being in this library. The original artifacts simply no longer exist.[34]

For this reason, the inferences Gmirkin makes about the Alexandrian library must be handled with great care. I certainly detected a number of speculations, albeit "informed" and "creative" speculations. This is also true of his proposition that the Pentateuch and the Hebrew Bible as a whole collection derive from the writings of Plato found at the Great Library of Alexandria.[35]

The extensive corpus of Greek legal writings at the Library of Alexandria (Mouseion) in the early Hellenistic era, according to Gmirkin,[36] raises the possibility that Jewish knowledge of Athenian legal institutions was mediated by Jewish access to Greek skills, drawing on the two stages of creation in Plato's *Timaeus*. (This suggestion is speculative, in my view.)

In what follows I briefly follow up on aspects of Gmirkin's *Plato and the Making of the Hebrew Bible* (2017). I cannot be exhaustive because of the limited space and time. It is furthermore also true that the author has broken new ground that will have to be dealt with by specialists.

Athenian and Pentateuchal Institutions

Gmirkin finds parallels between Athenian and pentateuchal institutions.[37] He argues that the *ktisis*, or literary genre of the foundation story, was one of the most popular among the ancient Greeks. In a typical Greek foundation story, negative circumstances lead to the sending forth of an expedition under the divinely sanctioned leadership of a founder figure, who leads his forces to establish a colony in a new land.[38] The founder

33. MacLeod, "Alexandria in History and Myth"; Collins, *Library in Alexandria*.
34. MacLeod, "Alexandria in History and Myth," 17.
35. Gmirkin, *Plato and the Making*, 1.
36. Gmirkin, *Plato and the Making*, 3.
37. Gmirkin, *Plato and the Making*, 9.
38. Gmirkin, *Plato and the Making*, 10.

figure acted as commander (leader), religious guide, and lawgiver. According to Gmirkin, conquering territory for settlement and apportioning of land, as well as the setting up of altars, were his responsibility.[39] This included the writing of a constitution and laws for the new nation. According to Gmirkin, the biblical story about the Israelite exodus and sojourn in the wilderness, under the leadership of Moses, and the conquest under his successor, Joshua, closely conform to this Greek literary genre.[40] The presentation of the Mosaic law codes within a recognizably Greek narrative framework, according to Gmirkin, raises the possibility that the law codes themselves may display influences from Greek legal genres and content.[41] Gmirkin posits two arguments to prove his point that Plato in fact influenced the Hebrew Bible: firstly, the contention that the content of the Hebrew Bible comes mainly from Plato, and secondly, that it has its origins in the Hellenistic era by virtue of the existence of Greek constitutional elements within the Pentateuch.[42]

In my opinion these aspects have not been established beyond any doubt. As a matter of fact, the same speculative approach detected in previous work by Gmirkin appears here again. This also applies to the methodological approach followed by the author. The research boundaries between the Greek and ancient Near Eastern worlds are not accounted for. This applies to authors in Hellenistic and Roman antiquity, who viewed the Torah as the authoritative constitutional document of the Jews. These authors included ancient Jewish writers and the church fathers as well as Ptolemaic, Seleucid, Jewish, and Roman regimes who all interpreted the Torah as the foundational document that recorded the ancestral laws and constitution of the Jews. This ancient interpretation of the Torah as possessing constitutional elements is, according to Gmirkin, supported by the biblical scholarship of recent decades that also detects Greek constitutional content in the Pentateuch, especially in Deuteronomy.[43]

As far as the second example is concerned, it is significant that the biblical tribal enrollment in Numbers was for the purpose of military organization.[44] Like the Athenian military structure, the biblical army was grouped into tribal divisions (Num 1–3, 10, 26) and biblical, ancient Near

39. Gmirkin, *Plato and the Making*, 11.

40. Gmirkin, *Plato and the Making*, 11.

41. Gmirkin, *Plato and the Making*, 12.

42. Gmirkin, *Plato and the Making*, 13.

43. Gmirkin, *Plato and the Making*, 9.

44. Gmirkin, *Plato and the Making*, 14.

Eastern, and Greek laws. This is a generalization by Gmirkin without any substantiating evidence that the biblical authors in fact had Plato in hand while construing Numbers. It cannot be denied that there is some general correspondence between these phrases, but this does not mean that the authors of the book of Numbers had Plato in hand (or in their heads, for that matter!) while formulating the text.

A final example occurs in the following statement by the author: "If it is accepted that the Pentateuch was authored at the Great Library of Alexandria, as evidenced by the various Greek sources the Pentateuch drew on, then this would provide an economical explanation for the international setting implicit in Deut. 4.6–8."[45] Legislative research conducted at Alexandria's library by the Jewish jurists who authored the Pentateuchal law collections could have exposed them to constitutions and laws found in city-states elsewhere in the Greek world, including Athens, providing the Deuteronomists with a comparison of Israelite law to those of other nations. Furthermore, the addition of the Pentateuch (in Greek translation) to the Great Library's holdings made the Mosaic laws immediately available to a wider international reading audience, much as Deut 4:6–8 envisioned. The laws of Moses were thus arguably composed and published in conversation with the legal traditions of the wider Mediterranean world.

According to Gmirkin it is entirely legitimate to view Mosaic and Greek legal traditions, including those at Athens, as part of the same historical stream during the early Hellenistic era, justifying a direct comparison of biblical and Greek laws.[46] Sources for the study of Greek laws are abundant and varied. The most important sources are legal inscriptions from Classical Greece, especially Athens, where there was a strong tradition of posting written laws for public display. Much of the original wording of Drakon's famous homicide law of ca. 620 BCE, for instance, has been preserved in an inscription discovered during nineteenth-century excavations in the Agora at Athens. A large number of Athenian laws are known from the forensic speeches of the classical Greek orators, which often quoted or summarized statutes relevant to the cases being argued. Many references to Greek laws appeared in historical works, poetry, and even Greek tragedies and comedies because of the important role written law played in the daily life of the *polis*. The Greek world also

45. Gmirkin, *Plato and the Making*, 298.

46. Gmirkin, *Plato and the Making*, 171.

produced a substantial body of prose literature devoted to legal topics. Ideal government was a common topic of the Classical Greek philosophers, with books that dealt with various aspects of politics that were authored by Plato, Aristotle, Theophrastus, Demetrius of Phalerum, and others. Some of these books dealt specifically with the constitution and laws of Greek city-states, most prominently Athens. Unfortunately, most of this literature has perished and is known to us only by author and title. In a few other cases, some fragments have survived in quotations from later authors. A handful of texts authored by the philosophers Plato and Aristotle have come down to us substantially intact.[47]

The problem remains, there is no proof that the Pentateuch was in fact authored at the Library of Alexandria![48]

Conclusions

Gmirkin has come up with interesting comparative material. However, there are no incontrovertible arguments to substantiate his conclusions. Gmirkin unfortunately adopts the same speculative approach that I detected in his earlier research. However, having said that, one has to give credit where it is due. He has ventured into speculative realms without a clear ideological basis. Yet in the process he has ventured beyond the boundaries set in previous scholarship. To me it is clear that his promising research findings must still be tested to the full.

Bibliography

Collins, Nina L. *The Library in Alexandria and the Bible in Greek*. Vetus Testamentum Supplements 82. Leiden: Brill, 2000.

Cook, Johann. "Judaism and Hellenism, Did They Ever Meet? Reflections on Biblical Creation Stories." In Cook and Kotzé, *The Septuagint South of Alexandria*, 50–69.

———. "Platonism and the 'Bible(s).'" *HTS Theological Studies* 78 (2022) 1–8. https://doi.org/10.4102/hts.v78i1.7432.

———. "Reflecting on the Creation (בְּרֵשִׁית)—Comparison of Genesis 1 in the Pentateuchal Targumim and the Septuagint." In *Septuagint, Targum and Beyond: Comparing Aramaic and Greek Versions from Jewish Antiquity*, edited by David J. Shepherd et al., 13–36. Leiden: Brill, 2022.

47. Gmirkin, *Plato and the Making*, 74.

48. I am aware of the research of Eckhard Otto on possible Platonic influence in the Hebrew Bible (see Otto, "Qahal und Ekklesia"). However, since my focus is on the Septuagint, I decided not to address these issues here.

Cook, Johann, and Gideon R. Kotzé, eds. *The Septuagint South of Alexandria. Essays on the Greek Translations and Other Ancient Versions by the Association for the Study of the Septuagint in South Africa (LXXSA).* Vetus Testamentum Supplements 193. Leiden: Brill, 2022.

Feldman, Louis H. *Jewish Culture in Judea, Judaism and Hellenism Reconsidered.* Supplements to the Journal for the Study of Judaism 107. Leiden: Brill, 2006.

Fraser, Peter M. *Ptolemaic Alexandria.* Oxford: Clarendon, 1977.

Gmirkin, Russell E. *Berossus and Genesis, Manetho and Exodus: Hellenistic Histories and the Date of the Pentateuch.* The Library of the Hebrew Bible / Old Testament Studies 433. New York: T&T Clark, 2006.

———. "The Historical Context of the Septuagint and Its Hebrew Vorlage." In Cook and Kotzé, *The Septuagint South of Alexandria*, 28–49.

———. *Plato and the Making of the Hebrew Bible.* New York: Routledge, 2017.

———. *Plato's Timaeus and the Biblical Creation Accounts: Cosmic Monotheism and Terrestrial Polytheism in the Primordial History*. New York: Routledge, 2020.

Hengel, Martin. "Judaism and Hellenism Revisited." In *Hellenism in the Land of Israel*, edited by John J. Collins and G. E. Sterling, 6–37. Notre Dame: University of Notre Dame Press, 2001.

Honigman, Sidnie. *The Septuagint and Homeric Scholarship. A Study in the Narrative of the Letter of Aristeas.* Routledge: London, 2003.

Kooij, Arie van der. "Perspectives on the Study of the Septuagint: Who Are the Translators?" In *Perspectives in the Study of the Old Testament and Early Judaism: A Symposium in Honour of Adam S. van der Woude on the Occasion of His 70th Birthday*, edited by Florentino García Martínez and Ed Noort, Vetus Testamentum Supplements 73, 214–29. Leiden: Brill, 1998.

———. "The Septuagint of the Pentateuch and Ptolemaic Rule." In *The Pentateuch as Torah: New Models for Understanding Its Promulgation and Acceptance*, edited by G. N. Knoppers and B. M. Levinson, 289–300. Winona Lake, IN: Eisenbrauns, 2007.

Lemche, Niels P. "The Old Testament—a Hellenistic Book?" *Scandinavian Journal of the Old Testament* 7 (1993) 163–93.

MacLeod, Roy. "Introduction: Alexandria in History and Myth." In *The Library of Alexandria: Center of Learning in the Ancient World*, edited by Roy MacLeod, 1–18. London: IB Tauris.

Nodet, Ettienne. "Editing the Bible, Palestine or Babylonia?" In *The Bible and Hellenism: Greek Influence on Jewish and Early Christian Literature*, edited by Thomas L. Thompson and P. Wajdenbaum, 36–55. New York: Routledge, 2011.

Otto, Eckhard. "Qahal und Ekklesia im Deuteronomium und in der politischen Theorie in Platons Nomoi." In *Qahal und Ekklesia: Typen und Funktionen von Versammlungen im Alten und Neuen Testament und ihren Umwelten*, edited by J. J. Krause et al., Studies in Cultural Contexts of the Bible 19, 221–48. Leiden: Brill, 2024.

Pietersma Albert. "The Interlinear Model and the Septuagint." In *Bible and Computer: The Stellenbosch AIBI-6 Conference; Proceedings of the Association Internationale Bible et Informatique "From Alpha to Byte" University of Stellenbosch 17–21 July, 2000*, edited by Johann Cook, 337–64. Leiden: Brill, 2002.

Wright, B. G. *The Letter of Aristeas: "Aristeas to Philocrates" or "On the Translation of the Law of the Jews."* Berlin: de Gruyter, 2015.

10

Chronicles and "Theodicy"

Related Concerns in Philosophy of Religion as Second-Order Discourse

Jaco Gericke

The word *theodicy* can be considered both a term of art and an essentially contested concept in contemporary research on the book(s) of Chronicles. More specifically, it often appears in, but is not limited to, scholarly remarks on how the Chronicler's concept(s) of God is perceived to be related to different degrees and kinds of evil and suffering in the world of the text.[1] An example of this would be the following attempt to clarify the inexact folk-metaphysics of causal relata combining divine rule and moral teleology within history-like narratives.

1. Which means all related research is somehow concerned therewith, even when not using the particular term, and perhaps opting for something similar in theology or the history of religion, and less obviously borrowed from philosophy of religion. This is evident in the commentary on the various relevant texts and contexts highlighted in the discussion to follow. For the broader introduction to all the associated background issues of interest in research on Chronicles that will be assumed in this article, the reader may consult leading commentaries and publications on theology and history in Chronicles. Examples include Ackroyd, "Theology of the Chronicler"; Braun, *1 Chronicles;* Japhet, *I and II Chronicles*; Japhet, *1 Chronik* and *2 Chronik*; Jonker, *1 and 2 Chronicles*; Klein, *1 Chronicles*; Knoppers, *I Chronicles 1–9* and *I Chronicles 10–29*; McKenzie, *1–2 Chronicles*; Tuell, *First and Second Chronicles.*

> For the Chronicler like for all biblical historians, the ultimate "cause" is God's rule of the world, determined by his attributes, the principles by which his rule can be comprehended. The most emphasised of these attributes in the Chronicler's view of history is God's justice, and one of the most significant goals of his history-writing is the demonstration of how the history of Israel is a constant and consistent application of God's just rule. Although this view applies to the entire work, its most pervasive expression is found in the book's third section, depicting the history of Israel during the reign of the Davidic dynasty (2 Chr. 10–36). Chr., very much like the Deuteronomistic historiography that preceded it, may thus be termed "a work of theodicy."[2]

However, the same author felt the need to qualify the claim just made:

> "The traditional concerns of theodicy, such as the origin of evil and its final requiting, are not really addressed in the book. Nor is there any attempt to answer (or repudiate) the question of innocent suffering, which we might expect as part of a rigorous theory of retribution." This is an example of a "circular argument," based on an *a priori* limited definition of theodicy and its goals.[3]

The interest in theodicy and its use in descriptions of one of the concerns of the Chronicler is hardly limited to the texts in question. This is itself implicit in the context in which the chosen example occurs—namely, an edited volume on theodicy in the biblical world:

> Is it justice when deities allow righteous human beings to suffer? This question has occupied the minds of theologians and philosophers for many centuries and is still hotly disputed. All kinds of argument have been developed to exonerate the "good God" of any guilt in this respect. Since Leibniz it has become

2. Japhet, "Theodicy," 449n41. Japhet also references a spectrum of different views on whether and how Chronicles can be described as a "theodicy" (e.g., among Old Testament theologians, someone like Eichrodt denied this possibility while Von Rad affirmed it). Compare this with the absence of a discussion of Chronicles and theodicy in the writings of a leading scholar on the subject, i.e., Crenshaw, *Theodicy in the Old Testament*, and more recently, *Defending God*. The difference between the two publications (edited volume vs. monograph) and in the wording ("Theodicy" vs. "Defending," "Responses," and "the Problem of Evil") are noteworthy for reasons that will become readily apparent in the discussion to follow.

3. Japhet, "Theodicy," 449n41; Japhet here is quoting from Kelly, *Eschatology and Retribution*, 107.

> customary to describe such attempts as "theodicy," the justification of God. In modern philosophical debate this use of "theodicy" has been questioned. However, this volume shows that it is still a workable term for a concept that originated much earlier than is commonly realised.[4]

This distinction between the biblical scholarly term and the religious-philosophical concept is of particular interest for the present discussion. More specifically, given the already acknowledged relations between discussions of theodicy and Chronicles and certain religious-philosophical presuppositions, problems, and perspectives, the originality of the present contribution will come from the ways in which it will raise and respond to the following questions.[5]

1. What are some of the epistemologically prior concepts, concerns, and categories contextualising constructions of theodicy within contemporary philosophy of religion?
2. What happens when said concepts, concerns, and categories are considered with special attention to their relation to theodicy, on the one hand, and the relation of their conjunction to Chronicles, on the other?
3. How might such an expansion of the theoretical framework benefit future research on Chronicles and theodicy?

In response to these questions, it is hypothesised that extending discussions of "theodicy" and Chronicles to correlate it with other issues of interest in contemporary analytic philosophy of religion will allow for a more nuanced and meaningful comparison between the first- and second-order religious language at play. The objectives of this article can be formulated in the mirror image of the research questions—that is, the identification of, experimentation with, and proposals for an informed application of the religious-philosophical auxiliary discourse supervening on the current debates. Concordantly, a theoretical, experimental, and comparative religious-philosophical approach will be adopted as method.[6] The relevance and motivation for doing so

4. Laato and de Moor, *Theodicy*, publisher's synopsis.

5. The present discussion within Hebrew Bible (HB) scholarship using philosophy of religion as an auxiliary discipline is to be distinguished from philosophers of religion reflecting on the HB with other ends in mind, e.g., Bergmann et al., *Divine Evil?*; Stump, *Wandering in Darkness*.

6. Additional methodological justification for this has been discussed elsewhere

is that it will allow exploring both biblical and philosophical contexts of discourse to be sampled with minimal risk of committing the kind of interpretative fallacies associated with doing so. Therein also lies the originality of the article.

As regards outline, the questions posed in the three points above will be discussed thematically and concurrently. The typical themes will be adopted, adapted, and applied from analytic philosophy of religion purely to structure the discussion and without ontological commitment to corresponding entities in the first-order discourse used to construct the world of the text. In this way, the perspective offered may be distinguished from interpretations where an external anachronistic philosophical framework is imposed on the data claiming shared interests in conceptually-historically anachronistic ways.

Chronicles and the Philosophy of Religion

Some additional qualifying preliminary remarks are in order before commencing with the comparison proper.

First, as with all auxiliary disciplines in Hebrew Bible / Old Testament scholarship, at the forefront of research there is no consensus on what is meant by philosophy[7] or religion[8] and concordantly their combination within the discipline of interest. However, in this chapter the focus is merely on some of the background concerns in philosophy of religion that contextualise and supervene on any discussion of the problem of evil. Doing so does not require Chronicles to be similarly concerned, a particular relation between the text and theodicy, or an argument showing its (ir)relevance for current debates philosophy of religion.

Second, it is not assumed that Chronicles is a theodicy or a "religious-philosophical treatise," only that one can enrich the discussion of its relation to theodicy by noting similarities and differences between the ontological commitments in its first-order discourse with that of the chosen idiom and current in philosophy of religion. More specifically, religious-philosophical discussions of theodicy cannot be clearly separated from trying to determine what is (not) incidentally assumed

---

and cannot be provided here. For the relevant arguments, see Gericke, *Hebrew Bible*.

7. For the relevant conceptual and fundamental differences, see Joll, "Metaphilosophy."

8. Schilbrack, "Concept of Religion."

by the Chronicler in relation to the problems of religious language, the concept of God, the existence of God, religion and morality, and most obviously, the problem of evil.

Third, in terms of structuring the discussion on Chronicles and theodicy, one would ideally start with a discussion of the problem of evil. After all, this is where theodicy is usually located as a response and therefore primarily at home at. However, since the Chronicler is not a philosopher of religion, reflection on more fundamental presuppositions related to supervening problems and perspectives must precede the discussion of theodicy proper.[9]

Fourth, the focus on specific words and concepts in texts from English translations is meant to highlight certain more explicit and surface-level comparative aspects within popular second-order discourses and not to be confused with proof texts in favour of a particular philosophical-theological doctrine or even exegetical claim. All available linguistic, literary-critical, historical-critical, social-scientific, religious-historical, and theological research are presupposed without it being possible to correlate the comments to the relevant considerations for each text in the set of samples illustrating a particular point. In this way the discussions can be distinguished from trying to force the text into a philosophical system or using it as a pretext to make a contemporary religious-philosophical argument better at home in reception history or philosophy proper.

Chronicles and the Problem of Religious Language

The term *religious language*[10] refers to all the statements or claims made about God or gods in the two books. For the purposes of discussing the concept of theodicy as a religious-philosophical category in relation to Chronicles, let us distinguish between RL1 which is the religious language of the books of Chronicles where philosophy of religion does not supervene, and RL2 or the language of biblical scholars about RL1 where it does. RL1 lacks many words in RL2 like *history* or *text* or *theodicy*, but

9. For a helpful overview of current related presuppositions, problems, and perspectives in different traditions and religions and in the analytic tradition especially, see Taliaferro, "Philosophy of Religion"; Taliaferro et al., *Companion to Philosophy of Religion*. For a more historical sense of the changing landscape and the anachronism of certain concepts and concerns, see Oppy, *Arguing About Gods*; Oppy and Trakakis, *Western Philosophy of Religion*.

10. For a philosophical overview of the relevant philosophical concepts, concerns, and categories, see Scott, "Religious Language"; Hart-Weed, "Religious Language."

these and the auxiliary disciplines from which they come are deemed useful for comparative and analytic purposes. Sometimes a concept in RL2 can be present in RL1 even if the word is not—e.g., reality—but usually the ontology[11] of RL1 and 2 can be distinguished, even if not coherently separated once a reading commences. That is, we know RL1 only through various forms of RL2, all of which target their own set of conceptual content in the world of the text (where no absolute separation is present, e.g., between religion and society, culture, history, etc.).

For example, are references to YHWH in relation to moral properties such as good and evil implicit but not distinguished in Chronicles,[12] assumed to have the same sense as when used of human characters (assuming the possibility of differences in nuance, a plurality of associated assumptions, and aside from axiological, aesthetic, and pragmatic senses of the terms, e.g., utility, etc.)? Another problem relates to the theory of the nature of RL1 most popular in RL2, i.e., that it is metaphorical. There is a sense in which describing RL1 as metaphorical is a non-informative trivial datum. This is partly since all language is so. That does not mean that there was no assumed difference between the deity and humans in drawing on certain source domains from socio-cultural contexts. The same is true for other supervening source domains and the roles related to them, i.e., kings, warriors, judges, spouses, artists, and sages. Likewise, the same words in the source and target domains themselves have histories, so simply repeating the Hebrew or translation is not in itself informative of associative meaning at all. Of course, the problem is not merely reading in context but also that contexts have to be reconstructed, and there is neither just one domain of discourse in RL2 nor a unified or descriptively adequate religious-philosophical

11. According to Moltmann, "natural language ontology is the study of the ontology (ontological categories, structures, and notions) implicit in natural language. Natural language ontology is part of 'descriptive metaphysics' . . . a sub-discipline of both philosophy and linguistics, more specifically, of metaphysics and natural language semantics." He continues, "The ontology of natural language is to be distinguished from the ontology a speaker accepts on the basis of philosophical or naïve reflection or reasoning using language, as well as from the ontology that is reflected in cognition in general. The ontology of a natural language is thus best characterized as the ontology competent speakers implicitly accept by way of using the language." Moltmann, "Natural Language Ontology."

12. Though other terms and names for the deity appears in Chronicles, the Tetragrammaton (or "God," or "the deity" or "the divine") will be used for the sake of simplicity while admitting doing so in any other context will sacrifice too much nuance and religious-historical specificity.

idiom to decide the matter with reference to theodicy (e.g., differences in analytic, continental, and other conceptualisations).

Another problem with relating theodicy to RL1 in Chronicles is simply the vagueness and inexact folk-metaphysics involved. Thus, the references to the deity as having certain properties, relations, kinds, agency seems to have elements of univocality, equivocality, and analogy. It can be difficult to tell if the Chronicler was ontologically committed to everything assumed by the sources used in relation to RL beyond the obvious revisionary aspects. One can reflect on the Chronicler's relation to other biblical (and associated) traditions, or on the socio-cultural context(s) in the world behind the text as condition of its possibility. Yet without triangulating one's findings with some comparative religious-philosophical conceptual framework, no descriptively apt account of the ontology of RL1 co-constituting the world of the text is possible.

In other words, it is one thing to describe the divine like a king or a warrior or a spouse, but how many of the properties in the source domain were assumed to apply in the target domain? It is another to ask what moral properties ascribed to moral agents in those contexts were assumed to mean. Likewise, where attribution occurs in the context of poetry and life settings derived from political flattery, how much of it can actually be meaningfully clarified as regards reference and associated qualitative and quantitative dimensions of moral properties? Without some attempt to provide answers to these questions, attempts to make sense of how Chronicles may or may not be related to theodicy will start off presumptuous and end likewise. What can and should be considered in this section is more than is presently practical. Suffice it to note that a comparative assessment of RL1 in relation to RL2 categories is required as the first point of conceptual clarification, as corrective of imported philosophical assumptions, or simply to conclude with a challenge of insurmountable obscurity.

Chronicles and Concepts of God

Since all readings are reductive and auxiliary, and there is no perfect or descriptively final RL2, it might be helpful to remember that speaking of the concept of God is itself philosophical language.[13] Historically it is

13. As is evident in the titles of, e.g., Morley, "God, Western Concepts of"; Buckareff and Nagasawa, *Alternative Concepts of God*.

the (neo-)Kantian heritage in psychology and cognitive science and both technical term and popular word in ordinary language. These senses mix in RL2 as do theories of concepts, as is evident when the same scholar refers to something akin to essential features, necessary conditions, typical traits, theoretical frameworks, etc. These in turn link up with different theories of concepts, themselves seldom noted in discussions of the concept of God in Chronicles. Even if one is reluctant to assign YHWH a nature and attributes in descriptive discourse, substitutions with other ontologically reductive alternatives, e.g., a character and characteristics, are themselves not without problems.[14] The use of concept or words, names, ideas, images, beliefs signs, or the intellectual world, Hebrew thought, worldview instead of philosophical (folk) assumptions are similarly overlapping and motivated by historical tensions.

For the purposes of considering theodicy, part of the problem in philosophy of religion stems from the presumptions of a concept of God instantiating certain sets of metaphysical and moral attributes. In an attempt to avoid imposing distortive philosophical frameworks, most of the discussion of Chronicles and theodicy emphasises the textual assumptions about divine justice in relation to suffering (on the etymology of the word). However, in a comparative approach there is no reason why one cannot try to determine what the Chronicler does and does not incidentally assume with reference to those divine attributes usually associated with the problem of evil to which theodicy is a response—namely, power, knowledge, and goodness. Of course, there is more to this than explicit references in RL2 translated to the same semantic field, yet for the purposes of illustration of the point of this section, the example given should suffice (without assuming conceptual coherency or normativity or intent or ontological commitment). The discussion below will only introduce the concepts, with special attention to more detailed instantiations of the particular property in the world of the text in the discussion to follow.

In terms of power (to prevent evil), the inexact metaphysical assumptions are hardly quantifiable. Translating associated Hebrew words in RL1 as "power," "might," or "strength" presents the reader only with more "fuzzy concepts." These do not feature exemplifications of the property by the deity in divine agency within the world of the text but are rather found in predication by other characters in the context of

14. See Gericke, *What Is a God*? and *Philosophical Theology*.

hyperbolic and vague rhetoric. From the samples below it should be clear that the ontological commitment involved and its relation to the concerns of theodicy do not allow for clear and concise restatement in the sort of propositional form required for conceptual clarification.

> Yours, O LORD, are the greatness, the power, the glory, the victory, and the majesty, for all that is in the heavens and on the earth is yours; yours is the kingdom, O LORD, and you are exalted as head above all. Riches and honor come from you, and you rule over all. In your hand are power and might, and it is in your hand to make great and to give strength to all. (1 Chr 29:11–12)[15]

> O LORD, God of our ancestors, are you not God in heaven? Do you not rule over all the kingdoms of the nations? In your hand are power and might, so that no one is able to withstand you. (2 Chr 20:6)

> Rather, go by yourself and act; be strong in battle, or God will fling you down before the enemy, for God has power to help or to overthrow. (2 Chr 25:8)

At the very least, texts like these and other explicit references to divine power can, however, *prima facie* still be related to theodicy in the following ways. First, divine power in these texts, however the words are translated or understood, is not omnipotence in the later senses debated in classical theism's perfect being theory. Second, maximal greatness in instantiation is relative to the function of divine power in divine relations to humans, and to the overlapping aspects of the source domain used in a particular context of analogical predication. Third, the deity is implicated in the folk-metaphysics of causal relations in the actualisation of good and evil. Fourth, divine power is what makes the deity worthy of worship, even more so than divine goodness, which in turn is something not unrelated to concerns in the problem of evil and theodicy.

The same challenges for conceptual clarification with reference to divine power also apply for making sense of divine knowledge (of evil). One condition of possibility for the meaningfulness of the language of the lament is the assumed link between divine power and divine knowledge. That is, the deity is not only able to stop suffering but is aware thereof (although prayer has its own philosophical assumptions about divine knowledge media or power actualisation). Here, what is in view is not omniscience but very specific types of knowing-that, knowing-how, and

15. All biblical verses are quoted from the NRSV.

knowledge by acquaintance (as is sometimes distinguished in discussions of kinds of knowledge in epistemology).[16] The kind is knowledge of moral status, and the degree is, from a consideration of the broader context, not always immediate, often mediated and requiring confirmation through evidence of object relations over time. As with power it is also implicit in the sharing of the property without diminishment in doing so.

> And what more can David say to you for honoring your servant? You know your servant. (1 Chr 17:18)

> Give me now wisdom and knowledge to go out and come in before this people, for who can rule this great people of yours? (2 Chr 1:10)

> Then hear from heaven, your dwelling place, forgive, and render to all whose hearts you know, according to all their ways, for only you know the human heart. (2 Chr 6:30)

> For the eyes of the LORD range throughout the entire earth to strengthen those whose heart is true to him. You have done foolishly in this, for from now on you will have wars. (2 Chr 16:9)

From the above it is clear that divine knowledge has both different senses and references, another challenge for conceptual clarification but not so much for comparative assessment limited to identifying ontological vagueness.

What about the other divine attribute of interest in the formulation of the problem of evil within which theodicy belongs as a type of response, i.e., divine goodness (wanting to oppose evil). Again, all the conditions and challenges related to divine power and knowledge apply to any attempted conceptual clarification of this property, which is mostly implicit in narration and explicit in RL1 predication by others. It is not limited to the exact abstract wording (goodness, as opposed to good and the semantic field) in English, of which the particular (NRSV) translation only has two instances:

> Now rise up, O LORD God, and go to your resting place, you and the ark of your might. Let your priests, O LORD God, be clothed with salvation, and let your faithful rejoice in your goodness. (2 Chr 6:41)

16. For the relevant religious-epistemological context of the related concerns, see Audi, *Rationality and Religious Commitment*, 925.

> On the twenty-third day of the seventh month he sent the people away to their homes, joyful and in good spirits because of the goodness that the LORD had shown to David and to Solomon and to his people Israel. (2 Chr 7:10)

Here too it is not goodness *simpliciter* or perfect goodness which is in view but a very specific kind relative to a utility function. Most of what should be included under divine goodness as concept is not so specifically worded and has already been discussed with reference to the Chronicler's own choice of words for justice, righteousness, and related. However, since the focus here is one comparison with the conceptual framework contextualising theodicy, these samples reveal the problems of identity conditions for the concepts involved along with differences already accumulating for the more detailed discussion later on. That being said, it would not be wrong to say that goodness was assumed to be a property of YHWH, and a higher-order one supervening on others (although the order of the supervenience relation could be reversed through power and knowledge). Even so, what is meant by goodness conceptually-historically, and its semantic field outlined by others, is substantially different from an attempted cross-culturally abstracted great-making property.

Though YHWH is never called evil, actualising good and evil were both powers of divinity in Chronicles. Though distinct, they were not seen as mutually exclusive. This point will be further explored below but will here be illustrated with a few samples in RL1 which show the absence of divine foreknowledge as it was later understood. A condition of possibility for the meaningfulness of divine motivation, divine anger, and repentance is a lack of immediate foreknowledge, and a context involving the deity as im/moral agency in the actualisation of evil.

> And God sent an angel to Jerusalem to destroy it, but when he was about to destroy it, the LORD took note and relented concerning the calamity; he said to the destroying angel, "Enough! Stay your hand." The angel of the LORD was standing by the threshing floor of Ornan the Jebusite. (1 Chr 21:15)

> Then the LORD saw that they had humbled themselves, the word of the LORD came to Shemaiah, saying, "They have humbled themselves; I will not destroy them, but I will grant them some deliverance, and my wrath shall not be poured out on Jerusalem by the hand of Shishak." (2 Chr 12:7)

> Then Micaiah said, "Therefore hear the word of the LORD: I saw the LORD sitting on his throne, with all the host of heaven standing to the right and to the left of him. And the LORD said, 'Who will entice King Ahab of Israel, so that he may go up and fall at Ramoth-gilead?' Then one said one thing, and another said another, until a certain spirit came forward and stood before the LORD, saying, 'I will entice him.' The LORD asked him, 'How?' He replied, 'I will go out and be a lying spirit in the mouth of all his prophets.' Then the LORD said, 'You are to entice him, and you shall succeed; go out and do it.'" (2 Chr 18:18–21)

All these texts are formulated in such a way that deconstructs a binary opposition between divine justice and injustice. It also involves an emergent form of precognition of evil because future states of affairs are not always already actualised but through a dualist and mediated metaphysics of causal relata. No genre considerations, appeals to primitive elements in source, or appeals to anthropomorphisms can be made without bordering on apology and anachronism, or as a result of an attempt at systematisation *ex post facto*.

Another way to approach this is through the religious-philosophical question of the relation between religion and morality, adapted to that of divinity and the moral order. In other words, before one can answer the question of assumed prevention capabilities or actions in Chronicles, another prior question to be answered can be formulated by rephrasing the so-called Euthyphro dilemma (on the gods and piety). Thus, we may ask whether the Chronicler assumed or implied (consistently or not) that something is good/evil because the divine thinks it so, or whether the divine thinks it so because it is good/evil. Indeed, elements of both moral realism and divine command theory overlap with what seems to be present in the ontological commitments related to this in RL1. The former is evident when the reason for calling YHWH *good* seems to be that the deity instantiates the property of goodness, the moral status of which is not ontologically dependent on divine axiological assessment. Here a distinction is evident in the text between moral and axiological types of goodness, i.e., goodness as a virtue of moral agents and goodness and the value of certain relations in certain events and states of affairs. Much of the description, however, appears in the context of metaphysically inexact hyperbolic theo-political flattery in contexts of worship.

> O give thanks to the LORD, for he is good, for his steadfast love endures forever! (1 Chr 16:34)

> And now, O LORD, you are God, and you have promised this good thing to your servant; therefore may it please you to bless the house of your servant so that it may continue forever before you. For you, O LORD, have blessed and are blessed forever. (1 Chr 17:26–27)

> On the twenty-third day of the seventh month he sent the people away to their homes, joyful and in good spirits because of the goodness that the LORD had shown to David and to Solomon and to his people Israel. (2 Chr 7:10)

In these texts the relationship between the divine and goodness assumes that the deity is good because the divine properties, relations, and agency exemplify the property of goodness. More to the point, YHWH in such texts is assumed to be good and so are the deity's actions in virtue of the beneficent effects of divine relation and agency being good for humans, i.e., conducive to happiness, prosperity, and, negatively, to the removal of unjust suffering, which is assumed to be intrinsically evil. As with the Euthyphro dilemma, the problem is that such a distinction between the relationship between the deity and goodness above suggests moral realism and a universal moral order with reference to which divine goodness is and can be verified as such. Yet this is not so much a problem for the Chronicler as an anomalous state of affairs resulting from the monotheistic tendencies which remove the conditions of possibility for the meaningfulness of certain forms of moral predication. Perhaps for this reason, but not limited to it, one also encounters in the text what is implied to be the opposite response to the dilemma. That is, what is good is such because it is good in the eyes of YHWH, leaving open the potential for provincialist forms of moral relativism.

> Be strong, and let us be courageous for our people and for the cities of our God, and may the LORD do what seems good to him. (1 Chr 19:13)

Alternative references are translated as *what is right*, as is found implicit in the narratives as contexts for the corresponding set of formulaic references.

> And X did what was good and right in the eyes of the LORD his God. (2 Chr 14:2, 20:32, 24:2, 25:2, 26:6, 27:2, and *passim*)

Whereas the relative perspective is sometimes that of YHWH with reference to divine agency, in other contexts like these it refers to the moral properties exemplified by human agency. It may thus be granted that the Chronicler assumed a mixture of relativism and objectivism here since the divine was conceived of as in the role of truth-maker of propositions of what counts as evil, and the deity called it evil because it was seen as a breach of the moral order (with some stability so that the opposite actions of humans would not be right in the eyes of the deity or inherently so). Hence the relevance for nuanced distinctions between different kinds of objective and relative good and evil and its relation to divinity in discussions of Chronicles and theodicy.

Chronicles and the Problem of Evil

In contemporary philosophy of religion, the problem of evil is typically seen as the problem of accounting for evil in a world created by an all-powerful, all-knowing, all-good God.[17] This is one of the reasons why the supervening concept of God from perfect being theology may motivate some scholars to consider the concept of theodicy, on the assumption it presupposes such RL, problematic. On the other hand, there is no reason why one cannot conceptually-historically reframe the problem of evil in relation to a deity who falls considerably short of omnipotence, omniscience, and moral perfection, but who could intervene in the world of the text to prevent many evils, and who knows of those evils, even if after the fact through testimony and mediated knowledge.[18]

To start with, before one can properly consider the nuances related to theodicy itself as a response to the problem of evil, it may be helpful to ask, What typology of evil can be put up for the envisaged comparison? This question is prior to asking about what evil meant in the context of Chronicles, not in the old way of imposing the philosophical framework but keeping it outside and comparing it properly. On this point, one possible distinction is between a broad and a narrow concept of evil.[19]

> The broad concept picks out any bad state of affairs, wrongful action, or character flaw, and has been divided into two categories: natural evil and moral evil. . . . In contrast to the broad concept of evil, the narrow concept of evil picks out only the

17. For the present section I am grateful for and indebted to the framework of the nuanced discussion in Tooley, "Problem of Evil." See also Meister and Moser, *Problem of Evil* as well as Meister and Taliaferro, *History of Evil*.

18. See Tooley, "Problem of Evil."

19. See Calder, "Concept of Evil."

> most morally despicable sorts of actions, characters, events, etc. . . . Since the narrow concept of evil involves moral condemnation, it is appropriately ascribed only to moral agents and their actions.[20]

Some would add metaphysical evil, following Leibniz and, as above, not without assumptions related to this in the ontology of RL1 even if it cannot be changed (e.g., elements of chaos in the cosmos not tamed completely by YHWH is a familiar theme in biblical theology and related to older mythological cosmogonies and theomachy). The other two evils often distinguished in philosophy of religion are that of natural and moral evils, associated with suffering caused by nonhuman and human causal agencies respectively (to oversimplify the conceptual complexities involved). The question is how the broad/narrow distinction, as well as those between metaphysical, natural, and moral evil, may be compared to and perhaps even distinguished, if not separated, in Chronicles. Not all explicit references should be taken at surface value, but these and others should be analysed with reference to implicit ontological commitments where discernible.

> And Ephraim went in to his wife, and she conceived and bore a son; and he called his name Beriah, because evil had befallen his house. (1 Chr 7:23)

> Then they will say, "Because they forsook the LORD the God of their fathers who brought them out of the land of Egypt, and laid hold on other gods, and worshiped them and served them; therefore he has brought all this evil upon them." (2 Chr 7:22)

> If disaster comes upon us, the sword, judgment, or pestilence, or famine, we will stand before this house, and before you, for your name is in this house, and cry to you in our distress, and you will hear and save. (2 Chr 20:9)

> Thus says the LORD: Behold, I will bring evil upon this place and upon its inhabitants, all the curses that are written in the book which was read before the king of Judah. Behold, I will gather you to your fathers, and you shall be gathered to your grave in peace, and your eyes shall not see all the evil which I will bring upon this place and its inhabitants. (2 Chr 34:24, 28)

It is important not to simply note the use of the word *evil* but to think about all the forms of suffering it is assumed to include for all involved.

20. Calder, "Concept of Evil."

Even in contexts of divine justice instantiated, it involves causing moral agents to commit moral evil for the actualisation of retribution (violence and other forms of suffering induced). However, as with the relationship between religion and morality or divinity and goodness discussed earlier, the same divergent paths are also evident with the relationship between the deity and evil. On the one hand, there is the assumption that moral evils are not just what is evil in the sight of YHWH. On the other hand, this is exactly what they are, and they are often intertwined with religion-specific cultural and contextual conditions of possibility for the meaningfulness of predicating the relevant negative moral properties in RL1. Here the moral evils as transgressions can be distinguished from those involved in retributions (but not always).

> And X did what was evil in the sight of the LORD.
> (2 Chr 22:4, 29:6, 33:2, and *passim*)

However, the relation between the deity and evil even in these texts is more complex in terms of the broader conceptual background. In the context of the problem of evil, moral evil relative to divine commands, when committed, involves retribution (as a consequence of divine goodness and justice), which itself includes the actualisation of evil states of affairs. That is, it invites punishment that includes causing other moral agents or personified nature (to use the anachronistic term) to themselves commit moral/natural evils as means of retribution. This means not only that divine goodness and justice do not have the same properties and are thus not one property but that where the former is conjoined with the latter, it is part of causal *relata* leading to the emergence of moral and natural evils through dual or multicausal agency. This is no necessary outcome, but in the world of the text the intertwining of good and evil in successive events is less problematic than it would be today. The reason for this includes the supervening considerations above, i.e., related to differences in the problem of RL, the concept of God, and the relation between religion and morality. This shows the relevance of incorporating a broader comparative conceptual framework when discussing theodicy and Chronicles.

Up to now no actual discussion of the term *theodicy* has taken place. Yet at this point the relevance of groundwork has clearly been established and partly illustrated. Consequently, the stage is set to consider the primary focus of this article, Chronicles and theodicy as already part of current research. In this regard, the first thing to note is philosophers of religion categorise theodicy as one of the possible "responses" to the problem of evil. These include "total refutations, theodicies, and defenses."[21] Such nuances are not always present in the research on Chronicles, yet failure to consider such might lead to those debating the matter talking past each other (aside from differences in assumptions related to RL, concepts of God, relation between religion / the deity and morality). As philosophers of religion use that term, theodicy

> involves the thesis that, for every actual evil found in the world, one can describe some state of affairs that it is reasonable to believe exists, and which is such that, if it exists, will provide an omnipotent and omniscient being with a morally sufficient reason for allowing the evil in question.[22]

Again, this is not the concept of God in Chronicles, so that even if it is not an argument[23] from evil, it is still a problem. It should be noted here that

> the term "theodicy" is sometimes used in a stronger sense, according to which a person who offers a theodicy is attempting to show not only that such morally sufficient reasons exist, but that the reasons cited are in fact God's reasons.[24]

This is often linked to the evidential version of the problem, not the logical one. Different scholars in philosophy of religion and in related contexts offer different typologies with different numbers of types of theodicies. Here other metaphysical concepts from the theological anthropology of the Chronicles (assumptions about personhood and personal identity, as opposed to social as well) supervene. An exhaustive survey is not possible here, but among the most important are theodicies that appeal to "the value of acquiring desirable traits of character in the face of suffering"; "libertarian free will" (an anachronism in the world of the text); thirdly, "the human and divine freedom to inflict horrendous evils upon others" (which the deity either prevents, interferes with, or only responds to later, complicating the problem); and a world of the text that is governed by divine laws (while leaving space for unforeseen and anomalous events).[25]

21. Calder, "Concept of Evil."
22. Calder, "Concept of Evil."
23. See Bergmann, "Rational Religious Belief."
24. Calder, "Concept of Evil."
25. Calder, "Concept of Evil."

Most of these concepts have already been discussed in research on Chronicles and theodicy and often include an additional background concern related to religious epistemology—that is, a concern with the rationality of beliefs about the relationship between the divine and evil in the world of the text, motivated by later concerns about the interplay between reason and faith in the world in front thereof. The assumptions implicit in RL1 that have already been identified in the literature are those in more explicit reasoning in religious thought. The relevant examples have already been identified[26] by noting the presence of argument markers (technically only indicative of arguments to morality, not informal logical arguments as found in later philosophy of religion). They include the following concepts and concerns frequently reappearing in different configurations in RL1:

- Why x? (raising a question in the context of genuine perplexity or as rhetorical at certain forms of moral or natural evil)
- Because x (where x is divine or human acts exemplifying the property of being evil and warranting divine retribution)
- Therefore x (the justification of the evil actualised by the divine)

If one pays attention to these bits of reasoning (already evidenced in some of the text quoted above), one encounters them not only sometimes conjoined but mostly appearing separately in translation on many occasions in Chronicles. They are technically not in themselves theodicies but bits and pieces of unstructured and incomplete components thereof. They quantify over divergent and piecemeal instances of (also) theodicy-like reasoning. Even so, given the complexity of divine and human relations to evil, and the inexact folk-metaphysical assumptions of causal relations involved, other terms like anthropodicy and atheodicy and a-anthropodicy would have their place. In other words, the sheer variety of idiosyncratic incidents involving suffering of any kind in the text is greater than the conceptual content generally considered relevant when reflecting on Chronicles and theodicy.

Metaphysical, natural, and moral evil are so interwoven with ordinary everyday existence that it is merely noted in passing, e.g., in agency related to basic human means of subsistence and survival. Though one could see the broader narrative frameworks as theodicy in story mode, the two books cannot be reduced to said purpose. Moreover, the distinction

26. Japhet, "Theodicy," 429–63.

between a concern with divine justice (as in theodicy) should not be confused with the Chronicler showing that individual and collective suffering at a certain point in time and over time have a sufficient reason and relate to moral evil. The mere description involving reasons given can occur even in legal settings without ever amounting to a theodicy. After all, much of the Chronicler's concern is not to show why YHWH allows and is justified in actualising evil but rather to describe divine retribution as reason for said evil. The distinction may seem trivial and pedantic. Yet at the intersection of the ontology of RL1 and RL2, it begs the question why "theodicy" remains the most popular philosophical category put up for comparison among the spectrum of possible responses to the problem of evil—even adapted to fit the Chronicler's own RL, concept of God, and assumptions about the relationship between divinity and morality. In response to this, it may be argued that because of its place in the history of RL2, even in non-philosophical readings, putting it up for comparison still amounts to some sort of conceptual clarification, even if this occurs only by way of contrast.

In discussions of Chronicles and theodicy, what philosophers of religion call "defenses" are often conflated with theodicy.[27] The former are more typically associated with the so-called argument from evil (against the existence of God). Different formulations are possible, and none are found in Chronicles. Even so, inductive and deductive formulations,[28] as well as deontological and axiological formulations of conceptual frameworks, are interesting and informative post facto abstractions that can likewise aid clarification via comparison.[29] Moreover, just because Chronicles does not try to defend the existence of the God of Israel, this does not mean nothing related is indeed present. From a comparative philosophical perspective, it is well-known that not all reasoning in religious thought appears in the form of abstracted premises and a conclusion. Moreover, there is no practical narrow atheism without unformulated theoretical assumptions that defensive reasoning (valid or not) is not present as condition of possibility for the meaningfulness in RL1.

For example, on some occasions in the world of the text, when evil occurs, it is seen as, among others, evidence of sorts for YHWH's reality and ability to cause evil in response to moral evil:

27. Crenshaw, *Defending God.*

28. For a helpful discussion on this, see Clayton, *Religion, Reasons and Gods.*

29. Calder, "Concept of Evil."

> Then they will say, "Because they abandoned the LORD the God of their ancestors who brought them out of the land of Egypt, and they embraced other gods and worshiped them and served them; therefore he has brought all this calamity upon them." (2 Chr 7:22)

It is also seen as justifying the belief that YHWH is greater than other gods and that it shows that their images, for all practical purposes, do not have existing counterparts.

> For great is the LORD and greatly to be praised; he is to be revered above all gods. For all the gods of the peoples are idols, but the LORD made the heavens. (1 Chr 16:25–26)

In this way the Chronicler's ontology allows for an argument from evil against other gods to be simultaneously a type of defense for the god of Israel. Yet there is a double standard at work in relation to other gods: when evil befalls those who worship YHWH, others are not deemed justified to infer YHWH's nonexistence, uselessness, lack of comparable greatness, or that it shows the reality of their gods.

> "Do you not know what I and my ancestors have done to all the peoples of other lands? Were the gods of the nations of those lands at all able to save their lands out of my hand? Who among all the gods of those nations that my ancestors utterly destroyed was able to save his people from my hand, that your God should be able to save you from my hand? Now, therefore, do not let Hezekiah deceive you or mislead you in this fashion, and do not believe him, for no god of any nation or kingdom has been able to save his people from my hand or from the hand of my ancestors. How much less will your God save you out of my hand!" His servants said still more against the Lord GOD and against his servant Hezekiah. He also wrote letters to throw contempt on the LORD the God of Israel and to speak against him, saying, "Just as the gods of the nations in other lands did not rescue their people from my hands, so the God of Hezekiah will not rescue his people from my hand." They shouted it with a loud voice in the language of Judah to the people of Jerusalem who were on the wall, to frighten and terrify them, in order that they might take the city. They spoke of the God of Jerusalem as if he were like the gods of the peoples of the earth, which are the work of human hands. (2 Chr 32:13–19)

One would think the opposite is the real concern, i.e., that they are speaking of the gods of the peoples as they spoke about the God of Jerusalem. However, when evil befalls those who do not worship YHWH, they are not deemed to be reasoning soundly, were they to see it as the just retribution of other gods and as the latter's response to the moral evils committed by their worshippers.

> The LORD was angry with Amaziah and sent to him a prophet, who said to him, "Why have you resorted to a people's gods who could not deliver their own people from your hand?" But as he was speaking, the king said to him, "Have we made you a royal counselor? Stop! Why should you be put to death?" So the prophet stopped but said, "I know that God has determined to destroy you because you have done this and have not listened to my advice." (2 Chr 25:15–16)

The result of this is a kind of "saving the phenomena" of suffering (assuming divine justice while not denying the events related to evil) and an error theory for apostasy and idolatry (why other gods are religious objects even when they do not exist).

> For he sacrificed to the gods of Damascus that had defeated him and said, "Because the gods of the kings of Aram helped them, I will sacrifice to them so that they may help me." But they were the ruin of him and of all Israel. Ahaz gathered together the utensils of the house of God and cut in pieces the utensils of the house of God. He shut up the doors of the house of the LORD and made himself altars in every corner of Jerusalem. In every city of Judah he made high places to make offerings to other gods, provoking to anger the LORD, the God of his ancestors. (2 Chr 28:23–25)

This becomes even more nuanced in the attempt to combine considerations related to the anomalies arising from any attempt to resolve some of the complexities that had emerged within the Chronicler's logic of belief revision. In the RL2 of reasoning in RL1, this included updating, revising, and recovering received ideas about individual and collective, ancestral and transgenerational, and ruler and ruled–related retribution. It also involved anomalous instances, reconciled by removing/reinserting exceptions to the rule into the broader belief base.

> "Thus says the LORD: I will indeed bring disaster upon this place and upon its inhabitants, all the curses that are written

> in the book that was read before the king of Judah. Because they have forsaken me and have made offerings to other gods, so that they have provoked me to anger with all the works of their hands, my wrath will be poured out on this place and will not be quenched." But as to the king of Judah, who sent you to inquire of the LORD, thus shall you say to him: Thus says the LORD, the God of Israel: "Regarding the words that you have heard, because your heart was penitent and you humbled yourself before God when you heard his words against this place and its inhabitants, and you have humbled yourself before me and have torn your clothes and wept before me, I also have heard you, says the LORD. I will gather you to your ancestors and you shall be gathered to your grave in peace; your eyes shall not see all the disaster that I will bring on this place and its inhabitants." (2 Chr 34:25–28)

With such a line of reasoning, the Chronicler has in effect immunised his RL against challenges posed by contextual historical grounds for verification and falsification of associated truth claims. The latter pertains also the limits of belief revision and conceptual change in the face of evil.

Conclusion

In view of the above, a distinction may be made between Chronicles and theodicy as part of the purpose of the broader historical narrative and defenses of YHWH that are related to unformulated arguments from evil against other gods. These in turn may be distinguished from general metaphysical evil and idiosyncratic or matter-of-fact instances of natural and moral evil, explicit rhetoric in RL1. Implicit background considerations as briefly introduced also clearly allow for comparison of purported Chronicles and theodicy relations to various loci in philosophy of religion as RL2. These including the problem of RL, certain concepts of God as condition of possibility for the problem of evil, the relationship between religion and morality, and the problem of evil. Whatever view one takes on this relation, without attempting to identify associated content or the lack thereof on their own terms even if not in them, existing auxiliary approaches will not be sufficiently complete. That is, without such a broader religious-philosophical approach to supervening concerns involved in the justification for any position on Chronicles and theodicy, one will be neglecting an important part of the reason why things in the world of the text (and in the scholarship in the world in front thereof) are construed in the ways they are, or why they are deemed worthy of consideration at all.

Bibliography

Ackroyd, Peter R. "The Theology of the Chronicler." In *The Chronicler in His Age*, edited by Peter R. Ackroyd, Journal for the Study of the Old Testament Supplements 101, 273–89. Sheffield: Sheffield Academic, 1991.

Audi, Robert. *Rationality and Religious Commitment*. Oxford: Clarendon, 2011.

Bergmann, Michael. "Rational Religious Belief Without Arguments." In *Philosophy of Religion: An Anthology*, edited by Louis Pojman and Michael Rea, 534–49. Boston: Wadsworth, 2012.

———. "Religious Disagreement and Rational Demotion." In *Oxford Studies in Philosophy of Religion*, edited by Jonathan Kvanvig, 6:21–57. Oxford: Oxford University Press, 2015.

Bergmann, Michael, et al., eds. *Divine Evil? The Moral Character of the God of Abraham*. Oxford: Oxford University Press, 2010.

Braun, Roddy L. *1 Chronicles*. World Biblical Commentary. Waco, TX: Zondervan, 1986.

Buckareff, Andre A., and Yujin Nagasawa, eds. *Alternative Concepts of God: Essays on the Metaphysics of the Divine*. Oxford: Oxford University Press, 2016.

Calder, Todd. "The Concept of Evil." In *The Stanford Encyclopedia of Philosophy*, Winter 2022 ed., edited by Edward N. Zalta and Uri Nodelman. https://plato.stanford.edu/archives/win2022/entries/concept-evil/.

Clayton, John. *Religion, Reasons and Gods: Essays in Cross-Cultural Philosophy of Religion*. Cambridge: Cambridge University Press, 2006.

Crenshaw, James L. *Defending God: Biblical Responses to the Problem of Evil*. Oxford: Oxford University Press, 2006.

———, ed. *Theodicy in the Old Testament*. Philadelphia: Fortress, 1983.

Gericke, Jaco. *The Hebrew Bible and Philosophy of Religion*. Resources in Biblical Literature 70. Atlanta: SBL, 2012.

———. *A Philosophical Theology of the Old Testament: A Historical, Comparative, Historical, Experimental and Analytic Perspective*. Routledge Series in Interdisciplinary Biblical Criticism. London: Routledge, 2020.

———. *What Is a God? Philosophical Perspectives on Divine Essence in the Hebrew Bible*. London: Bloomsbury, 2017.

Hart-Weed, Jennifer. "Religious Language." Internet Encyclopedia of Philosophy, 2006. https://iep.utm.edu/rel-lang/.

Japhet, Sara. *I and II Chronicles: A Commentary*. Old Testament Library. Louisville: Westminster John Knox, 1993.

———. *1 Chronik*. Herders theologischer Kommentar zum Alten Testament. Freiburg: Herder, 2002.

———. *2 Chronik*. Herders theologischer Kommentar zum Alten Testament. Freiburg: Herder, 2003.

———. "Theodicy in Ezra–Nehemiah and Chronicles." In Laato and de Moor, *Theodicy in the World of the Bible*, 429–68.

Joll, Nicholas. "Metaphilosophy." Internet Encyclopedia of Philosophy, 2010. https://iep.utm.edu/con-meta/.

Jonker, Louis, C. *1 and 2 Chronicles*. Understanding the Bible. Grand Rapids: Baker, 2013.

Kelly, Brian. *Retribution and Eschatology in Chronicles*. JSOT Supplements 211. Sheffield: Sheffield Phoenix, 1996.

Klein, Ralph W. *1 Chronicles: A Commentary*. Hermeneia. Minneapolis: Fortress, 2006.

Knoppers, Gary N. *I Chronicles 1–9: A New Translation with Introduction and Commentary*. Anchor Bible Commentary. New York: Doubleday, 2003.

———. *I Chronicles 10–29: A New Translation with Introduction and Commentary*. Anchor Bible Commentary. New York: Doubleday, 2004.

Laato, Antti, and Johannes C. de Moor. *Theodicy in the World of the Bible: The Goodness of God and the Problem of Evil*. Leiden: Brill, 2003.

McKenzie, Steven L. *1–2 Chronicles*. Abingdon Old Testament Commentaries. Nashville: Abingdon, 2004.

Meister, Chad, and Charles Taliaferro, eds. *History of Evil*. 6 vols. London: Routledge, 2018.

Meister, Chad, and Paul Moser, eds. *The Cambridge Companion to the Problem of Evil*. Cambridge: Cambridge University Press, 2017.

Moltmann, Friederike. "Natural Language Ontology." In *The Stanford Encyclopedia of Philosophy*, Winter 2022 ed., edited by Edward N. Zalta and Uri Nodelman. https://plato.stanford.edu/archives/win2022/entries/natural-language-ontology/.

Morley, Brian. "God, Western Concepts of." Internet Encyclopedia of Philosophy. https://iep.utm.edu/god-west/.

Oppy, Graham R. *Arguing About Gods*. Cambridge: Cambridge University Press, 2006.

Oppy, Graham R., and Nick Trakakis, eds. *The History of Western Philosophy of Religion*. 15 vols. New York: Oxford University Press, 2009.

Schilbrack, Kevin. "The Concept of Religion." In *The Stanford Encyclopedia of Philosophy*, Summer 2022 ed., edited by Edward N. Zalta and Uri Nodelman. https://plato.stanford.edu/archives/sum2022/entries/concept-religion/.

Scott, Michael. "Religious Language." In *The Stanford Encyclopedia of Philosophy*, Spring 2022 ed., edited by Edward N. Zalta and Uri Nodelman. https://plato.stanford.edu/archives/spr2022/entries/religious-language/.

Stump, Eleanor. *Wandering in Darkness: Narrative and the Problem of Suffering*. Oxford: Oxford University Press, 2010.

Taliaferro, Charles. "Philosophy of Religion." In *The Stanford Encyclopedia of Philosophy*, Fall 2024 ed., edited by Edward N. Zalta and Uri Nodelman. https://plato.stanford.edu/archives/fall2024/entries/philosophy-religion/.

Taliaferro, Charles, et al., eds. *A Companion to Philosophy of Religion*. 2nd ed. Blackwell Companions to Philosophy 9. Hoboken, NJ: Wiley-Blackwell, 2010.

Tooley, Michael. "The Problem of Evil." In *The Stanford Encyclopedia of Philosophy*, Winter 2024 ed., edited by Edward N. Zalta and Uri Nodelman. https://plato.stanford.edu/archives/win2021/entries/evil/.

Tuell, Steven S. *First and Second Chronicles*. Interpretation. Louisville: John Knox, 2001.

11

Imperial Economics and Divine Retribution

Economic and Theological Perspectives on Storage Cities in 2 Chronicles

Hendrik Bosman

References to "storage cities" (*'are miskenot*) in the Hebrew Bible or Old Testament are predominantly found in 2 Chronicles (8:4, 6; 16:4; 17:12; and 32:28), the Pentateuch (Exod 1:11), and the so-called Deuteronomistic History (1 Kgs 9:19). Similar to Mesopotamian (Assyrian, Babylonian, and Persian) royal inscriptions, the Hebrew Bible relates the building of storage cities to royal power in and close to Israel and Judah. In all seven references to storage cities, mention is made of a king: Pharaoh, Solomon (twice), Asa, Jehoshaphat, and Hezekiah. This makes a link between storage and state power likely.

The increase in references to "storage cities" in 2 Chronicles will be interpreted against the backdrop of the overlapping, but also diverging, depictions of Judahite kings in the books of 1 and 2 Kings and 2 Chronicles. These royal depictions seem to be modeled on Solomon as the builder of the temple in Jerusalem and storage cities.

The discussion of the significance of the increased references to storage cities in 2 Chronicles will pay close attention to some relevant aspects of the extensive research on Chronicles and Second Temple literature conducted by Louis Jonker, an esteemed colleague for more than two decades. This discussion of storage cities in 2 Chronicles will attempt to do justice to postexilic "reforming history" in Yehud that established a theological bridge between two worlds: the preexilic monarchy of Judah with its predominantly subsistence economy and the postexilic colony of Yehud with its redistributive (storage) type of imperial economy.

Brief Notes on Economies, Cities, and Storage in the Ancient Near East

Economies in the Ancient Near East

Despite many sterile debates amongst economic historians about the most appropriate model to do justice to our diverse economic past, brief attention still seems to be justified to provide context to the current understanding of storage in ancient Israel and Yehud. A perennial challenge in this regard is to what extent contemporary economic models correspond with the economic realities of the ancient Near East in general and Israel or Yehud in particular.[1]

Anyone interested in ancient civilisations and their economic systems must strive for greater clarity when analysing and conceptualising an ancient economy.[2] Johannes Renger distinguishes two ways in which the concept "market" can be used as a structural element of ancient Mesopotamian economy: (a) "as an abstract economic concept which serves to analyse all kinds of phenomena in economic terms" and considers it to be based "on the complex interaction between supply, demand, and price or equivalent"; (b) as "an actual process of exchange involving goods and services" that "often takes place in a specific spatial and temporal environment."[3] He considers "storage" so "intimately linked with the concept of redistribution that a redistributive economy is often described as storage economy," and he is convinced that "the need for security . . . prompts large households or the 'state' to build up stocks to weather bad

1. Master points out that archaeologists and historians "struggle to agree on even the basic framework for Iron Age exchange, divided between the familiar paradigms of an economy based on market forces versus one dependent on social networks." Master, "Economy and Exchange," 81.

2. Renger, "Economic Structures," 163.

3. Renger, "Economic Structures," 174.

times."[4] According to Renger it is lamentable that "direct evidence for storage of large quantities of grain or other staples is very scarce" and "very little has been done on the subject."[5]

According to Thomas Blanton, three "methodological trends" can be discerned in the ferment that the study of ancient economy currently seems to be in, of which two are pertinent to the study of the economic background of the Hebrew Bible: New Institutional Economics and Marxist-influenced economic theory.[6]

The Nobel Prize winner Douglass North summarises the New Institutional Economics (NIE) approach to economic history as follows: "It is the task of economic history to explain the structure and performance of economies through time"—in short, history matters![7] The institutional setting of economic growth becomes paramount, and therefore economic history must focus on how and why forms of economic and political organisation changed, and not get bogged down in the traditional market analysis. According to North, institutions can be formal or informal: on a formal level it manifests in laws and regulation, while on informal level they can be traced in codes of conduct, customs, and traditions.[8] It seems that NIE overcomes the somewhat stale debate on the prevalence of markets in ancient economies, oscillating between total dominance and complete absence, and provides a more nuanced and balanced approach to engage with ancient economies in a historical sensitive manner that takes note of institutional changes and the mentalities or mindsets that undergirded them.

Roland Boer's use of Marxist economics to study the so-called "sacred economy" of ancient Israel is rooted in his application of the "*Régulation* theory" that takes as point of departure that "specific economic systems stabilize crisis in order to gain some continuity for

4. Renger, "Economic Structures," 178. This also refers to the economic advice given by Joseph to Pharaoh in Gen 41 as a significant indication of "the notion the authors of Genesis had about a storage economy."

5. Renger, "Economic Structures," 204 and 208. Renger here agrees both with Karl Polanyi "that economic processes and economic behaviour in preindustrial economies are embedded into societal relationships and are influenced by socially determined behaviour," and with Douglass North "that the motive forces underlying classical and neo-classical economics are not amenable to analysing the ancient world"—see later discussion.

6. Blanton, "Theorizing 'the Ancient Economy.'"

7. North, *Structure and Change in Economic History*, 1–2.

8. North, *Institutions*, 3.

certain periods."[9] He identifies four phases in the development of ancient economies, starting with the basic subsistence survival system that allowed all members of a society to survive,[10] followed by the emerging of villages that consisted of kinship-households and related clans,[11] then the rise of estates and eventually city-states that developed systems of extraction from the subsistence and village economies to benefit the elite class,[12] while the last phase was that of empires (focusing on Neo-Assyrian, Neo-Babylonian, and Persian Empires) that thrived on plunder, tribute, and taxes—different forms of extraction.[13]

In recent South African scholarship, the economic aspects of Hebrew Bible contexts received little attention. A notable exception is Louis Jonker's study of the impact of the agrarian economy during the late Persian period on the genealogies of 1 Chr 1–9. Jonker is informed by Roland Boer's understanding of Jerusalem as a "sacred economy" with, at its centre, a "temple-city" complex.[14] The extensive genealogies of the first nine chapters of 1 Chronicles deal with the allocation of land to "all Israel," with a large section of the land given to the Levites. Despite the probability that the author of the genealogies was a member of the "urban elite" in Jerusalem, the focus is on rural areas and how they related to Jerusalem within the context of the imperial Persian administration.

9. Boer, *Sacred Economy*, 32. Boer defines "*Régulation* theory" as follows: "The key components of economic analysis are institutional forms, regimes, and modes of *régulation*, which form into new constellations within a mode of production," while the "mode of *regulation*" refers to the "behavioral patterns and institutions that ensure periods of relative stability (during a regime)," and it includes "cultural norms, ideologies, compromises, and above all, religion." Boer, *Sacred Economy*, 236–37.

10. Boer considers the "subsistence survival" to be the "crucial allocative institutional form of ancient Southwest Asia, focused on agriculture, both animal husbandry and crop growing . . . well tried and geared for survival by means of diversity, food security, risk-spreading . . ." Boer, *Sacred Economy*, 236.

11. Boer argues that the "kinship-household" was the "socially determining feature of subsistence survival" that combined "flexible kinship structures with equally flexible productions of lived space." Boer, *Sacred Economy*, 236.

12. Boer describes "states" as the "extractive system of palatine and temple estates, using indentured labor (temporary and permanent, including slaves) in order to supply the small ruling class . . . managed directly by palace functionaries or indirectly by landlords"; while the "extractive system" can be characterised as the "extraction of surplus from what one does not possess, but is possessed by another." Boer, *Sacred Economy*, 235–36.

13. Boer depicts "tribute exchange" as an "extractive form that used tribute, taxation, and exchange—all forms of plunder—as mechanisms for appropriating good that one did not produce." Boer, *Sacred Economy*, 236.

14. Jonker, "Agrarian Economy," 77–84, 96–101.

One can glean a few elements from the above debate on the history of ancient economies that seem to be pertinent for the study of storage cities in Israel and Yehud: to approach the topic from a comprehensive historical point of view (according to North) by interpreting the *why* and *how* of storage cities in the Hebrew Bible as economic institutions. Storage in general, and storage-cities in particular, seem to have developed due to different socio-economical (as well as religious or theological) forms of *régulation* as it evolved from subsistence survival economies, with little or no surplus available for storage, to different forms of central extraction (sacrifice, tax, tribute, etc.) by either temple, royal palace, or imperial capital that provided enough grain, oil, and wine for central storage.[15]

Cities in the Ancient Near East

In his research on the development of ancient Mesopotamian cities, Marc Van de Mieroop suggests that these cities developed due to an increase in population density as the result of more productive agriculture and stability of residence that did not require a nomadic or even seminomadic existence.[16] The development of cities in the ancient Near East was influenced by the access to and storage of water (rivers, springs, wells, cisterns, and reservoirs); that enabled improved agricultural production and the exchange of goods by means of markets and trade.[17]

The layout or design of ancient Near Eastern cities varied a lot, and their characteristics seemed to be area specific. Most inner cities were laid out as a large rectangle incorporating both temples and palaces that functioned as a dominating central administrative public space, often incorporating storage facilities for agricultural produce.[18]

The building of storage cities in this contribution will be interpreted as part of royal building activities within the economies of the ancient Near East. Due to the postexilic dating of Chronicles, specific attention is warranted for the economy of the Persian Empire.

15. Silver cautiously suggests that there "are indications that the Assyrian Empire moved from a policy of free trade to one of economic regulation" and that is possible that "the same trend manifested itself in Babylonian . . . and later on, in Persian policy." Silver, *Prophets and Markets*, 251.

16. Van de Mieroop, *Mesopotamian City*, 27.

17. Snell, *Life in the Ancient Near East*, 13–15.

18. Van de Mieroop, *Mesopotamian City*, 5, 88–89.

In his discussion of the impact of Achaemenid rule on Yehud, Josef Wiesehöfer argues that the success of the Persian Empire was based on granting qualified autonomy to subjugated nations while "maintaining austere supervision," as was reflected in their "economic and political ethnocentrism" where "Persians were in key positions and were the main beneficiaries of economic success."[19] Archaeological excavations at Ramat Raḥel, close to Jerusalem, found "an unusual concentration of *yhwd* stamp impressions on jar handles" that is most likely to be an indication that this centre of Persian administration also became "the most important tax collection centre of Yehud" with storage facilities for the taxes or tithes that were collected in kind, like olive oil or wheat.[20] Excavations at Tell el-Ḥesi, close to Lachish, indicate the Persian use of "subterranean storage pits" for wheat and barley; this corresponds with "more than fifty cylindrical pits" discovered near the Persian "Residency" at Lachish, suggesting a close relation between storage and Persian administration.[21]

Storage in Ancient Near East and Persian Yehud

"Storage" is interpreted as part of an economic system that facilitates the exchange of goods and services. Ancient Near Eastern economies start with production, move to storage in different formats, continue with distribution regulated by concentrations of power in society (temple and palace), and end with consumption by different target groups (local population, soldiers, international trade, etc.).

Although storage was found throughout the ancient Near East, the format of storage varied due to available resources (mainly agricultural) and the cultural context (socio-economic, political, and religious concerns). The following formats of storage have been found in the ancient Near East.

Buildings were used as *granaries* in urban areas to protect stored grains (like barley, millet, and wheat) from humidity and pests and

19. Wiesehöfer, "Achaemenid Rule," 171.

20. Wiesehöfer, "Achaemenid Rule," 182–83. He also points out here that the similar "storerooms" were "part of the Second Temple complex in Jerusalem" that laid the foundation for "the political and economic power of the Jerusalem High Priest in Hellenistic times."

21. Stager, "Climatic Conditions," 449–50. Stager disagrees with Flinders Petrie that this grain storage was intended for the use by Persian soldiers during their Egyptian military campaign, and he opts for food security as the reason for grain storage.

enabled "food security" during food shortages caused by drought or war—this is important to note in view of the subsequent focus on storage cities in 2 Chronicles. Subterranean *silos* provided a cooler and more stable environment for storage and reduced the risk of grain spoilage.[22] In most ancient Near Eastern cities, *temples and palaces* served as centres of economic activity where agricultural produce was used for religious offerings or sacrifices, royal tribute or taxes, and military provisions. Liquids, like olive oil and wine, were stored in sealed *amphorae and pottery jars* to prevent contamination and allow long-distance trading. These ceramic containers were also found in *storehouses* that provided storage along trade routes and therefore played an important role in the national and internation exchange of goods. In smaller villages and in extended family households, *storages pits* were used for more perishable goods and were often lined with straw or reeds.[23]

While acknowledging the risk-buffering function of grain storage, it is evident that the collected archaeological and textual evidence does not "map easily into the idealised image of a centripetally organised storage economy."[24] In their research on Late Bronze Age storage structures, Amir Golani and Eli Yannai argue that the Bronze Age shift "to centralised storage practices" during increasing urbanisation in the Southern Levant was probably the result of "the rapid development of a market-orientated economy and the ensuing empowerment of ruling elites."[25] The first part of this argument must be considered with caution, while the second part will inform the subsequent discussion of storage cities in 2 Chronicles.[26]

Storage in the early first millennium was investigated by Tim Frank, who scrutinised the archaeological and textual evidence for food storage in ancient Israel and Judah.[27] His most important research result

22. Golani and Yannai make a twofold distinction for "large-scale storage" facilities in the Southern Levant: "above-ground installations" are called "granaries" while "below-ground facilities are termed 'silos.'" Golani and Yannai, "Storage Structures," 14.

23. Golani and Yannai define a "storage structure" in the Bronze Age as "a built circular structure whose size is too large to be regarded as a simple pit yet is too small or otherwise unsuitable for a dwelling." Golani and Yannai, "Storage Structures," 9.

24. Tate, "Grain Storage," abstract.

25. Golani and Yannai, "Storage Structures," 37. They presuppose that the increase in "centralised storage" was "controlled by ruling (urban) elites."

26. It goes without saying that this survey of storage-related research in the ancient Near East covers several millennia and refers to a multitude of socio-economic cultures—it can at most produce a few working hypotheses that must be tested and verified by research in the future.

27. Frank, *Food Storage*.

was that there was a shift from shared community storage in Iron Age 1 to redistributive storage in Iron Age 2.[28] In their reconstruction of the Judean economy of the seventh century BCE, Avraham Faust and Ehud Weiss identified different agricultural zones in Palestine: outer coastal plain, with Ashkelon as the centre for wine; the inner coastal area and the Shephelah, with Ekron as the centre of the olive oil industry; Judah producing wheat and other grain surpluses (requiring storage); and the Negev for grazing husbandry.[29]

Grain storage in Late Achaemenid and Hellenistic Babylonia can be considered as a risk-management strategy "to minimize price volatility" in view of the data available in the Babylonian "astronomical diaries" that contain sales records of "old" and "new" grain (harvests from different seasons that imply the existence of storage facilities), especially barley.[30] According to these records there is "little evidence of substantial storage" because the storage costs outweighed its financial benefits because the regular seasonal availability of grain made the large-scale storage thereof unnecessary.[31] Here it must be pointed out that the more arid Yehud could not depend on the regular seasonal availability of grain and other foodstuffs, as in Babylonia, and therefore required substantial storage for food security during drought.

After studying the Persepolis Fortification Tablets, Makis Aperghis found that Achaemenid financial administration was comprised of a two-fold network of commodity storehouses: "a regional one of storehouses where commodity tax was collected, and a super-imposed flexible system of work-groups and animal management."[32] Aperghis concludes that "there was a definite system in place, centred on the 'public' storehouse and governed by established procedures," undergirded by an efficient "military-style organization."[33] It is probable that the same system was operational in Yehud because it existed in neighbouring countries and corresponded with Egyptian examples of the same period.[34]

28. Frank, *Food Storage*, 160–80.

29. Faust and Weiss, "Judah, Philistia, and the Mediterranean World," 71, 75, 79.

30. Van Leeuwen et al., "Storage in Hellenistic Babylonia," 169.

31. Van Leeuwen et al., "Storage in Hellenistic Babylonia," 190.

32. Aperghis, "Storehouses and Systems," 152. It describes how these "tablets" indicate "the collection, storage and distribution of commodities for the king, his family and priests" during the reign of Darius I (509–494 BCE).

33. Aperghis, "Storehouses and Systems," 191–92.

34. Aperghis, "Storehouses and Systems," 183, 188.

Yehud was under the jurisdiction of a satrap who governed the provinces of the Persian Empire. These satraps were charged to collect tributes or taxes and to store them in regional treasuries, as well as to secure the borders by means of royal garrisons to maintain "peace and order in the empire."[35] In contrast to previous empires, the Persian Empire was interested in maximising the productivity of a region, such as Yehud, that enabled the extraction of more taxation and tribute.[36]

Storage Cities According to the Pentateuch and Former Prophets

Exod 1:11

It seems clear that Exod 1:11–12 "reports the 'humiliation' of the Israelite people received at the hands of the Egyptians" by means of forced labour.[37] What is not that clear is when this description was written and to what Egyptian domination it refers.

For decades scholars have been at loggerheads about the dating of the building of the storage cities of Pithom and Raamses and the identification of the pharaoh for whom the Israelites had to perform the forced labour. The so-called "classic interpretation" of verse 11 is that the pharaoh was Raamses II and that the historical context was situated in the thirteenth century BCE.

Recent scholarship considers it significant that the words for *taskmasters* (שָׂרֵי) and *storage cities* (עָרֵי מִסְכְּנוֹת) are Akkadian loanwords "and can hardly have entered Judean vocabulary before the 7th century."[38] In a critical evaluation of the extensive research on the cities of Raamses and Pitom in Exod 1:11, Bernd Schipper considers a "historical background" of "the late 7th century" to be "more likely, when Judahites had to perform forced labour for the Egyptian hegemon in the Southern Levant."[39]

35. Wiesehöfer, "Achaemenid Rule," 172, 183.

36. Faust and Weiss, "Economic System," 85–86.

37. Utzschneider and Oswalt, *Exodus 1–15*, 67. They also point out that in the ancient Near East, ruling classes "often conscripted the general public for labor."

38. Utzschneider and Oswalt, *Exodus 1–15*, 72–73. They agree that the term *storage city* can apply to Pitom but not to the opulent capital city of Raamses II of the thirteenth century BCE—rather a city that was linked to Raamses II in a later period. Davies agrees that the meaning "storehouse, depot" is attested by "the very similar Akkadian word maškantu, . . . thus most likely to be a loanword." Davies, *Exodus 1–18*, 142, 157.

39. Schipper, "Raamses, Pithom," 265.

In view of archaeological and philological evidence, it now seems that Exod 1:11 reflects the historical context of "Judah as a vassal state under the Saite Pharaohs in the 7th to 6th centuries"—probably Pharaohs "Psammeticus I and Necho II" who took over "the former Assyrian administration and formed an Egyptian rulership" with storage cities that formed part of "an agricultural system controlled by the Egyptians."[40]

William Propp points out that the ancient translations "are divided in their understanding of *miskenôt*": the Targumim renders it as "storehouse" (*ʾosara*) and the Septuagint with "fortified" (*ochyrai*). Therefore, Propp suggests a combination of the terms by suggesting "fortified storage cities," especially in view of 2 Chr 32:27–28 "where reference is made of both the fortification of cities and the storage of grain, wine and oil."[41] The border cities of Pithom and Rameses are considered by James Bruckner to be "military supply cities for protection and campaigns."[42] Linkage between storage and fortification can be explained by the possibility that the storage was not primarily available for the local population but for military personnel that protected borders and trade routes.

The Latin translation in the Vulgate of the second half of Exod 1:11 is "*aedificaveruntque urbes tabernaculorum Pharoni Phiton et Ramesses*" (and built for Pharao cities of tabernacles, Pithom and Ramesses[43]). It seems as if the reception in the Vulgate is based on an association of *miskenôt* with the Hebrew root *skn*, that allowed the link with the building of the tabernacle discussed in the second half of the book of Exodus.[44] In similar vein, Victor Hamilton refers to the "similarity in sound between *miskenôt* ('storage') and *miškān* ('tabernacle') throughout Exod. 25–40."[45]

1 Kgs 9:19

From 1 Kgs 5:1—9:25 Solomon is described as builder of several impressive structures, starting with the building of the temple in Jerusalem (1

40. Utzschneider and Oswalt, *Exodus 1–15*, 74; Schipper, "Raamses, Pithom," 282.

41. Propp, *Exodus 1–18*, 132–33.

42. Bruckner, *Exodus*, 19.

43. My translation.

44. There is a possibility that this reception indicates an eventual link between the building of storage cities as expression of royal power and the manifestation of divine presence that resonates with the focus on the building of the temple (like the tabernacle) in Chronicles.

45. Hamilton, *Exodus*, 9–10.

Kgs 6), continuing with a description of its furnishings (1 Kgs 7:13–51), reaching a climax with the longest chapter in the book of Kings where the dedication of the temple described (1 Kgs 8), and also including the construction of the royal palace (1 Kgs 7:1–12). First Kings 9:15–23 forms part of the concluding section on the building endeavours of Solomon and describes how he made use of *corvée*, or conscripted labour, to erect numerous buildings in Israel—the workforce required for the building projects probably consisted of Canaanite "permanent *corvée* workers" and "Israelite temporary draftees."[46]

It starts in verse 15 with an account the building of the temple, royal palace, the Millo (filled terrace or citadel), and city walls in Jerusalem; it continues with reference to cities on major trading routes: Hazor (on the road from the north), Megiddo (on the road from Phoenicia), and Gezer (on the road from Philistia).[47] The list of cities continues in verses 17–18 with smaller cities, Lower Beth-Horon and Baalath, that were closer to Jerusalem, ending with an enigmatic reference to "Tadmor in the desert."[48] In 2007 Khirbet Qeiyafa was excavated on a hill west of Jerusalem overlooking the Elah Valley between Judah and Philistia, providing evidence of the existence of garrison or fortress towns with storage facilities that protected trade routes and vulnerable border areas as early as the tenth century BCE and later.[49]

According to Volkmar Fritz the terms for "storage cities," "cities for his chariots," and "cities for his cavalry" do not "denote a certain type of city but rather describe the functions connected with some of them."[50] The jury is still out whether "the so-called houses of poles" attached to "palaces at Megiddo, Samaria, and Lachish and the sanctuary at Arad" can be considered as public buildings for storage.[51] A final decision on the existence of urban storage spaces during the Israelite

46. House, *1, 2 Kings*, 158. See also 2 Kgs 9:20–22.

47. Wiseman, *1, 2 Kings*, 136.

48. While the *qere* of the Masoretic Text (MT) reads "Tadmor," the *ketiv* of the MT and LXX reads "Tamar."

49. Na'aman points out that no less than 693 "finger impressions on storage jar handles" were "discovered at Khirbet Qeiyafa." Na'aman, "Was Khirbet Qeiyafa," 9.

50. Fritz, *1 and 2 Kings*, 111. Fritz, *City in Ancient Israel*.

51. Fritz, *City in Ancient Israel*, 152. Slager concludes that "store-cities were towns that served for storage of government supplies, including food." Slager, *1 and 2 Kings*, 316–17.

monarchy depends on the verification that a "storage economy" existed "during the period of the monarchy.[52]

Storage Cities According to 2 Chronicles

Approaching 2 Chronicles

In agreement with Louis Jonker, the following sections in 2 Chronicles will be interpreted as "narratives" that retold "Judah's past" based on "probably earlier forms of Samuel and Kings."[53] The retelling of the reign of Judean kings most likely took place during the fourth century BCE when Yehud was a province of the Persian Empire, and despite tolerating the rebuilding of local shrines and temples, provinces had to "remain loyal to the empire in terms of tributes and military campaigns."[54]

The following references to storage cities in 2 Chronicles will be interpreted while hypothesising Chronicles as "reforming history" and as "an attempt to reformulate and sanitize the older traditions about the past, as well as an attempt to reformulate the identity of God's people in the changed sociohistorical circumstances of the late Persian era."[55]

2 Chr 8:4, 6

According to Jonker the references in 2 Chr 8:4 and 6 to "storage towns/cities" form part of the extensive discussion of the reign of Solomon in 2 Chr 1–9.[56] It is important to note that 2 Chr 8:1 introduces the description of building projects by Solomon (verses 1–6), with the mention of the duration of the temple construction being twenty years, and continues with a report on the use of forced labour for the completion of the buildings in

52. Fritz, *1 and 2 Kings*, 111. Fritz is cautious when he concludes that the term "storage cities" in verse 19 "refers to general provisions more than to concrete building projects by the king."

53. Jonker, *1 and 2 Chronicles*, 6–7. He does not presume a single author, "the Chronicler," but rather a group of authors and editors that were "interested in the Davidic dynasty, the temple in Jerusalem, its clergy, and its cult" combined with a "special" portrayal of the Levites.

54. Jonker, *1 and 2 Chronicles*, 8–9.

55. Jonker, *1 and 2 Chronicles*, 14.

56. Jonker, *1 and 2 Chronicles*, 4.

question.[57] There seems to be an "overall chiastic structure that shapes the Chronicler's account of Solomon," and those sections "have in common their emphasis on construction projects"—thus the thematic importance of royal building projects is undergirded by its literary construction.[58]

Amidst the similarities between 2 Chr 8:1–6 and 1 Kgs 9:10–17, there is an important difference: according to 1 Kgs 9:11–13, Solomon gave twenty towns in Galilea to the Phoenician King Hiram, but in 2 Chr 8:2 Solomon receives the cities from Hiram—possibly suggesting that in the relationship between Solomon and Hiram, the former was "the superior party."[59]

The close connection between Tadmor and Hamath in 2 Chr 8:4 might be an indication of "Solomon's sovereignty over all major arteries for trade with Mesopotamia."[60] This link with Mesopotamian trade possibly explains the references to the construction of "storage towns" in both verses 4 and 6. In this regard Sarah Japhet concludes that verses 1–6 entail "a well-planned composition having a definite goal: the systematic description of Solomon's settlement, development and fortification of the northern border of his kingdom."[61] The additional mentioning of "storage towns" suggests that trade also played a significant role in the fortification of the northern border area.[62] Over and above the reference to "storage towns" in verse 6, one should also take note of the mentioning of the building of towns for chariots and cavalry by Solomon. This is "the only reference in Chronicles to the military prowess of Solomon," who is usually depicted as "the man of peace" (1 Chr 22:9).[63]

It is important to take note of 2 Chr 8:16 (with no equivalent in 1 Kgs 9) where it "is suggested that all these other projects stood within the

57. Jonker, *1 and 2 Chronicles*, 195. He also points out the similarities and differences with 1 Kgs 9:10–28.

58. Dillard, *2 Chronicles*, 61, 62. Dillard considers 8:1–16 parallel to 2:17—5:1 and references to construction projects in 3:1—4:22 and 8:1–6.

59. Jonker, *1 and 2 Chronicles*, 195. This forms part of the overall emphasis on and glorification of Solomon by Chronicles.

60. Dillard, *2 Chronicles*, 64. Dillard points out that Hamath controlled the main overland trade route and Tadmor the desert shortcut—both important for Solomon's "commercial endeavours and wealth."

61. Japhet, *I and II Chronicles*, 619–20.

62. Merrill considers the excavations of fortifications at Khirbet el-Qeiyafa—as well as Hazor, Megiddo, and Gezer—to be a validation that fortress towns existed around Jerusalem during the monarchy. Merrill, *1 and 2 Chronicles*, 363.

63. Dillard, *2 Chronicles*, 64.

framework of the construction of the temple," and these projects include the "storage towns" of Solomon.[64] It can also be pointed out that the detailed description of Solomon's building activities is enclosed by "statements about the temple (vv. 1, 12–16)," as if the obedient construction of the Jerusalem temple enabled the other building projects, including the storage towns, that glorified Solomon.[65]

2 Chr 16:4

Jonker is of the opinion that 2 Chr 14–16 narrates the reign of King Asa (ca. 911–910 BCE) and corresponds with 1 Kgs 15:24 in an interesting manner. The latter provides "a positive image of Asa as a king who ensured religious-cultic-purity," while the former depicts Asa ambiguously: positively in 2 Chr 14–15 ("having rest / peace / not war") and negatively in 2 Chr 16 ("having wars from now on").[66] Asa is one of four "reformer kings" that Chronicles discusses in more detail—the other "reformers" being Jehoshaphat, Hezekiah, and Josiah—of which the first two are also linked to storage cities in following sections of 2 Chronicles.[67]

The reference to "storage cities" in 2 Chr 16:4 forms part of the negative description of Asa that commences with the announcement that King Baasha of Israel marched against Asa (verse 1). Asa responds by stripping the temple and royal palace in Jerusalem of its silver and gold to motivate the Aramean King Ben-hadad of Damascus to break his alliance with Baasha (verses 2–3); Ben-hadad listens to Asa's request and conquers three towns in Israel (Northern Kingdom) as well as unnamed storage cities of Naphtali (verse 4).

The first city or town (Ijon) was at the northern side of the Huleh Valley "on the main trade road from Israel to Syria," important for trading and the deployment of soldiers; the second city (Dan) is of strategic importance on the northern border of Israel and Syria; and the third (Abel-maim / Abel Beth Maakah) forms part of "the main international highway" taken

64. Jonker, *1 and 2 Chronicles*, 195.

65. Selman, *2 Chronicles*, 359–60; De Vries, *1 and 2 Chronicles*, 269.

66. Jonker, *1 and 2 Chronicles*, 221. Jonker identifies two "specific temporal indications (2 Chron. 15:19 and 16:1)" that "establish the break between the two."

67. Hubbard and Dearman argue that the Chronicler "offers more-expanded treatment of the four reformer kings" and with regards to Asa, downgrades him "a notch." Hubbard and Dearman, *Introducing the Old Testament*, 221.

by the soldiers of Ben-hadad.[68] No mention is made of these "storage cities of Naphtali" in the corresponding section in 1 Kgs 15:20.[69]

The references to three cities or towns close to the border between the Northern Kingdom and Syria, as well as the unnamed storage cities, seem to be linked with their strategic importance for international trade and the upkeep of the Aramean army of Ben-hadad—again a possible link between storage, trade, and military activity.

2 Chr 17:12

In one of the longest accounts of a king's reign, 2 Chr 17:1—21:1 provides a mainly positive account of Jehoshaphat (ca. 873–849 BCE) of Judah that "contains the most substantial portion of the Chronicler's own material."[70] The description of Jehoshaphat's reign in Chronicles is double that of Kings and "second only to that of Hezekiah (II Chron. 29–31)."[71] As part of the Chronicler's own material, 17:1–6 "introduces Jehoshaphat with references to his righteousness in the eyes of the Lord and to the successful establishment of his kingdom," while in the verses 7–11 following, the king's effort to teach Judah "the Book of the Law of the Lord" is described.[72]

Jonker is quite correct in pointing out that the reference to "storehouses for the yield of grain, wine, and oil" in verse 12 forms part of the description of Jehoshaphat's "growing military power" in 2 Chr 17:12–19.[73] This increasing military power of the king is illustrated by his building of storage towns and fortresses in Judah and his "enormous army."[74] The description of how Jehoshaphat constructed military for-

68. Japhet, *I and II Chronicles*, 125.

69. Ormanson and Ellington, *Handbook on 1 and 2 Chronicles*, 989.

70. Jonker, *1 and 2 Chronicles*, 227. Jonker distinguishes between 18:1–34 and 20:31—21:1 that corresponds with 1 Kgs 22:1–35 and 22:41–50, while "the rest of the Jehoshaphat account consists of the Chronicler's own material."

71. Japhet, *I and II Chronicles*, 743. Japhet also draws attention to the fact that the depiction of the same period in 1 Kings is focused on the reign of Ahab, while Chronicles emphasises Asa and Jehoshaphat.

72. Jonker, *1 and 2 Chronicles*, 227.

73. Jonker, *1 and 2 Chronicles*, 227.

74. Jonker, *1 and 2 Chronicles*, 228. Jonker cautions quite rightly that the numbers linked to Jehoshaphat's army (1,160,000 soldiers!) should "not be taken literally but is rather a sign of the importance the Chronicles attributes to his king." *1 and 2 Chronicles*, 232.

tifications and storage cities anticipates his battles reported in chapters 18 and 20.[75] Again it would seem as if the references to the building of military forts and supply cities form part of the Chronicler's depiction of a pious king that was blessed by YHWH. In fact, the references to the building activities by Jehoshaphat as signs of prosperity were due to "the fear of the Lord" mentioned in verse 10, combined with the acknowledgement that the king obeyed the commandments of God and removed the high places (verses 4–6).[76]

The reigns of Asa and Jehoshaphat agree with regards to the results of piety and distrust but differ in terms of the sequence: Asa and Jehoshaphat were both pious kings, but while Asa in the beginning trusted YHWH and was victorious over a foreign invader, he later on did not primarily depend on YHWH and suffered a military defeat as penalty, while Jehoshaphat initially suffers a military setback due to distrust and then renews his piety by trusting YHWH that leads to "victory over the foreign invader."[77]

2 Chr 32:28

The Chronicler's four-chapter account (2 Chr 29–32) of Hezekiah (ca. 727–697 BCE) is the third most extensive of the royal narratives, after David and Solomon. In view of the "general tendency of the Chronicler to abbreviate, the Chronistic additions are all the more significant."[78]

According to Jonker it is striking that no reference is made of the fall of Samaria and the demise of the Northern Kingdom in 722 BCE, but much emphasis is placed on "the theological unity" of "All-Israel" rooted in "the temple worship of Yahweh."[79]

The mentioning of "storehouses" in verse 28 forms part of 2 Chr 32:1–33 that makes "extensive use of source material" in 2 Kgs 18:13, 17–37; 19:35–37; and 20:1–21; but it "[moves] it from the realm of political history to the realm of cultic history" that incorporates descriptions of temple cleansing and the celebration of Passover, as well as the

75. Ormanson and Ellington, *1 and 2 Chronicles*, 1008.

76. Japhet, *I and II Chronicles*, 751.

77. De Vries, *1 and 2 Chronicles*, 309. Dillard confirms that "building programs and large armies (17:2, 12–19) are common items the author uses to show divine favor." Dillard, *2 Chronicles*, 132.

78. Japhet, *I and II Chronicles*, 976.

79. Jonker, *1 and 2 Chronicles*, 267.

organisation of Levites and priests.[80] More in particular, the reference to "storehouses" in 2 Chr 32:28 resonates with the general presupposition in Chronicles that "riches and building programs are among the tokens of divine favor."[81]

In the Chronicles version of the reign of Hezekiah, certain negative features of his reign are omitted, such as his pride, the removal of valuable vessels from the temple, his surrender to the Assyrians, etc. More emphasis is placed on how Hezekiah prayed to the Lord after becoming seriously ill (verse 24) and humbled himself (*kana'* in verse 26). The prayer and humbling of the king averts divine wrath and triggers abundant (*me'od* is used twice in verses 27–29) blessings by means of an elaborate description of wealth and honour that reminds one of David, Solomon, and Jehoshaphat. Parallel references to buildings related to the storage of grain, wine, and oil, as well as stalls for cattle and sheep, are linked to the acquisition of towns, large and small animals, and "the channelling of the Gihon spring into the City of David."[82]

Conclusion

The references to storage cities in 2 Chronicles are part of a "reforming history" attempted to bridge or relate the past of the Judean monarchy with the present of the Persian Empire—a theological retelling that bridged two worlds (preexilic Judean monarchy and the postexilic Persian province of Yehud). In agreement with Jonker, this bridging of past and present in Chronicles is done by evaluating the kings of Judah in terms of their relationship with and trust in Yahweh, as well as the importance of the Jerusalem temple as central sanctuary during the Persian and Hellenistic periods.[83]

The increase in references to storage cities in 2 Chronicles can be explained within the context the Persian imperial economy and in relation to the role storage cities played within the theological depiction of good kings in the Southern Kingdom.

While local domestic storage has been around for millennia to maintain food security within households, regional state storage

80. Jonker, *1 and 2 Chronicles*, 267–68.

81. Dillard, *2 Chronicles*, 259.

82. Jonker, *1 and 2 Chronicles*, 277.

83. Jonker, *1 and 2 Chronicles*, 15–23.

systems emerged in tandem with the development from a subsistence to a redistributive economy in the Iron Age ancient Near East. With the emergence of empires in the ancient Near East, storage became part of a well-organised system of state extraction through tribute and taxation. Excavations at Ramat Raḥel and Lachish indicate a clear link between regional storage and Persian administration due to the proximity of the respective buildings. Beneath a benevolent façade, the Persian Empire was ruthlessly efficient in maximising the economic production of their subjugated nations, and storage played an important part in this system. Therefore, urban storage facilities in Yehud were often found close to trade routes and borders with neighbouring countries, where military garrisons were stationed for the protection of storage for food security and defence of national territorial integrity.

It is striking that all the kings of Judah related to "storage cities" were considered good kings. Few kings of Judah received a positive description, and this was embedded in the postexilic theological focus on the Jerusalem temple (divine presence) and a double-edged retribution theology. Kings who trusted YHWH were blessed, and those who distrusted YHWH by establishing alliances with foreign kings were punished. From within an oppressive economic system of imperial extraction and redistribution through regional storage in Persian Yehud, the "reforming history" highlights the existence of storage cities within the reign of good kings. Storage cities are now redefined, not as instruments of imperial oppression in colonial Yehud but as visible manifestations of divine blessings during the Judahite monarchy.

Bibliography

Aperghis, Gerasimos G. "Storehouses and Systems at Persepolis: Evidence from the Persepolis Fortification Tablets." *Journal of the Economic and Social History of the Orient* 42 (1999) 152–93.

Blanton, Thomas R., IV. "Theorizing 'the Ancient Economy': Three Paradigms." *Ancient Jew Review* (2017) 1–6.

Boer, Roland. *The Sacred Economy of Ancient Israel*. Library of Ancient Israel. Louisville: Westminster John Knox, 2015.

Bruckner, James K. *Exodus: Understanding the Bible Commentary*. Grand Rapids: Baker, 2012.

Davies, Gerald I. *A Critical and Exegetical Commentary on Exodus 1–18*. International Critical Commentary. London: T&T Clark, 2020.

De Vries, Simon. *1 and 2 Chronicles*. Forms of the Old Testament Literature 11. Grand Rapids: Eerdmans, 1989.

Dillard, Raymond. *2 Chronicles*. Word Commentaries 36. Waco, TX: Word, 1987.

Faust, Avraham, and Jehud Weiss. "Judah, Philistia, and the Mediterranean World: Reconstructing the Economic System of the Seventh Century BCE." *Bulletin of the American Schools of Oriental Research* 338 (2013) 71–92.

Frank, Tim. *Household Food Storage in Ancient Israel and Judah*. Oxford: Archaeopress, 2018.

Fritz, Volkmar. *The City in Ancient Israel*. Biblical Seminar 29. Sheffield: Sheffield Academic, 1995.

———. *1 and 2 Kings*. Continental Commentary. Minneapolis: Fortress, 2003.

Golani, Amir, and Eli Yannai. "Storage Structures of the Late Early Bronze I in the Southern Levant and the Urbanisation Process." *Palestine Exploration Quarterly* 148 (2016) 8–41.

Hamilton, Victor P. *Exodus: An Exegetical Commentary*. Grand Rapids: Baker Academic, 2011.

House, Paul R. *1, 2 Kings*. New American Commentary 8. Nashville: Broadman & Holman, 1995.

Hubbard, Robert L., and J. Andrew Dearman. *Introducing the Old Testament*. Grand Rapids: Eerdmans, 2018.

Japhet, Sara. *I and II Chronicles*. Old Testament Library. London: SCM, 1993.

Jonker, Louis, C. "Agrarian Economy Through City-Elites' Eyes: Reflections of Late Persian Period Yehud Economy in the Genealogies of Chronicles." In *The Economy of Ancient Judah in Its Historical Context*, edited by Marvin Lloyd Miller et al., 77–101. Winona Lake, IN: Eisenbrauns, 2015.

———. *1 and 2 Chronicles*. Understanding the Bible. Grand Rapids: Baker, 2013.

Master, Daniel M. "Economy and Exchange in the Iron Age Kingdoms of the Southern Levant." *Bulletin of the American Schools of Oriental Research* 372 (2014) 81–97.

Merrill, Eugene. *A Commentary on 1 and 2 Chronicles*. Kregel Exegetical Library. Grand Rapids: Kregel Academic, 2015.

Na'aman, Nadav. "Was Khirbet Qeiyafa a Judahite City? The Case Against It." *Journal of Hebrew Scriptures* 17 (2017) 1–40.

North, Douglass C. *Institutions, Institutional Change, and Economic Performance*. Cambridge: Cambridge University Press, 1990.

———. *Structure and Change in Economic History*. London: Norton, 1981.

Ormanson, Roger L., and John E. Ellington. *A Handbook on 1 and 2 Chronicles*. UBS Handbooks. Miami: UBS, 2014.

Propp, William H. *Exodus 1–18: A New Translation with Introduction and Commentary*. Anchor Bible Commentary. New Haven: Yale University Press, 2008.

Renger, Johannes. "On Economic Structures in Ancient Mesopotamia." *Orientalia* 63.3 (1994) 157–208.

Schipper, Bernd Ulrich. "Raamses, Pithom, and the Exodus: A Critical Evaluation of Ex 1:11." *Vetus Testamentum* 65 (2014) 265–88.

Selman, Martin. *2 Chronicles: An Introduction and Commentary*. Tyndale Old Testament Commentaries 11. Downers Grove, IL: IVP, 1994.

Silver, Morris. *Prophets and Markets: The Political Economy of Ancient Israel*. Boston: Kluwer-Nijhoff, 1983.

Slager, Donald. *A Handbook on 1 and 2 Kings*. New York: United Bible Societies, 2008.

Snell, Daniel C. *Life in the Ancient Near East 3100–332 BC*. New Haven: Yale University Press, 1997.

Stager, Lawrence. "Climatic Conditions and Grain Storage in the Persian Period." *Harvard Theological Review* 64 (1971) 448–50.

Tate, Paulette. "Grain Storage and the Moral Economy in Mesopotamia (3000–2000 BC)." PhD diss., University of Chicago, 2015.

Utzschneider, Helmut, and Wolfgang Oswalt. *Exodus 1–15*. International Exegetical Commentary on the Old Testament. Stuttgart: Kohlhammer, 2015.

Van de Mieroop, Marc. *The Ancient Mesopotamian City*. Oxford: Clarendon, 1997.

Van Leeuwen, Bas, et al. "Markets in Pre-Industrial Societies: Storage in Hellenistic Babylonia in the Medieval English Mirror." *Journal of Global History* 6 (2011) 169–93.

Wiesehöfer, Josef. "Achaemenid Rule and Its Impact on Yehud." In *Texts, Contexts and Readings in Postexilic Literature: Explorations into Historiography*, edited by Louis C. Jonker, Forschungen zum Alten Testament II 53, 171–85. Tübingen: Mohr Siebeck, 2011.

Wiseman, Donald J. *1, 2 Kings*. Tyndale Old Testament Commentaries. Downers Grove, IL: IVP, 1993.

12

The Use of Chronicles in the Gospel of Matthew

Marius J. Nel

The focus of this chapter is primarily on the use of Chronicles[1] as source by the author of the Gospel of Matthew. Its secondary focus is on the possible influence of the redactional approach evident in Chronicles's use of Samuel–Kings on Matthew. Since Chronicles is an interpretive retelling of Samuel–Kings,[2] a better understanding of its redactional approach can be valuable for understanding the literary relationship between the Synoptic Gospels, as the recent studies of Giacobbe and Myers have indicated.[3] In its focus on how Matthew reused, reinterpreted, rearranged, and supplemented Chronicles, this chapter connects with the work of Louis Jonker[4] on how Chronicles maintains continuity and discontinuity with past traditions while (re)formulating

1. In this chapter LXX, or Chronicles LXX, refers to the Greek translation of Chronicles. In Greek manuscripts, it is referred to as Παραλειπομένων ("[Of] the things left out"; Klein, *1 Chronicles*, 26), reflecting the ancient understanding of its relationship with Samuel–Kings. In the Masoretic Text, 1 and 2 Chronicles form one book. It was the translators of the LXX Chronicles that divided it into two books and renamed it; Good, "1–2 Chronicles (Paraleipomena)," 168.

2. Giacobbe, *Luke the Chronicler*, 57.

3. Giacobbe, *Luke the Chronicler*; Myers, "Synoptic Singularity."

4. See also Jonker, "David's Officials," 67, which lists some of his relevant studies.

his contemporary readers' identity. The primary engagement of this chapter will be with Jonker's *Defining All-Israel in Chronicles: Multi-Levelled Identity Negotiation in Late Persian-Period Yehud*.[5]

The Use of Chronicles by Matthew

To describe and understand the possible ways in which Matthew used Chronicles in composing his Gospel, this chapter will use the common differentiation made between quotations, allusions, and echoes in intertextual studies of the New Testament.

Quotations are typically indicated by a citation formula, such as "it is written" (Mark 1:2) or "this was to fulfill" (Matt 2:15),[6] although some scholars warn against rigidly applying these formulas in identifying quotations since there could be some that lack them.[7] The fifth edition of the Greek New Testament published by the United Bible Society lists fifty-four quotations in Matthew. None of these are, however, from Chronicles. There are thus no quotations of Chronicles that can be studied to determine what Matthew's redactional strategy was when using it as a source. It also makes it very difficult to determine the specific Greek or Hebrew version of Chronicles that was used by Matthew.[8]

Allusions are less precise than quotations in that they are comprised of a few key words that are woven into a new composition.[9] They are more difficult to detect than quotations due to their less precise nature, and therefore clear criteria for identifying them need to be set. To qualify as an allusion according to the criteria of Beale, a passage's wording should closely resemble the source text (it must contain an "incomparable or unique parallel in wording, syntax, concept, or cluster of motifs in the same order or structure"), possess the same general meaning, and not reasonably originate from elsewhere.[10] According to

5. Jonker, *Defining All-Israel.*

6. Beale, *Handbook on the New Testament*, 29–30.

7. Moyise, *Old Testament in the New*, 5.

8. This is also the case with Luke. It does appear, however, that when Luke cites the Old Testament, he has a preference for the text that has been preserved in Codex Alexandrinus (LXX^{A}); Giacobbe, *Luke the Chronicler*, 46.

9. Moyise, *Old Testament in the New*, 6.

10. Beale, *Handbook on the New Testament*, 31–32. The expression "like sheep who have no shepherd" (ὡς πρόβατα οἷς οὐκ ἔστιν ποιμήν) that is used in 2 Chr 18:16 occurs in Matt 9:36 (ὡσεὶ πρόβατα μὴ ἔχοντα ποιμένα). It, however, also occurs in Num 27:17 (ὡσεὶ πρόβατα, οἷς οὐκ ἔστιν ποιμήν), and it is thus not apparent that Matt 9:36 is an

this set of criteria, there are various allusions to Chronicles in the Gospel of Matthew that can be analysed.

Lastly, scholars refer to *echoes* when an allusion is so subtle that its conscious use by its author is unlikely. This is especially the case with biblical authors deeply immersed in Scripture who naturally incorporated its idioms and expressions in their own writings. Their intention was often not to explicitly allude to a text as part of an argument or as a significant element of their composition; the allusion simply emerged naturally when creating a text.[11] In his seminal work, *Echoes of Scripture in the Letters of Paul*, Richard B. Hays has provided clear criteria for identifying possible echoes in New Testament texts.[12] These criteria have been incorporated into Beale's approach, though he prefers the term "allusion" to "echo."[13]

In view of the abovementioned distinction made between quotations, allusions, and echoes, it is apparent that while there are no direct quotations of Chronicles in the Gospel of Matthew, there are allusions and echoes to it that are noteworthy.[14] This chapter will specifically focus on two pericopae in Matthew that contain possible allusions to Chronicles. The first is the genealogy of Jesus in Matt 1:1–17 that uses 1 Chr 1–3 to construct Jesus' genealogy. Due to the overlap between 1 Chr 1–3 and Ruth 4:18–22, it is necessary to determine to which of these sources Matthew is alluding to. The second is a possible allusion in Matt 23:35 to 2 Chr 24:1–32. Both pericopae will be analysed using Leslie Allen's[15] approach

allusion to specifically 2 Chr 18:16; Good, "1–2 Chronicles (Paraleipomena)," 174.

11. Moyise, *Old Testament in the New*, 6.

12. According to Hays, identifying scriptural echoes in Paul's writings requires a nuanced approach involving seven key criteria: verifying the availability of the source text to Paul and his readers, assessing the volume and explicit repetition of textual elements, examining the recurrence of similar scriptural references, evaluating thematic coherence with Paul's broader argument, considering historical plausibility of interpretation, reviewing the history of previous interpretations, and ultimately determining the overall satisfaction and illuminative power of the proposed reading. These criteria provide a sophisticated hermeneutical framework for discerning intertextual connections, while acknowledging that certainty remains elusive and interpretive judgment is inherently contextual; Hays, *Echoes of Scripture*, 29–32.

13. Beale, *Handbook on the New Testament*, 33–34.

14. A possible echo of Chronicles is the reference to the Queen of Sheba who is referred to as the "Queen of the South" (*βασίλισσα νότου*) in Matt 12:42. This reference may allude to 2 Chr 9:1 (*βασίλισσα Σαβα*), but this is impossible to determine conclusively as there are also other Old Testament references to her; Good, "1–2 Chronicles (Paraleipomena)," 175.

15. Allen, *Greek Chronicles*, conducted an extensive study of the LXX translation

to describing the relationship between the Septuagint (LXX) and the Masoretic Text (MT) by considering additions, omissions, possible errors, and deliberate changes evident in Matthew's use of Chronicles. It will also be attempted to determine if Matthew used the LXX or the MT text of Chronicles and if he preferred Ruth as a source over Chronicles.

Before undertaking the task described above, it is necessary to note what this chapter, due to its limited scope (along with the already-noted lack of quotations of Chronicles in Matthew), will not attempt to do. This chapter will only investigate the possible LXX and MT texts used by Matthew and not the relationships between different versions of the LXX or its sources. It is important to acknowledge this since in considering how Matthew uses the LXX[16] translation of the MT,[17] the clear differences between the LXX and Matthew's versions of particular texts ultimately needs to be accounted for. This is, however, a very difficult process since the differences could be attributed to Matthean redaction, the translation process that produced the LXX, differences in the textual tradition of the LXX, or the texts it is based on in that it could reflect variances in the MT textual tradition or its *Vorlage*. When encountering a variation between the LXX wording of Chronicles and the MT, for example, it is thus crucial to determine when and why the divergence occurred. It is also important to determine if they are deliberate deviations by the translators of the LXX from the MT, or as Allen claims in numerous instances, the result of differences that occur within the Greek tradition.[18] While determining the specific LXX version of Chronicles used by Matthew is not the focus

of the MT that still informs contemporary studies. Allen concluded that behind the notable Greek corruptions and unique characteristics of the translation, there exists a Hebrew text that, in many instances, can be compared to the MT. Allen's second volume focuses specifically on identifying and analysing the differences between Chronicles LXX and Chronicles MT. See also Klein, *1 Chronicles*, 26.

16. The Septuagint text used in the chapter is that of Rahlfs and Hanhart *Septuaginta: SESB Edition.*

17. The Masoretic Text used is that of the second edition of the *Biblia Hebraica Stuttgartensia.*

18. Allen is confident that in most instances the Greek text can be corrected with reasonable confidence, often with the assistance of text forms other than the Groningen Codex. This is necessary since while the Groningen Codex represents the oldest text form of Chronicles, it is corrupted. This is particularly evident in cases involving variations in the form of names, which is important for any investigation into the use of the LXX version of Chronicles in Matt 1:1–17. There are also apparently instances where it is not only the corruption of the Greek text that creates variations in that the LXX's source text that was translated. The variations could, for instance, reflect the MT's *Vorlage* instead of the transmitted MT; Allen, *Greek Chronicles*, 1.

of this chapter, engaging with this complex issue is an important one for fully understanding how he redacted the Jewish Scriptures. As already stated, the lack of direct quotations of Chronicles by Matthew, however, makes it an almost impossible task to undertake.

Matthew's Redactional Approach to the LXX

In the following section, the way Matt 1:1–17 uses 1 Chr 1–3 to construct Jesus' genealogy and the possible allusion in Matt 23:35 to 2 Chr 24:1–32 will be analysed.

Chronistic Allusions in Matt 1:1–17

The most extensive use of Chronicles by Matthew occurs in Jesus' genealogy. The genealogy of Jesus in Matt 1:1–17 is comprised of a string of allusions to Chronicles. Since Matthew does not simply take over all the genealogies in Chronicles, it is best to understand him alluding to Chronicles rather than him quoting it.

Using the criteria of Beale that in the case of an allusion, a passage's wording should closely resemble the source text (it must contain an "incomparable or unique parallel in wording, syntax, concept, or cluster of motifs in the same order or structure"), possess the same general meaning, and not reasonably originate from elsewhere, it is possible to identify allusions to 1 Chr 1:28, 1:34, and 2:1–15 in Matt 1:2–6a. There are a number of wording parallels of identical names that occur in identical sequence: Abraham, Isaac, Jacob, Judah, Perez, Hezron, Ram, Amminadab, Nahshon, Salmon, Boaz, Obed, Jesse, and David. There are furthermore syntactical parallels in the genealogical structure of the texts. There are also conceptual parallels in that Matthew, like Chronicles, traces the Israelite patriarchal lineage, establishes Davidic royal ancestry, and demonstrates covenantal continuity. They likewise have the same general meaning in that both 1 Chr 1–3 and Matt 1:1–17 describe genealogical progression and emphasise divine covenant transmission through specific family lines. In terms of distinctiveness, the name sequence is unique with no extant alternative textual sources for this precise lineage. The inclusion of notable women (Tamar, Rahab, Ruth) is also somewhat unusual for genealogical records. In view of Beale's assessment that a proposed allusion takes on greater probability if both unique wording and verbal and thematic coherence are found, it is thus justified to describe elements in Matt 1:1–17 as probable allusions to 1 Chr 1–3. It should be noted that Beale stresses that recognising allusions results in degrees of probability and possibility, not full certainty.[19]

Chronicles is, however, not the only textual source used by Matthew in composing the genealogy. Matthew 1:2–6a utilises the summaries in 1 Chr 1:28, 34; 2:1–15; and Ruth 4:18–22 for the names of persons from Abraham to David that are also mentioned in Genesis and other historical sections of the Jewish Scriptures.[20] The historical events presupposed by Matt 1:6b–11 are described in the two books of Kings, while the succession of named kings is summarised in 1 Chr 3:5, 10–17.[21] They are, however, not part of the mini-genealogy found in Ruth 4:18–22.[22] Matthew 1:12 agrees with 1 Chr 3:17 MT that has Jechoniah (יְכָנְיָה) as the father of Shealtiel, while 1 Chr 3:17 LXX has Ιεχονια-ασιρ (Jechoniah-Asir). According to 1 Chr 3:19 LXX, Jechoniah was the father of Zerubbabel, whereas 1 Chr 3:19 MT has Zerubbabel as the son of Pedaiah (apparently a brother of Shealtiel).[23] Matthew 1:12 thus follows the LXX's general identification pattern for Zerubbabel's lineage.[24] In using his source material from the Jewish Scriptures, it is thus clear that Matthew makes a number of additions, omissions, and changes. Matthew 1:13–16 has no parallels in the Jewish Scriptures.[25]

Additions

In addition to mentioning Judah in Matt 1:2, the ancestor of the tribe to which the Davidic dynasty belongs (as described in Gen 49:8–12), Matthew adds a reference to Judah's brothers.

> Matt 1:2—Ἀβραὰμ ἐγέννησεν τὸν Ἰσαάκ, Ἰσαὰκ δὲ ἐγέννησεν τὸν Ἰακώβ, Ἰακὼβ δὲ ἐγέννησεν τὸν Ἰούδαν καὶ τοὺς ἀδελφοὺς αὐτοῦ.

19. Beale, *Handbook on the New Testament*, 31–32.
20. Hagner, *Matthew 1–13*, 7.
21. Gundry, *Matthew*, 15; France, *Gospel of Matthew*, 38.
22. Nolland, *Gospel of Matthew*, 79.
23. Nolland, *Gospel of Matthew*, 84–85.
24. The text of the New Testament used in this chapter is the Nestle et al., *Novum Testamentum Graece*.
25. Nolland, *Gospel of Matthew*, 84–85.

1 Chr 1:34—Καὶ ἐγέννησεν Αβρααμ τὸν Ισαακ. καὶ υἱοὶ Ισαακ Ησαυ καὶ Ιακωβ.

This reference, although not essential to the genealogy itself, may have been inspired by the list of Judah's brothers found in 1 Chr 2:1–2 and used by Matthew due to his interest in depicting the church as a brotherhood.[26] In 1:11 Matthew again mentions brothers, specifically those of Jeconiah, also known as Jehoiachin in the Jewish Scriptures. However, 1 Chr 3:16 only mentions one brother of Jeconiah.

Matt 1:11—Ἰωσίας δὲ ἐγέννησεν ⸆ τὸν Ἰεχονίαν καὶ τοὺς ἀδελφοὺς αὐτοῦ ἐπὶ τῆς μετοικεσίας Βαβυλῶνος.

1 Chr 3:16—καὶ υἱοὶ Ιωακιμ· Ιεχονιας υἱὸς αὐτοῦ, Σεδεκιας υἱὸς αὐτοῦ. (The sons of Jehoiakim: his son Jehoiachin and his son Zedekiah.)

The mention of brothers in the plural by Matthew has led to the suggestion of an early scribal error. A copyist may have mistakenly written Jeconiah's name where Matthew originally referred to Jehoiakim, whose brothers are mentioned in 1 Chr 3:15.[27] This supposition allows for the inclusion of Jeconiah in the third set of fourteen generations (1:17). Matthew links Jeconiah with the deportation to Babylon (τῆς μετοικεσίας Βαβυλῶνος), an apparent reference to the Chronicler's description of Jeconiah, not Jehoiakim, as "the captive" (1 Chr 3:17 in the MT).[28] It could thus be that Matthew intentionally skips Jehoiakim[29] and that the brothers of Jeconiah referred to his fellow Jews and not his family members.[30] This understanding of Jeconiah's brothers suggests that the concept of brotherhood is employed throughout Matthew's narrative in a broader theological sense to indicate that the brotherhood that originated with Jacob's twelve sons culminated in Jeconiah's fellow Jews (his "brothers") being taken into exile, before a new brotherhood comprised of Jesus' disciples are commissioned to make disciples of all nations (Matt 28:19).[31]

26. Gundry, *Matthew*, 14.

27. Gundry, *Matthew*, 16.

28. Gundry, *Matthew*, 16.

29. The LXX uses Ιωακιμ for both Jehoiakim (1 Chr 3:16) and Jehoiachin (1 Chr 3:17). Matthew, however, does not mention Jehoiakim; France, *Gospel of Matthew*, 27.

30. Like Judah's brothers are to be understood as the people of God in their time (Matt 1:2), the "brothers" of Jeconiah are thus the people of God who went into exile and not solely the family of Jeconiah; Gundry, *Matthew*, 17.

31. Gundry, *Matthew*, 17.

Another inclusion in Matthew is the mentioning of Ruth (τῆς Ῥούθ) in verse 5 when discussing Rahab (τῆς Ῥαχάβ) since she is not mentioned in lists in the Jewish Scriptures that serve as source for Matthew (cf. 1 Chr 2:12; Ruth 4:21).[32]

> Matt 1:5—Σαλμὼν δὲ ἐγέννησεν τὸν ⸀Βόες ἐκ τῆς Ῥαχάβ, Βόες δὲ ἐγέννησεν τὸν Ἰωβὴδ ἐκ τῆς Ῥούθ, Ἰωβὴδ δὲ ἐγέννησεν τὸν Ἰεσσαί.

Rahab was a Canaanite woman revered by Jewish rabbis as a gentile convert. She serves as a foreshadowing, alongside Tamar, of the inclusion of gentiles into the community of believers.[33] First Chronicles (and Luke) does not mention Ruth as the mother of Obed, but in Ruth 4:9–22, which presents a parallel genealogy, there is a connection between Ruth and Tamar. It is thus possible that to align with this association and to present Ruth as another prototype of gentiles entering the church,[34] Matthew includes her in the genealogy of Jesus.[35] This use of the book of Ruth indicates that Matthew is not restricted to using 1 Chronicles as source.

> Matt 1:6—Ἰεσσαὶ δὲ ἐγέννησεν τὸν Δαυὶδ τὸν βασιλέα. Δαυὶδ δὲ ⸆ ἐγέννησεν τὸν Σολομῶνα ἐκ τῆς τοῦ Οὐρίου.

The description of David as "the king" (τὸν βασιλέα) in 1:6 is not used in 1 Chr 1–3,[36] although it is frequently associated with his name in other writings of the Jewish Scriptures (e.g., 2 Sam 6:12, 7:18).[37] By employing this designation from the Jewish Scriptures, Matthew presents David as a prototype of Jesus and signifies the conclusion of the initial section of the genealogy (Matt 1:17).[38]

32. Hagner, *Matthew 1–13*, 11.

33. Gundry, *Matthew*, 14–15.

34. Gundry, *Matthew*, 15.

35. Rahab, the prostitute mentioned in Joshua 2:1–21, lived at least a century too early to be the wife of David's great-grandfather. If she is thus to be understood as the Rahab referred to by Matthew, the genealogy of Jesus is incomplete here; France, *Gospel of Matthew*, 36.

36. Nolland, *Gospel of Matthew*, 77.

37. The LXX^{A} text of Ruth 4:22 refers to "David the king," but according to Nolland, this may reflect the influence of Matthew; Nolland, *Gospel of Matthew*, 78.

38. Gundry, *Matthew*, 15.

Omissions

Besides the abovementioned additions by Matthew to the LXX version of 1 Chronicles, there are also a number of omissions. In 1:6 an unnamed woman is introduced into Matthew's genealogy, marking the fourth occurrence of a woman in the genealogy of Jesus.

> Matt 1:6—'Ιεσσαὶ δὲ ἐγέννησεν τὸν Δαυὶδ τὸν βασιλέα. Δαυὶδ δὲ ᵀ ἐγέννησεν τὸν Σολομῶνα ἐκ τῆς [. . .] τοῦ Οὐρίου.

The source of the unnamed woman is 1 Chr 3:5, where she is referred to as "Bathshua" (daughter of Shua) in the MT (בַּת־שׁוּעַ) and "Bathsheba" (Βηρσαβεέ) in the LXX. She is identified as Solomon's mother in both the MT and LXX versions of 1 Chr 3:5. Matthew, however, omits her name and departs from the Chronicler's description of her as "the daughter of Ammiel."[39] Matthew instead highlights her relationship with her husband by describing her as "the [wife] of Uriah" (cf. 2 Sam 11:26; 12:10, 15).

> 1 Chr 3:5—καὶ οὗτοι ἐτέχθησαν αὐτῷ ἐν Ιερουσαλημ· Σαμαα, Σωβαβ, Ναθαν καὶ Σαλωμων, τέσσαρες τῇ [Βηρσαβεε] θυγατρὶ Αμιηλ.
>
> וְאֵ֥לֶּה נוּלְּדוּ־ל֖וֹ בִּירוּשָׁלָ֑יִם שִׁמְעָא וְשׁוֹבָ֔ב וְנָתָ֖ן וּשְׁלֹמֹ֑ה אַרְבָּעָ֔ה לְבַת־שׁ֖וּעַ בַּת־עַמִּיאֵֽל׃

The changes made by Matthew in identifying Solomon's mother draw attention to her transformation into a gentile through her marriage to Uriah, who is identified as a Hittite in the Jewish Scriptures.[40] Once again, the Matthean genealogy thus anticipates the inclusion of gentiles in the church.[41]

While Matthew draws attention to her marriage to Uriah, who is identified as a Hittite and thus a gentile, to possibly anticipate the inclusion of gentiles in the church, by highlighting Bathsheba's transformation into a gentile through marriage, the Chronicler's view of intermarriage with non-Israelites is more complex. Knoppers has identified at least six instances of intermarriage with non-Israelites that the Chronicler includes without criticism of these unions.[42] He does, however, criticise some of the actions of those involved. The Chronicler's purpose in including these instances of intermarriage with non-Israelites is not

39. Gundry, *Matthew*, 15.

40. Gundry, *Matthew*, 15.

41. Gundry, *Matthew*, 15.

42. Knoppers, "Intermarriage, Social Complexity."

to exclude but to include a range of groups into the broader Judahite identity. The Chronicler's inclusive approach in this regard differs from that of Ezra and Nehemiah, who sought to preserve a distinct Israelite identity by mandating the divorce of those who had intermarried with native peoples. Therefore, while the author of the Gospel of Matthew may have used Bathsheba's marriage to Uriah to foreshadow the inclusion of gentiles in the church, the Chronicler's perspective is more nuanced. The Chronicler's genealogies do not suggest that marriage to a non-Israelite would automatically transform someone into a gentile. Instead, the Chronicler emphasises the ethnic diversity within Judah and the inclusion of non-Israelites into the community.

To achieve the required number of fourteen generations leading up to the Babylonian exile (as mentioned in 1:17), Matthew in 1:8 excludes three successive kings (Ahaziah, Joash, and Amaziah), as found in 1 Chr 3:11–12, from Jesus' genealogy that should have linked Joram to Uzziah. He also omits the brothers Jehoahaz and Jehoiakim that came between Josiah and Jehoiachin.[43]

> Matt 1:8—Ἀσὰφ δὲ ἐγέννησεν τὸν Ἰωσαφάτ, Ἰωσαφὰτ δὲ ἐγέννησεν τὸν Ἰωράμ, Ἰωρὰμ δὲ ἐγέννησεν τὸν Ὀζίαν.
>
> 1 Chr 3:11–12—Ιωραμ υἱὸς αὐτοῦ, Οχοζια υἱὸς αὐτοῦ, Ιωας υἱὸς αὐτοῦ, Αμασιας υἱὸς αὐτοῦ, Αζαρια υἱὸς αὐτοῦ, Ιωαθαν υἱὸς αὐτοῦ.

The omission of some of the first three kings omitted (Ahaziah, Joash, and Amaziah)[44] could be an error due to the confusion of Ahaziah (Ὀχοζίας, or Ὀζείας according to Codex B) with Uzziah (Ὀζίας) (alternatively known as Azariah) in Greek.[45] While 1 Chr 3:12 LXX has Οχοζια for Ahaziah, it has Ἀζαρίας (Azariah) for Uzziah while Matt 1:9 has Ὀζίας. Matthew may thus have used the LXX form Ὀζ(ε)ία(ς)[46] that

43. France, *Gospel of Matthew*, 30.

44. Second Kings 23:30—24:20 mention three brothers (Jehoahaz, Jehoiakim, and Zedekiah) who ruled in succession. France states that "according to 2 Kings the three omitted rulers were not Jehoiachin's brothers, but his father and uncles, but 2 Chr 36:10 (cf. also 1 Chr 3:16) says Zedekiah was Jehoiachin's 'brother' (though LXX has 'father's brother'), while LXX 4 Kgdms 24:17 makes him the 'son' of the exiled king, whom it calls by the same name as his father, 'Ioakim.'" France, *Gospel of Matthew*, 38. Johnson argues from the LXX textual confusion that the omission of the three kings was originally accidental, but that then "the accident was turned into virtue" and Matthew's scheme of fourteens was the result. Johnson, *Genealogies*, 181–82.

45. Hagner, *Matthew 1–13*, 7–8.

46. Gundry, *Matthew*, 16.

originally referred to Ahaziah (rendered ᾿Οχοζ[ε]ία[ς] in the LXX) to refer to Uzziah (Azariah).[47] A similar confusion could have occurred with the names of Jehoiakim (omitted by Matthew) and Jehoiachin, which the LXX does not differentiate in that it uses ᾿Ιωακιμ for both names.[48] The brief reign of Jehoahaz of only three months could in turn explain why he does not represent a separate "generation."[49] The name Jeconiah (᾿Ιεχονίας) in verse 11 follows the LXX in giving an alternative name for Jehoiachin, son of Jehoiakim.[50]

> Matt 1:8—Ἀσὰφ δὲ ἐγέννησεν τὸν ᾿Ιωσαφάτ, ᾿Ιωσαφὰτ δὲ ἐγέννησεν τὸν ᾿Ιωράμ, ᾿Ιωρὰμ δὲ ἐγέννησεν τὸν ᾿Οζίαν, 9 ᾿Οζίας δὲ ἐγέννησεν τὸν ᾿Ιωαθάμ, ᾿Ιωαθὰμ δὲ ἐγέννησεν τὸν ⸀Ἀχάζ, Ἀχὰζ δὲ ἐγέννησεν τὸν ῾Εζεκίαν.

> 1 Chr 3:11–12—Ιωραμ υἱὸς αὐτοῦ, Οχοζια υἱὸς αὐτοῦ, Ιωας υἱὸς αὐτοῦ, † Αμασιας υἱὸς αὐτοῦ, Αζαρια υἱὸς αὐτοῦ, Ιωαθαν υἱὸς αὐτοῦ. (Joram his son, Ahaziah his son, Joash his son, Amaziah his son, Azariah his son, Jotham his son.)

First Chronicles 3:15 names four sons of Josiah: Johanan, Jehoiakim, Zedekiah, and Shallum, of which all but Jeconiah in the place of "Jehoiakim" are omitted by Matthew in verse 11 to ensure that the second section of the genealogy concludes with the Babylonian exile while maintaining a count of only fourteen generations.[51] Matthew 1:11 again refers to brothers in line with his focus on brotherhood.

> Matt 1:11—᾿Ιωσίας δὲ ἐγέννησεν ⸆ τὸν ᾿Ιεχονίαν καὶ <u>τοὺς ἀδελφοὺς αὐτοῦ</u> ἐπὶ τῆς μετοικεσίας Βαβυλῶνος.

> 1 Chr 3:15—καὶ υἱοὶ Ιωσια· πρωτότοκος Ιωαναν, ὁ δεύτερος Ιωακιμ, ὁ τρίτος Σεδεκια, ὁ τέταρτος Σαλουμ.

47. According to Nolland, "Ahaziah is normally rendered ᾿Οχοζ(ε)ία(ς) in the LXX, but in 1 Ch. 3:11 the B text has ᾿Οζεία, and A, V, and Lucian have ᾿Οζιάς. For Uzziah = Azariah the LXX normally has ᾿Οζ(ε)ίας or Ἀζαρία(ς). In 1 Ch. 3:12 the B text has Ἀζαρία, the A text Ἀζαρίας, and Lucian ᾿Οζιάς." Nolland, *Gospel of Matthew*, 80.

48. Nolland, *Gospel of Matthew*, 82; France, *Gospel of Matthew*, 30.

49. France, *Gospel of Matthew*, 30.

50. The form *Jeconiah* occurs in both the Hebrew and LXX versions of 1 Chr 3:16–17; France, *Gospel of Matthew*, 30.

51. Gundry, *Matthew*, 16. See Nolland, *Gospel of Matthew*, 81–84, for a discussion of other possible reasons for the omission of Jehoiakim's name.

The names listed in Matt 1:6–11[52] are all derived from 1 Chr 3:5, 10–16 in that the genealogy in Ruth 4:18–22 ends with David.[53] Matthew does not here provide a genealogy based on physical descent for Joseph, who was Jesus' foster father according to Luke 3:23. He instead presents a list of royal figures who serve as prototypes of Jesus, the King of the Jews.[54] The list, based on 1 Chr 1:34 and 2:1–15, provides him with fourteen generations from Abraham through David.[55]

Changes

There are some of the names in Matthew's genealogy that differ from how they are spelled in the LXX.

Matthew, firstly, appends a φ to Asa's name mentioned in 1 Chr 3:10 in Matt 1:7–8.

> Matt 1:7–8—Σολομὼν δὲ ἐγέννησεν τὸν Ῥοβοάμ, Ῥοβοὰμ δὲ ἐγέννησεν τὸν ⸀Ἀβιά, Ἀβιὰ δὲ ἐγέννησεν τὸν ⸁Ἀσάφ, Ἀσὰφ δὲ ἐγέννησεν τὸν Ἰωσαφάτ, Ἰωσαφὰτ δὲ ἐγέννησεν τὸν Ἰωράμ, Ἰωρὰμ δὲ ἐγέννησεν τὸν Ὀζίαν.
>
> 1 Chr 3:10—Υἱοὶ Σαλωμων· Ροβοαμ, Αβια υἱὸς αὐτοῦ, Ασα υἱὸς αὐτοῦ, Ιωσαφατ υἱὸς αὐτοῦ.

Matthew's spelling, secondly, of Ἰωαθάμ in 1:9 for Jotham follows the common LXX spelling but differs from that found at 1 Chr 3:12 (Ἰωαθάν).[56] Matthew 1:10, thirdly, also deviates from the name "Amon" (Αμων) as found in 1 Chr 3:14 in it being rendered as "Amos" (Ἀμώς).

> Matt 1:10—Ἑζεκίας δὲ ἐγέννησεν τὸν ⸀Μανασσῆ, ⸁Μανασσῆς δὲ ἐγέννησεν τὸν ⸀Ἀμώς, Ἀμὼς δὲ ἐγέννησεν τὸν Ἰωσίαν.
>
> 1 Chr 3:14—Αμων υἱὸς αὐτοῦ, Ιωσια υἱὸς αὐτοῦ.

52. These names differ from the corresponding names in Luke's genealogy and represent the descendants of David who succeeded him as rulers until the time of the Babylonian exile.

53. Ruth 4:18–22 presents a parallel genealogy that traces the lineage from Perez to David.

54. Gundry, *Matthew*, 15.

55. Gundry, *Matthew*, 18.

56. Nolland, *Gospel of Matthew*, 80.

This change can be attributed to either orthographical variation or a simple confusion of names within the textual tradition of the LXX[57] since Ἀμώς does occur in the LXX instead of Αμων.[58] It could also be that Matthew is here recalling the prophet Amos instead of Manasseh's son Amon.[59]

Matthew's Sources for Composing the Genealogy of Jesus

In noting Matthew's redactional activity in Matt 1:1–17, it can be asked whether he used the LXX or MT versions of his sources from the Jewish Scriptures and if he preferred Chronicles to Ruth as a source.

LXX or MT as Source?

There is clear evidence that Matthew customarily utilises the LXX in composing the genealogy of Jesus. The names of Jacob (1:2), Judah (1:2–3), Perez (1:3), Zerah (1:3), Tamar (1:3), Hezron (1:3), Aram (1:3–4), Amminadab (1:4), Nahshon (1:4), Salmon[60] (1:4–5), Boaz (1:5), Obed (1:5), Jesse (1:5–6), and David (1:6) are all derived from 1 Chr 1:34a in the LXX. The LXX versions of 1 Chr 2:1, 4, 5, 9 (deviating from "Ram" in the MT) and 2:10, 11 (differing from "Salma" in the MT) and 2:12 also provides a possible source for these names.[61] Matthew 1:4, that refers to Aram, moreover, aligns with the LXX version of 1 Chr 2:9–10 that provides additional details beyond the core list found in Ruth 4:18–22 in that it mentions four sons for Hezron in contrast to the three of the MT.

> Matt 1:3–4—Ἰούδας δὲ ἐγέννησεν τὸν Φάρες καὶ τὸν ⸀Ζάρα ἐκ τῆς Θαμάρ, Φάρες δὲ ἐγέννησεν τὸν Ἑσρώμ, Ἑσρὼμ δὲ ἐγέννησεν τὸν Ἀράμ, Ἀρὰμ δὲ ἐγέννησεν τὸν Ἀμιναδάβ, Ἀμιναδὰβ δὲ ἐγέννησεν τὸν Ναασσών, Ναασσὼν δὲ ἐγέννησεν τὸν Σαλμών.
>
> Ruth 4:19—Εσρων δὲ ἐγέννησεν τὸν Αρραν, καὶ Αρραν ἐγέννησεν τὸν Αμιναδαβ. (Ruth 4:19, Ἀρραν = "Arran")

57. Gundry, *Matthew*, 16.
58. Nolland, *Gospel of Matthew*, 81.
59. France, *Gospel of Matthew*, 27.
60. The spelling of Salmon is also that of 1 Chr 2:11 LXX; Nolland, *Gospel of Matthew*, 77.
61. Gundry, *Matthew*, 14.

1 Chr 2:9–10—καὶ υἱοὶ Εσερων, οἳ ἐτέχθησαν αὐτῷ· ὁ Ιραμεηλ καὶ ὁ Ραμ καὶ ὁ Χαλεβ καὶ Αραμ. καὶ Αραμ ἐγέννησεν τὸν Αμιναδαβ, καὶ Αμιναδαβ ἐγέννησεν τὸν Ναασσων ἄρχοντα τοῦ οἴκου Ιουδα. (1 Chr 2:9–10, Ἀραμ = "Aram")

1 Chr 2:9–11—

וּבְנֵ֥י חֶצְר֖וֹן אֲשֶׁ֣ר נוֹלַד־ל֑וֹ אֶת־יְרַחְמְאֵ֥ל וְאֶת־רָ֖ם וְאֶת־כְּלוּבָֽי׃

וְרָ֖ם הוֹלִ֣יד אֶת־עַמִּינָדָ֑ב וְעַמִּֽינָדָב֙ הוֹלִ֣יד אֶת־נַחְשׁ֔וֹן נְשִׂ֖יא בְּנֵ֥י יְהוּדָֽה׃

The additional son that is mentioned by Matthew, Aram, is furthermore named by him as the father of Amminadab, and not Ram as in the MT.[62] Matthew also substitutes Salmon for Sala (mentioned in Luke 3:32) in 1:4 to correspond with 1 Chr 2:11 in the LXX,[63] as he does with Obed in 1:5 which reflects the LXXA reading of 1 Chr 2:12.[64] Matthew and Luke also align when it comes to Salathiel and Zerubbabel in Matt 1:12, with both Gospel writers agreeing with the LXX version of 1 Chr 3:17–19 while deviating from the MT by stating that Salathiel, instead of Pedaiah, was the father of Zerubbabel.[65]

There is thus ample evidence that Matt 1:1–17 depends on the LXX rather than the MT as source. There are, however, exceptions that need to be taken into consideration. The Matthean Βόες in 1:5 for "Boaz" differs from the LXX Βόος or Βόοζ.[66] In the same verse the name Rahab is also spelled in accordance with the Hebrew text rather than the LXX[67] (Ῥαχάβ instead of Ῥαάβ in the LXX as in Josh 2:1, 3; 6:17, 23, 25; and rest of the NT as in Heb 11:31, Jas 2:25).[68] There is thus a possibility that in some instances Matthew preferred to work with a Hebrew text.

62. Nolland suggests that Aram and Ram may have been variant transliterations of the Hebrew *rm* that were subsequently mistaken to refer to different persons, resulting in the additional name occurring in the LXX version of 1 Chr 2:9–10. It is also conversely possible that one of two similar names has dropped out of the MT version of 1 Chr 2:9 and that the following verse was subsequently adjusted (*rm* for *ʾrm*). In this case Ruth 4:18–22 (MT and LXX) could possibly have used this version of 1 Chr 2:9–10; Nolland, *Gospel of Matthew*, 77.

63. Gundry, *Matthew*, 14.

64. Nolland, *Gospel of Matthew*, 78.

65. Gundry, *Matthew*, 17.

66. Nolland, *Gospel of Matthew*, 78.

67. Nolland, *Gospel of Matthew*, 78.

68. There is no support in the Old Testament for her role as the mother of Boaz; Gundry, *Matthew*, 14.

Ruth or 1 Chronicles as Primary Source

In light of Matt 1:3–4 including Aram from the LXX version of 1 Chr 2:9–10 who is not mentioned in Ruth 4:18–22, the question arises, Which of these Jewish Scripture books, Ruth or Chronicles, served as Matthew's primary source? As indicated previously it seems as if Matthew here follows 1 Chr 2:9–10 LXX in which the form "Aram" (Ἀραμ) is used instead of the "Arran" (Ἀρραν) in Ruth 4:19. The names Zerah,[69] Tamar, Aram, and Salmon used by Matthew in verse 3 also align only with the LXX version of 1 Chronicles and not with the parallel genealogy provided by Ruth 4:18–22. First Chronicles 3:19–20 furthermore provides the names of seven sons (and one daughter) of Zerubbabel, as well as names from several subsequent generations. Matthew, however, at times deviates from 1 Chronicles while aligning with Luke.[70] This suggests that Matthew could also have used a different, unknown, genealogy as a source that was similar to the one found in Luke. In view of the above, it can be concluded that while Matthew usually follows 1 Chronicles, he supplements it with material found in Ruth as well as other texts. He also used various sources in composing the final section of Jesus' genealogy.[71]

Chronistic Allusion in Matt 23:35

In Matt 23:35 (par. Luke 11:50–51)[72] Jesus refers "the blood of righteous Abel to the blood of Zechariah son of Berechiah,[73] whom you murdered between the temple and the altar."

69. The inclusion in verse 3 of Zerah, who was likely a Canaanite (as seen in Gen 38), alongside Perez and their mother Tamar differs from Luke's account. This choice aligns with 1 Chr 2:4 and highlights Tamar as a representative of the gentiles, whose inclusion Matthew advocates for; see Gundry, *Matthew*, 14.

70. The main difference is that Matthew does not trace the succession of kings through any of Zerubbabel's sons listed in 1 Chr 3:19–20; France, *Gospel of Matthew*, 39. This supports the claim that Matthew's intention with his genealogy is not to present a line of physical descent, as is evident in his substitution of reigning kings.

71. Gundry, *Matthew*, 17–18.

72. Luke 11:51, unlike Matt 23:35, does not mention Zechariah being the son of Berechiah (υἱοῦ Βαραχίου) and thus escapes the problem of the Zechariah he mentions having a different father than in Chronicles. It could have been added to Q by Matthew, or less likely, deleted from Q by Luke; Hagner, *Matthew 14–28*, 676–77.

73. The only extant manuscript of Matthew which omits the problematic reference to Zechariah being the "son of Berechiah" is Codex Sinaiticus. The phrase was, however, restored by a corrector; France, *Gospel of Matthew*, 881.

Matt 23:35—ὅπως ἔλθῃ ἐφ' ὑμᾶς πᾶν αἷμα δίκαιον ἐκχυννόμενον ἐπὶ τῆς γῆς ἀπὸ τοῦ αἵματος Ἅβελ τοῦ δικαίου ἕως τοῦ αἵματος Ζαχαρίου ⸋υἱοῦ Βαραχίου⸌, ὃν ἐφονεύσατε μεταξὺ τοῦ ναοῦ καὶ τοῦ θυσιαστηρίου.

2 Chr 24:20–21—καὶ πνεῦμα θεοῦ ἐνέδυσεν τὸν Αζαριαν τὸν τοῦ Ιωδαε τὸν ἱερέα, καὶ ἀνέστη ἐπάνω τοῦ λαοῦ καὶ εἶπεν Τάδε λέγει κύριος Τί παραπορεύεσθε τὰς ἐντολὰς κυρίου; καὶ οὐκ εὐοδωθήσεσθε, ὅτι ἐγκατελίπετε τὸν κύριον, καὶ ἐγκαταλείψει ὑμᾶς. καὶ ἐπέθεντο αὐτῷ καὶ ἐλιθοβόλησαν αὐτὸν δι' ἐντολῆς Ιωας τοῦ βασιλέως ἐν αὐλῇ οἴκου κυρίου.

2 Chr 24:20–21—

וְרוּחַ אֱלֹהִים לָבְשָׁה אֶת־זְכַרְיָה בֶּן־יְהוֹיָדָע הַכֹּהֵן וַיַּעֲמֹד מֵעַל לָע וַיֹּאמֶר לָהֶם כֹּה אָמַר הָאֱלֹהִים לָמָּה אַתֶּם עֹבְרִים אֶת־מִצְוֹת יהוה וְלֹא תַצְלִיחוּ כִּי־עֲזַבְתֶּם אֶת־יהוה וַיַּעֲזֹב אֶתְכֶם׃

וַיִּקְשְׁרוּ עָלָיו וַיִּרְגְּמֻהוּ אֶבֶן בְּמִצְוַת הַמֶּלֶךְ בַּחֲצַר בֵּית יהוה׃

The murder of Zechariah the son of Jehoiada, not Berechiah, is mentioned in 2 Chr 24:1–21 (MT). The LXX makes Zechariah the son of Jeberechiah, with it being the longer form of Berechiah. The difficulty is that Berechiah is most likely the father of the prophet Zechariah (Zech 1:1) who lived three hundred years after the death of the priest Zechariah conveyed in 2 Chr 24.[74] While the father of the murdered Zechariah in Matthew thus differs from Chronicles, the manner of his death is similar. The priest was killed between the sanctuary and the altar according to Matt 23, which correlates with the description of him being killed in the court of the temple (2 Chr 24:21). There is, however, no tradition[75] of the prophet Zechariah (the son of Berechiah) being killed in the temple since the temple was in ruins in his time.[76] There is in fact no record of him being killed at any locale. According to Jewish tradition he instead died peacefully at an advanced age (Lives of the

74. France, *Gospel of Matthew*, 880.

75. There is also the possibility that Matthew knew about Zechariah, the son of Baris (or Bariscaeus or Baruch), a wealthy man that was killed by the Zealots in about 69 CE during the first Jewish war that is mentioned by Josephus (*Jewish War* 4.334–44); Davies and Allison, *Matthew 19–28*, 318; Turner, *Matthew*, 558. This option would mean that the reference was the creation of Matthew. This possibility cannot be discarded in that it would refer to the very first murder in the OT and to the most recent murder known to him; Hagner, *Matthew 14–28*, 676–77.

76. Davies and Allison, *Matthew 19–28*, 318; Nolland, *Gospel of Matthew*, 946–47.

Prophets 15:6).[77] It thus seems as if Matthew confused the postexilic prophet Zechariah[78] with the preexilic priest Zechariah. This confusion is possible because there are more than thirty Zechariahs identified in the Old Testament, presenting the possibility of them being confused or even intentionally conflated with each other![79] Gundry suggests that Matthew's conflation of the two Zechariahs was influenced by him using the prophecy of Zechariah son of Berechiah in Matt 27:9–10 to explain the betrayal of Jesus' "innocent blood" (27:4).[80]

The intent of Matt 23:35 (par. Luke 11:50–51 and thus from Q) is probably to illustrate the persecution faced by God's messengers throughout the ages since the murders of Abel (Gen 4:8) and Zechariah (2 Chr 24:20–22) represent the first and last murders in the Jewish Scriptures,[81] if Chronicles is seen as the last book of the Jewish Scriptures.[82] In this case the dying curse the priest Zechariah uttered that Yahweh might hear and avenge his words would link Matt 23:35 to the cry of the spilled blood of Abel in Gen 4:10.[83] As with the murder of Abel, the murder of Zechariah cried out for vengeance (2 Chr 24:22).[84] It is thus a question if Matthew in describing the death of Zechariah is dependent on the MT, and not the LXX, since the inclusion between the first and last murders in the Old Testament depend on Chronicles being its final book. This is, however, a matter of debate. Goswell has indicated that the book of Chronicles is found in more than one position in the MT and the LXX canons, reflecting different post-authorial evaluations of Chronicles and its contents.[85] There is furthermore nothing to indicate that any of these positions are the earliest or best. In discussing Matt 23:35, Goswell indicates that while the reference to the blood of Abel and Zechariah could reflect a canonical arrangement beginning with Genesis and ending with Chronicles, the same sweep of Jewish history could be referred to if Chronicles was placed

77. France, *Gospel of Matthew*, 880.

78. Cited in Matt 27:9–10.

79. France, *Gospel of Matthew*, 881.

80. Gundry, *Matthew*, 471.

81. Dillard, *2 Chronicles*, 193.

82. It is, however, a question whether the order of the canonical books in the Hebrew Bible was fixed at the time Matthew was written so that 2 Chronicles could have been considered the last book of the Hebrew Bible; Hagner, *Matthew 14–28*, 676–77.

83. Nolland, *Gospel of Matthew*, 947.

84. Davies and Allison, *Matthew 19–28*, 318; France, *Gospel of Matthew*, 880.

85. Goswell, "Putting the Book of Chronicles," 283, 298–99.

after Kings. While Chronicles occupied the final position in some Jewish Scripture canons, neither literary nor historical considerations prove that this was its original position. The notion that Matthew is referring to the first and last murders mentioned in the Jewish Scriptures can thus not be used to determine if Matthew is using the MT or LXX. The possibility that Matt 23:35 uses the MT and not the LXX as source is, however, strengthened by the LXX naming the killed priest Azarias (Αζαριαν) and his father Jehoiada, and not Zechariah (זְכַרְיָה) as in the MT. Neither of Matthew's names for the priest and his father (Ζαχαρίας τοῦ Βαραχίου)[86] thus correspond to the LXX version of 2 Chr 24:20.[87]

In using Beale's criteria,[88] it is apparent that there are some unique parallels between Matt 23:35 and the MT or LXX text of 2 Chr 24:20–21. Both Matthew and 2 Chr 24:20–21 mention a righteous person being killed in a sacred space evoking Divine judgment. There are thus strong thematic similarities between these texts with a prophetic figure speaking truth, a violent response from religious/political leaders, and a death in proximity to sacred space. There are, however, also variations in specific wording, as indicated above with Matthew's naming differing from both the MT and the LXX, that make it difficult to determine conclusively if Matthew is alluding to the MT or LXX versions of 2 Chronicles. The allusion to the MT text by Matthew, as discussed above, however, seems the more probable possibility.

The Influence of the Redactional Approach of the Chronicler on the Author of Matthew

As stated in the introduction, the secondary focus of this chapter is to determine if the redactional strategy of the Chronicler influenced that of the author of Matthew since a better understanding of the Chronicler as a redactor can help in classifying the authors of the Synoptic Gospels as redactors and in clarifying their redactional intent.

86. Zech 1:1 refers to its author as "Zechariah, son of Βαραχίου."

87. France, *Gospel of Matthew*, 881.

88. Beale, *Handbook on the New Testament*, 31–32.

The Chronicler as Redactor

Determining the redactional approach of the Chronicler is possible since Chronicles extensively utilised Samuel–Kings to retell Israel's history along with a sweeping portrayal of human history, spanning from Adam to Cyrus.[89] It is also possible to describe the relationship between the LXX and MT versions of 1 Chr 1–3 to determine the redactional activity of the respective translators of Samuel–Kings and Chronicles.[90]

Giacobbe[91] has summarised the similarities between Samuel–Kings and Chronicles as their having similar basic *content* (the reign of David and Solomon, the construction of the temple, and the succession of kings up to the Babylonian exile), *structure* (2 Samuel and 1 Chr 9–29 in the LXX focus on David, 1 Kings and 2 Chronicles the succession from David to Solomon, and 1–2 Kings and 2 Chronicles on the succession of kings in the two kingdoms), and *themes* (the nature and quality of the monarchy, the kingdom of Yahweh, temple and worship, reward and retribution, and eschatological hope). There are, however, also notable differences that Giacobbe lists. Structurally Chronicles is more condensed compared to Samuel–Kings (in the LXX the four books of the MT become two), it contains material that does not occur in Samuel–Kings, and has a different perspective on the material that does. Chronicles also alters some of the themes of Samuel–Kings (especially regarding David and retribution). Chronicles furthermore has a clear hope for the restoration of Israel and the temple and for a future Davidic king.

According to Good[92] the differences between the book of Chronicles and Samuel–Kings reflect the ideology of Chronicles, which privileges the temple, David, and the Levites. Chronicles was, however, not composed as a substitute for the primary history of Samuel–Kings but rather as an alternative to it. The Chronicler's skillful reinterpretation, rearrangement, and substantial augmentation of sections of the primary history resulted in a distinctly different work aligned with the writer's ideology.[93] This

89. Allen, *1 and 2 Chronicles*, 1.

90. While most of the Hebrew version of Chronicles was probably written in the early Persian period (539–460 BCE), its genealogical material (cf. 1 Chr 3:19–24) appears to have been completed no earlier than 400 BCE; Good, "1–2 Chronicles (Paraleipomena)," 169. The Greek translation was probably undertaken in Egypt in the second century BCE; Klein, *1 Chronicles*, 26; Good, "1–2 Chronicles (Paraleipomena)," 169.

91. Giacobbe, *Luke the Chronicler*, 56–58.

92. Good, "1–2 Chronicles (Paraleipomena)," 173.

93. Knoppers, *I Chronicles 10–29*, 133–34.

ideological perspective evident in the MT was taken over by the translators of the LXX since it addressed the dire historical circumstances at the time of its translation—the most notable being the Maccabean revolt against the Syrian King Antiochus IV (180–161 BCE). Both the redaction of Samuel–Kings by the Chronicler and the LXX translation thereof testify to the freedom of interpretative communities to reimagine and rework their authoritative text to provide a fresh perspective that addresses the needs of their respective contexts.

Matthew as Chronicler

While both the sources used by Chronicles and its possible translation from Hebrew to Greek provide invaluable insight into both intra-canonical reinterpretation and the utilisation of different source material in general, there is a problem with this approach in attempting to specifically compare Matthew to the Chronicler (or his translators) in that 1 Chr 1–3, which is the primary source for Matt 1:1–17, has no parallel in Samuel–Kings. It is in this instance not possible to describe the use of Samuel–Kings by Chronicles before comparing it to Matthew's redaction of Chronicles. It is, however, on the other hand possible to compare the Chronicler's general redaction of Samuel–Kings to that of the Synoptic authors' redaction of all their sources. Myers,[94] for example, has recently analysed the Chronicler's redaction of Samuel–Kings to refute the notion that there are no precedents in ancient literature for the way in which the Synoptists utilised their sources, as claimed by scholars like Sanders and Davies.[95] It is especially the inconsistent manner with which the Synoptics utilised their sources that is used to support the claim that their redactional approach is unique. This inconsistency is evident in that while there are in some instances almost verbatim quotations between the Synoptics and their sources, they in other instances paraphrased, or even rewrote, their sources. They thus did not simply copy their sources without making substantial modifications, additions, and omissions.[96] What is noteworthy of their approach is their freedom to change the manner in which they redact their sources. At times they even change their redactional approach within a single pericope. While this is evident in how Matthew utilised Q

94. Myers, "Synoptic Singularity," 234–37.

95. Sanders and Davies, *Studying the Synoptic Gospels*, 51.

96. Myers, "Synoptic Singularity," 235.

and Mark, it is also according to Myers evident in the redactional approach of the Chronicler. Matthew thus continues the tradition of the Chronicler and his translators in reimagining and reworking the authoritative texts of his community to provide them with a fresh perspective in order to address the needs of their context. According to Kirk[97] the way the Synoptists act as redactors suggests that they should understood as belonging to the ranks of the low-status Greco-Roman scribes who transmitted and enriched traditional material with moderate sophisticated composition. Other scholars like Kloppenborg, who has investigated the different compositional techniques in ancient Jewish, Christian, and Greco-Roman literature, situate the Synoptists closer to the wooden copyists of texts like the Serek Hayahad from Qumran than to the free composers of Greco-Roman historiography and biography.[98]

The Chronicler and Matthew as Redactors

As indicated above, both the authors of Chronicles and the Gospel of Matthew can be viewed as redactors since they both employ redactional techniques, such as adapting, omitting, and adding to existing texts. They use these techniques to create new works with specific theological and social purposes to address the needs of their communities. They both also engage in intertextuality, using allusions, echoes, and quotations from earlier texts to construct their narratives in addressing these needs. Matthew uses a similar approach to the Chronicler by reinterpreting, rearranging, and supplementing his source material (Mark and Q). His reworking of an earlier narrative like the Gospel of Mark into a new one is thus not a novel approach, as indicated by the Chronicler's approach. In this sense his use of Chronicles is not just restricted to his intertextual use of it. It is also evident in his methodology and redactional freedom in that Matthew, like the Chronicler, was willing to adapt the past to fit his own theological and social contexts. Neither redactor was bound to a rigid interpretation of tradition. The Chronicler engages in what is described by Jonker as "reforming history,"[99] which means he is not just recounting the past but actively reshaping it to give new meaning to his contemporary readers. This involves maintaining continuity with past traditions while

97. Kirk, *Q in Matthew*, 40–42, 71.

98. Kloppenborg, "Variation," 77–80.

99. Jonker, *Defining All-Israel*, 11–13.

also introducing new interpretations that reflect the Chronicler's present circumstances. Matthew's theological and social agenda is similar in that he was also concerned with how his community understood their place in the world within the context of the Roman Empire amidst growing conflict with Judaism and internal strife.[100] Like the Chronicler, Matthew did not simply relay historical facts but rather actively reinterpreted Jewish texts to shape his audiences' identities. Both the books of Chronicles and the Gospel of Matthew thus exemplify sophisticated approaches to reinterpreting historical traditions, demonstrating how textual narratives actively shape communal identities.

Jonker's major work on Chronicles, *Defining All-Israel*, provides a comprehensive framework for understanding how the Chronicler constructed a sense of identity by reforming history. It serves as a valuable guide for understanding the mechanisms of social and theological meaning-making that influenced not only Chronicles but also later texts like the Gospel of Matthew that were likewise created within a Jewish conceptual world. In *Defining All-Israel* Jonker uses the term "identity negotiation" to describe the processes by which the community in the late-Persian province of Yehud defined itself.[101] He contrasts it with terms like "identity formation" to emphasise that identity is a dynamic and ongoing process. The identity negotiation in Chronicles is done by defining a restored community in terms of the Chronicler's own time. He envisions this restored community centred on the temple as כל-ישראל, "All-Israel." According to Jonker, Chronicles reinterprets older historiographical traditions and "reforms" history to create this new identity.[102] This negotiation of identity is not linear, but rather multidirectional and flexible.[103] According to Jonker the Chronicler's work addresses four levels of socio-historical existence in the Persian period: the Persian imperial context, the provincial dynamics of Yehud, the tribal relationship between Judah and Benjamin, and the inner-cultic dynamics of Jerusalem.[104] This approach considers different power relations and the need for both continuity and change. Identity negotiation in Chronicles is thus

100. Nel, "Mission and Ethics," 89–97.
101. Jonker, *Defining All-Israel*, 13–16.
102. Jonker, *Defining All-Israel*, 27.
103. Jonker, *Defining All-Israel*, 63.
104. Jonker, *Defining All-Israel*, 72–73.

not a simple, one-dimensional process but a complex interaction of these various levels that involves the past, present, and future.[105]

Jonker highlights the prominent block of genealogical material at the beginning of Chronicles (1 Chr 1–9) and notes that it serves to position the entire work within the framework of the identity of "All Israel."[106] The genealogies thus establish a sense of continuity and define the boundaries of "All-Israel." Jonker points out that the Chronicler uses earlier traditions and also constructs some of his own genealogies, arranging them in a specific order to emphasise the position of the Levites, Judah, and Benjamin.[107] Jonker notes that these genealogies include not only persons from the former Southern Kingdom's sphere of influence, but also the Northern Kingdom's, indicating what might be considered to be a utopian description of who belongs to "All-Israel."[108] The Chronicler furthermore portrays the relationships between Judah and other groups (such as Benjamin and Samaria) with a degree of ambiguity. This reflects the complex realities of the time, where the need for unity and the need for differentiation was in tension.

Matthew, like Chronicles, uses genealogies and prophecies from the Jewish Scriptures to establish Jesus' lineage and authority as the promised Messiah in his prologue (Matt 1–2). This is a key aspect of Matthew's effort to integrate Jesus into the historical and religious traditions of Israel. While the Matthean Jesus' primary focus is initially on the Jewish community, his genealogy, following Chronicles, includes non-Jewish women, such as Rahab and Ruth, suggesting a potentially inclusive understanding of identity by the Matthean community as is gradually revealed in Matthew's narrative.[109] According to Jonker the Chronicler's attention is on the situation in Yehud and on the second temple cult in Jerusalem.[110] A key element of the Chronicler's identity construction is his focus on the Jerusalem temple and its cult to foster a new understanding of the restored community centred on the temple ("All-Israel"). He emphasises the importance of proper worship and the roles of priests and Levites, suggesting that the authorship of Chronicles should be sought among the literati who were influential

105. Jonker, *Defining All-Israel*, 73.

106. Jonker, *Defining All-Israel*, 117.

107. Jonker, *Defining All-Israel*, 14, 227–76.

108. Jonker, *Defining All-Israel*, 156.

109. Amante, "Role of Genealogies," 112–14.

110. Jonker, *Defining All-Israel*, 68.

in the Jerusalem temple cult.[111] This emphasis on cultic practices helps the Chronicler to differentiate the Jerusalem community from other groups, while also providing a basis for internal cohesion.

Matthew's use of his sources is in turn determined by both christological and social identity concerns that stand in opposition to the temple and its functionaries. This is evidenced in his strategic use of references from the Jewish Scriptures to position Jesus within the context of God's promises. For Matthew, Jesus is the fulfillment of Israel's hopes and the foundation for a new community.[112] Matthew furthermore challenges the Jerusalem elite with his depiction of their response to the birth of Jesus (Matt 2:1–12) and the ministry of John the Baptist (Matt 3:1–12), which occurs outside the confines of the cult in Jerusalem. He does not employ a consistent redactional approach that results in his conclusions. His theological intent instead determines his redactional approach. The Gospel of Matthew strategically uses references from Chronicles to establish Jesus' lineage, highlight his authority as the promised Messiah, provide historical context for his ministry, and emphasise the significance of Jesus' ministry in light of God's promises in the Jewish Scriptures. The promise-fulfillment motif is an important one in Matthew's redaction of the Jewish Scriptures to align the promises made in them and their realisation in his Gospel's narrative. The ordering of Jesus' ancestors into three groups of fourteen in his genealogy is especially important in this regard to demonstrate God's commitment to his covenant. Jesus is also specifically linked to his ancestors who were kings, prophets, and priests to cement his identity as the promised Messiah.[113] In terms of social identity Matthew develops the motif of the inclusion of gentiles and women[114] into the new brotherhood of Jesus followers. He also highlights the dangers of being faithful to God. In Matt 23:35, Jesus references 2 Chr 24:1–19, mentioning

111. Jonker, *Defining All-Israel*, 70.

112. Nel, "Mission and Ethics," 89–95.

113. There is a danger of over interpretation of some of the changes made by Matthew of his source material in this regard. The addition of φ to Asa's name in verse 7–8 is for example seen by Gundry and France as possibly creating a secondary reference to the psalmist Asaph; Gundry, *Matthew*, 15; France, *Gospel of Matthew*, 27. According to the early tradition found in the psalm's title, Asaph is credited with writing Ps 78, of which Matt 13:35 cites a section as being fulfilled; Gundry, *Matthew*, 15. In contrast, Nolland states that Ἀσάφ ("Asaph") instead of Ἀσα ("Asa"), the consistent LXX name for this king, could simply be a mistake; Nolland, *Gospel of Matthew*, 79.

114. Chronicles is also an example of mothers being included in genealogies, like that of Jesus' in Matthew, with fourteen mothers being mentioned in 1 Chr 2 alone; France, *Gospel of Matthew*, 36.

the blood of the prophets shed from Abel to Zechariah, to highlight the history of persecution faced by God's messengers like himself throughout the ages. When comparing the redactional approach of Matthew, it thus apparent that he too was a skillful Chronicler of God's ongoing involvement in the history of his people. For Matthew, as for the Chronicler, there is a surprising freedom to rework and interpret the source texts used. Chronicles does not only provide Matthew with the relevant information with which to compose the genealogy of Jesus; it also provides the formulation for Matthew's genealogy of Jesus.[115] Matthew, however, does not (like Luke) follow the precedent in Chronicles of tracing Israel's history from Adam.[116] He instead begins his genealogy of Jesus with Abraham (Matt 1:2) when following the order of 1 Chr 1–3.[117]

Conclusion

Both the Chronicler and Matthew are active interpreters of tradition, who use their texts to shape the social identity of their respective communities. They achieve this by strategically reinterpreting existing traditions and narratives, by addressing community needs, and by creating a sense of continuity and purpose. The Chronicler emphasises a unified "All-Israel" centered on Jerusalem, while Matthew presents Jesus as the fulfillment of Israel's hopes and the basis for a new community.[118] Their texts demonstrate the power of narratives to define and shape group identities within their unique socio-historical contexts. To achieve this, they reveal remarkable hermeneutical creativity. Their authors freely adapt, omit, and supplement source materials, revealing an approach to tradition that prioritises contemporary meaning-making over strict historical preservation.

While there are no direct quotations of Chronicles in the Gospel of Matthew, there are allusions and echoes to Chronicles that can be analysed to understand how Matthew used it as a literary source. In composing the genealogy of Jesus (Matt 1:1–17), Matthew generally

115. The mention of Abraham "begetting" (γεννάω) Isaac in 1:2 can be traced back to 1 Chr 1:34a LXX (Καὶ ἐγέννησεν Αβρααμ τὸν Ισαακ). Although the verb appears irregularly in 1 Chr 1–3 LXX, Matthew chooses to use it here for the purpose of maintaining parallelism; Gundry, *Matthew*, 14.

116. Giacobbe, *Luke the Chronicler*, 52.

117. Gundry, *Matthew*, 14.

118. Nel et al., "Matthew's Reconfiguration," 4–14.

follows 1 Chronicles. He, however, also supplements it with material from Ruth as well as other sources that are no longer extant. Matthew 23:35 seems to interact with the MT version of 2 Chr 24. It apparently assumes, as does Q, that Chronicles is the last book of the Jewish Scriptures. There could thus be instances where Matthew switches to the MT as his primary source or uses a Greek translation of the MT that is closer to it than the extant version of the LXX. What is apparent is that Matthew uses a variety of sources and that he omits, adds, and modifies material taken over from them. The way with which Matthew uses his Jewish Scriptures sources (LXX and MT) is thus similar to how he uses Mark and Q as sources.

In studying Chronicles' transformative power in constructing and negotiating group identities, the lasting scholarly significance of Jonker's work lies not just in understanding specific texts like Chronicles, but in recognising how narratives like Chronicles and the Gospel of Matthew becomes a dynamic tool for social and theological meaning-making.

Bibliography

Aland, Barbara, et al., eds. *The Greek New Testament*. 5th rev. ed. Stuttgart: Deutsche Bibelgesellschaft, American Bible Society, United Bible Societies, 2014.

Allen, Leslie C. *1 and 2 Chronicles: A Message for Yehud: An Introduction and Study Guide*. T&T Clark's Study Guides to the Old Testament. London: Bloomsbury, 2021.

———. *The Greek Chronicles: The Relation of the Septuagint of I and II Chronicles to the Massoretic Text; The Translator's Craft*. Vetus Testamentum Supplements 1. Leiden: Brill, 1974.

Amante, Motuma Badassa. "The Role of Genealogies in the Antiquities of the Jews and the Gospel of Matthew: A Comparative Study." PhD diss., Stellenbosch University, 2024.

Beale, G. K. *Handbook on the New Testament Use of the Old Testament: Exegesis and Interpretation*. Grand Rapids: Baker Academic, 2012.

Davies, William David, and Dale C. Allison. *Commentary on Matthew 19–28*. Vol. 3 of *A Critical and Exegetical Commentary on the Gospel According to Saint Matthew*. Edinburgh: T&T Clark, 1997.

Dillard, Raymond B. *2 Chronicles*. Word Biblical Commentary 15. Nashville: Thomas Nelson, 2000.

Elliger, K., et al., eds. *Biblia Hebraica Stuttgartensia*. 2nd ed. Stuttgart: Deutsche Bibelgesellschaft, 1997.

France, R. T. *The Gospel of Matthew*. Grand Rapids: Eerdmans, 2007.

Giacobbe, Mark S. *Luke the Chronicler: The Narrative Arc of Samuel–Kings and Chronicles in Luke–Acts*. Biblical Interpretation Series. Leiden: Brill, 2023.

Good, Roger. "1–2 Chronicles (Paraleipomena)." In *The T&T Clark Companion to the Septuagint*, edited by James K. Aitken, 167–77. London: T&T Clark, 2016.

Goswell, Gregory. "Putting the Book of Chronicles in Its Place." *Journal of the Evangelical Theological Society* 60.2 (2017) 283–99.

Gundry, Robert Horton. *Matthew: A Commentary on His Literary and Theological Art*. Grand Rapids: Eerdmans, 1982.

Hagner, Donald Alfred. *Matthew 1–13*. Dallas: Word, 1993.

———. *Matthew 14–28*. Dallas: Word, 1995.

Hays, Richard B. *Echoes of Scripture in the Letters of Paul*. New Haven: Yale University Press, 1986.

Jonker, Louis C. "David's Officials According to the Chronicler (1 Chronicles 23–27): A Reflection of Second Temple Self-Categorization?" In *Historiography and Identity (Re)Formulation in Second Temple Historiographical Literature*, edited by Louis C. Jonker, T&T Clark Library of Biblical Studies, 65–92. New York: T&T Clark, 2010.

———. *Defining All-Israel in Chronicles: Multi-Levelled Identity Negotiation in Late Persian-Period Yehud*. Forschungen Zum Alten Testament 106. Tübingen: Mohr Siebeck, 2016.

Kirk, Alan. *Q in Matthew: Ancient Media, Memory, and Early Scribal Transmission of the Jesus Tradition*. Library of New Testament Studies 564. London: Bloomsbury T&T Clark, 2016.

Klein, Thomas. *1 Chronicles: A Commentary*. Hermeneia. Minneapolis: Fortress, 2006.

Kloppenborg, John S. "Variation in the Reproduction of the Double Tradition and an Oral Q?" *Ephemerides Theologicae Lovanienses* 83 (2007) 53–80.

Knoppers, Gary N. *I Chronicles 10–29: A New Translation with Introduction and Commentary*. New Haven: Yale University Press, 2007.

———. "Intermarriage, Social Complexity, and Ethnic Diversity in the Genealogy of Judah." *Journal of Biblical Literature* 120 (2001) 15–30. https://doi.org/10.2307/3268591.

Moyise, Steve. *The Old Testament in the New: An Introduction*. London: T&T Clark International, 2001.

Myers, Jimmy. "Synoptic Singularity? The Chronicler's Redaction of Samuel–Kings and Gospel Composition." *Journal for the Study of the New Testament* 46 (2023) 233–57.

Nel, Marius J. "Mission and Ethics: Sensitivity to Outsiders in Matthew." In *Insiders Versus Outsiders: Exploring the Dynamic Relationship Between Mission and Ethos in the New Testament*, edited by Jacobus Kok and John Anthony Dunne, 85–103. Piscataway, NJ: Gorgias, 2014.

Nel, Marius J., et al. "Matthew's Reconfiguration of Salvation in a Context of Oppression." In *Reconciliation, Forgiveness and Violence in Africa: Biblical, Pastoral and Ethical Perspectives*, edited by Christo H. Thesnaar et al., 1–16. Stellenbosch: Sun, 2020.

Nestle, Eberhard, et al. *Novum Testamentum Graece with Dictionary*. 28th ed. Stuttgart: Deutsche Bibelgesellschaft, 2013.

Nolland, John. *The Gospel of Matthew: A Commentary on the Greek Text*. Grand Rapids: Eerdmans, 2005.

Rahlfs, Robert, and Alfred Hanhart, eds. *Septuaginta: SESB Edition*. Rev. ed. Stuttgart: Deutsche Bibelgesellschaft, 2006.

Sanders, E. P., and Margaret Davies. *Studying the Synoptic Gospels*. London: SCM, 1989.

Turner, David L. *Matthew*. Grand Rapids: Baker Academic, 2008.

13

Discourses of Difference and Sameness

Pauline Othering and Its Reception

JEREMY PUNT

THE MODERN WORLD ACROSS the globe as much as locally is characterised by the ongoing anomalies that difference is celebrated *but* also feared while sameness is disparaged *but* also treasured.[1] Recent examples include the continual reoccurrence of pernicious xenophobia in South Africa;[2] popular (and populist) reactions to the ongoing so-called migrant problem in Europe; and the virulence of racially based protests about police actions in the United States and elsewhere—incidences which no one will dare suggest are identical, but in which notions of Self and Other appear to be central. But these and other events raise the question whether, and how, fear of Otherness or the idolisation of Sameness impacts social locations, and what feeds into such perceptions. In other words, are these events

1. Louis C. Jonker has been a friend, colleague, and academic conversation partner for several decades; I celebrate his scholarship and collegiality, his various contributions to biblical hermeneutics and studies on our African continent, his insistence on the importance of the contexts of texts, and especially his concern for exploring connections between Global South and North interpretation and the importance that contextual framings of identity play in both contexts.

2. When does xenophobia become an excuse, in fact, seen almost as a legitimate response to that which is different but at the same time threatening to a sense of self, including sense of self-value and self-worth, prosperity, etc.?

related to perceptions about others or rather about their own group, or both, and on what are such perceptions built? At least at times, Self and Other notions are not self-contradictory and only apparently anomalous since the fear of the Other often seems to be informed and held in place by a (overdeveloped) sense of group identity or belonging.[3]

This chapter suggests that the Self and Other discourse provides a useful grid for making sense of New Testament (NT) texts, being invested in identity and its construction. Such social construction is evident in how Paul manoeuvred himself and those he addressed from his hybrid but strongly Jewish perspective. Since language and discourse is not primarily about conveying information but about action and affiliation,[4] constituting reality rather than representing or reflecting it, social reality including personal and group consciousness and relations are established through language.[5] What Martin claimed for gender in late antiquity, being "socially constructed, textually inscribed, and literarily interpreted," is true also for identity in the NT.[6] My argument traces the Pauline rhetoric of Othering, showing how it rested both upon strong insider positions and the vilification of the Other, amidst the ambivalent role of Others in the first-century Roman context. Subsequent Pauline reception continued the rhetoric of Othering through the artificial construct of Christian universality. Cultural discourses of difference and sameness that take a Pauline rhetoric of Othering in one way or another as point of departure established a grid that in our (post)modern day runs analogous and arguably feeds into both the celebration of difference and the fear of the Other. The identity constructions accomplished in the Pauline letters are vast, and their socio-historical settings are important[7]—but first a look at the broader NT situation is warranted.

3. Emmanuel Levinas critiqued Western philosophy's "insurmountable allergy" to "the other that remains other," the other that is not assimilated into the fold of selfness. Levinas's understanding of the Other is as both untranslatable, beyond representation and thus "otherwise than being," or "non-totalizable," or "a transcendence inconvertible to immanence," and nevertheless also that for which humans are especially responsible. Levinas, "Trace of the Other," 346.

4. Gee, *Introduction to Discourse Analysis*, 1.

5. "The idea that identities are discursive constructions is underpinned by a view of language in which there are no essences to which language refers and therefore no essential identities." Barker, *Television*, 23–24.

6. Martin, introduction to *Cultural Turn*, 10.

7. While Roman imperial rule had shaped and changed Jewish cultures and customs, Paul's Jewishness impacted also his perception of the Romans. "Accepting Taubes's emphasis on Paul's radical political challenge to the Hellenic political world, as well as to

Identity and Othering in the New Testament

Identity is a social construct, shaped according to mutable descriptions,[8] with features dropped or added over time so that differences connected to an ethnic identity are real and observable, while the power granted to such differences is synthetic and can be regulated.[9] At the same time, identity is polythetic and based on association and differentiation.[10] In antiquity, binary thinking in terms of identity was less typical among Roman imperial authorities and more common among Greeks and Jews. The Romans were not only more aware about human diversity than most other groups in antiquity, but contrasts made with other peoples as barbarians were mostly on the basis of "cultural deficiencies" rather than "with ethnic difference per se."[11] Confronted by Persian imperial

---

the imperial organizational matrix with Rome at its center, we argue that this challenge was performed first and foremost through the 'conversion' of Romans, Corinthians, and Galatians into gentiles." Rosen-Zvi and Ophir, "Invention of the Gentiles," 40.

8. Even ethnic identity is a social construct, as Barth pointed out: "Ethnic groups are categories of ascription and identification by the actors themselves, and thus have the characteristic of organizing interaction between people"; Barth, *Ethnic Groups and Boundaries*, 10. Otherness in the first century cannot be restricted to notions of ethnicity only, a fluid and a pliable construct whose morphology depended upon those using it. Besides conceptual dexterity, ethnic identity was not devoid of other social aspects, e.g., constellations of culture, politics, religion, and economics. See, e.g., Baumann, "Grammars of Identity/Alterity" on framing identity through others; for the ancient context, see Nasrallah and Schüssler Fiorenza, *Prejudice and Christian Beginnings*.

9. In contrast, an essentialist position of identity such as found in attempts at an "ontology of Judaism" reduces ethnicity to irreducible qualities, appealing to bloodline and kinship, insisting upon demonstrable links to land, history, language, culture, religion, or myth of origins. Lines between insiders and outsiders are conceived as rigid and unbroken, with the boundaries themselves taking on an inviolable status; Wan, "Letter to the Galatians," 13:246–47.

10. Brown and Breed, "Social Identity and Scriptural Interpretation." Jonker, *Defining All-Israel*, especially 16–143, also treated the concept of "identity" with dexterity when he used it to understand the book of Chronicles in the Hebrew Bible. He not only explored various sociological models to see how well they work for this purpose, acknowledging their strengths and weaknesses, but in the end offers a more complex view of the historical and social context of the late Persian period when these biblical texts were written. Dividing this period into four distinct social layers, each with its own unique power dynamics, he demonstrated how the negotiation of identity was a multifaceted process influenced by the shifting power relationships within and between these different social levels.

11. Stanley, "Paul the Ethnic Hybrid," 125. Stanley argues that Roman anxiety about their status in comparison with the revered histories of the Egyptians and the Greeks, and the special privileges accorded to Jews in many parts of the Empire, is testimony to Roman lenience regarding identity categories.

influence, Greeks were concerned with identity already since the fifth century BCE to be Hellenes, and to distinguish between Hellenes and barbarians. In the Jewish Scriptures the often stark contrast made between Israel and the nations is accentuated by the variety of ethnic and political entities also represented in these texts.[12]

The NT texts, including Paul's on whom our attention will be here, straddle such positions regarding identity claims for their communities. At times the claims, overtly or subtly, extended also to those outside of these communities. Identity claims cannot, however, be posited as generally exclusive or hostile, as much as sweeping demands about their promotion of inclusivity and harmony equally fail to convince. Harsh language including exclusivist or hostile claims points to Othering at work,[13] even if tough language was conventional first-century rhetoric, and severe expressions in the NT were hardly unique for the era.[14] Hard sayings or polemical passages include the Gospel of Matthew, which has "all the people" baying for Jesus' crucifixion and them demanding that "his blood be on our heads and on our children" (Matt 27:25); Jesus in the Fourth Gospel telling the Jews, "You are from your father the devil, and you choose to do your father's desires" (John 8:44); and Paul referring to (presumably) his fellow Jews as people "who killed both the Lord Jesus and the prophets. . . . They displease God and oppose everyone" (1 Thess 2:15).[15] The provenance of the NT's polemical language cannot avoid its Jewish setting. Already in the Hebrew Bible / Old Testament,

12. See Punt, "Identity Claims," 84–85. In this regard, see (for example) Jonker's investigation of the relationship between the late stages of literature formation of the Hebrew Bible, shedding light on the complex interplay of ideological beliefs and power struggles that characterised the late Persian and early Hellenistic periods; Jonker, "Melting Pots and Rejoinders?"

13. See also Punt, "Bible and Others."

14. The role of language both in polemics as well as in configuring insider-outsider categories is important. As Rhoads notes, "Speech, particularly rhetorical speech, is sometimes agonistic, because it often occurs in contexts in which there is an in-group and an out-group." Rhoads, "Performance Criticism," 121.

15. All translations throughout are the author's own, unless otherwise indicated. The Pauline letters articulated a new identity both by building upon the history of the Jewish people and in juxtaposition with the Roman Empire and its ideology of power. Those who resisted the contemporary dominance through visions of future utopia nonetheless were obliged to use the language and images of the current social system to formulate and construct a new world that could be considered attainable and conceivable; Perkins, *Roman Imperial Identities*, 176. Paul's redescriptions of his communities' identity took up the scripts of the religiously influential (Jewish), the politically dominant (Roman), and the socio-culturally normative (Greek/Hellenistic).

Amos, Jeremiah, Nahum, and Ezekiel criticised neighbouring countries and the authorities of the priestly establishment in less than civil tones. Comparably, the Qumran Scrolls denounced fellow Jews in harsh terms: the "sons of darkness" are full of "wickedness and lies, haughtiness and pride, falseness and deceit, cruelty and abundant evil, ill-temper and much folly" (Serek Hayahad 4.9–14). First-century Jewish writers often responded in harsh terms to fellow Jews with whom they disagreed, and in even stronger terms about gentiles.[16]

However, the pervasiveness and subtlety of the insider-outsider mentality in the NT is a complex matter reaching far beyond harsh language. "We-they perspectives" are present in all the major corpora of the NT, revolving largely around matters of identity, influenced as they were by social, political, economic, and other concerns. Some people were defined as outsiders from the outset; some first became insiders but over time and for different reasons turned into outsiders again. The NT shows lines of demarcation broken through, if not broken down, but also sees other divisions reinforced. The strong tone of intra-Jewish conflict surfaces repeatedly in the Gospels, revealing two strata of the Jesus story. On one level, the relatively simple story of Jesus is primary, but amidst the reinterpretation of the events taking place after his death, Jesus' story was retold with the communities' concerns in mind. The Fourth Gospel expresses anger against Jews who became the symbol for all who rejected God (John 5:16, 8:57–59, 18:12, 19:10) in a context where the early Jesus followers dreaded the Jewish authorities for fear of exclusion and the might of the Roman Empire to annihilate whole communities for dissent.[17] Echoes of the concern with insiders and outsiders are heard throughout the associated Johannine writings, invoking categories like the saved and the damned.[18] Binary opposites in the NT often play on

16. Levine, "What Jews (and Christians Too) Should Know," 1–3. Josephus called the Sicarii, the "dagger men" who promoted the revolt against Rome in 66–70 CE, "slaves, the scum, and the spurious and abortive offspring of our nation" (*Jewish War* 5.443) who "left no words of reproach unsaid, and no works of perdition untried, in order to destroy those whom their contrivances affected" (*Jewish War* 7.262). Philo criticised fellow exegetes in Alexandria who did not read Scripture as he did as "impious ones" who "use these and similar passages as stepping stones as it were for their godlessness." *Confusion of Tongues* 2.1.

17. The Johannine writings provide interesting parallels: the Fourth Gospel begins with a (negative) reference to the insiders, *οἱ ἴδιοι αὐτὸν οὐ παρέλαβον* (John 1:11; "and his own [people] did not receive him"), a phrase that set the tone for the Gospel's strong self-other binaries and exclusionist tendencies.

18. The boundaries of the new covenant group in Rev 21 and 22, with their decided

religious or spiritual distinctions and employ symbolic language, such as to be free or enslaved, children of the light or children of the darkness, the faithful or the apostates, those on the narrow or those on the broad way, the wheat or the chaff, the sheep or the goats, the strong or the weak. Some opposites invoked sentiments that entail going beyond religious categories for explaining the force of the contrast and even the original identity concerns, and might be related to categories of privilege and marginalisation, wealth and poverty, and other socio-political configurations.[19] Some of the clearest attempts at scripting identity through a rhetoric of Othering, both scripting as well as impacting insiders as much as outsiders, are found in the Pauline letters—marked by binaries stronger than most other NT documents.

The Pauline Rhetoric of Othering

The gist of the Pauline letters, addressed to communities of Jesus followers, is to encourage an identity formed around Christ, with an associated worldview and ethos.[20] Rather than some theological programme, the thrust of the letters is to encourage a renewed social location for community members, both insiders and outsiders. Ironically, the implications of attempting to forge a single community at times mitigated against that very goal, leaving what can be summarised as a politics or rhetoric of Othering in its wake.[21] The identification of the discourse of power in

gendered angles, are clearly marked: "The boundary of the redeemed sets up a system of opposites expressed as insider and outsider, Christian and non-Christian, and fornicators and virgins. There is no room for dissent and no place for women's power and women's voices." Pippin, *Death and Desire*, 55–56. See Lieu on insiders and outsiders in 2 and 3 John: *Epistles of John*, 125–65, especially 145–48.

19. For a longer argument on a Pauline rhetoric of Othering, see Punt, "Paul and the Others"; the relationship with and impact on violence, also in contemporary contexts, was addressed in Punt, "Bible and Others."

20. This is not to argue for the historical existence of the so-called third race which, as Zetterholm, "Will the Real Gentile-Christian" argues, may have stayed little more than a laudable dream.

21. A case can be made for Paul's advocacy of the inclusivity of the reign of God and its earthly manifestations as seen for example in Rom 1:14 and 13:1–14; Jewett, "Exegetical Support," 62–68. However, Paul generally made such inclusiveness dependent on the communities' assent to his visions, understandings, and praxis so that people in the Pauline community had access to spiritual information and knowledge not available to others, an ambiguity that emerges clearly in Galatians with Paul's explanation of the covenant; Dunn, *Epistle to the Galatians*, 249. The choice is not for or against Jews, for or against gentiles, but an inclusive choice for all people—see Park, *Either Jew or*

the Pauline letters uncovers the disempowerment of others and those on the margins of the Pauline communities.[22] Without looking to excuse the Pauline rhetoric of Othering, it was embedded in the first-century Mediterranean imperialist context of oppression and want, marked by dispossession and persecution, in which communities were very aware of foreigners and especially opponents.

Before Roman imperial times, already the Greek *polis* reflected patterns of identification and domination, marginalisation, and exclusion.[23] The patriarchal city-state embodied political-philosophical values in accordance with an androcentric understanding of democracy. Political and social power belonged to elite, propertied men, excluding slave men and women, free-born propertied women, poor men and women, and of course barbarian (i.e., not Greek) men and women. Notwithstanding beliefs such as the Sophists' notion that all people are equal by nature, socio-political arrangements were given ideological justification through articulating dualisms[24] and notions of natural superiority and inferiority of some people.[25] In the end, however, it was during Roman imperial times that a practice, which has through the centuries become the norm in hegemonic and colonialist discourse, was firmly established—simply put, the politics of Othering did not intend to describe the generic person but, rather, generalised the imperial standard as the universal subject.[26] The dynamics of a politics of Othering meant that once hierarchy was established and legitimated, systems of domination and subordination acted as mechanisms of control, with a validating discourse obscuring such practices as natural and/or (divinely) ordained.[27]

Gentile—but such inclusion is according to the requirements of Paul's understanding.

22. Polaski, *Paul and the Discourse*, 136. The focus here is on the communities Paul addressed rather than on his autobiographical claims such as in Gal 1–2, Phil 3, and in the Corinthian correspondence; see Punt, "Identity Claims," 91–92.

23. E.g., the distinction between the public and private realms of life leaves the civic public inhabited by an "impartial and universal point of view of normative reason," and the private with its emphasis on the family seen as the domain of women, and thus of "the body, affectivity and desire." Schüssler Fiorenza, "Politics of Interpretation," 45.

24. Such as human-animal, male-female, slave-free, native-alien; Schüssler Fiorenza, "Politics of Interpretation," 46. For the stratified society, see, e.g., Meeks, *Moral World*, 32–38.

25. It was predominantly about the assertion of the inferiority of slaves and (free-born) women as the targets of the ideological constructs on the inferiority of these groups, and the concomitant need to treat them accordingly.

26. See Schüssler Fiorenza, "Politics of Interpretation," 46.

27. Dorothy Smith calls these "relationships of ruling." Smith, *Texts, Facts, and*

However, first-century identity politics did not construe real or imagined Others simply in oppositional terms.[28] Constructions of the Other were certainly vital for framing and sustaining identity, but at times collective identity was developed *in terms of* rather than *in contrast to* another group. The imperial divide and rule strategy deliberately set different nations against one another,[29] but ancient societies saw themselves connected to a broader cultural heritage too,[30] entailing perceived links between societies and framing own social memories in terms of an adopted past.[31] Tracing "foreign" cultural influences included the interaction with and embracing elements of others' identity, reconstructing such elements into their own sense of identity.[32] Aware of differences between themselves and others, identity could still be fabricated in comparison with neighbouring peoples[33] so that both distinctiveness and connectedness were at play. In short, the complex negotiation of identities in self-sustaining binaries[34] cannot be resolved through emphasis on simple contrasts.[35] Ancient notions of identity fed off others but did not lead to an amalgam of

Femininity.

28. Wills defines nine theorems about the construction of the Other applicable to the Bible and elsewhere: construction of self through others; construction of Others through self; Others as similar to self; Others' seductive power; distorting Others; constructing internal Others; reassignment of ambiguous groups; reassignment of origins of practices; constructing eternal Others. Wills, *Not God's People*, 12–14, 217–18.

29. E.g., Lopez, *Apostle to the Conquered*, 56–118; Lopez, "Visualizing Significant Otherness," 85–89. Encapsulated in Tacitus's words (*Germania* 33.2), "May the Gods continue and perpetuate amongst these nations, if not any love for us, yet by all means this their animosity and hate towards each other: since whilst the destiny of the Empire thus urges it, fortune cannot more signally befriend us, than in sowing strife amongst our foes" (Thomas Gordon translation).

30. "When ancients reconstructed their roots or fashioned their history, they often did so by associating themselves with the legends and traditions of others." Gruen, *Cultural Identity*, 3–4.

31. "That practice [associating themselves with the traditions of others] affords a . . . revealing insight into the mentalities of Mediterranean folk in antiquity. It discloses not how they *distinguished* themselves from others but how they transformed or reimagined them for their own purposes. . . . It represents a more circuitous and a more creative mode of fashioning a collective self-consciousness." Gruen, *Cultural Identity*, 4; emphasis original.

32. Gruen, *Cultural Identity*, 5.

33. See Mendels, *Identity, Religion and Historiography*, 19.

34. Gruen, *Cultural Identity*, 1–2; see Gruen, *Rethinking the Other*, 1–5.

35. Stanley makes a somewhat similar claim about Paul: "His [Paul's] preference for binary modes of categorization is real, but so is the dexterity with which he applies those categories to concrete situations." Stanley, "Paul the Ethnic Hybrid," 120.

convoluted identities nor to some idealised universal identity.[36] The Other was important in ancient identity negotiations but was appropriated not only in opposition—not only vilified but also retooled for own use. Even when Paul appropriated "his" and "his people's" Abraham narrative in Galatians and elsewhere, his language about the Others was less than favourable ("slave children"). With Paul's rhetorical strategy sharply pointed, challenging and even decrying their tradition *and* position, his negotiation of identity included binaries more complex than mere contrasts.[37] An intricate web of relations meant that also Paul at times appropriated existing identities, retooling them for further use.[38]

However, in Pauline rhetoric, identity establishment and maintenance evidently required the construction of borders. Their purpose was to provide a social location for the insiders as much as it was to fend off outsiders, whether or not they challenged the insiders and their sense of identity. Even without the benefit of Girard's scapegoat theory,[39] it is possible to understand how keeping the outsiders at bay, even to the extent of their elimination, is considered vital in intentional communities, especially in their early days of formulating new, or different at least, senses of identity. In effect, a politics of Othering is predominantly a rhetoric of legitimisation, constructing a discourse replete with cause, development, and effect. People are scripted not only in distinction from but also in contrast to the selves and are therefore deemed deserving of exclusion,

36. Even in Claudius's insistence to include some Romanised Gallic notables in the Senate (48 CE), an event remembered and recalled in both the (but for two lacunae, well-preserved) bronze Lyons tablet and in Tacitus (*Annales* 11.23–24), the emperor towards the end of his oration defaults to the us-them binary, ironically when insisting upon the full inclusion of these Gauls into the Roman society.

37. Although, it can be debated whether Paul's affirmation of Abraham as ancestor from the ranks of the Other and criticism of the contemporary Other does not imply Pauline criticism of the Other's interpretation and use of Abraham in "their" traditions and claims.

38. Punt, "Identity Claims," 85–86. Other moderating features in Paul's politics of Othering included that boundary lines were generally not fixed, since the missionary drive allowed for the outsider to be seen as a potential insider. Attempts to break through insider-outsider, us-them moulds are found in celebrated texts such as Gal 3:28 and other baptismal formulae. Calls for inclusivity, tolerance, and respect for difference are found in Rom 12:3–8 (esp. 4–5), 1:14, and 15:7–13. See also Jewett, "Exegetical Support," 62–65, 69–71. A niggling question is whether such calls were limited to the intra-communal situation, restricted to the different groups of factions inside the early Christian church.

39. See Selengut, *Sacred Fury*, 53.

marginalisation, vilification, and even brutalisation.[40] Strong invectives originating from Paul's politics of Othering focused on the opponents in Galatians, Philippians, and Corinthians (e.g., Phil 3:2, 2 Cor 11:1–15). His politics of Othering, however, also included strategies of marginalisation and silencing, when variously defined groups both inside and outside these communities became targets of Pauline controls.

In the Pauline letters, insiders were positioned against outsiders, reminding insiders of hostile people who threaten them, increasing the degree of hostility as can be seen in the vice catalogues (e.g., 1 Cor 6:9–11) and the frequent virulent attacks on opponents.[41] Significantly, the substantiated use of the adverb ἔξω occurs, with one exception (Mark 4:11), only in the Pauline tradition (1 Cor 5:12, 13; 1 Thess 4:12; cf. Col 4:5).[42] Communities are encouraged to develop a sense of belonging, and in this regard familial and affectionate terms (e.g., 1 Thess 2:7–8) are often encountered, and the body metaphor (Rom 12:3–5, 1 Cor 10–12, etc.) is of specific significance.[43] Baptismal discourse (Gal 3:27–28, 1 Cor 12:12–13; cf. Col 3:9–11) underscores the notion that a community of people with the same focus is established through their commitment to Christ. In some Pauline letters (e.g., Galatians and Philippians), inclusivity turns into sharp exclusion when those threatening the fibre of the community or the

40. The Pauline discourse is gendered, often claiming Paul as the *father* of the communities and the one who will present the community as *bride* to her husband (e.g., 2 Cor 11:2–3). The negative overtones in gendering the community relate to the narrative of the seduction of Eve. Such a symbolic construct of gender dualism at once coheres in and undermines the other dualistic oppositions insofar as it casts all speaking subjects (Paul, the opponents, contemporary interpreters, and so on) as masculine and construe their audience (the Corinthian community, Judaism, or contemporary readers, etc.) in feminine terms as passive, immature, and gullible; Schüssler Fiorenza, "Politics of Interpretation," 47.

41. At times, conflicts provide the context and requirement to define identity, e.g., Paul in Galatia. See Taylor, "Conflict as Context," 915–45.

42. In the NT, the adjectival adverb ἔξω (outside) is used a total of sixty-three times, six instances in which it is substantiated, and in five of these it expresses the notion of the outsiders, those outside the community, the people not part of the in-group—the others. In the other instance, ὁ ἔξω refers to corporeality, the external or outer side of being human, as opposed to the inner being, ὁ ἔσω (2 Cor 4:16). Tracing single words (such as ἀδελφός) or phrases (such as with ἴδιος) through the NT writings leads to limited, and even incomplete, pictures. Since words and phrases—and their particular usage—are reflective and representative of one tradition, the contributions of other NT traditions are then often marginalised or even excluded.

43. In later Pauline tradition, the body metaphor is altered in Colossians and Ephesians, with Jesus Christ now portrayed as the head of the body, while Christians make up the rest of the body (Col 1:18; Eph 1:22, 4:15).

veracity of Paul's expressed convictions and commitments are vilified and marginalised. Those who reject the Christian message fall into a different category of human beings and are accused of vile acts.

The Pauline letters, then, focused on communal identity through us-them discourse and engaged a rhetoric of Othering. Paul wielded the yardstick for aspirant insiders and determined which actions and convictions were to be considered as appropriate for belonging to the community and for maintaining community solidarity.[44] But it is especially the differentiation between insiders and outsiders which proves potentially hazardous and ultimately destructive: the insistence on an in-group in possession of all truth and essentially superior to all others.

Pauline Reception and Christian Generalisation

The Pauline letters' dangerous tendency of Othering presented a rhetoric poised on the justification of insider claims, a vilifying rhetoric directed at outsiders, and a rhetoric which legitimated the imperialising ideal as norm. The Pauline letters went beyond Roman Othering trends in the sharp tone with which Others were denounced. "[Paul] initiates a discourse that in many cases validates sameness, that condemns certain kinds of difference and by means of silence renders others unthinkable, that promotes community cohesion by self-discipline and outright self-denial."[45] In the history of interpretation this compromising discourse became problematic when the Pauline letters were generalised, a movement which aided the larger discourse of generalised and generalising Christianity, in a trend which prevails to this day. Pauline sentiments became an enduring presence in Christian identity construction, with such interpretation steeped in concern with distinctiveness, including the ongoing debate about his Jewishness and relationship to the Torah.[46]

44. Segal reckons that Paul saw the terms of commitment and choice more rigidly than many other contemporary Jews. As a recent convert, he considered no middle-positions; Segal, "Some Aspects of Conversion," 186–87. Castelli, *Imitating Paul*, finds in Paul's frequent calls for imitation a (warped) discourse of power; see Polaski, *Paul and the Discourse.*

45. Polaski, *Paul and the Discourse*, 136.

46. Daniel Boyarin puts it succinctly: "[Paul's discourse on the Law and Judaism is] forever caught in a paradox of identity and difference." Boyarin, *Radical Jew*, 204; cf. Matlock, "Almost Cultural Studies," 7:450. Boyarin criticises the coercive "universalising" or multicultural transformation of Jewish tradition, contending that Paul generalised Jewishness to the extent that he in the end destroyed it; Boyarin, *Radical Jew*, 228–60.

These debates are framed by claims that Paul eschewed particular ethnic identities[47] in favour of an all-inclusive community of the Lord—but these claims ignore the evidence: the basis for exclusion was often not ethnic identity as such, but rather the position people assumed toward such identity.[48] The unbridgeable divide between Judaism and Hellenism is a conventional construct,[49] as Paul's thinking can after all not be divorced from the story of Israel. He wrote not as a Christian theologian but as a first-century Jewish teacher of gentiles responding to concrete situations in early communities of Christ-followers. The Pauline letters were not aimed at rejecting Judaism, but the letters were a response to God's call to be a "light to the nations."[50] Caroline Johnson Hodge emphasises how Christianity has de-ethnicised the Jesus movement, transforming it into "general Christianity" so that the religion was reduced to generalisation, which left little space outside of conformity.

The dejudaising of the NT texts works hand in hand with the idea held by Christians that their religion transcends ethnicity, often accompanied by the promotion of a universal Christianity, harbouring an essence reaching beyond (or above) human culture. The de-Judaised essentialism of the NT and early Christianity fails to appreciate its relation to Jewish belief and practice especially in comparison with contemporary polytheistic cultures. The normativity of much of Jewish culture is signalled by the NT authors' uptake of Israel's Scriptures through quotations, allusions, and echoes. Not only texts, the early Jesus followers chose to accept the master narrative of ancient Israelites, not the myths and narratives of the ancient Greeks or the contemporary Romans. "They have accepted the story of this particular ethnic people, the God of their homeland, their myths about creation and the ordering

47. "Sometimes Paul's opponents must be Christians as well as, presumably, Jews. I would include in that category gentile Christians who had already been circumcised, making them Jews for all intents and purposes." Segal, "Some Aspects of Conversion," 186.

48. Jewett claims, "Paul's mission implies an alternative vision of the path toward global reconciliation. It runs neither through Roman propaganda and imperial rule nor through conversion to a single ethnic identity or theological orientation," and, "Since God's grace is equally available to all, no claim of superiority remains valid and therewith the basis for every kind of imperialism has been removed." Jewett, "Exegetical Support," 71. These claims are fair as they go, but leave a vital point out of consideration: Paul's notion of identity ruled the day.

49. Engberg-Pedersen, *Judaism/Hellenism Divide*; Gerdmar, *Roots of Theological Anti-Semitism.*

50. Johnson Hodge, *If Sons, Then Heirs.*

of the cosmos, and the morals inscribed in their sacred scripture." Later, along with theological interpretation of the NT, Christians took over Jewish identity markers, translating them into "an ethnically neutral, all-inclusive tradition which is somehow beyond the normal human characteristics of culture, its discourses and practices."[51] The resilient F. C. Baur–inspired template of Christian universalism versus Jewish particularism in Pauline studies continues to skew interpretation into the modern era.[52] The NT's ghettoising came to rest upon theological interpretation averse to the texts' ethnic and political nature, texts purged in the process of their Jewishness and its significance.[53]

Sameness and Difference: Ancient and Contemporary Worlds

In today's identity politics, insider-outsider notions tend to justify negative and even hostile reactions towards the Other. Such Othering practices have come a long way, and as we have seen, the NT shows similar identity politics among early Jesus followers, which was tied to beliefs and practices in incipient Christianity, and much earlier, inherited beliefs and traditions and their prevailing legacy(ies). Religion as social reference did not and is not putting an end to demarcation but underlines that "perception of differences between groups constitutes the presupposition of any 'identity.'"[54] The NT documents attest to the erection of borders between people, the construction of "us" and "them," the selves and the others, and the subsequent consequences. The NT's saturation with language of identification renders images, processes, and structures of claiming and disavowing identity, of tracing insiders

51. Johnson Hodge, *If Sons, Then Heirs*, 4.

52. F. C. Baur's postulation of the universality of Christianity versus the exclusivity of Judaism has proven difficult to eradicate. With the origin of Paul's shift from Judaism to "Christianity" located in the Damascus-road events, he moved "from the bodiliness of genealogy to the pure spirituality of faith, from the particularity of 'peoplehood' to the universality of multiculturality, from the locality of land to the globality of the world." Volf, *Exclusion and Embrace*, 43–50; see, e.g., Boyarin, *Radical Jew*, 228–60; Dunn, *Romans 1–8*, 72. However, the presence of both universalist and particularist sentiments in most religious and other institutions (Park, *Either Jew or Gentile*, 3) were common in the first century, as were the ensuing tensions. For the recent invocation of universalist categories in Pauline literature, see Worthington "Alternative Perspectives," 368–71, on Badiou, Žižek, and other continental philosophers.

53. Punt, "New Testament as Political Documents."

54. Riesebrodt, *Promise of Salvation*, 23.

and allocating status, pointing to outsiders and marginalising them or appealing for their marginalisation. Like other first-century, and unlike twenty-first-century, communities, the NT did not idealise diversity, flexibility, and being open-ended.[55] In the long reception history of the Bible, and especially since the post-fourth-century influence if not dominance of Christianity, the us-them perspective already present in the NT has grown ever stronger and more dominant.

The NT's strong notions of identity and efforts to maintain and elaborate notions of identity required procedures of demarcation and identification. The formation and evolution of biblical texts and constantly changing constructions of identity are linked.[56] With the inability to determine their own psychological, social, and cultural identity as the defining characteristic of Otherness,[57] the sharp side of negotiating identity and Otherness comes into focus. Paul's letters (and other NT documents) that were written in varied social locations and perceptions of identity of who or what constituted "self" and "Other," shared in these constructive but often ambivalent energies. When it comes to identity, similarity implies difference—that is, constructing the self invokes and construes others,[58] which is not without danger given that identity formation at times is a hairbreadth away from violence.[59] Paul's rhetorics of Othering scripted counter-identity in two particular ways: through assimilating the differences of the other to the self (but, of course, an inferior version of the self), and vilifying and idealising difference as otherness.[60] Claims to identity and exclusion from identity, and subsequent structures of domination and subordination, rested on an appeal to naturalised differences, as embodied in a perceived or even revealed *natural* order.[61] And as mentioned earlier, generalising the imperial standard as the universal subject is a practice which through the centuries became the norm in hegemonic and

55. Even today, the notion of human diversity as a "great resource, which is underpinned—this is our strength—by universal cultural values that must be passed on from the cradle to the grave" often remains idealist. Mayor, "Human Right to Peace," 2.

56. See Wills, *Not God's People*, 3.

57. Stimpson, "Feminist Criticism," 252.

58. Lieu, *Christian Identity*, 15.

59. Schwartz, *Curse of Cain*, 5.

60. Schüssler Fiorenza, "Politics of Interpretation," 45–57.

61. "And if we think after the critique of metaphysics of substance—say, with Judith Butler—then we no longer think that the quest is to find substances in their pre-discursive authenticity. Instead, we try to think about how substances are produced." Povinelli in DiFruscia, "Shapes of Freedom."

colonialist discourse. Only through recognising such appeals as part of a historical political process rather than transcultural natural order can the process of dismantling a politics of Othering begin.

The canonical texts and their history of their interpretation are implicated in the Pauline politics of Othering. "This Western 'politics of identity' and 'rhetorics of othering' establishes identity either by comparison to the other as an inferior 'same' or by emphasizing and stereotyping difference as the otherness of the other."[62] Beyond the texts themselves, two illegitimate processes of identification contribute to a hegemonic politics of Pauline interpretation: "malestream" interpreters identify themselves with Paul and assume Paul to be identical with the communities he addressed.[63] Theological as well as sociological angles on the disputes recalled in the letters accord Paul's voice pride of place, dismissing the positions of the opponents of Paul as either heretical challenges to orthodoxy or sectarian deviance.[64] Differences are taken by the powerful as legitimate warrant to control and rule, and differences with the powerless as natural or divinely ordained sanction for subordination. Pauline rhetorics and politics of meaning requires attention, as much as the valorisation and reinscribing of a (Pauline) rhetoric and politics of Othering remains problematic. A starting point for biblical interpreters is to avoid a hermeneutics of identification with Paul as a "master-voice" in the NT through an investigation of the politics of meaning in contemporary interpretation and by holding on to an appropriate ethics of interpretation!

In Edward Said's groundbreaking work on the topic, he describes how the West invented the idea of the Orient and its people with the purpose both to describe the Other but also, in that way, exercise and authorise control over the Other. Orientalism as "corporate institution for dealing with the Orient" was the mechanism by which Western

62. Schüssler Fiorenza, "Politics of Interpretation," 46. A rhetoric of Othering deals with ideological justification and can, in its more well-known forms, be traced back to the "classic undemocratic discourses" of Plato and Aristotle, even if they were later refined and continued by the post-Enlightenment philosophers such as Locke, Hobbes, Rousseau, and Hegel. "Not just religious studies but all modern theories of political and moral life are shot through with the politics of Othering, that is, with ideologies of sexism, colonialism and racism, the systems and discourses of marginalization, vilification, and dehumanization." Schüssler Fiorenza, "Politics of Interpretation," 45.

63. Schüssler Fiorenza, "Politics of Interpretation," 44.

64. Schüssler Fiorenza, "Politics of Interpretation," 46–47.

colonial powers created a manageable and controllable entity.[65] In conjuring up the Orient, essentialist ideas dominated, "its sensuality, its tendency to despotism, its aberrant mentality, its habits of inaccuracy, its backwardness," which were now grouped together into "a separate and an unchallenged coherence."[66] Power was unilaterally exercised through this construct, wherein "West is the actor, the Orient a passive reactor,"[67] also raising the question not only about the possibility of representing others but the inevitable and accompanying effects (and likely, motive) of control over the Other.[68] More recently, Clingman referred to this as the "pathology" of oneness or singularity in identity concerns and how they play out in terms of ethnicity, nationality, or religion.[69]

The existence of powerful social structures in the (post)modern world challenges established identities, also those religious in nature.[70] The interesting paradox inherent in *globalisation* is that it challenges inherited particularist cultures and identities but also contributes to the invention (reinforcing) of other cultures and identities as a measure of taking control over systemic power.[71] Amidst the real or perceived threat which globalisation poses to local identities, religion can become the last sanctuary within which a particular identity is fostered.[72] Such religiously justified consciousness often proves more recalcitrant to accepting change

65. Said, *Orientalism*, 3.

66. Said, *Orientalism*, 205.

67. Said, *Orientalism*, 109.

68. Said, *Orientalism*, 325–26.

69. Clingman, *Grammar of Identity*, 5.

70. In our postmodern times, a politics of location that allows for a "fluid, shifting, and generally context-dependent" view of identity is called for. Rather than some essential category, identity depends on location, which again is determined by "facts of blood"—social, personal, and familial alignments—and "facts of bread"—national, economic, and political matters—which are often elements at violent odds with one another. Tolbert, "Politics and Poetics of Location," 305.

71. "Globalisation carries with it a danger of uniformity and increases the temptation to turn inwards and take refuge in all kinds of convictions—religious, ideological, cultural, or nationalistic." Mayor, "Human Right to Peace," 2. On the abuse of multiculturalism in order to maintain a new form of monoculturalism, see Povinelli, *Economies of Abandonment*, 574; on the contribution of multiculturalism in Britain to "the reinforcement of centralized state power and the aestheticization of moral identities," see Asad, *Genealogies of Religion*, esp. 266; and see Žižek, "Multiculturalism," for seeing multiculturalism as an excuse for imposing capitalism.

72. More ominously, "various kinds of cultural *'cleansings'* demand of us *to place identity and otherness at the center of theological reflection* on social realities." Volf, *Exclusion and Embrace*, 17; emphasis original.

and adjustments and can even lead to societal conflict when the actions and aims of such communities clash with those of broader society.

Ecclesiocentric theologies continue to create problems regarding religious pluralism—the saved community against the unsaved world[73]—and, depending on the boundaries of the *ekklesia*, potentially also among different faith communities. The danger is always there that the insider-outsider rhetoric will mutate into the call for holy war, "the earliest and most elemental expression of religious violence"[74]—as recent times have shown in some parts of the world. The underlying problem is the formulation of identity (consciousness) and the construction of community (boundaries). Marginalised groups can claim their detrimental status as both an indication of their special status before God and as a warrant for venting anger and violence on their opponents and the rest of society in general.[75] Groups who feel exposed, ignored, and humiliated, with frustrated expectations, are fertile feeding grounds for anger and violence.[76] Assuming a special status with God, they believe they are endowed with unique rights to punish their victimisers and perpetrators to gain their rightful place in society and undo their position as a persecuted and stigmatised community. With identities of the Self and Other often textually inscribed, the link between normative writings (Scripture) and a sense of identity rests on self-definition but also the identification of the Other through appropriation of the biblical texts. The relation between hermeneutical processes of identity and Othering and then social identity and Othering is worth noting, especially against the background of a pragmatist or interpersonal hermeneutic: hermeneutical and social "otherness" is interrelated.[77]

73. Ariarajah, *Bible and People*, 69.

74. Selengut, *Sacred Fury*, 17.

75. *Multiculturalism* often equals tension and conflict, especially where "identity with itself" is found, as is the case with the identity of modern Europe with its history of colonisation, oppression, and destruction of cultures and imposition of its religion, all in the name of its "identity with itself"; Volf, *Exclusion and Embrace*. This resulted in a totalising, absolutizing self-identity, therefore exclusivist and oppressive and often violent towards the other.

76. Selengut, *Sacred Fury*, 85.

77. See Punt, "Empire, Messiah and Violence."

Conclusion

Proving direct and consequential links between the Bible, NT, and Pauline insider-outsider rhetoric and instances of modern politics of identity is neither possible nor the point, but should not discourage investigation of biblical-rhetorical patterns whose perceived influence still prevails. Despite utilising binary contrasts throughout his writings, Paul's rhetoric has not proven particularly effective in establishing and enforcing political regulations. His analogies, often drawing upon biblical binaries such as sin and salvation, destiny and the future, or ethnicity and communal status, have not been widely adopted as tools for governance. However, at a hermeneutical and even epistemological level, the Pauline rhetoric of Othering as well as its reception could have contributed to formatting and securing a politics of identity, expedient for defining and justifying both demarcation lines and for delineating the positions of people on either side of it. Questions posed centuries later moved beyond a politics of Othering, inquiring about perceptions of alterity that do not reduce otherness to sameness but allow for disturbance of sameness (Levinas), to break through normalising, regulating regimes of sameness. Which leaves the question, How do we celebrate our differences as human beings, working toward understanding rather than assimilation of others (Others)?

Bibliography

Ariarajah, Wesley. *The Bible and People of Other Faiths*. RISK Series. Geneva: WCC, 1985.

Asad, Talal. *Genealogies of Religion: Discipline and Reasons of Power in Christianity and Islam*. Baltimore: Johns Hopkins University Press, 1993.

Barker, Chris. *Television, Globalization and Cultural Identities*. Maidenhead: Open University Press, 1999.

Barth, Frederick. *Ethnic Groups and Boundaries: The Social Organization of Culture Difference*. Boston: Little, Brown, 1969.

Baumann, Gerd. "Grammars of Identity/Alterity: A Structural Approach." In *Grammars of Identity/Alterity*, edited by Gerd Baumann and Andre Gingrich, European Association of Social Anthropologists 3, 18–50. New York: Berghahn, 2004.

Boyarin, Daniel. *A Radical Jew: Paul and the Politics of Identity*. Berkeley: University of California Press, 1994.

Brown, Ken, and Brennan W. Breed. "Social Identity and Scriptural Interpretation: An Introduction." In *Reading Other Peoples' Texts: Social Identity and the Reception of Authoritative Traditions*, edited by Ken Brown et al., Library of Hebrew Bible / Old Testament Studies 692, 1–32. New York: T&T Clark, 2020.

Castelli, Elizabeth. *Imitating Paul: A Discourse of Power*. Louisville: Westminster John Knox, 1991.

Clingman, Stephen. *The Grammar of Identity: Transnational Fiction and the Nature of the Boundary*. Oxford: Oxford University Press, 2009.

DiFruscia, Kim Turcot. "Shapes of Freedom: A Conversation with Elizabeth A. Povinelli." *E-Flux Journal* 53 (2014). https://www.e-flux.com/journal/53/59889/shapes-of-freedom-a-conversation-with-elizabeth-a-povinelli/.

Dunn, James D. G. *The Epistle to the Galatians*. Peabody, MA: Hendrickson, 1993.

———. *Romans 1–8*. Word Biblical Commentary 38a. Dallas: Word, 1988.

Engberg-Pedersen, Troels. *Paul Beyond the Judaism/Hellenism Divide*. Louisville: Westminster John Knox, 2001.

Gee, James Paul. *An Introduction to Discourse Analysis: Theory and Method*. 2nd ed. London: Routledge, 2005.

Gerdmar, Anders. *Roots of Theological Anti-Semitism: German Biblical Interpretation and the Jews, from Herder and Semler to Kittel and Bultmann*. Studies in Jewish History and Culture 20. Leiden: Brill, 2009.

Gruen, Erich S., ed. *Cultural Identity in the Ancient Mediterranean*. Issues and Debates. Los Angeles: Getty Research Institute, 2011.

———. *Rethinking the Other in Antiquity*. Martin Classical Lectures. Princeton: Princeton University Press, 2011.

Horsley, Richard A. *Paul and Politics: Ekklesia, Israel, Imperium, Interpretation; Essays in Honor of Krister Stendahl*. Harrisville: Trinity International, 2000.

Jewett, Robert. "Response: Exegetical Support from Romans and Other Letters." In Horsley, *Paul and Politics*, 58–71.

Johnson Hodge, Caroline. *If Sons, Then Heirs: A Study of Kinship and Ethnicity in the Letters of Paul*. Oxford: Oxford University Press, 2007.

Jonker, Louis C. *Defining All-Israel in Chronicles: Multi-Levelled Identity Negotiation in Late Persian-Period Yehud*. Forschungen Zum Alten Testament 106. Tübingen: Mohr Siebeck, 2016.

———. "Melting Pots and Rejoinders? The Interplay Among Literature Formation Processes During the Late Persian and Early Hellenistic Periods." *Vetus Testamentum* 70 (2020) 42–54.

Levinas, Emmanuel. "The Trace of the Other." In *Deconstruction in Context: Literature and Philosophy*, edited by Mark C. Taylor, 345–59. Chicago: University of Chicago Press, 1986.

Levine, Amy-Jill. "What Jews (and Christians Too) Should Know About the New Testament." *Biblical Archeology Review* 38.2 (2012) 1–3.

Lieu, Judith M. *Christian Identity in the Jewish and Graeco-Roman World*. Oxford: Oxford University Press, 2004.

———. *The Second and Third Epistles of John: History and Background*. Studies of the New Testament and Its World. Edinburgh: T&T Clark, 1986.

Lopez, Davina C. *Apostle to the Conquered: Reimagining Paul's Mission*. Minneapolis: Fortress, 2008.

———. "Visualizing Significant Otherness: Reimagining Paul(ine Studies) Through Hybrid Lenses." In Stanley, *The Colonized Apostle*, 74–94.

Martin, Dale B. Introduction to *The Cultural Turn in Late Ancient Studies: Gender, Asceticism, and Historiography*, edited by Dale B. Martin and Patricia Cox Miller, 1–21. London: Duke University Press, 2005.

Matlock, R. Barry. "Almost Cultural Studies? Reflections on the 'New Perspective' on Paul." In *Biblical Studies/Cultural Studies: The Third Sheffield Colloquium*, edited by J. Carol Exum and Stephen D. Moore, 7:433–59. Gender, Culture, Theory. Sheffield: Sheffield Academic, 1998.

Mayor, Federico. "The Human Right to Peace." *Bulletin* 4.4 (1997) 1–2.

Meeks, Wayne A. *The Moral World of the First Christians*. Louisville: Westminster John Knox, 1986.

Mendels, Doron. *Identity, Religion and Historiography: Studies in Hellenistic History*. Sheffield: Sheffield Academic, 1998.

Nasrallah, Laura Salah, and Elisabeth Schüssler Fiorenza, eds. *Prejudice and Christian Beginnings: Investigating Race, Gender, and Ethnicity in Early Christian Studies*. Minneapolis: Fortress, 2009.

Park, Eung Chun. *Either Jew or Gentile: Paul's Unfolding Theology of Inclusivity*. Louisville: Westminster John Knox, 2003.

Perkins, Judith. *Roman Imperial Identities in the Early Christian Era*. London: Routledge, 2009.

Pippin, Tina. *Death and Desire: The Rhetoric of Gender in the Apocalypse of John*. Louisville: Westminster John Knox, 1992.

Polaski, Sandra Hack. *Paul and the Discourse of Power*. Sheffield: Sheffield Academic, 1999.

Povinelli, Elizabeth. *Economies of Abandonment: Social Belonging and Endurance in Late Liberalism*. Durham: Duke University Press, 2011.

Punt, Jeremy. "The Bible and Others: Root of Violence in Africa?" In *The Bible and Violence in Africa: Papers Presented at the BiAS Meeting 2014 in Windhoek (Namibia), with Some Additional Contributions*, edited by Jannie Hunter and Joachim Kügler, Bible in Africa Studies 20, 35–57. Bamberg: University of Bamberg Press, 2016.

———. "Empire, Messiah and Violence: A Contemporary View." *Scriptura* 80 (2002) 259–74.

———. "Identity Claims, Texts, Rome and Galatians." *Acta Theologica Supplementum* 19 (2014) 81–104.

———. "The New Testament as Political Documents." *Scriptura* 116 (2017) 1–15.

———. "Paul and the Others: Insiders, Outsiders and Animosity." In *Animosity, the Bible, and Us: Some European, North American, and South African Perspectives*, edited by John T. Fitzgerald et al., SBL Global Perspectives on Biblical Scholarship 12, 137–52. Atlanta: SBL, 2009.

Rhoads, David. "Performance Criticism: An Emerging Methodology in Second Testament Studies—Part 1." *Biblical Theology Bulletin: Journal of Bible and Culture* 36 (2006) 118–33.

Riesebrodt, Martin. *The Promise of Salvation: A Theory of Religion*. Translated by Steven Rendall. London: University of Chicago Press, 2010.

Rosen-Zvi, Ishay, and Adi Ophir. "Paul and the Invention of the Gentiles." *Jewish Quarterly Review* 105 (2015) 1–41.

Said, Edward. *Orientalism*. 2nd ed. New York: Vintage, 1994.

Schüssler Fiorenza, Elisabeth. "Paul and the Politics of Interpretation." In Horsley, *Paul and Politics*, 40–57.

Schwartz, Regina M. *The Curse of Cain: The Violent Legacy of Monotheism*. London: University of Chicago Press, 1997.

Segal, Alan F. "Response: Some Aspects of Conversion and Identity Formation in the Christian Community of Paul's Time." In Horsley, *Paul and Politics*, 184–90.

Selengut, Charles. *Sacred Fury: Understanding Religious Violence*. Walnut Creek, CA: AltaMira, 2003.

Smith, Dorothy E. *Texts, Facts, and Femininity: Exploring the Relations of Ruling*. London: Routledge, 1990.

Stanley, Christopher D., ed. *The Colonized Apostle: Paul Through Postcolonial Eyes*. Paul in Critical Contexts. Minneapolis: Fortress, 2011.

———. "Paul the Ethnic Hybrid? Postcolonial Perspectives on Paul's Ethnic Categorizations." In Stanley, *The Colonized Apostle*, 110–26.

Stimpson, Catharine R. "Feminist Criticism." In *Redrawing the Boundaries: The Transformation of English and American Literary Studies*, edited by Stephen Greenblatt and Giles Gunn, 251–70. New York: Modern Language Association of America, 1992.

Tacitus. *Tacitus on Germany*. Translated by Thomas Gordon. New York: P. F. Collier & Son, 1910.

Taylor, Nicholas H. "Conflict as Context for Defining Identity: A Study of Apostleship in the Galatian and Corinthian Letters." *HTS Theological Studies* 59 (2003) 915–45.

Tolbert, Mary Ann. "Afterwords: The Politics and Poetics of Location." In *Social Location and Biblical Interpretation in the United States*, edited by Fernando F. Segovia and Mary A. Tolbert, 305–17. Vol. 1 of *Reading from This Place*. Minneapolis: Fortress, 1995.

Volf, Miroslav. *Exclusion and Embrace: A Theological Exploration of Identity, Otherness, and Reconciliation*. Nashville: Abingdon, 1996.

Wan, Sze-Kar. "The Letter to the Galatians." In *A Postcolonial Commentary on the New Testament Writings*, edited by Fernando F. Segovia and Rasiah Sugi Sugirtharajah, The Bible and Postcolonialism, 13:246–64. New York: T&T Clark, 2007.

Wills, Lawrence M. *Not God's People: Insiders and Outsiders in the Biblical World*. Lanham, MD: Rowman & Littlefield, 2008.

Worthington, Bruce. "Alternative Perspectives Beyond the Perspectives: A Summary of Pauline Studies That Has Nothing to Do with Piper or Wright." *Currents in Biblical Research* 11 (2013) 366–87.

Zetterholm, Magnus. "'Will the Real Gentile-Christian Please Stand Up!' Torah and the Crisis of Identity Formation." In *The Making of Christianity: Conflicts, Contacts, and Constructions; Essays in Honor of Bengt Holmberg*, Coniectanea Biblica New Testament Series, edited by Magnus Zetterholm and Samuel Byrskog, 373–93. Winona Lake, IN: Eisenbrauns, 2012.

Žižek, Slavoj. "Multiculturalism, or, the Cultural Logic of Multinational Capitalism." *New Left Review* 225 (1997) 28–51.

14

The Implicated Subject and Epistemic Vulnerability in the Story of Josiah in 2 Chronicles 35:25

Gerrie Snyman

A large part of Louis Jonker's work on Chronicles focuses on identity formation as well as identity negotiation in the early Second Temple period.[1] His argument is that the books of Chronicles speak into the imperium in a multileveled process of identity negotiation by engaging overlapping yet clearly distinguishable socio-political and socio-religious contexts.[2] This essay will, in turn, speak into his argument by adding the topics of the implicated subject and epistemic vulnerability with a reading of the Josiah narrative in 2 Chr 34–35.

The description of Josiah's reign in 2 Chronicles alludes to various kings, like Saul, Ahab, Manasseh, Ahaziah, Hezekiah. Some are regarded as good kings, like Hezekiah, but others like Saul, Ahab, and Ahaziah are usually regarded as bad kings, with Manasseh redeemed at the last minute.[3] Yet we know that at least the reigns of Ahab and Manasseh were

1. I wish to thank the Collège de France and Prof. Thomas Römer in particular who have enabled me to utilize the resources in the ancient Near Eastern library to work on this celebratory essay in November and December 2023.

2. Jonker, "Engaging with Different Contexts."

3. Mitchell compares Josiah's death with Saul, Ahab, Amaziah, and Ahaziah.

relatively long, and longevity is a sign of royal success in the political and diplomatic domain. But the Chronicler sees them differently; something in their lines of causality went awry.[4] Josiah is seen as having walked in the ways of his ancestor David (2 Chr 34:1–2).

Second Chronicles 34:3–7 summarizes Josiah's actions towards the worship of foreign and deities and idolatry: he tore down the altars and the Asherahs, pulverized them, and scattered the ashes and powders over the graves. He even burned the bones of the priests associated with them. He restored the temple (2 Chr 34:8–13) and in the process found a copy of the law of Moses (2 Chr 34:14–21). The discovery of the law humbled Josiah to consult the prophetess Huldah (2 Chr 34:22–28), who proclaimed death and destruction to the people (verses 24–25) but a good death to Josiah:

> Because your heart was penitent and you humbled yourself before God when you heard his words against this place and its inhabitants, and you have humbled yourself before me, and have rent your clothes and wept before me, I also have heard you, says the LORD. Behold, I will gather you to your fathers, and you shall be gathered to your grave in peace, and your eyes shall not see all the evil which I will bring upon this place and its inhabitants. (2 Chr 34:27–28 RSV)

Following the prophecy Josiah renewed his efforts of reform and renewed the covenant with Yahweh (2 Chr 34:29–33) and reinstituted the Passover (2 Chr 35:1–18). His reforms followed the law that was discovered (2 Chr 34:12). Second Chronicles 35:20–26 describes his death: he was heavily wounded in battle with Pharaoh Necho in Megiddo and died either in Jerusalem or on his way back to Jerusalem. As the prophetess proclaimed, Josiah was united with his ancestors ("gathered with his fathers"), but the part that bothers me as reader is the proclamation of not seeing the evil that Yahweh will bring to the people. In a literal way, he did not, but the evil Yahweh usually brought over his people time and again was to subject them to foreign rule, which Josiah went to stop by going to Megiddo against the Egyptian army.

Regarding Josiah's death, she says, "When the prophetic word comes, therefore, it is a warning against some act already committed." The warning is against the inhabitants of Judah and acts "like a call to repentance, and a comment on an ordained outcome. It is not a warning against a contemplated action." Mitchell, "Ironic Death of Josiah," 425.

4. Talshir, "Three Deaths of Josiah," 230.

It appears he did not recognize the voice of Yahweh in Pharaoh Necho's words. Second Kings 22–23 gives much more detail in terms of the associated violence and destruction that accompanied Josiah's reform. It is violent and bloodied. Nevertheless, from the law's requirement to destroy foreign cults, and the political successes of the reigns of Ahab and Manasseh, a reader gathers that the problem in the kingdom of Judah always was that they were most of the time subjected to the power of foreign rulers with which they had to enter into vassal treaties. In order to accommodate these foreign interventions, foreign cults had to be allowed. In the end the foreign powers became too strong, and the small kingdoms of Israel and Judah were run over with the ruling elite evicted to be closer to the seat of the foreign imperial power.

It is in one such setting that I would suggest for the world of text production of Chronicles—a reflection within this small group of removed ruling elites regarding their history and current socio-political position for being without a monarchy and removed from Jerusalem. They sought the reason for their calamity in the way power was used in relation to the Yahweh cult: what the king allowed regarding foreign worship, what the population did, and what they did. It started with the Deuteronomistic History whose aim was, according to Römer,

> to show that the destruction of Jerusalem and the exile were not the result of Yhwh's weakness, but instead were the work of Yhwh himself, who was at the origin of the catastrophe: he used the Babylonians to punish his people and his kings, because they had not respected the divine commandments, which had been entrusted to them in Deuteronomy. If Yhwh can make use of the Babylonians, that means he can control them; therefore, he is more powerful than the gods of Babylon.[5]

The deported ruling elite, or their offspring, realized they were now without a monarchy, a temple, and a place which they can call home. Looking back on their past, they imposed on themselves the current weight of the destruction and loss by constructing a history where the king and his people carry the blame for the destruction and loss of the kingdom and temple. But they did it with a sense of a different identity.

I do not think it was an easy task. The elite accepted the imperium, but as Mary Beard recently pointed out in an interview,[6] people

5. Römer, *Invention of God*, 252.

6. In an interview regarding her latest book *Emperor of Rome*, Beard stated that

work around an obstacle without getting in its way. The institutions of the temple and the Yahweh cult were fragile, and they needed to be strengthened. It is in this process that I think the notion of epistemic vulnerability may be helpful. The hallmark of the latter is change and renewal, and similarly, the book of Chronicles broadly tries to provide something better in lieu of the first written history (Deuteronomistic) that they already possessed, as Jonker states:

> Differently from the Deuteronomists who wanted to give an explanation for the fatal destruction of Judah through the exile, the Chronicler was taking part in a process of reconstruction. Not only does the Chronicler contribute to the identity negotiation process of defining All-Israel in the Persian period, but he also contributes to finding new ways and means of existence in a socio-political dispensation of being a dependent province in the Persian Empire.[7]

More specifically, regarding the version on Josiah's reign (2 Chr 34–35), Jonker argues that instead of idealizing King Josiah by focusing on his religious reforms, especially regarding the Passover, his narrative instrumentalizes him to focus on the Passover.[8] I agree that Josiah is not idealized here, but why let him die in Megiddo leaving the reader with the idea he did not listen to the pharaoh's message from Yahweh? In Jonker's terms, Josiah has fulfilled his duty with the reinstatement of the Passover, and his death should not be the focus. I beg to differ. The royal history described in Chronicles ends with the enthronement of Cyrus: what the kings failed to achieve will be achieved by Cyrus—he will allow

---

people accept dictatorship. An emperor gets away with violence because people do not stand up to him or her. Ordinary people go on with their daily task, probably murmur against it at night in secret, but they know how the world works for them. It is a rather dystopian outlook. With the start of Christianity in the third and fourth century, Roman Christians were still ambivalent, and in the face of danger they would still sacrifice to the emperor. Would it be a fair assumption that in Judah and Israel that has been always the case: the Yahweh cult was always present, but to survive they had to sacrifice to whichever deity was prevalent at the time? No wonder the inhabitants and ruling elite are implicated in Chronicles. La Vita, "'Ons sal laaglê.'"

7. Jonker, "Was the Chronicler More Deuteronomic," 196–97. Römer concludes by saying "the whole history is conceived in an exilic perspective, and it is no wonder that the 'exile' becomes during the Persian period a new foundation myth for the 'real Israel'"; Römer, *So-Called Deuteronomistic History*, 164. Given the importance of the exile, the Deuteronomists were most probably part of the deportees who became employed by the Babylonians as interpreters and scribes.

8. Jonker, *1 and 2 Chronicles*, 287–88.

the people to return and rebuild Jerusalem. In the light of Cyrus, I would argue for a nuanced portrayal of Josiah. His failure to recognize a divine prophecy and his subsequent death illustrate a certain vulnerability and implication in his own demise.

The sense of a different identity in the early Persian period brought with it a sense of being implicated historically—that is, being closely connected with the events and persons of the past. Whereas all the people are implicated in the destruction of Jerusalem and the temple, some kings are implicated more than others. Josiah remains implicated though not culpable, yet he could not avert the destruction of Jerusalem. Does the Chronicler make King Josiah a figure of solidarity in turning him from a perpetrator (like Ahab, Ahaziah, Amaziah) into a more nuanced figure implicated by the events in Chronicles? Ristau suggests as much: "However, despite the insecurities, they [the people responsible for the books of Chronicles] remain committed to a theological tradition, which they understand in continuity with past communities that wrote and disseminated the Torah and also, though perhaps less deferentially, Samuel–Kings and other books of the Hebrew Bible."[9]

Louis Jonker started his studies in Chronicles shortly after I finished my doctoral dissertation on Chronicles in 1991.[10] Whereas my focus remained within the field of hermeneutics concentrating on a variety of postexilic texts, Jonker's focus continued to proceed with Chronicles, ultimately providing us with a remarkable scholarship on the book. It is an honor to participate in a Festschrift that would celebrate his work. I sincerely hope my own contribution helps towards looking at the book in new ways.

With the consequences of identity definition and negotiation in mind, and knowing that the process can be far from peaceful, I take up in this essay the issue of identity formulation and negotiation which Jonker pushed in his work,[11] and I want to ask the narrative on Josiah in 2 Chr 34–35 about vulnerability and being implicated. My contribution here has a distinctive humanistic critical slant, since I stand in community with other interpreters in other socio-historical contexts. Whereas Jonker is perhaps more traditional in his theological and historical-critical focus, the perspective I bring within a hermeneutic of vulnerability deals more with human agency. Given the current context, looking at human agency

9. Ristau, "Reading and Rereading Josiah," 247.

10. Snyman, "Biblical Hermeneutics."

11. See Jonker, "Engaging with Different Contexts."

is, in the words of Said, the "final resistance we have against the inhuman practices and injustices that disfigure human history."[12]

The first section is about epistemic vulnerability and being an implicated subject. The Chronicler reveals a different view on the royal history of Judah because the context in which he writes demands a different look at the past in the light of the arrival of a new power, Cyrus on the Persian throne (2 Chr 36:22–3). But in writing a new history (assuming a new or a different epistemology), the assumed readers (inter alia scribes and those whose ancestors were part of the captured ruling elite taken from Jerusalem) became implicated subjects. The Chronicler's history shows despite all the good things the kings did, the destruction of the temple and of Jerusalem did take place as the people were at fault. The kings also died because a chain of causality demanded sins to be punished. In the second section I will try to interpret 2 Chr 34–35 in terms of the notions of epistemic vulnerability and the implicated subject.

Vulnerability and Implicated Subject

Epistemic Vulnerability

Vulnerability refers to, in its basic meaning, the susceptibility to harm and injury. According to Erinn Gilson, vulnerability can have positive manifestations and value, resulting in empathy, compassion, and community.[13] To her, vulnerability is a basic human condition that is managed and kept in place by ethical and political principles.[14] Because it links up with ethics, vulnerability has a normative force; it requests a response that usually intends to minimize damage. But vulnerability also relates to political and social frameworks because it is a precondition to harm.

In terms of its negative understanding, there is a strong movement that demands for the avoidance and minimization of vulnerability. For example, within research in bioethics and human rights, certain vulnerable groups of people are specifically mentioned in Article 8 of the 2005

12. Said, "Window on the World." Said's words here just before his death resound vividly in the light of the current violence (since October 7, 2023) that is gripping Gaza, Lebanon, and the state of Israel. Harm and injury are inflicted upon Israelis and Palestinians with human dignity taking a back seat.

13. Gilson, *Ethics of Vulnerability*, 8. For a discussion on Gilson's concept of vulnerability, see Snyman, "Read as/with the Perpetrator."

14. Gilson, *Ethics of Vulnerability*, 15.

UN Universal Declaration on Bioethics and Human Rights.[15] Special care should be taken of these groups. The downside is that in naming them they can be easily relegated to the margin.

Gilson argues that we stigmatize vulnerability out of fear for the way vulnerability can affect us.[16] Vulnerability as a negative concept thrives where exploitation takes place and invulnerability is prized; vulnerability is seriously devalued.[17] But a dichotomous view on vulnerability disables one from working with the ethical difficulties surrounding and cultural baggage towards the notion of vulnerability. She argues the following:

> An ethics of vulnerability thus has at least two dimensions that are emphasized to varying degrees: on the one hand, recognizing vulnerability as a fundamental and unavoidable feature of life necessitates more extensive responsibility for and responsiveness to others who are especially vulnerable; on the other hand, such ethical responsiveness is elicited through experiences of vulnerability and a process of reckoning with and/or assuming one's own vulnerability.[18]

In overcoming the negative connotation of vulnerability, Gilson pushes the sense from passivity as a specific mode of receptivity towards a condition of potentiality that becomes a condition to openness and alteration. It also comes with an experience that is ambivalent and ambiguous, underlining an intersectionality in a complex of racial, ethnic, national, and linguistic identity. She argues, "Vulnerability as strength brings with it vulnerability as exposure to those who would thwart one's attempts to undo the dominant order or undermine one's mode of being in general."[19]

The kind of vulnerability Gilson works toward is what she calls an epistemic vulnerability.[20] It is a vulnerability which brings an openness

15. Article 8, titled "Respect for human vulnerability and personal integrity," states, "In applying and advancing scientific knowledge, medical practice and associated technologies, human vulnerability should be taken into account. Individuals and groups of special vulnerability should be protected and the personal integrity of such individuals respected." UNESCO, "Universal Declaration."

16. Gilson, *Ethics of Vulnerability*, 127.

17. Gilson, *Ethics of Vulnerability*, 144.

18. Gilson, *Ethics of Vulnerability*, 128.

19. Gilson, *Ethics of Vulnerability*, 144. Gilson bases her notion of an ethics of vulnerability on Merleau-Ponty, Gilles Deleuze, and Hélène Cixous. See Cixous, "Sorties"; Deleuze, *Différence et répétition*; and Merleau-Ponty, *Visible and the Invisible.*

20. Gilson, *Ethics of Vulnerability*, 73–97.

to being affected and altered. Epistemic vulnerability makes learning possible and forces the reduction of ignorance. Instead of proclaiming oneself "a masterful, invulnerable knower who has nothing to learn from others or for whom others are merely vehicles for the transmission of information,"[21] epistemic vulnerability acknowledges that "we all have lapses, gaps in our experience and atonement that demand alterations in our knowing attitudes."[22]

It is not only an openness to not knowing, recognizing ignorance, but also an openness to be wrong yet venture one's own ideas and beliefs, not closing off to other people. Moreover, an important aspect of epistemic vulnerability is to put yourself in an unsettling situation, a context in which one is foreign and strange, in order to overcome one's own ignorance and engage others.[23] Discomfort enables learning. The dispelling of ignorance is important to epistemic vulnerability because here it is the "deeply rooted, wilful form of ignorance that entails not just beliefs but unconscious commitments and habits" that get destabilized.[24] It entails an emotional as well as a bodily response, making vulnerability corporeal. For example, Gilson refers to racial discrimination and oppression that provides one with knowledge that needs to sink in to our emotional responses and physical bodies. It is not superficial but ultimately affects our basic understanding of the world, for example, that every human being is vulnerable and needs to be treated with respect. Habits are habits because they are repeated, and re-habituation too requires repetition. Epistemic vulnerability goes deep into the self, in the end affecting what one does and how one behaves, ultimately facing the consequences of one's self-understanding and actions. Challenging what one is and what one says is unsettling, but it allows for change in knowledge and ways of knowing.[25] Epistemic vulnerability challenges the notion of "this is the way things are," the ideal of invulnerability over against the cultivation of a process of being open to revise the self and what or how one knows.

21. Gilson, *Ethics of Vulnerability*, 93.

22. Gilson, *Ethics of Vulnerability*, 93. Gilson inserts here a reference to feminist theory as an example of opposing oppression of women, yet full of its own gaps of information and ignorance about its own oppressive ways. I think the same is true from whichever intersect one perceives, as long one keeps in mind an epistemic vulnerability.

23. Gilson, *Ethics of Vulnerability*, 94.

24. Gilson, *Ethics of Vulnerability*, 94.

25. Gilson, *Ethics of Vulnerability*, 96.

Given the notion of epistemic vulnerability, what would one have to assume about the author(s) of Chronicles? From the representations on the Chronicler and the text of Chronicles, would one assume they were aware of their own vulnerability, or, given their relationship with the Persian imperial power, would one not rather accept a stance of invulnerability? After all, they are privileged and possess a skill those who remained behind in the land did not have—namely, writing or a scribal culture.[26] The Persian period is credited with a large and significant amount of literary activity. Despite being a small agrarian community, the urban population of Yehud was "responsible for a wide variety of social, political and religious functions."[27] The elite would have focused on various skills while extracting surplus from the surrounding agrarian communities. But with heavy taxation and probable internal Yehudite maladministration, the people were fragile and sold themselves into debt. The result was a negative vulnerability in terms of a breakdown of the family structure and general economic malaise. It was only later with the fortification of Jerusalem that it became more important to secure western Palestine and not merely due to the good will of the Persian emperor. What also happened was that some Jews remained behind in Persia. Others returned but did not live in Jerusalem or Yehud; they rather went to Samaria, Ashdod, or other provinces.[28] The size and status of Yehud increased with time. That meant economic growth but also instability and rivalries, for example with the Edomites who started to populate the south.

The socio-historical, political, and religious context in this period I would relate to vulnerability in a negative sense: poverty, bad harvests, taxation, drought, destruction for those who remained, estrangement for those in captivity. However, when one looks at the Chronicler's work, he is taking part in what is called a project of reconstruction.

26. See Carter, *Emergence of Yehud*. One would then accept the idea that one deals with a low literacy in Yehud at the time, with about only 1–4 percent of the population able to read and write. Add to this the smallness of Yehud with a population in Jerusalem of less than fifteen hundred (*Emergence of Yehud*, 249–324), the question is how a small province could have maintained such a large corpus of texts. When looking at the biblical traditions, the skilled workers would have been professional members of the cult, singers, temple servants, gatekeepers, and a scribal class. Add to this the staff of the governor, soldiers, goldsmiths, perfumers, masons, and carpenters (*Emergence of Yehud*, 287–88).

27. Carter, *Emergence of Yehud*, 287.

28. Carter, *Emergence of Yehud*, 294.

The assumption would be that the Chronicler have to work through his epistemic vulnerability and construct a new text presenting the reader with new knowledge and a new sense of self, new hope. If the Chronicler's aim is reconstruction, one can expect a measure of destabilization among the audience, as what they know, or thought they knew, is changing and perhaps indicated as ignorance, at best, or willful ignorance, at worst. But the Chronicler has imperial support and participates in the power structures that would cause discomfort ideologically. Does he not become an implicated subject too?

The Implicated Subject

The Chronicler follows the Deuteronomistic History in his presentation of royal history, yet his differences with Deuteronomistic History clearly reflect his own ideological purposes. His text becomes an apologia for the centrality of Jerusalem, the temple cult, and the absolute centrality of Yahweh.[29] And in the case of Josiah, it is the latter principle that is not obeyed: Josiah is unable to see the word of Yahweh in someone else's speech. But is the Chronicler fair to blame Josiah for not listening to Necho?

The Chronicler seeks an answer to what got Josiah killed in Megiddo since the Deuteronomistic History does not provide one. Römer says the death notice in 2 Kgs 22–23 is a "lakonische Notiz," rather cryptic and not saying anything about military intentions, but Necho becomes nonetheless a "legetime Vermittler des gottlichen Willens."[30] The Chronicler needs a death that will fit his ideological frame. Was it simply "un évènement ponctuel" and the logical result of his obstinacy, as Bürki suggests?[31] Na'aman regards the Chronicler's version as far-ranging and speculative in his attempt to highlight his rendering of the doctrine of retribution.[32] Mitchell, having difficulty with modern scholarship's efforts to explain Josiah's death, suggests three other possibilities: Josiah the good king in 2 Kings is a backsliding, prideful, or afflicted with hubris king in Chronicles; his is a foolish death in thinking

29. Ristau, "Reading and Rereading Josiah," 241.

30. Römer, "Der Pharao als Gotteswortvermittler," 340.

31. Bürki, "Les notices funérairers," 265.

32. Na'aman, "Kingdom of Judah," 54.

he is furthering Hezekiah's work; his is an ironic death, as he dies in peace (*shalom*) in Jerusalem and not somewhere else.[33]

I regard the Chronicler as author part of a particular class of people closely related to power—scribes. Firstly, given they are associated with the evidence of the biblical texts as texts, scribes can be linked to the temple as an institutional and intellectual center. Thinking of a scribe, one has to think about "scholars committed to the transmission, interpretation, and divulgation of the traditional scriptures they had received from their fathers and ancestors."[34] If one looks at the education of the time in the early Persian period, van der Toorn argues for a first phase in which students were taught writing, composition, and eloquence. In the second phase they will learn the skill of memorization and will study classic texts of their trade and culture. Deuteronomy, thinks van der Toorn, was one of these texts.[35]

From van der Toorn, one can also gather the following about scribes:[36] Scribes were constituted as a publicly funded guild through tax on agricultural products. Scribes belonged to the upper middle class with mere copyists drawn from lower classes. Being a scribe meant upward mobility with knowing wisdom (reading texts) the one thing that was recognized by the public. Van der Toorn says they distinguished themselves from the rest by being a literate minority in an oral community while Judaism developed into a book religion. They had been privy to the deeper meaning or the symbolic capital of the text, which required an understanding of a language quite different from that of the general population. Being the inheritors of Moses and the prophets, they had social standing to claim office and authority of the spiritual ancestors—their authority was passed on to the scribes. Their power lay "in their position as mediators and brokers of a body of knowledge that was inaccessible to those not initiated into the arts of writing and interpretation."[37] They are part and parcel of the entire process and will be implicated by the ideology employed: they cannot distance themselves from what they wrote or copied. The Chronicler's role as implicated subject lies in his construction of a new story for a ruling elite returning to Jerusalem, claiming the seat of power in the emerging province of Yehud with the blessing

33. Mitchell, "Ironic Death of Josiah," 434–35.

34. Toorn, *Scribal Culture*, 96.

35. Toorn, *Scribal Culture*, 98, 102.

36. Toorn, *Scribal Culture*, 105–8.

37. Toorn, *Scribal Culture*, 108.

of Persian authority over-against other possible claims from the people of the land. It is an act of grabbing power and specific jobs by claiming political and cultic superiority in a vacuum left by a more relaxed Persian administration.[38] Moreover, the Chronicler had to be careful since his claims could be interpreted differently by yet another group—namely, a remnant of Israel (Ephraim, Manasseh, and Benjamin) who also contributed to the restoration of the temple. Jonker sees him walking a thin line, as a Yehudite distancing himself from the Benjaminites to an extent yet claiming to be an "all Israelite," and an inhabitant of the Persian province of Yehud within the Persian Empire.[39]

Michael Rothberg's point of departure with the word *implicated* in his book *The Implicated Subject: Beyond Victims and Perpetrators* is that the word alludes to entanglement, involvement, or being closely connected. The concept stands in a close relationship with power: "Implicated subjects occupy positions aligned with power and privilege without being themselves direct agents of harm; they contribute to, inhabit, inherit, or benefit from regimes of power of domination but do not originate or control such regimes."[40]

An implicated subject is someone who participates in a history that delivers victims and perpetrators but becomes neither. As Rothberg puts it, "Implicated subjects help propagate the legacies of historical violence and prop up the structures of inequality that mar the present; apparently direct forms of violence turn out to rely on indirection. Modes of implication—entanglement in historical and present-day injustices—are complex, multifaceted, and sometimes contradictory, but are nonetheless essential to confront the pursuit of justice."[41]

The Chronicler as scribe with a text from a particular ideological viewpoint constructs a religious community with a new history, described by Handy as "massive reorientations of long-established state-sponsored and social-identity traditions."[42] This means one needs to look at the Chronicler in a context of a socio-historical (real) world as a representation for a position in a world that is constantly shifting, socially

38. Jonker, "Engaging with Different Contexts," 381.

39. Jonker, "Engaging with Different Contexts," 381.

40. Rothberg, *Implicated Subject*, 14. For a more in-depth discussion on the concept of the implicated subject, see Snyman, "Hermeneutic of Vulnerability."

41. Rothberg, *Implicated Subject*, 14.

42. Handy, *Josiah*, 165.

constituted, and contingent.[43] The Chronicler becomes a figure to think with and through. He remains imaginary but is a very real part of political, economic, and religious machinery that will affect others.

At present, anybody thinking about the Chronicler and the narrative he presented would see him in correspondence or difference from 1 and 2 Samuel and 1 and 2 Kings. But back then, it is more than likely that the history he presented was heard without knowledge of these two books (except those who are closely related to the Chronicler as scribe; see below). Was he an effective agent for a different royal history, or does his new knowledge constitute yet another form of social ignorance? Obviously, without the knowledge of Samuel–Kings, his audience would not have had that knowledge, creating a gap or ignorance. It is clear certain people would have benefitted from his new view on past history, the high officials or "mandarins"[44] in the foreign seat of power. The new story he created opens the story to others and creates a sense of solidarity with those left behind. King Josiah becomes a figure of solidarity in the book, a perpetrator in the book of Kings who turned into a more nuanced implicated figure in Chronicles. Let us now look at the story of Josiah.

Vulnerability and Implicated Subject in the Chronicler's Story of Josiah

Jonker describes Josiah's death a false note to his reign.[45] Mitchell warns against modern scholarship buying into the ideology of 2 Kgs 22–23, whereas the Chronicler's version may have another message than the one of our expectations.[46] Hasegawa says Josiah's death was since antiquity a mystery.[47] It is puzzling that a foreign king, Pharaoh Necho II, would know the will of Yahweh better than Josiah. The Chronicler seems to clear up the puzzle: since the death of the pious king is not congruous to his system of retribution, a perfect explanation would be that Josiah failed to listen to the words of Necho.[48] But Josiah never fought in a battle, except the one he died in. In fact, it seems he entered

43. Rothberg, *Implicated Subject*, 275.

44. Römer, "L'école Deutéronomiste," 182; Römer, *Invention of God*, 214–16.

45. Jonker, *Reflections of King Josiah*, 32.

46. Mitchell, "Ironic Death of Josiah," 434.

47. Hasegawa, "Josiah's Death," 534.

48. Talshir, "Three Deaths of Josiah," 230.

his kingship with multiple violent deaths and ends it with one, and he is comparable to Ahaziah, Ahab, Hezekiah, and Manasseh.[49] Josiah did one thing the other kings did not and which is alluded to eight times in Chronicles but once in 2 Kgs 10:31: he followed the law.[50] Being a good king does not necessarily entail a good death. Hezekiah was a righteous man, but dies a horrible death. Manasseh ruled for fifty-five years and thus a successful king, but his reign is portrayed as wicked and despicable. Despite annulling Manasseh's religious cultic institutions, Josiah was also unable to waive the judgment on the people.[51]

Did the Chronicler then mean to cast Josiah in a less sympathetic manner, a perpetrator of sorts? Jarrard thinks so: etching Josiah with the likes of Ahab, Ahaziah, Amaziah, and even Saul, the Chronicler is constantly sharpening the social memory of Josiah.[52] Despite Josiah's religious reforms and the celebration of Passover, his confrontation with Necho and subsequent death puts his story in the new political realities of the province of Yehud. In Exodus, the pharaoh as the antagonist ignores Moses and his army drowns. In the story of Josiah, the king acts like Moses with a Passover celebration, with the reader expecting him to exhibit the authority of Moses and recognizing his divine mandate. Instead, he acts not like Moses and fails to believe Pharaoh Necho. Josiah seems to act like the pharaoh in Exodus: "By depicting Josiah's

49. The deaths of Josiah and Ahaziah are comparable (Megiddo is central to the battle). According to Bürki ("Les Notices Funérairers," 265) there are three correspondences between the two regarding the place and circumstances of the death, the funeral procession, and the place of burial. However, the two kings can also not be more in opposition to each other: Ahaziah is closely associated with Athaliah, a descendant of Omri and a hugely problematic and infidel house towards Yahweh. Josiah is one of the best kings of Judah due to his cultic reform. Hence, he cannot be buried in the same way as Ahaziah, and the report around his death is changed: "Le Chroniste présente ensuite la mort d'Achazia comme celle d'un lâche qui fuit le champ de bataille et se terre dans Samarie où il sera retrouvé et mis à mort par les hommes de Jéhu. Il sera enterré en souvenir de la justice de son père mais le Chroniste ne donne aucune information sur cette tombe (2 Chr 22, 7–9)"; "Les Notices Funérairers," 265. In turn Bürki refers to Josiah's death as a "le scandale de la mort subite et brutale de Josias dont le règne a pourtant été si brilliant" (265), but to him the Chronicler also show brutal deaths of kings whose reign was good. The death of Josiah does not resemble his reign but is simply "un évènement ponctuel" and the logical result of his obstinacy.

50. Smiley, "Rescinding the Rewritten," 317–26. See also 1 Chr 16:40, 22:12; 2 Chr 12:1, 17:9, 31:3–4, 34:14, 35:26.

51. Smiley, "Rescinding the Rewritten," 320–22. Manasseh is redeemed in Chronicles, and he is no longer given any blame for the exile. See also Snyman, "Read as/with the Perpetrator."

52. Jarrard, "Pharaonic Paradox," 644.

actions as pharaoh like, the Chronicler effectively accounts for why the righteous King Josiah died a violent and untimely death, especially after his (re)institution of the law (see 2 Chr 21:13; 22:3–4)."[53] Jarrard turns Josiah here into some kind of wrongdoer.

Jonker, in turn, suggests the Chronicler builds a bridge between the past of Israel and the present in Yehud.[54] Necho, the pharaoh once "an axiomatic metaphor for foreignness and villainy," becomes a divine agent of Yahweh, but for the Judean king under foreign tutelage, it was "too hard a pill to swallow."[55] Römer also thinks along the lines of Necho as a divine spokesman, as it is not the first time such a situation occurred.[56] Na'aman,[57] Talshir,[58] and Hasegawa[59] find a historical credible reason for Josiah to meet up with Necho II: Necho II has just assumed his position as pharaoh and was moving around in his kingdom to compel his vassals' loyalty. Given Josiah's reforms and liberties he took, it is suggested that Necho killed him because of suspected disloyalty. Here Josiah becomes a victim of Necho II.

Would the audience have understood it? After all, under Persian rule, before being allowed to return, they were no longer an independent territory or kingdom with a cult and a deity. Handy describes their identity as "a Slavic-nestling-doll of identities."[60] They are heirs to a nonexistent state with a religious center and a loyalty to a specific deity, yet as residents of the Persian Empire it is physically impossible for them to gather at the religious center. The Chronicler seems to unite them in the very last two verses of his text by proclaiming Cyrus to be a servant

53. Jarrard, "Pharaonic Paradox," 661. Jarrard calls the depiction of Josiah by the Chronicler "character assassination."

54. Jonker, *Reflections of King Josiah*, 29–32.

55. Jarrard, "Pharaonic Paradox," 665. It was also a hard pill for others to swallow, because in the rendering of the story in 1 Esdras, Jeremiah takes over Necho's role.

56. Römer, "Der Pharao als Gotteswortvermittler," 344. He noticed that later authors changed the origin of the words, i.e., Jeremiah, Schicksal, gods. Even Japhet thought it proper to put the words of Necho in the mouth of an Egyptian deity; Japhet, *I and II Chronicles*, 1056.

57. Na'aman, "Kingdom of Judah," 58.

58. Talshir finds substantiation in the Babylonian Chronicle of 609 BCE for Necho's campaign when a large Egyptian army crossed the Euphrates; Talshir, "Three Deaths of Josiah," 213.

59. Hasegawa argues that with Necho ascending the Egyptian throne, Josiah became his vassal who went to Necho to request confirmation of his own power in the kingdom of Judah; Hasegawa, "Josiah's Death," 524–25.

60. Handy, "References Relating to Josiah," 212.

of Yahweh commanded to build a temple in Jerusalem, the center of legitimate devotion.[61] Jonker argues (see above) that the restoration of the temple service and the reinstitution of the Passover underscores the value of Josiah in making Jerusalem the cultic center again.[62]

But perhaps one should be more specific about the audience, as Ristau is.[63] Ristau distinguishes three different kinds of audiences. The first relates to the world of text production. They are the inner audience who had direct access to the text. They could read it and study it, and they were aware of the primary issues discussed. They would have been able to accept, reject, rewrite, and eventually disseminate the text. They would have adhered to the conventions of writing and the school of thought and methodology to which they belonged. They would have been the primary audience. It would be on this level that knowledge of the Deuteronomistic History can be assumed and that the Chronicler, in terms of Römer's notion of canonical history, aims to change the ideology with which the past is being looked at.

The Deuteronomistic History's formation is to Römer the beginning of "un canon vétérotestamentaire" and "une historiographie canonique,"[64] with a different authoritative history by way of a new imperative of centralization and monotheistic cult. While the destruction of the temple and the loss of the monarchy initiated an ideology of the centralization of the cult, the physical presence of a written history in the form of a scroll gradually replaced the ideologies found in the traditional cult.[65] In the Persian period the discovery of the scroll in Josiah's story served to replace the temple cult with the reading of the book.

The informed audience is followed by a slightly wider audience, the lay participants in the cult. They would have received the text filtered

61. Handy, "References Relating to Josiah," 213.

62. To Jonker the Chronicler's focus was the cult, as can be seen in his presentation of the Passover and the temple building during his reign. The Passover served as the proper celebration and completion of the building of the temple. See Jonker, "Completing the Temple," 391; Jonker, "Finding a New Identity," 406; Jonker, *Reflections of King Josiah*, 59.

63. Ristau, "Reading and Rereading Josiah," 240–41. Ristau bases his differentiation on the work of Liverani, "Deeds of Ancient Mesopotamian Kings."

64. Römer, "L'école Deutéronomiste," 183.

65. Römer, *Invention of God*, 205. The ideology of centralization resulted in the following: a singular god to be worshiped at a unique singular sanctuary within a specific selected tribe coupled with the rejection of other sacred places and slaughterhouses and other tribes (the Northern Kingdom). In the Chronicler's version of Josiah's kingship, the rejection of sacred places and slaughterhouses is shortened.

through the inner audience who read it to them and educated the lay cultic audience on it. They are the targets of the primary ideology of the text. I am not sure what level of knowledge one can expect them to have to fulfill the conditions for an epistemic vulnerability. What would the effect have been on the readers when they had knowledge of the Deuteronomistic History of the kings? It would have been part of their public transcript and official ideology. Hearing a new or somewhat different history from the book of Chronicles would have thrown their previous knowledge off balance. It would have changed the way things were.[66] Would it have been disconcerting to them to realize that Josiah was subordinate to Necho II, because from a Deuteronomistic outlook that would have been unfitting for such a righteous king.[67]

A third audience would be the wider public, an outer audience consisting of people who do not necessarily participate in the cult (women, slaves, foreigners). If they receive the text, it would be filtered by the wider audience. They would not specifically be addressed by the text nor would they necessarily know other texts. There is a real possibility that they did not know the Deuteronomistic History since they remained in the land and the new history was constructed by those who were taken captive.

Nonetheless, if one looks at the dissemination process, all three audiences become implicated subjects in the new royal history: "Through reading and rereading the Josiah narrative in Chronicles, and reading it to others, the community of the text advances and promotes its own ideals and values and receives encouragement in its present situation and future goals."[68] Jonker refers to the golden thread in Chronicles—namely, peace, rest and quietness, although he acknowledges strife was always present.[69] His idea of identity *negotiation* implies difference and struggle, especially within the three groups just mentioned, because in the text of Chronicles a particular social order is being set up that is enforced by the returning elite. That would relegate other groups to less important positions of power, making them more vulnerable in a

66. Talshir remarks that one wonders whether the report on Josiah's death in 2 Kgs 23:29 would have been understood as an allusion to a battle were it not for the Chronicler's rendition of the story; Talshir, "Three Deaths of Josiah," 215.

67. Na'aman, "Kingdom of Judah," 41.

68. Ristau, "Reading and Rereading Josiah," 246.

69. Jonker, "Engaging with Different Contexts," 389–90. Take note that Jonker does not distinguish between different audiences but rather opts for different levels of identity negotiation. A specific group would theoretically be able to participate in more than one level.

negative sense. But since the groups are all implicated subjects in this new history, they are expected to accept the new order as the will of Yahweh. Here enters epistemic vulnerability.

Ristau seems to pour some cold water on an association between a positive new identity for Yehud and the notion of epistemic vulnerability. He is more pessimistic about the context in which the Chronicler wrote. He acknowledges the following: "From the Josiah narrative, in particular, it is clear that the Chronicler and the primary community of the text are passionate Yahwists concerned with monotheistic worship centred in Jerusalem and its temple. They are interested in questions about leadership and temple organization and deeply concerned with the intersection of praxis and ideology in the cult and life of the community."[70] Seeing themselves in line with past communities, and thus implicated subjects, this continuity is supposed to provide "the community with its self-identity, its sense of purpose in the world, its source of joy, and also, as evident from the Josiah narrative, its validation of lament. In a world of tragedy, perhaps the last of these is one of the most important legacies of the Josiah narrative."[71]

In 2 Chr 35:25 Jeremiah is said to have written laments for Josiah, pushing a dark cloud over his story. But Handy sees the dark cloud in an earlier event: the people at the Passover did not rejoice, whereas joy was a mark of all the festivities in Chronicles.[72] Ristau also notices a darker tone in the story but finds it bearable: "The pall is palatable through the absence of the joy and blessing paradigms, the specter of the exile, the finding of the book of law, the encounter with Huldah, and the despondency of the king."[73] These events hang like a sword over the entire narrative. This is in stark contrast with the joy and Yahweh's blessings in response

70. Ristau, "Reading and Rereading Josiah," 247.

71. Ristau, "Reading and Rereading Josiah," 247.

72. Handy, "References Relating to Josiah," 203.

73. Ristau, "Reading and Rereading Josiah," 224–25. Ristau elaborates on five things that darkens the narrative (226–28): The temple repairs already reflect the language of the exile, for example, the kings are seen as temple destroyers and the specter of the exile threatens to destroy the kingdoms. The book of the law that has been found foregrounds the covenant and the eventual Passover celebration, but it also exposes the failure of the kings and people in the past to keep the covenant. When seeking Yahweh on the discovery of the book, the language of the exile rears its head again with reference to the rest of Israel. The reader would realize the audience was already in exile and a remnant. Huldah's prophecy verbalizes the exile and turn it into a judgment. But Huldah's prophecy causes the king to be depressed, tear his clothes, and weep. There is clearly no paradigm of joy in Chronicles as with other "good" kings.

to a faithful king. There seems to be no joy and blessing in the narrative, especially the Passover, of Josiah, one of the supposedly greatest Israelite kings who proceeded with comprehensive reforms and (re)instituted the most important religious festival within Judaism.[74]

Would the darkness have been unsettling for the audience of Chronicles? Josiah was the last to attempt religious and cultic reforms. Quite a few tried their hand before him, but it seems Josiah was more successful, especially with his Passover which the Chronicler describes in glowing terms while giving less attention to Hezekiah's, which he does not label with a Passover. But the story starts with violence (2 Chr 34:3–6), alluding to an implicated subject of being king. Amon, the king before Josiah, dies a violent death and so does Josiah, all of which implies divine displeasure. Destruction of Judah was a long time in the offing; Josiah just could not avert it.[75] It was inevitable, and by the time the Chronicler wrote, it already happened. The people in the world of text production were confronted by a new political reality they had to navigate. Furthermore, they were a small community where a theology of blessings for faithfulness may seem strange and inadequate because, according to Ristau, they were "too small, too beset by difficulties, too confined in its influence, too poor, too powerless to claim that it was a faithful community in the tradition of David, Solomon, Hezekiah, and Josiah—all kings who, blessed by Yahweh, reigned over a glorious people in a promised land and established an authentic cult."[76]

Josiah's death in 2 Kings and 2 Chronicles indicates the end of the monarchy in Judah and of Judah itself. With the end of Josiah, both books end their narrative shortly after. In Kings there is no prophetic possibility;[77] in Chronicles hope enters the scene with Cyrus as a new favorite of Yahweh.

Josiah is not mentioned in Ezekiel or in Jeremiah, but his story functioned as the foundational myth or *pia fraus* (Römer) of the Deuteronomistic History.[78] I have mentioned the aim of the Deuteronomists earlier,

74. Ristau, "Reading and Rereading Josiah," 225.

75. Smiley, "Rescinding the Rewritten," 320.

76. Ristau, "Reading and Rereading Josiah," 242.

77. Handy, *Josiah*, 40.

78. Early Jewish commentators and the church fathers identified the scroll as the book of Deuteronomy, since Josiah's reform corresponds with the prescriptions in Deuteronomy (Deut 17:1–3 and 2 Kgs 23:4–5; Deut 12:2–3 and 2 Kgs 23:6, 14; Deut 23:18 and 2 Kgs 23:7; Deut 18:10–11 and 2 Kgs 23:24). Römer refers to the *pia fraus* (pious lie) where the first edition of Deuteronomy was written to promote the Josianic reform

but it is necessary to add the following, as it is valid for the Chronicler too: they conceived the history from an exilic perspective—no monarchy, no temple, no Jerusalem. But in contrast, the Chronicler adopted an attitude filled with what some scholars would term utopian ideas.[79] The Chronicler recognizes the crisis the Deuteronomists identified, but he provides a way forward in the crisis in suggesting a different ideology with a different medium: a written authoritative text.

Conclusion

The crisis was that the destruction of the temple, the removal of the king, and the fall of Jerusalem indicated that the Babylonian gods conquered Yahweh and that Yahweh abandoned them. This was the reality of the Chronicler's audience. And the Chronicler, in line with the Deuteronomist school and beyond,[80] by analyzing the crisis in giving an account that could explain the destruction of the previous dispensation, argues that it is not the Babylonian gods who conquered Yahweh but rather the wrath and anger of Yahweh that caused the collapse of the kingdom.[81]

The Chronicler accepted that the institution of the monarchy could not return, as Yahweh had a new favorite in the Persian emperor. The Chronicler does not write a history of how it really happened but "an ideological re-presentation of the community's historical traditions with the purpose of making them (intellectually and/or pragmatically) relevant to the community's present."[82] It is a revised history where all the negative events were deemed to be the logical consequences of the disobedience of the people and its leaders to the will of Yahweh. And here enters the

(*So-Called Deuteronomistic History*, 50). It was disguised as a testament of Moses and hidden in the temple to be discovered. Moreover, "the discovery of the book offered the possibility to *understand* this destruction [of the temple and kingdom], and to worship Yahweh *without any temple*" (*So-Called Deuteronomistic History*, 51). The story of the discovery of the book as a foundational myth is not strange in ancient Near Eastern literature. The book-finding myth can be found in the foundational tablets of Mesopotamian sanctuaries where kings rediscover them and undertake restoration works. Similarly in Egypt, where chapter 64 of the Egyptian Book of the Dead is presented as having been found in the Sokaris temple. Babylonian Nabonidus is also portrayed as a discoverer of quite a few foundational documents.

79. Uhlenbruch and Schweitzer, *Worlds That Could Not Be*.

80. Jonker, "Was the Chronicler More Deuteronomic," 185–97.

81. Römer, *Invention of God*, 217.

82. Ristau, "Reading and Rereading Josiah," 240.

notion of epistemic vulnerability and the implicated subject: in as much as the audience is open to change, they will accept the text's ideological representation of them as implicated subjects and be persuaded to a different and new worldview that will suit their context. Texts are shaped by communities, be they part of the world of text production or text reception. The Chronicler, in turn, uses an authoritative text to counter the destabilization of his audience in creatively turning around an ambiguous "canonical" story into a new, canonical, identity-stabilizing text, fulfilling his role of the scribe as guardian of the written tradition.[83] With his text he becomes an implicated subject with his ties to the power of the returning elite who would push themselves into a power vacuum in Yehud and relegate others to the margins, i.e., those in Ezra and Nehemiah who would resist aspects of the reconstruction.

Bibliography

Beard, Mary. *Emperor of Rome: Ruling the Ancient Roman World.* New York: Liveright, 2023.

Bürki, Michael. "Les notices funérairers des rois dans le livre des Chroniques." In *Les vivants et leurs morts: Actes du colloque organisé par le Collège de France, Paris, les 14–15 avril 2010*, edited by Thomas Römer et al., 253–66. Göttingen: Vandenhoeck & Ruprecht, 2012.

Carter, Charles E. *The Emergence of Yehud in the Persian Period.* Sheffield: Sheffield Academic, 1999.

Cixous, Hélène. "Sorties: Out and Out; Attacks/Ways Out/Forays." In *La jeune née*, edited by Hélène Cixous and Catherine Clément, 90–98. Paris: 10/18 Union Générale d'Editions, 1975.

Deleuze, Gilles. *Différence et répétition.* Paris: Presses Universitaires de France, 1968.

Erickson, Amy. *Jonah: Introduction and Commentary.* Grand Rapids: Eerdmans, 2021.

Gilson, Erinn. *The Ethics of Vulnerability: A Feminist Analysis of Social Life and Practice.* London: Routledge, 2016.

Handy, Lowell K. *Josiah: From Improbable Stories to Inventive Historiography.* Sheffield: Equinox, 2020.

———. "References Relating to Josiah in the Chronicles' Narrative." In *The Hunt for Ancient Israel: Essays in Honour of Diana V. Edelman*, edited by Cynthia Schafer-Elliott et al., 195–217. Sheffield: Equinox, 2022.

Hasegawa, Shuichi. "Josiah's Death: Its Reception History as Reflected in the Books of Kings and Chronicles." *Zeitschrift für die alttestamentliche Wissenschaft* 129 (2017) 522–35.

Japhet, Sara. *I and II Chronicles: A Commentary.* Old Testament Library. Louisville: Westminster John Knox, 1993.

83. Erickson, *Jonah*, 32–33.

Jarrard, Eric. "Pharaonic Paradox: Josiah's Tragic Role Reversal in 2 Chronicles 35." *Catholic Biblical Quarterly* 85 (2023) 640–65.

Jonker, Louis C. "Completing the Temple with the Celebration of Josiah's Passover?" *Old Testament Essays* 15 (2002) 381–97.

———. "Engaging with Different Contexts: A Survey of the Various Levels of Identity Negotiation in Chronicles." In *Texts, Contexts and Readings in Postexilic Literature: Explorations into Historiography and Identity Negotiation in Hebrew Bible and Related Texts*, edited by Louis C. Jonker, 381–97. Tübingen: Mohr Siebeck, 2011.

———. "Human Dignity and the Construction of Identity in the Old Testament." *Scriptura* 105 (2010) 594–607.

———. *Reflections of King Josiah in Chronicles: Late Stages of the Josiah Reception in II Chr. 34f.* Gütersloh: Gütersloher, 2003.

———. "The Rhetorics of Finding a New Identity in a Multi-Religious and Multi-Ethnic Society: The Case of the Book of Chronicles." *Verbum et Ecclesia* 24 (2003) 396–416.

———. "Was the Chronicler More Deuteronomic Than the Deuteronomist? Explorations into the Chronicler's Relationship with Deuteronomic Legal Traditions." *Scandinavian Journal of the Old Testament* 27 (2013) 185–97.

La Vita, Murray. "Ons sal laaglê en die diktatorskap aanvaar." Netwerk24, Dec. 1, 2023. https://www.netwerk24.com/stemme/profiele/ons-sal-laagle-en-die-diktatorskap-aanvaar-20231201.

Liverani, Mario. "The Deeds of Ancient Mesopotamian Kings." In *Civilizations of the Ancient Near East*, edited by Jack M. Sasson, 4:2353–66. New York: Simon & Schuster Macmillan, 1995.

Merleau-Ponty, Maurice. *The Visible and the Invisible: Followed by Working Notes.* Evanston, IL: Northwestern University Press, 1968.

Mitchell, Christine. "The Ironic Death of Josiah in 2 Chronicles." *Catholic Biblical Quarterly* 68 (2006) 421–35.

Na'aman, Nadav. "The Kingdom of Judah Under Josiah." *Tel Aviv* 18 (1991) 3–71.

Ristau, Kenneth A. "Reading and Rereading Josiah: The Chronicler's Representation of Josiah for the Postexilic Community." In *Community Identity in Judean Historiography*, edited by Gary N. Knopper and Kenneth A. Ristau, 219–47. Winona Lake, IN: Eisenbrauns, 2009.

Römer, Thomas. "L'école deutéronomiste et la formation de la Bible hébraïque." In *The Future of the Deuteronomistic History*, edited by Thomas Römer, 179–93. Leuven: Leuven University Press, 2000.

———. *The Invention of God.* Translated by Raymond Geuss. Cambridge: Harvard University Press, 2015.

———."Der Pharao als Gotteswortvermittler: Josia und Josef." In *Nächstenliebe und Gottesfurcht: Beiträge aus alttestamentlicher, semitischer und altorientalisher Wissenschaft für Hans-Peter Mathys zum 65. Geburtstag*, edited by Hanna Jenni and Markus Saur, 339–49. Münster: Ugarit-Verlag, 2016.

———. *The So-Called Deuteronomistic History: A Sociological, Historical and Literary Introduction.* London: T&T Clark, 2007.

Rothberg, Michael. *The Implicated Subject: Beyond Victims and Perpetrators.* Stanford, CA: Stanford University Press, 2019.

Said, Edward. "A Window on the World." *Guardian*, Aug. 1, 2003. https://www.theguardian.com/books/2003/aug/02/alqaida.highereducation.

Smiley, David M. "Rescinding the Rewritten: Receiving the Death of Josiah in Paraleipomena." *Scandinavian Journal of the Old Testament* 36 (2022) 317–26.

Snyman, Gerrie F. "Biblical Hermeneutics and Reception Theory: The Authority of Biblical Text and the Chronicler's Interpretation of the Sacred Story of the Ark." PhD diss., University of South Africa, 1991.

———. "A Hermeneutic of Vulnerability: Difficult Empathy in Response to Moral Injury Within Whiteness." *Koers: Bulletin for Christian Scholarship* 86 (2021) 1–17.

———. "Read as/with the Perpetrator: Manasseh's Vulnerability in 2 Kings 21:1–18 and 2 Chronicles 33:1–20." *Scriptura* 116 (2017) 188–207.

Talshir, Zipora. "The Three Deaths of Josiah and the Strata of Biblical Historiography (2 Kings XXIII 29–30; 2 Chronicles XXXV 20–5; 1 Esdras I 23–31)." *Vetus Testamentum* 46 (1996) 213–36.

Toorn, Karel van der. *Scribal Culture and the Making of the Hebrew Bible.* Cambridge: Harvard University Press, 2007.

Uhlenbruch, Frauke, and Steven J. Schweitzer, eds. *Worlds That Could Not Be: Utopia in Chronicles, Ezra and Nehemiah.* Library of Hebrew Bible / Old Testament Studies 620. New York: Bloomsbury T&T Clark, 2016.

UNESCO. "Universal Declaration on Bioethics and Human Rights." Oct. 19, 2005. https://www.unesco.org/en/legal-affairs/universal-declaration-bioethics-and-human-rights?hub=66535.

15

Second Isaiah's Reception of Deuteronomy's Monolatry as Protective Strategy

How Do Previously Known "Gods" Become Unknown Again?

Benjamin D. Giffone

The Challenge

Building on the work of Louis Jonker in the areas of identity formation/negotiation and intercultural readings of biblical texts, this essay situates Isa 40–55's reception of Deuteronomy's aniconic and monolatrous rhetoric within a polytheistic milieu.[1]

In Deuteronomy's various sections, worship of deities other than YHWH is portrayed as pointless and degrading due to the nonresponsiveness of handmade images. Within the putative setting of Deuteronomy, this is "predicted" to be Israel's punishment for disobedience: serving

1. I acknowledge with gratitude the continuing support provided to me as a research associate in the Faculty of Theology, Stellenbosch University, including access to library resources, as well as several research grants from the Department of Higher Education and Training (South Africa). Portions of this work were read at the November 2023 meeting of the Evangelical Theological Society (San Antonio, TX, USA). I am grateful to the participants for feedback received on that occasion.

the images of the nations. Yet also sometimes paired with the "serving-images" warning is the qualification, "gods which you / your fathers have not known" or "gods not allotted to them" (e.g., Deut 11:28; 13; 28:64; 29:26; 32:17).[2] This is puzzling on the grounds of Deuteronomy's own internal theological logic, and in its reception within the biblical story. In Israel's origin mythology, Abraham and Terah worshiped Mesopotamian deities in the lands of Ur and Harran. The threat of "gods your fathers have not known" seems to imply that captivity to the gods served by Israel's Mesopotamian ancestors would have somehow been *less bad* for Israel than serving other pantheons—for example, the gods of Egypt or Canaan (Josh 24:2–3, 14–15). Moreover, the biblical metanarrative does present the people of Israel and Judah *in fact* "returning" to Assyria and Babylon as captives, where they were forced to serve Mesopotamian gods—which would seem to be "gods their ancestors *had* known."

Both of these observations present difficulties for the monotheistic, aniconic outlook of Isa 40–55, whose image-polemics are indebted to the language of Deuteronomy. The author[3] of Isa 40–55 therefore deploys a protective theological strategy in a new cultural setting. In Isa 40–55, the exile "predicted" in Deuteronomy represents Israel's full regression: Abraham's descendants are now right back in Mesopotamia where they began, captive to Babylonian gods. They are as blind, deaf, and hard-hearted as the idols they worship (Isa 42–44). Yet this is worse than the original situation of Abraham because Israel has no longer been apportioned to the Mesopotamian gods (Deut 32:8–9); Israel has been identified with YHWH through the covenants with Abraham and Moses; and Israel has "known" YHWH experientially. Thus, Israel serving and being identified with "gods their ancestors *had* known" would further degrade YHWH's people and bring more shame upon YHWH. In Isa 40–55, it is now even more urgent that YHWH rescue his people out of enslavement to other deities than it was for Abraham to leave Mesopotamia or for Israel to leave Egypt.

This interpretive move of simultaneously "remembering" and "forgetting the former things" is a survival strategy for the Isa 40–55

2. Scripture translations are the author's, unless otherwise noted.

3. While not precluding the possibility of multiple authorial/editorial hands in Isa 40–55, I describe the author of this section in the singular (e.g., "the Second Isaiah prophet"), for simplicity. Isaiah 40–55 certainly addresses the situation of the Babylonian exile, with a voice and perspective distinct from those of the portions of Isaiah that come before and after. See Giffone, *My Salvation Is Close at Hand*, 35–42.

community, which places the "familiar" (and ancestral) Mesopotamian deities off-limits for the Yehudians, and asserts YHWH's covenantal "known-ness" by Israel.

Warrant and Justification

This study is inspired not only by a close reading of the biblical texts but by the insights and methods of Louis Jonker: an eminent and creative scholar, a mentor, a colleague, and a friend.

First of all, "adequate biblical interpretation" is itself a justification: trying to understand the Bible's meaning and implications. Broadly speaking, both traditional and modern interpreters have struggled to account for this phrase in Deuteronomy, either using synchronic approaches that simply enfold this threat into others around it, or using diachronic approaches that attempt to explain this "previously unknown gods" phrase as remnants of earlier polytheism or tolerant monolatry (before the full-blown monotheism of Second Isaiah). Both of these approaches lead to a flattened, deficient view of monotheism; they miss the richness of YHWH's relationship with the patriarchs, and how God is "known" by them. The diachronic approaches have been used as well to drive an unnecessary wedge between parts of Deuteronomy, and between Deuteronomy and, among other texts, Second Isaiah.

Additionally, the puzzle of "gods whom you / your ancestors have not known" presents an opportunity to move "from adequate biblical interpretation to transformative intercultural hermeneutics," as Jonker has titled one of his books.[4] The plurality of analytical approaches to the "previously unknown gods" puzzle provides resources not just for exegesis and biblical criticism, but also for thinking about missions, spiritual warfare, evangelism, and Bible-reading in secular, post-secular, pre-Christendom, and post-Christendom contexts. International experience has shaped my thinking in this regard—I was born and raised in North America, completed doctoral studies in South Africa, and then worked in theological education in Lithuania for six years, with opportunities to teach in Ukraine, Singapore, and India along the way. Many Christian believers in regions other than North America and Western Europe have a robust conception of the existence of other gods, specifically the activity of malevolent spiritual beings tied to places and nations/peoples.

4. Jonker, *From Adequate Biblical Interpretation.*

Third, a more nuanced interpretation of "previously unknown gods" in Deuteronomy provides an opportunity to learn from Second Isaiah's interpretation of earlier scriptural traditions. In another of his significant contributions to scholarship, Jonker has directed our attention to the ways that later biblical writers reconstrue earlier traditions to address new situations. In his work on Chronicles, Jonker has dubbed this phenomenon "reforming history": history that is re-formed (i.e., reworked) in service of the Chronicler's agenda, and history that reforms (i.e., regathers and redefines) the "All-Israel" community in the Chronicler's present.[5]

Like the Chronicler, the Second Isaiah prophet is attempting to protect and to reconstitute the community of faith on the other side of catastrophe: the Babylonian invasion, and the apparent victory of Babylonian gods over YHWH. In this essay, I argue that Second Isaiah's protective strategy involves not *changing* Deuteronomy's theology of other gods and account of YHWH's relationship to Israel, but rather, a creative *retelling* of that theology and tradition. When both Deuteronomy's and Second Isaiah's "monotheisms" are contextualized correctly, we see that a *hermeneutical* move rather than a *redactional* move is required to solve this puzzle of "previously unknown gods." As a protective strategy, Second Isaiah "doubles down" on the past rather than innovating.

Modern Western readers misunderstand Second Isaiah's protective strategy vis-à-vis Deuteronomy when we impose modern "monotheism" on both texts. So also, today, Western missionaries and theologians do the same regarding "spirits" and the invisible realm as experienced in non-Western cultures. The necessary corrective is a retrieval of a nuanced understanding of "other gods" in the Bible, including what it means to be "known" by a deity.

The Three Puzzles

In Deuteronomy's passages describing the worship of other deities besides YHWH, several passages add an additional qualification: "gods which you / your ancestors have not known." Sometimes this is connected to warnings against serving other gods (Deut 13); in other places, serving "previously unknown gods" is part of the punishment of

5. Jonker, "Reforming History." See also Jonker, *Defining All-Israel*, 12–13.

exile (e.g., Deut 11:28). This specification is puzzling in its implication, and in its eventual "fulfillment."

(1) The "serving other gods" punishment is sometimes paired with language that apparently presumes that "gods of wood and stone" are unresponsive idols without correspondence to any spiritual reality. Worshiping such idols is therefore fruitless and degrading for Israel (and the nations), but serving Mesopotamian idols would not necessarily be any more harmful than others.

(2) Another possibility is that the nations (and Israel, voluntarily or in captivity) who reverence those images in fact serve rebellious *elohim*, former members of YHWH's divine council. If spiritual realities stand behind the idols of the nations, then one might assume that worship of all "other gods" would be equally offensive to YHWH (Deut 5:7) and destructive/degrading for Israel. Would serving gods that *did have* some similarity to the gods served by Israel's Mesopotamian ancestors ("the devil you know") have been any *less bad* for Israel than serving random gods—or the gods of Egypt or Canaan, for that matter ("the devil you don't know")?[6] If not, then the "gods your ancestors have not known" threat seems pointless.

(3) Finally, in the eventual "fulfillment" of Deuteronomy's warnings, the people of Israel and Judah *did* in fact return to Assyria and Babylon as captives and were forced to serve Mesopotamian gods. How then are these "gods which you / your ancestors have not known"?

The Puzzles: "Previously Unknown Gods" Threat/Warning in Deuteronomy

There are numerous warnings in Deuteronomy against serving other deities, making images for the purpose of worship, or using images for worshiping YHWH. Most notably, the Decalogue contains both prohibitions: Israelites must worship no other gods besides YHWH (Deut 5:7) and must not make any images of anything to worship (5:8–11), including YHWH (see 4:12, 15). Beyond these basic commands, many questions are left unanswered, or the texts imply different answers: Do other deities exist besides YHWH? If so, are those deities in some sense equivalent in power or nature to YHWH, or is he qualitatively different? Even if

6. On the origins of this English phrase/proverb, see "Better the Devil You Know Than the Devil You Don't Know," in Speake, *Oxford Dictionary of Proverbs*, 22.

it is improper for Israelites to worship deities other than YHWH, is it appropriate for other peoples to worship these other gods? In addition to prompting these questions, the negative prohibitions on polylatry (worshiping many deities) and idolatry (worshiping using images) imply different facets of what is true worship in the eyes of the final editors of Deuteronomy (i.e., exclusive, aniconic worship of YHWH).

Serving Unresponsive Images

It is important to distinguish between the punishments and plights of directing worship at someone/something other than YHWH. There is the pointlessness of cultivating a reverential relationship to an idol that is unresponsive to its human servant. The other tragic plight is being captive in an abusive relationship to a malevolent spiritual being. Both of these plights tell us something about the blessing, safety, and fruitfulness of serving YHWH. In the Hebrew Bible we find texts that describe both plights.

Modern monotheistic readers tend to conceptualize the tragedy of idolatry more in terms of the former—and there is no shortage of passages that describe the pointlessness of worshiping idols. A well-known example outside of the corpora that are the subject of this chapter (Deuteronomy and Isa 40–55) is the first half of Ps 115. The nations mock Israel because their deity cannot be seen, but the counter is that he is living and present, in the heavens (115:2–3). The gods of the nations are "made by human hands" (115:4). They have nonfunctioning body parts (mouths, eyes, ears, noses, hands, feet, throats)—they are nonresponsive (115:5–7).[7] Those who make them and those who trust in them "will become like them" (115:8), i.e., non-responsive/dead.[8] Similar sentiments are found in Ps 96:5 // 1 Chr 16:26 ("The gods of the nations are אלילים, but YHWH made the heavens," implying that the images did not make anything); Jer 10:8, 14 (images are deceitful, because they have no breath); Jer 14:22 (images cannot send rain).

Turning to Deuteronomy and Second Isaiah, the plight of serving nonresponsive images is one aspect of the punishment of exile. "There

7. See parallels in Ps 135:15–18.

8. The psalm concludes by contrasting the living humans (not YHWH, interestingly) with such images: "The dead do not praise YHWH . . . but as for us, we will bless YHWH" (115:17–18). This points to the Israelite conception of humans as living images of YHWH.

you will serve gods, the work of human hands, wood and stone, which neither see nor hear, nor eat nor smell anything" (Deut 4:28; see also 28:36, 64). In Isa 44:9–20, the most famous of the "idol polemic" passages, the prophet draws attention to the frail humanity of the craftsman who hopes to create something lasting and beneficial (44:12; so, the irony of the human "creator"). He benefits from part of the wood used to fashion the image, burning for heat and for cooking (44:15–16, 19)—that would be a more profitable use of wood than an image. He says to the image, "Save me, for you are my god" (44:17). Those who worship images have covered eyes and deceived hearts (44:18, 20). Calling on such a god through an image is compared to eating ashes (44:20).

The plight of worshiping unresponsive images is easy for modern monotheistic readers to comprehend, so we will not belabor this point but rather move on to the more difficult polemics that presume spiritual realities behind images. Of course, there are some passages in the Hebrew Bible that speak of both unresponsive idols and other gods.[9]

Parallel Threat: Serving Spiritual Beings Other than YHWH

On the other hand, "a god you have known" would be a god that is assumed to exist as *knowable* in some way. Numerous texts in the Hebrew Scriptures state or assume that the Israelites and their ancestors actually served other spiritual beings, variously called *elohim*, sons of *elohim*, *elim*, or sons of *elim*. Heiser has provided a valuable attempt at a coherent portrait of the descriptions of these beings.[10] Without reproducing Heiser's analysis, it is important here to consider a few relevant texts.

Psalm 82 is a crucial text that describes the existence of gods other than the God of Israel. YHWH is not mentioned by name, but the singular masculine אלהים (82:1, 8) is contrasted with (and judges / rules over) the "divine council" (82:1, עדת אל) and the plural אלהים (82:1, 6), who are

9. "Let all those be ashamed who serve an image, who boast-themselves in idols; worship him, all you gods!" (יבשו כל עבדי פסל המתהללים באלילים השתחוו לו כל אלהים, Ps 97:7). Other passages refer to "foreign gods/images"—for example, Jer 8:19c: מדוע הכעסוני בפסליהם בהבלי נכר ("Why have they provoked me with their *carved-images* and the worthlessnesses-of foreigners?"). נכר is a nonsensical adjective to add to the condemnation of images, if the images do not have any real divine referent behind them (they are הבל, "vanity"/"vapor"). The prophet could just have easily condemned "images" or "non-gods."

10. Heiser, "Monotheism"; Heiser, *Unseen Realm*.

also called "sons of the Most High" (82:6, בני עליון).[11] A "divine council" comprised of other spiritual beings loyal to YHWH may be seen in Job 1:6, where the beings who "present themselves to YHWH" include בני האלהים and "the adversary" (השטן), and in 1 Kgs 22:19–22, which calls the other spiritual beings "all the host of heaven" (כל צבא השמים), including several beings each called a "spirit" (רוח).

In addition to the divine council, other evidence of the activity of foreign gods can be found. In 2 Kgs 3:26–27 the god of Moab is understood to have acted in response to Mesha's sacrificing the crown prince in desperation—thus "great wrath came upon Israel" (ויהי קצף גדול על ישראל; 2 Kgs 3:27).[12] The Israelites are apparently not protected from Chemosh's wrath by YHWH because they are not particularly loyal to YHWH at this time.

The Hebrew Bible contains both sorts of passages: those that portray the gods of other nations as existing, and those that portray gods as figments of human imagination, mere idols. The ideas are not mutually exclusive. The cumulative evidence indicates that at least some Yahwists (including exclusivists!) believed that some of the nations served deities that actually existed and—as we will see below—that Israel and her ancestors served these gods at times (willingly or unwillingly).

Threats in Proximity: "Unresponsive Images" and "Unknown Gods"

Having made this distinction between serving unresponsive images and serving other spiritual beings/deities, we see that Deuteronomy in its received form contains both sorts of warnings, sometimes in close proximity to one another.

Alongside (#1) "unresponsive images" warnings/threats (Deut 4:28; 28:36, 64), there are at least three other sorts of warnings/threats that presume other deities exist: (#2) threats/warnings against serving "gods not allotted to them" or "gods allotted to the nations" (Deut 4:19, 29:25[29:26]); (#3) threats/warnings against serving "the host of heaven" (Deut 4:19, 17:3); and (#4) threats/warnings against serving gods previously unknown to them or ancestors (Deut 11:28b; 13 [thrice]; 29:25[29:26]). Closely related language is found in Deut 28:36, which

11. Heiser, *Unseen Realm*, 25–32.

12. Margalit, "King Mesha of Moab"; Stern, "Of Kings and Moabites"; Giffone, *Storymaking*, 183–84.

predicts that in the exile Israel will serve "nations" previously unknown to them or ancestors.

Some passages combine two of these phrases (emphasized in italics):

- (#2) and (#3) are found in 4:19: ". . . And lest you lift up your eyes to heaven and see the sun and the moon and the stars, all the host of heaven [כל צבא השמים], and be drawn away and worship them and serve them, those which YHWH your God has allotted [חלק] to all the peoples under the whole heaven." This is in close proximity to warning/threat (1), found in 4:28.
- (#2) and (#4) are found in 29:25[29:26]: "They went and served other gods, and bowed down to them, gods which *they had not known* and which he had *not allotted to them*" (וילכו ויעבדו אלהים אחרים וישתחוו להם אלהים אשר לא ידעום ולא חלק להם).
- (#1) and (#4) are woven together in Deut 28:
  - 28:36b: ". . . a nation which neither you nor your ancestors *have known*, and there you shall serve other gods, *wood and stone*." (אל גוי אשר לא ידעת אתה ואבתיך ועבדת שם אלהים אחרים עץ ואבן)
  - 28:64b: "And there you will serve other gods which neither you nor your ancestors *have known, wood and stone*." (ועבדת שם אלהים אחרים אשר לא ידעת אתה ואבתיך עץ ואבן)

Deuteronomy 32 is very different in its language and quality but contains similar ideas, in close proximity to one another. Deuteronomy 32:8–9 indicates that Israel is YHWH's "portion" (חלק), while the other nations are the portions of the "sons of God" (בני אלהים).[13] In the wilderness, no "foreign god" (אל נכר) was with Israel (32:12). In 32:15–17, eventually Israel abandoned "the deity who made him" (אלוה עשהו), went after זרים, and sacrificed to שדים. The language of 32:17 elides the distinction between nonexistent entities, spiritual entities that are not "gods," and gods not previously known to ancestors:

יזבחו לשדים לא אלה	They sacrificed to שדים, not a god
אלהים לא ידעום	gods they had not known[14]

13. For an explanation of why the 4QDeut[j] reading בני אלהים was replaced by the MT בני ישראל, see Pakkala, *God's Word Omitted*, 185–87.

14. "Although the poem has just denied their divinity, it continues to use the word

חדשים מקרב באו	new [ones] who had come lately
לא שערום אבתיכם	whom your fathers had not dreaded

Similarly, 32:21a places "not a god" in parallel with "vapor/vanity":

הם קנאוני בלא אל	They made-me-jealous with not-a-god
כעסוני בהבליהם	They provoked me with their vanities

Yet a few verses later (32:37–39), the poem inquires tauntingly after the gods that Israel served (אי אלהימו), suggesting that these gods actually took something from Israel—the fat of their sacrifices and the wine of their libations (32:38)—without actually providing salvation in return. Immediately afterward, the poet places this claim in YHWH's mouth: "I am he, there is no god besides me" (32:39a). The claim is therefore not that no other spiritual beings exist (ontology) but rather that YHWH is unique among spiritual beings, demonstrating his divinity soteriologically: through "saving," "covering" (32:38), giving and taking life, and "rescuing" (32:39).

Next Puzzle: Why Are "Unknown" Gods Worse for Israel?

Having established that Deuteronomy contains both sorts of threats—"Serving Unresponsive Images" (#1) and "Serving Spiritual Beings" (#2, #3, #4)—we might ask, What difference (if any) is understood between the various sets of "other gods" that Israel was not to worship? As noted previously, one might presume that Israel's worship of all "other gods," including "gods not allotted to them" (#2) and "the host of heaven" (#3), would be equally offensive to YHWH. How does "previously unknown gods" strengthen the threat/warning? Would serving gods that *did have* some similarity to the gods served by Israel's Mesopotamian ancestors have been any *less bad* for Israel than serving other pantheons?[15]

ʾelohim for these beings. This is due to the ambiguity of the word. . . . Possibly *ʾelohim* is used for 'spirits' here, or else the word is used as if in quotation marks, meaning 'so-called gods.'" Tigay, *Deuteronomy*, 306.

15. MacDonald points out that the חרם mandate, which was applied to Canaanite cities (Deut 7:1–6), in Deut 13 is extended to anyone who worships other deities; MacDonald, *Deuteronomy*, 115. Even though 13:7[6] implies "gods your fathers *have* known" as a possible exclusion, 13:8[7] speaks about the gods of the surrounding peoples near and far, to the ends of the earth/land, being off-limits. This would presumably

The answer must be sought in what is implied by the notion that a human "knows" or "is known by" a deity. As we will see below, "knowing" entails some sort of experience of the god through worship or a display of power, especially power to rescue.

Unsatisfactory Answers

We now turn to the problem of "previously known gods" or "not-allotted gods" amid "pure monotheism" in Deuteronomy, for traditional[16] and modern readers. If we start with the assumption of "pure monotheism" as usually defined in deistic, Judeo-Christian, or Islamic conception(s), then numerous instances of these phrases in Deuteronomy are difficult to explain. The answers offered by source- and redaction-critical approaches are similarly unsatisfactory, given that editors of Deuteronomy could presumably have made changes to ensure a more consistently "monotheistic" text.

Diachronic Analysis and Developmental Suppositions

Heiser has articulated well the difficulty with the concept of "monotheism" in Deuteronomy and the explanations offered by exegetes and redaction critics:

> The consensus view argues that Deuteronomy provides evidence of an evolution of Israelite religion toward an exclusivistic monotheism. The argument is offered on the basis of passages that forcefully contend there are "no other gods besides Yahweh." This view seems coherent until one realizes that these "denial phrases" occur in the same chapters of Deuteronomy that

include Mesopotamia. Perhaps this is what prompts MacDonald to explain the phrase "which you / your ancestors have not known" *merely* as worshiping gods other than YHWH (*Deuteronomy*, 106)—an oversimplification in my view.

16. It is worth noting that, long before the Enlightenment and modern definitions of monotheism, premodern interpreters expressed their discomfort with the notion of a divine council or divine plurality through the changes they made to biblical traditions. As noted above, the Masoretes apparently changed "sons of God" in Deut 32:8 to "sons of Israel." TgPss 82 changes "gods" to "judges" (82:1, דינין), "angels" (82:6, מלאכיא), and "angels of the height" (82:6, אנגלי מרומא). As I will demonstrate below, there is also a tendency among ancient interpreters to downplay Abraham's relationship with the gods of Babylon, making him an early intuitor of monotheism even prior to being called out of Mesopotamia.

> assume and affirm the existence of other gods (Deuteronomy 4 and 32). In answer to the juxtaposition of polytheistic and monotheistic material in these passages, scholars argue that this phenomenon indicates either a rhetorical merging of polytheistic and monotheistic traditions or blunders by the redactors when updating the older traditions to monotheism. Since the evolutionary trajectory is assumed from the outset, an either-or fallacy is set forth for discussion.[17]

Similarly, MacDonald has articulated the evolutionary view of Isa 40–55's contribution to monotheism:

> Most recent work on monotheism and Isaiah has assumed a relatively uncomplicated critical account of Isaiah and monotheism. Second Isaiah, understood as Isaiah 40–55, is recognized as an early, if not the earliest, proponent of a full monotheism. That this is the case is demonstrated not only by unambiguous monotheistic formulae, but by the presence of other ideas consequent upon monotheism. These include YHWH's complete mastery of nature and history, derision of cultic images, and a generous universalism.[18]

The approach offered by Juha Pakkala in *Intolerant Monolatry in the Deuteronomistic History* is a helpful example. Pakkala defines polytheism, monolatry, and monotheism on a spectrum:

> Many polytheistic religions show features of monolatry. . . . Monolatry should be distinguished from monotheism and polytheism, but it can also be understood as a stage between the two, for it shares features with them both.[19]

Pakkala further distinguishes between *tolerant* and *intolerant* monolatry. Tolerant monolatry, which he says is the "general stand" of the Old Testament (OT), holds that "Yahwe is unique and clearly above all other gods, but the co-existence of other divinities, at least at some level and to a certain point, is allowed."[20] Later "monotheistic" editors who objected to this view edited or omitted some of this monolatry material.[21] Another perspective represented in strands of OT texts is intolerant monolatry:

17. Heiser, "Monotheism," 4.

18. MacDonald, "Monotheism and Isaiah," 45.

19. Pakkala, *Intolerant Monolatry*, 16.

20. Pakkala, *Intolerant Monolatry*, 18.

21. "In most of the OT one finds a clearly predominant Yahwe who is the unquestioned God of Israel. He is unique and His position is not challenged in any way. No

> The OT contains some passages that are ferociously and intrinsically intolerant of other gods. The other gods are actively antagonized and attacked with the main aim of hindering the Israelites from worshipping them. These passages, on the one hand, stand out from the OT's overall tranquil attitude, and on the other hand, often stick out from their contexts. They do not deny the existence of other gods, a feature which separates the stand from monotheism, but polemic against the other gods is forcible and systematic so as to undermine their power and to make them look unappealing and ridiculous. The difference to tolerant monolatry is evident. *It is not possible to explain away the difference between these two stands as two aspects of one theology. On the contrary, it seems reasonable to regard them as two distinct religious attitudes with a very different background and theology.*[22]

Pakkala thus distinguishes between the monolatry of Deut 4:19–20 and the full monotheism of 4:28 and Second Isaiah.

> [Regarding the "host of heaven" in 4:19–20:]The writer is not calling for the general worship of Yahwe among all nations. Quite the opposite, he wants them to continue in their indigenous religions. Only the Israelites should and may worship Yahwe. The difference between the writer and Deutero-Isaiah, who calls for the universal worship of Yahwe, is manifest.[23]

> Verse 28 evidently describes the situation where the [*later*] author lived: The Israelites worshipping other gods in a foreign land. It is a problem of the author's own situation. He wants to convince his contemporaries that these gods are only of wood and stone, and hence not worthy of worship and no comparison to Yahwe.[24]

This approach fundamentally fails on its own terms to explain how such wide-ranging development can be reflected within the book itself. If later editors made changes to a Deuteronomistic or pre-Deuteronomistic

---

polemic against other gods can be found however, and some passages reveal that the divine was not limited to Yahwe and that other divinities were accepted up to a certain extent. In any case, they are neither a threat nor a problem to Yahwe. These passages may only be vestiges of a richer realm of the divine that the Israelites worshipped or paid some devotion to. Later editors who had a stricter view on other divinities probably edited out or omitted some of the embarrassing material." Pakkala, *Intolerant Monolatry*, 18.

22. Pakkala, *Intolerant Monolatry*, 18; emphasis added.

23. Pakkala, *Intolerant Monolatry*, 91.

24. Pakkala, *Intolerant Monolatry*, 92.

core that represented polytheism or tolerant monolatry, then the retention of phrases acknowledging "previously known gods" or "gods allotted to the nations" in Deuteronomy might be seen as contradicting later Second Isaiah–style full monotheism. Why would these later editors have left so-called "polytheism" or "monolatry" phrases in the book at all? One standard critical answer is to appeal to the so-called "principle of addition/preservation": the idea that later editors and scribes never subtracted from holy writ, only added. But in his later work, *God's Word Omitted*, Pakkala admits that later editors could have taken things out, and we would never know.[25] Besides Pakkala himself, many biblical critics have begun to challenge this "principle of addition," including David Carr, Joshua Berman, Benjamin Ziemer, and my own recent contribution.[26]

Even if the premises and methods of source criticism are accepted to some degree, we are left with a received text that appears theologically incoherent—at least, based on the modern definition of "monotheism."

Western Readers: Examples

For source- and redaction-critics, the presumption that "simple/radical monotheism" is the latest development in Israelite religion leads to analysis that simply pulls apart the strands/layers of presumed development.

For Western readers who hold to historic Christian belief, the phrases "gods you / your ancestors have not known" and "gods not allotted to you/them" complicate the warnings against serving idols or supposedly nonexistent gods. Commentators have taken different kinds of approaches to the phrase "gods you / your fathers have not known." Many exegetes simply enfold this aspect of the warning into the other aspect, the "unresponsive gods" warnings (such as Deut 4:28[27] and Deut 28:36[28]).

25. Pakkala, *God's Word Omitted*, 379.

26. Carr, *Formation of the Hebrew Bible*; Berman, *Inconsistency in the Torah*; Ziemer, *Kritik des Wachstumsmodells*; Ziemer, "Radical Versus Conservative," 304; Giffone, *Storymaking*, 32–74, 225–27.

27. "The outcome of YHWH's jealousy is 'scattering' (exile) where Israel will be recruited into false worship, an unbearable fate for a community belonging to YHWH." Brueggemann, *Deuteronomy*, 56. "Ironically, the punishment for idolatry will be the worship of man-made gods in exile, which cannot relate to any of Israel's needs, because they are completely lifeless (v. 28). Then Israel will discover how frustratingly impotent these gods have been. Such gods contrast sharply with Yahweh's active power in verses 32–40." Woods, *Deuteronomy*, 112.

28. "Although the memory of Egypt no doubt lies behind this curse, it is not Egypt

Others admit early Israelite monolatry but still wish to appeal to later religious developments that place "pure monotheism" texts at a later stage, when Israel/Judah has experience of exile in Mesopotamia.[29]

Arnold, interestingly, observes the parallels between 4:28 and the idol polemics[30] but also rightly interprets "there is none besides him" (אין עוד מלבדו; 4:35) as a statement of YHWH's uniqueness among beings that were thought to exist: "The confession therefore asserts more than simple monotheism (a mere denial of the existence of other deities), while also contributing to the Old Testament's nature as a 'monotheizing' document."[31]

On "gods which you have not known" in Deut 11:28, commentators tend to emphasize the uselessness of those gods to Israel as compared to YHWH, while not explicitly admitting that the passage acknowledges the existence of those gods. The "knownness" of YHWH to Israel for these

---

that would be the instrument of God in the curse, but rather *a nation whom neither you nor your fathers have known*. Having lost the privileges of the covenant, the Israelites would be forced into the service of strange gods, not a living God like their Lord, but lifeless gods of wood and stone." Craigie, *Book of Deuteronomy*, 346; emphasis original.

29. Biddle is already reaching for a developmental explanation, attributing the idol polemic of 4:28 to a later period in Israel's history: "Ironically, expelled from the land for idolatry, they will be reduced to worshiping foreign gods of human manufacture, mere wood and stone (Deut 29:16, 36, 64; 2 Kgs 19:18 [= Isa 37:19]; Jer 2:27; Ezek 20:32). Once again, the language of the anti-idol polemic seems to derive from the rhetoric of a late period in Israel's history and manifests very strong affinities with the prophets, especially Jeremiah." Biddle, *Deuteronomy*, 87.

30. "If they provoke YHWH by worshiping him like any other god, they will find themselves dependent upon those other gods. And the deities they worship will become the gods they serve. But those deities are merely human products, idols made from *wood and stone*, incapable of the lifelike activities attributed to them by the pagan artisans who created them: seeing, hearing, eating, smelling." Arnold, *Deuteronomy Chapters 1–11*, 269; emphasis original.

31. Arnold, *Deuteronomy Chapters 1–11*, 282.

commentators is focused on YHWH's saving acts for Israel.[32] A similar approach is taken to Deut 32:16–18.[33]

In short, most Western interpreters in a more traditional stream have not been able to confront the issue of the "previously unknown deities" threats/warnings in Deuteronomy because of a default definition of monotheism as "simple monotheism." The fact that "malignant spiritual beings" threats/warnings are often bundled with "unresponsive idols" threats/warnings allows traditional interpreters to sidestep the issue and focus on the latter.

Dissolving the Puzzle: Monotheism Re(de)fined

I have indicated my view that more fruitful analysis has been offered by Nathan MacDonald in *Deuteronomy and the Meaning of "Monotheism"* and a subsequent essay on "Monotheism and Isaiah,"[34] and by Michael Heiser, starting with "Monotheism, Polytheism, Monolatry, or Henotheism," and then presenting his full thesis in *The Unseen Realm*.[35] A fuller

32. "That is, 'gods who have not proved themselves to you.' The Lord's claim on Israel's loyalty is based on the fact that He alone has acted on Israel's behalf (see 5:6). From other gods Israel has experienced nothing. Compare Hosea 13:4: 'Only I the LORD have been your God ever since the land of Egypt; you have never experienced a God but Me, you have never had a helper but Me.'" Tigay, *Deuteronomy*, 116.

"That the false gods are ones Israel has *not known* contrasts strongly with YHWH, whom they have been made to 'know' (*yd'*) as alone worthy of the designation 'God,' and who saved them from Egypt, sustained them in the desert, and loved them enough to give them the Torah (see 4:35, 39; 7:9; 8:5; 9:3)." Arnold, *Deuteronomy Chapters 1–11*, 604; emphasis original.

"The choice is not between God and a life without God; it is between YHWH and other gods (v 28); it is between a sovereign Lord who controls our destiny and lesser powers who become gods, for all practical purposes, who do not deliver what they promise. These latter are the 'other gods whom you have not known' (v 28); they did not create the nation, nor have they done anything to sustain it." Christensen, *Deuteronomy 1:1—21:9*, 229.

33. Woods comments on 32:16–18: "Forgetting the Lord consequently leads to idolatry (cf. 8:19–20; Hos 4:17), making Yahweh jealous of their *foreign gods* and angry at their *detestable idols* (cf. v. 12; 6:14–15; 7:25). Other gods are exposed as demons (*shedim*; cf. Ps. 106:37), which are *not god*, gods they had *not known*, which had *recently appeared* in the land, and whom the fathers had not feared/worshipped (or were 'acquainted' with), as a parallel to *not known*." Woods, *Deuteronomy*, 313; emphasis original. However, Woods never addresses what it might mean for Israelites to serve gods their ancestors *had* known, and why this qualification is necessary.

34. MacDonald, *Deuteronomy*; MacDonald, "Monotheism and Isaiah."

35. Heiser, "Monotheism"; Heiser, *Unseen Realm*.

view of "divine council monotheism," which accounts for the existence of other spiritual beings, may seem incoherent to Western readers but is more at home in African belief systems.

Snapshots of Monotheism in Deuteronomy and Second Isaiah

Heiser demonstrates through careful reading not only that Deuteronomy is a coherent document on the issue of monotheism when it is defined properly as "divine council monotheism," but also that Deuteronomy's monotheism is not incompatible with that of Second Isaiah.[36]

MacDonald outlines Deuteronomy's rich depiction of YHWH's character and the relationship that Israel should have to YHWH, for which "monotheism" (as traditionally defined) is an inadequate descriptor:

> Modern "monotheism" represents a call to recognize the objective state of metaphysical affairs. There is only one God, other deities are mythical, figments of the imagination, divinized natural forces or projections of psychological needs. The primary (only?) sin is ignorance. . . . In Deuteronomy, however, the recognition of YHWH'S oneness is a call to love YHWH, a love expressed in obedience and worship. The demand to show exclusive loyalty to YHWH depends, for its rhetorical effectiveness, on a common recognition that other gods exist and represent a serious challenge to Israel's commitment to YHWH. For Deuteronomy, the primary sin is disloyalty.[37]

Similar language in Second Isaiah means that the same must be said of that text's views of the existence of other divine beings.[38] Heiser

36. Contra, inter alia, Mark S. Smith, who holds that Second Isaiah uses Deut 32, supposedly a henotheistic/monolatrous text, as an "ideological template" to *develop* a rhetoric of full monotheism; Smith, *Origins of Biblical Monotheism*, 191. "Second Isaiah, however, provides us with what is the revolutionary breakthrough to monotheism, and most scholars acknowledge that his is an absolute and universalistic monotheism developed well beyond the thought of his predecessors." Gnuse, *No Other Gods*, 207.

Heiser rather argues, "Deutero-Isaiah is consistent with Deuteronomy since the phrases in his work on which scholars depend for arguing other gods do not exist, are the same, or are similar to those just discussed in Deuteronomy 4 and 32. There is also solid evidence that Isaiah utilizes the worldview of Deuteronomy 4 and 32, as well as Psalm 82. If so, then his alleged denials of the existence of other gods must be contextualized by his broader theology." Heiser, "Monotheism," 13.

37. MacDonald, *Deuteronomy*, 210.

38. "This work is not an exercise in rejecting the claims of Deuteronomy to 'true monotheism' so that Ezekiel, Deutero-Isaiah or the priestly material can claim the

surveys the scholarship that has recognized divine council language in Isa 40:1–8, and the language of the dwelling place of El and princes in the heavenly realm in 40:22–26.[39] Moreover, the "denial phrases" (Isa 43:10–12; 44:6–8; 45:5–7, 14, 18, 21–22) have near-exact parallels to Deut 4:35, 39 and 32:12, 39 and should be understood as statements of incomparability, not denials of other divine beings' existence.[40]

Holter, in his careful literary study of Deut 4 and analysis particularly of 4:19–20, cautiously focuses on the impotence of the astral gods whom the nations worship, rather than their supposed "nonexistence": "Israel has been saved by Yahweh from Egypt; this means that she has an experience of a *relationship to an acting and potent* God (v. 20a), whereas the other peoples are allotted, by the same God, to *non-acting and impotent* astral deities (v. 19b, cf. also v. 28)."[41] Holter also rightly observes that the comparisons to other nations and their gods in Deut 4's interpretation of the Second Commandment (against images) has more to do with the story of Israel: what YHWH has done for Israel, rather than YHWH's ontology.[42]

---

crown that is rightly theirs. My argument that 'monotheism' is a creation of the modern world prohibits the term's simple application to any other biblical book." MacDonald, *Deuteronomy*, 219. See also Barr, "Problem of Israelite Monotheism," 53–54, as quoted in Heiser, "Monotheism," 13; Moberly, "How Appropriate Is 'Monotheism,'" 229–31. On Isa 40–55, Moberly concludes, "The consensus that Isa. 40–55 (and related texts) expresses an understanding other than that of the *Shema*ʿ or the rest of the Old Testament is, I suggest, a misreading of the texts." Moberly, "How Appropriate Is 'Monotheism,'" 231.

39. Heiser, "Monotheism," 14–15.

40. Heiser, "Monotheism," 15–18.

41. Holter, *Deuteronomy 4*, 79; emphasis added.

42. "When the text talks about the cultic life of other peoples, claiming that Yahweh has allotted worship of astral deities to them, the motivation is mainly to point out the unique position of Yahweh. He is Lord of everything, even of the other peoples and their gods, and his own people Israel is expected to reflect this. The reference to the exodus experience serves to express this. Partly, this reference is part of an interpretive tendency throughout Deut 4 of relating the Second commandment to major phases in the history of Israel. Partly, however, the reference to the exodus experience also serves a more particular role here in v. 20, as exodus from Egypt is the central example in the Deuteronomistic literature that Yahweh is stronger than other gods and peoples. A similar thought is found also in the frame texts of this chapter. Vv. 6–8 and 32–34, each of them in a series of rhetorical questions, express how the other peoples will be amazed by watching a people living near its God, through decrees and judgements, vv. 6–8, and a God living near its people, through theophany and salvation, vv. 32–34. In other words, the function of the references to the other peoples and their relationship to the astral deities is to create a contrastive background for an understanding of the particular relationship between Yahweh and Israel." Holter, *Deuteronomy 4*, 80.

Divine Council Monotheism in African Context

It is not possible for me—nor is it necessary—to survey all of African scholarship on Deuteronomy, Isaiah, or "monotheism." It is also not possible, of course, to describe a single "African perspective" on the existence of spirits/gods. It can be said that certain notions are somewhat more common, or held in common, across African cultures. Several are particularly illuminating for the study of "previously known gods" in Deuteronomy.

African traditional religions and African Christians generally acknowledge that spiritual beings are active in the world, even under a high deity that is unique in his nature.[43] Darko writes,

> Some Western scholars and missionaries contend that African beliefs, outside Islam and Christianity, subscribe to polytheism and they resist the thought of any African reference to God being associated with the Christian God. Conversely, African scholars have argued against what they deem to be mischaracterization of traditional African beliefs during and after the colonial era. Some argue that African cultures adhere to belief in one Supreme God who works through mediators and subsidiary gods/goddesses, and who may be approached by the agency of other spirit or human agents. African monotheism then may not be misconstrued, in this reasoning. That God (one Supreme being) is responsible for creation is a widespread belief that preceded Christianity and Islam in Africa.[44]

Even perspectives that see the Bible as prescriptive for all cultures will find the notion of a "divine council" more at home in African belief systems than in Western belief systems.[45]

Second, African readers will be familiar with the notion that ancestors' past relationships to a deity or spirit would have significance for a present generation. For example, Mafico explains,

> In African worship and society, the community was a vital aspect of the *Mwari* tradition. To be in good relationship with

43. "The spirits in general belong to the ontological mode of existence between God and man. Broadly speaking, we can recognize two categories of spiritual beings: those which were created as such, and those which were once human beings. These can also be subdivided into divinities, associates of God, ordinary spirits and the living-dead." Mbiti, *African Religions and Philosophy*, 97.

44. Darko, *Against Principalities and Powers*, 166–67.

45. For example, MacDonald, *Demonology for the Global Church*, 54–59, 138–41.

> God meant that one was in a harmonious relationship with members of the community (see 1 John 3:20). The African social structure explains why Africans found it difficult to accept God as introduced by missionaries. They found it inconceivable that an individual could approach God for every personal need, bypassing their ancestral spirits. . . .
>
> The African approach to God is in many ways similar to that of the Israelites. Both the African and Israelite communities were organized along family hierarchical structures. While the Israelites approached God through the gods of their progenitors, their spiritual patrons, the Africans did so through the ancestors. Most remarkable is the fact that Africans, except in West Africa where the Semitic influence was strong, believed in one God. This God, *Mwari*, was called by different names according to national languages and tribal dialects. The names reflected God's attributes. The Israelites, who at first were as polytheistic as the other nations of the ancient Near East, in the end merged the gods of their progenitors and ended up worshipping one God, Yahweh, who remained closely related to the *Elohim*, "the gods" or ancestors of their progenitors.[46]

Mafico is no doubt correct that the individualism of Christian missionaries undermined traditional family structures and understandings of ancestors in relation to God.[47] His developmental understanding of Israelite religion as YHWH representing a "merger" of various ancestral gods is not a necessary or most natural reading of the biblical text. However, comparisons to African understandings help to illumine for Western readers just how challenging it would have been for the Israelites in the biblical story to disentangle themselves from the spiritual beings with whom their ancestors had previous relationships.

Third, African readers of the Bible will also be comfortable describing a deity/spirit based what it *does* for a person or a group, rather than a spiritual being's attributes described abstractly—i.e., the soteriology versus ontology distinction. Commenting on Deut 11:28, Chianeque and Ngewa emphasize the "knowing" of YHWH and Israel as creational and experiential.[48] Kunhiyop describes knowing the biblical

46. Mafico, "Biblical God of the Fathers," 488.

47. This acknowledgment does not preclude the possibility that the Bible itself in fact teaches, against some belief systems, the importance of individual, unmediated relationship to the Creator God. Direct access and loyalty to YHWH is a feature of both the OT (Deut 13) and the NT (through Christ; 1 Tim 2:5; Heb 4:14—5:10, 8–10).

48. "If Israel rejects Yahweh, it will be giving allegiance to *other gods, which you*

God as a protection against demons.[49] On "knowing" through naming of individuals, Adeboye describes the practice of African Christians changing names/surnames that honor or refer to gods or occultism (e.g., the Yoruba name Ogungbemi means "god of iron protects me," and Awokoya means "occultism has relieved me of suffering") to more neutral or "Christian" names, and the claims that subsequently negative trends/patterns in those individuals' lives were reversed.[50]

The brief sampling of African perspectives offered here are closer to those represented in Deuteronomy and its cultural milieu than those of Western "monotheistic" interpreters. Even though, to my knowledge, not many African commentators have commented specifically on "gods you / your ancestors have not known" in Deuteronomy, the interpretive puzzle would appear to be less puzzling within theological frameworks at the intersection of African Christianity and African indigenous religion.

Moving Forward

There is no need to resort to developmental models or source criticism in pulling apart the strands of Deuteronomy,[51] or separating Deuteronomy from Second Isaiah on these terms. Rather, with a doctrine of God defined by the texts themselves, we can then attend to the narrative of the Pentateuch and the Second Isaiah prophet's reflection on it. In order to understand "gods which you / your ancestors have not known," we must consider this within the narrative of the Pentateuch: when/how did the patriarchs "know" the gods of the nations, and—the "theological payoff"—how is it that they came to "know" YHWH? (And thus, how might subsequent readers of the Hebrew Bible, the other peoples of the world, come to "know" YHWH?)

---

have not known (11:28). The verb 'know' here refers to more than merely intellectual knowledge. It is the same word used of the intimate acquaintance of marriage partners. Yahweh was the one who had created Israel and cared for it, who knew it most intimately and who was known by the people in a way that no other god could be known." Chianeque and Ngewa, "Deuteronomy," 227; emphasis original.

49. Kunhiyop, *African Christian Theology*, 86, 89–90.

50. Adeboye, *Can a Christian Be Cursed*, 95–97.

51. "From the breakthrough of modern Deuteronomy research in the 19th century . . . there has been a strong tendency of focusing on questions related to the textual genesis of the book, often at the cost of questions related to the literary organizing of the transmitted and final version of the book." Holter, *Deuteronomy 4*, 6–7.

The problem of the patriarchs having indeed "known" Mesopotamian gods in ancient times is a real problem for Deuteronomy's "fulfilment" in the biblical presentation of Israel/Judah's story: they are indeed described as serving "gods their ancestors had known." I propose that Second Isaiah solves this problem by arguing that the exodus event and the accompanying revelation of YHWH's name forges a relationship between YHWH and Israel that erases all previous "known-ness" of the patriarchs by Mesopotamian deities. This hermeneutical move as a strategy of protecting the Judahite community is particularly urgent (and admittedly audacious) in response to the conquest by Babylon specifically, as contrasted with conquest by an imperial force from somewhere else.

What Gods Did Israel's Ancestors "Know," and When Did They Know Them?

An important part of this argument is to articulate the nature of the relationships that Abraham and the patriarchs had with other "gods" of Mesopotamia, and the relationships that the Israelites had with other gods. Scripture presents a picture of these relationships that is more nuanced and complex than simply humans serving unresponsive idols with no spiritual beings behind them.

The Patriarchs Worshiped Mesopotamian Gods and Their Images

According to the Hebrew Bible, the patriarchs were polytheists and idolators, and continued to be so even after encountering the deity who eventually revealed himself as YHWH. This seems like a bold statement but is actually evident from close reading of the Pentateuch and the Prophets.

Joshua 24 clearly states that Israel's ancestors from Mesopotamia served other gods:

> Then Joshua said to all the people, "Thus says YHWH, God of Israel: 'In Beyond-the-River, your fathers, from-time-immemorial [מעולם]—Terah, father of Abraham and father of Nahor—they served other gods. Then I took your father, Abraham, from Beyond-the-River, and I brought him through all the land of Canaan, and I made his offspring numerous, and I gave him Isaac.'" (Josh 24:2–3)

> And now, fear YHWH and serve him in wholeness and in truth, and put away the gods which your ancestors have served in Beyond-the-River and in Egypt, and serve YHWH. (Josh 24:14)

We might observe two important features of the received narrative of the Pentateuch. Exodus 6:2–8 claims that Israel's deity never revealed his personal name, YHWH, to the patriarchs, who knew him only as *El-Shaddai* (and other "El"-based epithets in Genesis).[52] Second, in Genesis, the deity whom Abraham and his descendants serve never insists on exclusive worship. Rather, by Gen 35, Jacob finally requires that his household put away the "gods of strangeness" (אלהי הנכר), which are buried under the oak near Shechem (35:2–4)—supposedly the site of the Josh 24 ceremony. Thus, it seems presumptuous to call Abraham a "monotheist" in the strictest sense.[53] Rather, a deity whom Abraham had not previously known, identifying himself as "God Most High" or "God of Mountains," draws Abraham and his offspring into a relationship that gradually becomes exclusive (or nearly so). The patriarchs' loyalty is a response to the deity repeatedly proving himself faithful and powerful (though acts of salvation from numerous threats, and wilderness provision). The ancestral gods have now become נכר (see Deut 31:16, 32:12).

The biblical portrait of Abraham as polytheist and idolator, at least for a significant part of his life, was sufficiently troubling for early Jewish interpreters that they sought other explanations for Josh 24:2–4. Kugel contends, "Ancient interpreters concluded that Abraham must somehow have been different from Terah and Nahor—that is why he is singled out."[54] Thus, in Judith 5:6–9, a character states that the ancestors of the Jews were driven out of "Chaldea" by the inhabitants because they refused to worship "the gods of their fathers" and instead worshiped "the God

52. Giffone, *Storymaking*, 133.

53. Note the apparent reference to plural gods in Gen 31:53: "god(s) of Abraham and god(s) of Nahor will judge [ישפטו, plural] between us, the god(s) of their father." Pakkala notes that the SamP and LXX change this verb to singular so that the three instances of אלהי can be understood as singular: "Whether the plural is a reference to several gods that both of them had or two gods only—one of Abraham, the other of Nahor—cannot be determined. If one divinity was meant, one would expect the text to read אלהי אברהם ונחור. The SP and LXX have changed the plural verb to singular, ישפט and κρινεῖ respectively. It is very likely that the SP and LXX are secondary here, because a tendency to remove the polytheistic elements would be expected from many later authors, while the opposite direction of development would be difficult to explain." Pakkala, *God's Word Omitted*, 101–2.

54. Kugel, *Traditions of the Bible*, 245.

of heaven, a god they had come to acknowledge [Thus, ᾧ ἐπέγνωσαν]" (NETS). In Jubilees, this becomes a more pronounced divide between young Abraham, who intuits from a young age that worshiping idols is worthless and that people should worship the God of heaven, and his father who fears the people of the land (Jub. 11:16–17, 12:2–7). Eventually, Philo comes to the view that Abraham intuited monotheism:

> In this creed Abraham had been reared, and for a long time remained a Chaldean. Then opening the soul's eye as though after profound sleep, and beginning to see the pure beam instead of the deep darkness, he followed the ray and discerned what he had not beheld before, a charioteer and pilot presiding over the world and directing in safety his own work, assuming the charge and superintendence of that work and of all such parts of it as are worthy of the divine care.[55]

These interpretations, though understandable, retroject later ideas onto the biblical portrait of the patriarchs' conception of the spiritual realm. In Mesopotamia, Abraham, Terah, and their clan "served other gods" (ויעבדו אלהים אחרים; Josh 24:2). Though Abraham and his descendants worshiped the deity who called them (whom they knew only by *El-* epithets) to Canaan, they were never disabused of polytheism (see Gen 35:2–4). YHWH *drew* Abraham to himself through the "knowing" of "redeeming him" out of Mesopotamia, and this led the patriarchs gradually to wholehearted devotion. The devotion is represented not in a mental assent or verbal confession of monotheism but in acts of trust (e.g., Gen 22:1–19, 35:2–4).[56] Through the exodus and Sinai events, he revealed his name and communicated he was the god worthy of exclusive worship (Exod 6:2–8, 20:2–3), the "God of gods" (Deut 10:17; see also Exod 15:11).

55. Philo, *On Abraham* 70 (LCL).

56. "[For Kuehnen and Schleiermacher,] the intellectual coherence of 'monotheism' is so persuasive that once proclaimed by Deutero-Isaiah it must necessarily permeate the whole of exilic and post-exilic Judaism such that a return to polytheism is inconceivable. In stark contrast, the account of YHWH'S oneness in Deuteronomy suggests that recognizing and correctly responding to YHWH'S lordship with wholehearted loyalty is a duty that is extremely taxing. Israel's propensity to idolatry is not solved by the recognition of a simple fact. Instead, the discipline of humility so that she can recognize the one who says 'I am YHWH' (29.5) is something that takes many years. Even with the discipline of the wilderness, Israel needs constant reminders, like the Song, and continued discipline (8.5) in order not to forget YHWH when she enters the bountiful land." MacDonald, *Deuteronomy*, 213.

Israel and the Pantheons of Egypt, Canaan, and Mesopotamia

In the Hebrew Bible's narrations and reflections on Israel's beginnings and story, there are at least three phases of worshiping other deities/pantheons. While in Egypt, the Israelites were compelled to serve the gods of Egypt. Ezekiel 20:7–8 makes this accusation, and it is confirmed in Josh 24:14. It is also implied in Deut 29:15–17[16–18].[57] This makes sense of their lives there: there was no freedom of religion—so if the Israelites served the Egyptians and the Egyptians served the Egyptian gods, the Israelites served the Egyptian gods, "knowing" them through their worship and their ways (and perhaps through apparent miraculous signs). Even Joseph is said to have "engaged in divination" (והוא נחש ינחש בו; Gen 44:5).[58] Eventually, the Israelites voluntarily served the gods of Canaan, despite the warning/offer in Josh 24:15. Psalm 106:34–39 seems to imply that they were "ensnared" by worshiping the images of Canaanite gods. This could be the pleasurable nature of Canaanite practices such as ritual prostitution, or the draw of pagan religion on some level. But it seems to imply that the gods were in some way responsive to the worship of the Canaanite people (and of the Israelites). Finally, as exiles in Assyria and Babylon, the Israelites served those gods as they had served the Egyptian gods in Egypt.[59]

If, according to these passages, the deities of the nations indeed exist (not mere unresponsive idols) and have some power to ensnare, then it makes more sense of other passages that speak of YHWH rescuing the people and commanding them to serve him only. The judgment upon Egypt is said to be judgment upon their gods (Exod 12:12; see also 15:11, 18:11). Israel appears to have had trouble extricating themselves from the gods of Egypt (Ezek 20:7–11). Thus, at Sinai, Israel was commanded to worship YHWH alone, without images (Exod 20:2–4). Despite this, Israel was drawn into ways of worshiping YHWH that echoed that of the

57. Giffone, "YHWH's Name in Ezekiel 20," 9–10.

58. It is fair to ask whether this testimony in the mouth of the steward can be trusted. Yet it does not seem inconceivable that Joseph, married to the daughter of an Egyptian high priest, would have accessed supernatural forces through divination. Jacob appears to make use of some sort of superstition or magic in making the strong flocks give birth to speckled/spotted offspring (Gen 30:37–43).

59. This might be inferred from 2 Kgs 17:24–28, in which Mesopotamians are deported to Northern Israel and are taught to serve "the god of the land"—the implication being that the Israelites would have been required to do the same for the Mesopotamian gods of their captivity. On YHWH's apparent partial responsiveness to this Bethel-style worship by Mesopotamian deportees, see Giffone, *Storymaking*, 182–83.

Egyptians and the Canaanites, and even adopting the gods of Canaan and the practice of human sacrifice (Ezek 20:25, "laws that were not good"). Eventually, Israel and Judah were sent to Mesopotamia to serve both unresponsive images and abusive spiritual beings.[60]

Second Isaiah's Hermeneutical Move

Second Isaiah's hermeneutical move is bold: the "knownness" of deity and people through the salvation act (a re-creative act) means that the Mesopotamian gods are "unknown" to Israel.

In both Deuteronomy and Second Isaiah, we are presented with the idea that Israel's deity is known by (his) humans not through the presence of an image but through his spoken words, his formative/redemptive power, and his ability to declare the future. (These three concepts are intertwined: his ability to create and to redeem are related, and his ability to form the future means that his spoken declarations about the future can be trusted.) The existence of a deity in an ontological sense is not at issue—rather, the experience of the deity (knownness) by the people. So also, the ontological existence of other deities is not a primary concern—but rather, the fact that those deities have no ability to form people and events, to save the people, and to declare the future.

It is not possible or necessary to expound Second Isaiah's theology at length, but here it will suffice to examine some key metaphors and concepts in Second Isaiah that have parallels in Deuteronomy (see table). Through these concepts, the implication is that Israel in exile in Mesopotamia experiences the foreign gods through worship and subservience. Even though those gods "exist" as spiritual entities, they cannot compare to the power, love, and loyalty displayed by YHWH to the patriarchs and to Israel in ages past.

60. Would Abraham have worshiped the same gods as the Judahite exiles in the sixth century? Perhaps. Abusch concludes that in the Old Babylonian period, "Marduk seems neither to have replaced the high gods of Babylonia nor to have ascended to the head of the pantheon. Only late in the second millennium does he take on many of Enlil's roles and become not only lord of the land but also king of the gods." By the time of Second Isaiah, "certainly, during the Neo-Babylonian empire, Marduk was the supreme god of a universal empire ruled from Babylon." Abusch, "Marduk," 545.

Rhetorically, what matters is the *perception* of the audiences of Deuteronomy and Second Isaiah that the Mesopotamian deities had stayed mainly the same, or been part of the same family of "gods"/spiritual beings from ancient times.

Second Isaiah	Deuteronomy parallel	Idea
"I am YHWH, [and] there is no other" (Isa 45:5–6, 14, 18, 21–22; 46:9)	Deut 4:35 and 39	YHWH's incomparability
Isa 43:8–13	Particularly Deut 4 and 32	Ability to save and create a new people
Witnesses summoned, including divine council and nations and the Servant (Isa 43:8–9)	Deut 4:26, 30:19, 32:1	Witness to YHWH's identity and works
"I am he; before me, no god was formed; and after me, none will be" (אני הוא לפני לא נוצר אל ואחרי לא יהיה; Isa 43:10b–c)	Deut 32:39 "there is no god besides me" (ואין אלהים עמדי) 4:34–35	YHWH's uniqueness and eternality
"I, I am YHWH; besides me, there is no savior" (אנכי אנכי יהוה ואין מבלעדי מושיע; Isa 43:11)	Deut 32:39	Ability to save
"I myself declared and saved and proclaimed; there was no strange [god] among you; you are my witnesses—utterance of YHWH—that I am God" (אנכי הגדתי והושעתי והשמעתי ואין בכם זר ואתם עדי נאם יהוה ואני אל; Isa 43:12)	Deut 4:34–35	Saving tied to knowing
YHWH "acts, and who can reverse it" (אפעל ומי ישיבנה; Isa 43:13)	Deut 32:39 (ואין מידי מציל), 32:27, YHWH's concern that Israel's enemies might say, "Our hand is exalted—YHWH did not do all this!" (ידינו רמה ולא יהוה פעל כל זאת)	Ability to save

Figure 5: Second Isaiah and Deuteronomy Parallels

Two well-recognized dimensions of Second Isaiah's monotheism are YHWH's identity as the Creator of all things ("the Everlasting God, the LORD, the Creator of the ends of the earth," Isa 40:28) and his incomparability, often indicated by the saying "I am YHWH, [and] there is no other" (45:5–6, 14, 18, 21–22; 46:9). These refrains closely parallel Deut 4:35 and 4:39.[61]

In several Second Isaiah passages, his uniqueness as a deity is explicitly tied to his ability to save and create a new people. Isaiah 43:8–13 is an instructive example. YHWH calls the heavenly audience (perhaps a divine council or astral deities, as in Isa 40:22–26[62]) to summon "nations and peoples" (43:9) who are blind and deaf though they have eyes and ears (43:8), and also YHWH's chosen servant (אתם עדי נאם יהוה ועבדי אשר בחרתי; 43:10) to witness that "I am he; before me, no god was formed; and after me, none will be" (אני הוא לפני לא נוצר אל ואחרי לא יהיה; 43:10b–c). Immediately following, YHWH's uniqueness and eternality is demonstrated by his ability to save: "I, I am YHWH; besides me, there is no savior" (אנכי אנכי יהוה ואין מבלעדי מושיע; 43:11). The "saving" is then tied to the "knowing" relationship between the deity and the people: "I myself declared and saved and proclaimed; there was no strange [god] among you; you are my witnesses—utterance of YHWH—that I am God" (אנכי הגדתי והושעתי והשמעתי ואין בכם זר ואתם עדי נאם יהוה ואני אל; 43:12). Finally, the decisive saving power of YHWH is reemphasized (43:13). All of these concepts have parallels in Deuteronomy, especially chapters 4 and 32. "Heaven and earth" are called as witnesses to YHWH's prediction and his covenant warnings against Israel (Deut 4:26, 30:19, 32:1). The claim in Isa 43:13 that no one can deliver from YHWH's hand parallels verbatim Deut 32:39 (ואין מידי מציל), which also states, "There is no god besides me" (ואין אלהים עמדי). Indeed, YHWH's ability to deliver a nation from the midst of another nation is celebrated as a once-in-a-universe event that demonstrates YHWH's power (Deut 4:34–35). The claim in Isa 43:13 that YHWH "acts, and who can reverse it" (אפעל ומי ישיבנה) finds its basis in Deut 32:27, YHWH's concern that Israel's enemies might say, "Our hand is exalted—YHWH did not do all this!" (ידינו רמה ולא יהוה פעל כל זאת).

Idol polemics in Second Isaiah (Isa 40:18–20, 41:6–7, 41:21–29, 42:17, 44:9–20, 46:1–7) emphasize the inability of images as gods to do anything for the people who make and worship them, especially to "help" (41:6–7) and to "save" (43:11–13; 44:17, 20; 45:20; 46:4, 7)—as contrasted with YHWH as deity, who has those abilities. However, Holter has pointed out that another relevant contrast is drawn between YHWH and

61. Heiser, "Monotheism," 16–17; MacDonald, "Monotheism and Isaiah," 50.

62. Heiser, "Monotheism," 14–15.

the image-makers, and between flourishing human images of YHWH and humans who become like the images they worship—unresponsive.[63] YHWH gives breath and spirit to people (42:5); people have become unresponsive like the images (42:16–20, 43:8–9), who know nothing (44:18–20). These critiques of idols as unresponsive, as we have seen, find parallels in Deuteronomy (Deut 4:28; 28:36, 64), but notably alongside passages that presume the existence (and impotence) of the gods of the nations (as noted previously in this essay).

The "creating" of a human people and the humans fashioning images are linked by the repeated use of the verb יצר, which occurs eighteen times in Second Isaiah (out of only sixty-seven occurrences in all of the Hebrew Bible). Images are formed by humans (Isa 44:9–10, 12), but no god formed YHWH or was formed before YHWH (43:10), who also formed elements of creation (45:7, 18). YHWH formed Israel/Jacob (43:1, 7, 21; 44:2, 21, 24; 45:9, 11) and the servant/prophet (49:5). YHWH formed "one from the north" who would rescue his people (41:25). He achieves all this because he forms history / the future (46:11).[64]

Second Isaiah contains numerous references to the patriarchs and their origins. Some of the twenty-two references to "Jacob" no doubt represent the nation as a whole,[65] but other verses refer to Israel's origins and ancestors. These verses, like Deut 4:37, 7:7–10, and 32, paint a picture of YHWH as the maker of a particular people who were supposed to know and serve him in a way that was deeper than the other peoples. YHWH "formed" this people from the womb (Isa 43:1; 44:2, 24). YHWH says of Israel, Jacob, and Abraham, "I chose you from the ends of the earth, took you" (41:8–9), and calls them "ancient people" (עם־עולם; 44:7). YHWH's people are reminded to "look to the rock from which you were hewn": Abraham and Sarah, many people created out of just one family (51:1–2). Israel, as opposed to the nations, who are not weighty (40:15–17, 41:2, 43:3–4), is the portion of YHWH, worth preserving.

Some verses even appear to reference the sojournings of the patriarchs and YHWH's struggle to get them to recognize and acknowledge him. "Why do you complain, Jacob, 'My way is hidden from YHWH'?" (Isa 40:27) reads well alongside Gen 28:16. YHWH claims to have

63. Holter, *Second Isaiah's Idol-Fabrication*, 30, 239.

64. The remaining use of יצר in Second Isaiah is in 54:17, human weapons fashioned against YHWH's people.

65. Isa 40:27; 41:8, 14, 21; 42:24; 43:1, 22; 43:28—44:2; 44:5, 21, 23; 45:4, 19; 46:3; 48:1, 12, 20; 49:5–6, 26.

carried Jacob since the day he was born (Isa 46:3–4), a parallel to Deut 1:31. YHWH says, "I have not said to Jacob's descendants, 'seek me in תהו'" (45:19), a reference both to Jacob's sojournings and to the wanderings of Exodus–Numbers. In response, Jacob has not called upon YHWH but has been sinful instead (43:22).

Yet despite this, YHWH is resolved to redeem Jacob's people (Isa 48:1—49:6), and he predicted that he would do so—unlike the images and other deities. The goal is that "all humanity will know that I, YHWH, am your Savior, your redeemer, mighty one of Jacob" (49:26), that "my people shall know my name" (52:6). Moreover, the nations have roles to play. In Isa 45:3–6, Cyrus has not "known" YHWH, but YHWH is using him so that men may "know" that he is YHWH. The other nations will serve Zion "so that you will know [ידע] that I am YHWH" (49:23, 26). Ultimately, other nations who don't "know" Israel (Deut 28:36) will run to her (Isa 55:5). In Deut 4, the nations have "the host of heaven," other deities allotted to them (4:19), but are envious of Israel's special relationship with YHWH (4:6–8). In Deut 32, when Israel spurned YHWH and made him jealous with other deities ("not-a-god," 32:17, 21), YHWH determined to make Israel jealous by establishing relationships with other nations ("not-a-people," 32:21; also, "nations," 32:43).

Another relevant metaphor of "knowing," which is not prominent in Deuteronomy, may nevertheless be found in the second half of Second Isaiah—namely, the marriage of YHWH and Zion, and the "children" of that union (the people of Israel). The sexual "knowing" of husband and wife establishes a bond that supersedes all previous relationships. Thus, Israel was "sent away" and "sold" but not divorced by YHWH (Isa 50:1). Zion has become drunk on YHWH's cup of wrath, and so she has been abused, with no children to console her (51:17–20). Yet YHWH will "contend" for his people (51:22), give the cup of wrath to Zion's enemies, and redeem her in the sight of the nations (52:3–6); the "uncircumcised" nations that had taken advantage of Zion will "no longer come into" her (כי לא יוסיף יבא בך עוד ערל וטמא; 52:1). The result is the people "knowing" YHWH's name (52:6). The previously infertile, disgraced, shamed, and widowed Zion will be made as a "wife of youth" when YHWH has compassion on his people (54:1–8).

All of this is possible because YHWH is not only the knower of the future but also the one who forms history. No one explained the future to YHWH or gave him "knowledge" (40:14). YHWH taunts the other gods: "Declare to us the things which will come afterward, so we may *know* that you are gods" (41:23, emphasis added; ונדעה כי אלהים אתם). With echoes of Deut 32,[66] YHWH claims that there is no other god or "rock" (צור) besides him, because he declared events before they happened (44:8). The premise of the threats/warnings of exile in Deut 4, 28, 29, 30, and 32 is that YHWH, unlike other gods or unresponsive idols, has the power to declare the future and accomplish it.

Second Isaiah's (re)interpretation of Israel's story—the ancestors' relationship to YHWH and other gods, Israel's relationship to YHWH—is presented as part of his audacious contention that YHWH, rather than Marduk, is responsible for the situation of Judah in the Babylonian period. It would be logical for Judah to assume that, because the servants of Marduk had sacked the land and the sanctuary of YHWH and subjugated, abused, and deported YHWH's people, Marduk is more powerful than YHWH. Given the perceived origins of Judah's ancestors in Mesopotamia, it would be natural and logical for Judahites to begin worshiping the Babylonian gods (perhaps following the same reasoning as those who advocate the resumption of Queen of Heaven worship in Jer 44:15–19).

Against this argument, Second Isaiah forcefully contends that (1) YHWH is unique and the lone Creator; (2) YHWH has an ancient "knowing" relationship with Israel's ancestors; (3) YHWH has a saving/redeeming/"knowing" relationship with Israel at the exodus; and (4) YHWH continues to "know" Israel in covenant (marriage) despite all that has occurred between them. Thus, in the paradox of "remember the former things" / "do not remember the former things" (Isa 46:9, 48:18), the uniqueness of the exodus event (see Deut 4:32–34) will be duplicated but superseded when YHWH redeems his "known" people from captivity in Babylon. The gods of Babylon have become those whom their "ancestors have not known and which He has not allotted to them" because Israel has now known YHWH.

Conclusion

In this study, we have seen that in order for the language of the Deuteronomy threat/warning "gods which you / your ancestors have not known" to make sense, the gods must exist—but also, "knownness" must be defined in terms of an experiential, creating/forming or saving/redeeming interaction. This becomes clearer when Deuteronomy

66. Israel's deity is referred to as צור in 32:4, 15, 18, 30–31, 37.

is read through the lens of Second Isaiah's interpretation of YHWH's relationship to other gods, Israel's ancestors, and Israel.

The patriarchs were not "monotheists" in the strict, modern Western sense of that term. Rather, YHWH revealed himself progressively through acts of salvation and loyalty, such that the patriarchs eventually dropped their other loyalties (Gen 22, 35). The "knowing" relationship between YHWH and the patriarchs is not through their recognition of YHWH's ontology but through experience of salvation and provision.

Deuteronomy describes the relationship of Israel to other gods (including Mesopotamian gods) as transforming from being "previously known" in relationship to Israel's fathers, to being off-limits for Israel (Deut 13:7). This tells us something about the exclusive worship and relationship that YHWH desires. Thus, the Deuteronomy "threat" (whether preemptive, or *ex eventu*) of serving "unknown gods" becomes intelligible and legitimate.

The Babylonian exile is presented in Deuteronomy, and also in passages in Second Isaiah, as Israel going "back to square one." Abraham's descendants are now right back in Mesopotamia where they began, captive to Babylonian gods. They are blind, deaf, and as hard-hearted as the images they worship. Israel being "known" by Mesopotamian gods is worse this time because they have "known" YHWH experientially in the time of the patriarchs and soteriologically through the exodus. Israel has no longer been apportioned to the Mesopotamian gods. To serve "gods their ancestors had [historically] known" is actually worse-than-square-one: "unknowing" YHWH. In Second Isaiah, a "new exodus" from Babylon is now more urgent than it was when YHWH rescued Abraham from Babylon and Israel from Egypt.

In this essay, I have extended further the insights of MacDonald and Heiser to explain the phrase "gods you / your ancestors have not known" in Deuteronomy. It is my contention that Second Isaiah, rather than representing an innovation ("simple" or "full" monotheism), provides an account of YHWH's identity that is fully consistent with that of Deuteronomy. Progressive developmental models of Israel's religion and redaction-critical theories of Deuteronomy based on those models do not explain the complex "divine council monotheism" of both Deuteronomy and Second Isaiah. Rather, the "known gods" versus "unknown gods" warning/threat points to how YHWH is known *soteriologically*:

through acts on behalf of his people.[67] Second Isaiah's protective strategy may thus be understood as a hermeneutical move, not a theological innovation of "pure monotheism."

Postscript

At the beginning of this essay, I suggested that the puzzle of the phrase "gods which you / your ancestors have not known" is not only interesting from the standpoint of exegesis, but also provides an opportunity for conversations between Bible readers from different cultures and assumptions, present and past. I have suggested that modern/post-Reformation Western interpretation has misunderstood monotheism, and so also this phrase. Traditional commentators have tried to avoid it by conflating idolatry with polytheism. Others have turned to source-critical explanations, which fail to explain why, if a text advocating "simple monotheism" was the goal of later redactors, they did not remove this confusing phrase and others like it.

Non-Western Christian readers of Scripture can offer Western readers a perspective from cultures with more robust understandings of the spiritual realm. In Deuteronomy and in Second Isaiah, YHWH's ontology is not in view—rather, soteriology and the "knowing" relationship between a deity and a people is signified by this phrase.

There are two sets of implications which I think are relevant in this line of thinking, related to the New Testament and the mission of the church.

The Returning Unclean Spirit

Jesus tells the parable of the cleaned-and-swept house in Matt 12:43–45.[68] If a spirit is cast out of a house—usually understood to be a human

67. MacDonald rightly states, "The monotheism of Second Isaiah is soteriologically, not ontologically, orientated." "Monotheism and Isaiah," 59.

68. Earlier in the chapter, the evangelist quotes Isa 42:1–4 LXX describing Jesus as the Servant in whom dwells "the Spirit" of YHWH, and the "hope" of the nations (Matt 12:17–21). We then read of an exorcism performed on a man who was blind and mute (12:22–23) and the religious leaders' attribution of Jesus' works to Beelzebub (12:24–37). The unclean spirit had made the man a deficient "servant" á la Isa 42:7, 16, 18–19; 43:8 ("Who is blind but my servant, or so deaf as the messenger whom I send?!" 43:19a), but Jesus healed the man and transformed him into a suitable "house" for the Spirit of God.

person, but perhaps could also refer to a place—but the Spirit of God has not subsequently indwelled that person/place, then the unclean spirit will return with seven more spirits, resulting in a worse situation than previously.

This parable helps to understand this trajectory in Israel's history. "Serving other gods" in exile, especially the more "familiar" (familial?) gods their ancestors had previously served in Mesopotamia, is not a consolation—"the devil you know is better than the devil you don't know"—but is actually even more disastrous than the original situation, analogous to the unclean spirit who was forced out of the house bringing seven others back with it. Israel's return to serving Mesopotamian gods (and more) is worse than the patriarchs' worship of Mesopotamian gods, precisely because Israel had known what it was like to "know" YHWH.

Christian Mission in Pre- and Post-Christendom Nations

The New Testament describes the relationship of other nations to other gods in the same way as Deut 4:19–20 and 32:8. What other nations sacrifice to idols, they offer to "demons" (1 Cor 10:20). In the past, YHWH let the nations go their own way (Acts 14:16), but now they are summoned to serve a "previously unknown God" (Acts 17:22–31). The solution alluded to in both Second Isaiah and Matt 12 (not to mention Rom 9–11 and 15, which quote Isaiah heavily, including Isa 42:1–4 LXX like Matt 12:18–21) is that YHWH must act to ransom both the people who are his portion, Israel, per Deut 32:9, *and* the nations who have been under the sway of these other gods since Babel (Deut 32:8, Ps 82).

As I noted in at the beginning, my experience has been shaped by studies and teaching on four continents, mainly Europe and North America but also Africa and Asia. My students (mainly current and future pastors and church leaders) often speak about the spiritual realm as if there are particular areas where particular rebellious divine beings hold sway.

For example, from personal conversations with Christians from Lithuania, I know that many of them believe that there is some unique spiritual force of darkness that holds sway over that nation. Rates of depression, alcoholism, child abuse, and especially suicide are sky-high, even compared to countries with similar histories of oppression and the same dark, depressive winter months. Some say it has to do with the

Lithuanians being the last people in Europe to convert from paganism to Christianity; others say it has to do with Lithuanian leaders' complicity in the Holocaust.

Here is where the soteriological "knownness" of YHWH—by the patriarchs, by preexilic Israel, and by Second Isaiah's captives in Babylon—provides a hermeneutical lens for contemporary interpretation. Speaking from a "national" perspective, Europeans have "previously known" the biblical deity after the pagan gods had been repelled—but now in the post-Christendom era, those gods are coming back with a vengeance. This gives the challenge of Christian mission to European individuals a particular flavor: trying to help Europeans "know again" the deity who still haunts their societies. (This spiritual dimension is different than what my students and colleagues in South Asia describe to me because that land has not yet "known," by and large, the Triune God.) Second Isaiah's reaffirmation of Deuteronomy's soteriological case for YHWH's uniqueness offers hope for a different trajectory in Europe (and North America).

Bibliography

Abusch, Tzvi. "Marduk." In *Dictionary of Deities and Demons*, 2nd ed., edited by Karel van der Toorn et al., 543–49. Leiden: Brill, 1999.

Adeboye, Godwin. *Can a Christian Be Cursed? An African Evangelical Response to the Problem of Curses*. Bukuru: HippoBooks, 2023.

Arnold, Bill T. *The Book of Deuteronomy Chapters 1–11*. New International Commentary on the Old Testament. Grand Rapids: Eerdmans, 2022.

Barr, James. "The Problem of Israelite Monotheism." *Glasgow University Oriental Society* 17 (1957–1958) 52–62.

Berman, Joshua A. *Inconsistency in the Torah: Ancient Literary Convention and the Limits of Source Criticism*. New York: Oxford University Press, 2017.

Biddle, Mark E. *Deuteronomy*. Smyth & Helwys Bible Commentary. Macon, GA: Smyth & Helwys, 2003.

Brueggemann, Walter. *Deuteronomy*. Abingdon Old Testament Commentaries. Nashville: Abingdon, 2001.

Carr, David M. *The Formation of the Hebrew Bible: A New Reconstruction*. New York: Oxford University Press, 2011.

Chianeque, Luciano C., and Samuel Ngewa. "Deuteronomy." In *Africa Bible Commentary*, edited by Tokunboh Adeyemo et al., 209–54. Grand Rapids: Zondervan, 2006.

Christensen, Duane L. *Deuteronomy 1:1—21:9*. Rev. ed. Word Biblical Commentary 6a. Nashville: Nelson, 2001.

Craigie, Peter C. *The Book of Deuteronomy*. New International Commentary on the Old Testament. Grand Rapids: Eerdmans, 1976.

Darko, Daniel K. *Against Principalities and Powers: Spiritual Beings in Relation to Communal Identity and the Moral Discourse of Ephesians*. Bukuru: HippoBooks, 2020.

Giffone, Benjamin D. "'Anger Exhausted' for the Sake of YHWH's Name in Ezekiel 20: Did YHWH Really Relent from Wrath Poured out on Israel?" *Biblische Zeitschrift* 66 (2022) 1–15.

———. *My Salvation Is Close at Hand: Isaiah 56–66 for the Church After Christendom*. Eugene, OR: Wipf & Stock, 2025.

———. *Storymaking, Textual Development, and Varying Cultic Centralizations: Gathering and Fitting Unhewn Stones*. Forschungen zum Alten Testament II 142. Tübingen: Mohr Siebeck, 2023.

Gnuse, Robert Karl. *No Other Gods: Emergent Monotheism in Israel*. Journal for the Study of the Old Testament Supplement 241. Sheffield: Sheffield Academic, 1997.

Heiser, Michael S. "Monotheism, Polytheism, Monolatry, or Henotheism? Toward an Assessment of Divine Plurality in the Hebrew Bible." *Bulletin for Biblical Research* 18 (2008) 1–30.

———. *The Unseen Realm*. Bellingham, WA: Lexham, 2015.

Holter, Knut. *Deuteronomy 4 and the Second Commandment*. Studies in Biblical Literature 60. New York: Lang, 2003.

———. *Second Isaiah's Idol-Fabrication Passages*. Beiträge zur biblischen Exegese und Theologie 28. Frankfurt: Lang, 1995.

Jonker, Louis C. *Defining All-Israel in Chronicles: Multi-Levelled Identity Negotiation in Late Persian-Period Yehud*. Forschungen Zum Alten Testament 106. Tübingen: Mohr Siebeck, 2016.

———. *From Adequate Biblical Interpretation to Transformative Intercultural Hermeneutics: Chronicling a Personal Journey*. Intercultural Biblical Hermeneutics Series 3. Elkhart, IN: Institute for Mennonite Studies, 2015.

———. "Reforming History: The Hermeneutical Significance of the Books of Chronicles." *Vetus Testamentum* 57 (2007) 21–44.

Kugel, James L. *Traditions of the Bible: A Guide to the Bible as It Was at the Start of the Common Era*. Cambridge: Harvard University Press, 1998.

Kunhiyop, Samuel Waje. *African Christian Theology*. Grand Rapids: Zondervan, 2012.

MacDonald, Nathan. *Deuteronomy and the Meaning of "Monotheism."* Corrected 2nd ed. Forschungen zum Alten Testament II 1. Tübingen: Mohr Siebeck, 2012.

———. "Monotheism and Isaiah." In *Interpreting Isaiah: Issues and Approaches*, edited by David G. Firth and H. G. M. Williamson, 43–61. Nottingham: Apollos, 2009.

MacDonald, Scott D. *Demonology for the Global Church: A Biblical Approach in a Multicultural Age*. Carlisle: Langham Global Library, 2021.

Mafico, Temba L. J. "The Biblical God of the Fathers and the African Ancestors." In *The Bible in Africa: Transactions, Trajectories, and Trends*, edited by Gerald O. West and Musa W. Dube, 481–89. Leiden: Brill, 2000.

Margalit, Baruch. "Why King Mesha of Moab Sacrificed His Oldest Son." *Biblical Archaeology Review* 12.6 (1986) 62–63.

Mbiti, John. *African Religions and Philosophy*. Garden City, NY: Anchor, 1970.

Moberly, R. W. L. "How Appropriate Is 'Monotheism' as a Category for Biblical Interpretation?" In *Early Jewish and Christian Monotheism*, edited by Loren T. Stuckenbruck and Wendy E. S. North, Journal for the Study of the Old Testament Supplement 263, 216–34. London: T&T Clark, 2004.

Pakkala, Juha. *God's Word Omitted: Omissions in the Transmission of the Hebrew Bible.* Forschungen zur Religion und Literatur des Alten und Neuen Testaments 251. Göttingen: Vandenhoeck & Ruprecht, 2013.

———. *Intolerant Monolatry in the Deuteronomistic History.* Publications of the Finnish Exegetical Society 76. Göttingen: Vandenhoeck & Ruprecht, 1999.

Philo. Translated by F. H. Colson and G. H. Whitaker. 10 vols. Loeb Classical Library. Cambridge: Harvard University Press, 1929–1962.

Smith, Mark S. *The Origins of Biblical Monotheism: Israel's Polytheistic Background and the Ugaritic Texts.* New York: Oxford University Press, 2001.

Speake, Jennifer, ed. *The Oxford Dictionary of Proverbs.* 6th ed. Oxford: Oxford University Press, 2015.

Stern, Philip D. "Of Kings and Moabites: History and Theology in 2 Kings 3 and the Mesha Inscription." *Hebrew Union College Annual* 64 (1993) 1–14.

Tigay, Jeffrey H. *Deuteronomy: The JPS Torah Commentary.* Philadelphia: Jewish Publication Society, 1996.

Woods, Edward J. *Deuteronomy: An Introduction and Commentary.* Tyndale Old Testament Commentaries 5. Downers Grove, IL: InterVarsity, 2011.

Ziemer, Benjamin. *Kritik des Wachstumsmodells: Die Grenzen alttestamentlicher Redaktionsgeschichte im Lichte empirischer Evidenz.* Supplements to Vetus Testamentum 182. Leiden: Brill, 2020.

———. "Radical Versus Conservative? How Scribes Conventionally Used Books While Writing Books." In *Inscribe It in a Book: Scribal Practice, Cultural Memory, and the Making of the Hebrew Scriptures*, edited by Johannes Unsok Ro and Benjamin D. Giffone, Forschungen zum Alten Testament II 139, 301–28. Tübingen: Mohr Siebeck, 2022.

List of Contributors

Solomon Amao
Faculty of Biblical Studies, ECWA Theological Seminary, Jos (JETS)
solomonamao@yahoo.com

Hendrik Bosman
Professor Emeritus, Department of Old and New Testament, Stellenbosch University
hlb1@sun.ac.za

Ntozakhe Simon Cezula
Senior Lecturer, Department of Old and New Testament, Stellenbosch University
cezulans@sun.ac.za

Johann Cook
Professor Emeritus, Department of Ancient Studies, Stellenbosch University
cook@sun.ac.za

Beth E. Elness-Hanson

Marie Skłodowska-Curie Postdoctoral Fellow and Associate Professor, VID Specialized University / Associate Professor of Hebrew Bible, Wartburg Theological Seminary

beth.elness-hanson@vid.no

Jaco Gericke

Associate Research Professor, Ancient Texts, Faculty of Theology, North-West University

jaco.gericke@nwu.ac.za

Benjamin D. Giffone

Research Associate, Faculty of Theology, Stellenbosch University / Visiting Associate Professor of Old Testament, Hindustan Bible Institute and College

giffone@sun.ac.za

Knut Holter

Professor of Biblical Studies, NLA University College, Bergen and Oslo / Extraordinary Professor, Stellenbosch University

knut.holter@nla.no

Marta Høyland Lavik

Professor, Stavanger University Hospital / Research Associate, Faculty of Theology, Stellenbosch University

marta.hoyland.lavik@sus.no

Christo Lombaard

Professor and Head of Department, Practical Theology and Mission Studies, Faculty of Theology, University of Pretoria / Researcher on Spirituality, Department of Theology, University of Latvia

CJS.Lombaard@up.ac.za

Lerato L. D. Mokoena
Senior Lecturer (Humanities), Department of Biblical and Ancient Studies, University of South Africa
mokoell@unisa.ac.za

Marius J. Nel
Professor of New Testament, Department of Old and New Testament, Stellenbosch University
mjnel@sun.ac.za

Jeremy Punt
Professor of New Testament, Department of Old and New Testament, Stellenbosch University
jpunt@sun.ac.za

Gerrie F. Snyman
Research Associate and Professor Extraordinarius in the Department of Biblical and Ancient Near Eastern Studies, University of South Africa
gfsnyman@global.co.za

Slindile Thabede
Postdoctoral Fellow, University of the Free State
thabede.s@ufs.ac.za

Gerald O. West
Senior Professor, School of Religion, Philosophy, and Classics, University of KwaZulu-Natal
west@ukzn.ac.za

Index

Hebrew Bible

Deuteronomy (continued)

Joshua

Judges

1 Samuel

2 Samuel

1 Kings

2 Kings

Isaiah

Isaiah (continued)

Jeremiah

Ezekiel

Hosea

Amos

Zechariah

Psalms

Luke

John

Acts

Romans

1 Corinthians

2 Corinthians

Galatians

Ephesians

Philippians

Colossians

1 Thessalonians

1 Timothy

Hebrews

James

1 Peter

1 John

Revelation

Ancient and Medieval Sources

Works Written or Co-written by Louis Jonker

www.ingramcontent.com/pod-product-compliance
Lightning Source LLC
LaVergne TN
LVHW020528100826
845148LV00010B/1380

* 9 7 9 8 3 8 5 2 5 1 9 0 2 *